SOLDIERS AND KINSMEN IN UGANDA
The Making of a Military Ethnocracy

SAGE SERIES ON ARMED FORCES AND SOCIETY

INTER-UNIVERSITY SEMINAR ON ARMED FORCES AND SOCIETY

Morris Janowitz, *University of Chicago*
Chairman and Series Editor

Charles C. Moskos, Jr., *Northwestern University*
Associate Chairman and Series Editor

SOLDIERS AND KINSMEN

IN UGANDA

The Making of a
Military Ethnocracy

Ali A. Mazrui

The University of Michigan

SAGE PUBLICATIONS   Beverly Hills / London

For information address:

SAGE PUBLICATIONS, INC.
275 South Beverly Drive
Beverly Hills, California 90212

SAGE PUBLICATIONS LTD
St George's House
London EC1N 8ER

Printed in the United States of America
International Standard Book Number 0-8039-0427-4
Library of Congress Catalog Card No. 75-5017

FIRST PRINTING

CONTENTS

V. POLICY-MAKING AND NEW NATIONAL IMAGES

To the living and dead of Uganda

ACKNOWLEDGMENTS

Before this book was written one major decision had to be made. Should it be a book which brought together all my material on the military whether it concerned Uganda or not? Or should it be a book which brought together all my material on Uganda whether it concerned the military or not? Or should it be a book about military rule in Uganda?

The third idea triumphed—but not entirely. I felt that military rule in Uganda could not be adequately understood without looking at other aspects of Uganda society. I also felt that Uganda society in turn could not be fully understood without placing it in the broader stream of Africa's cultural and political history.

I am greatly indebted to Morris Janowitz and the Inter-University Committee on Armed Forces and Society for encouraging me to write this book and for making publication arrangements. Professor Janowitz's encouragement to the author is much older than this book, going back over the years as a result of a shared interest in the social and political significance of the armed forces in different parts of the world. We also served together on the Research Committee on Military Sociology of the International Sociological Association for a number of years.

Most of the preliminary work on this book was done when I was Professor of Political Science at Makerere University, Kampala. I am greatly indebted to my former colleagues at Makerere, and to many others in Uganda, for stimulation and information pertinent to this work which I received from them during my years at Makerere. Much of the initial writing of the book was done when I was a Fellow at the Center for Advanced Study in the Behavioral Sciences at Stanford (1972-73). The book was completed when I was a Visiting Fellow at the Hoover Institution on War, Revolution and Peace, at Stanford (1973-74). To that extent the book is a product not only of my association with Makerere but also of my association with these two research institutions at Stanford. I am grateful to all those who made this possible.

A number of people were involved in getting the final manuscript ready. Especially active in the typing effort at Stanford were Ms. Penny McMullen, Ms. Jean Antonini, and Mrs. Valerie Faulkenberg. As a volunteer Mrs. Lawrence Kocher privately helped to keep my press clippings on Uganda up to date in the critical period before the book was completed. I greatly

[2]

appreciate the sense of commitment to the enterprise which all of them showed.

My ideas about the influence of culture on military behavior were developed partly in connection with my other work for the World Order Models Project. The first phase of this latter work was funded by the Institute for World Order and the Carnegie Endowment for International Peace, and culminated in a new book, *A World Federation of Cultures: An African Perspective,* scheduled for publication by Freeman Press, New York. But this Uganda book has also benefited by or borrowed from my other previous works. I am indebted to the relevant journals and publishers for permission to borrow from some of those previous writings.

Once again my wife, Molly, has served as editor, proofreader, literary consultant, and general intellectual companion. Her involvement in the work was second only to that of the author. Others are excused all responsibility for any faults in the book—but, alas, Molly has to share the burden of accountability inherent in a joint effort of this kind.

Ali A. Mazrui

PREFACE

In the effort to understand the significance of General Idi Amin in the history of both Uganda and Africa as a whole, this book has sought the assistance of a number of disciplines. It has benefited especially from insights provided by social psychology, cultural anthropology, as well as by political science. The book has also not hesitated to draw from social philosophy in the attempt to relate Uganda's experience to wider issues concerning man and society generally.

The author was on the faculty of Makerere University in Uganda for about ten years. Partly as a political scientist, and partly as a social critic, the author was a participant observer within Uganda's political system under a Milton Obote's presidency (1966-71) and continued to be so for the first two years of Idi Amin's presidency (1971-73). There were times when the author was under a political cloud under both governments because of political positions he had taken; there were other times when he was consulted on policy matters by the two presidents. His position in relation to the two governments had a continuing ambivalence throughout this period, but it was a position which enabled him to observe certain central areas of the political system while at the same time performing certain functions in the system.

This book is not about Uganda since independence. The author hopes to write another book in the future which would discuss more fully Milton Obote's contribution to his country.

For the time being the author focuses on Idi Amin, who is a fascinating phenomenon in his own right, and whose political significance goes far beyond the borders of his own country. At the time of writing it is not clear how long Idi Amin will remain in power. But he has been in power long enough to acquire a historical meaning for the African continent as a whole.

In addition, Amin's social origins and his political style raise new questions about the relationship between class, culture, ethnicity, and military behavior in post-colonial Africa. Amin's views on kinship, valor, and manliness raise questions about a psychological and sociological factor of primordial significance—the interaction between *martial qualities* and *sexual symbolism* in military history. This book will address itself to all these elements of the evolving phenomenon called Idi Amin, but within a context broader than Amin and his country.

Especially important among the continuing themes of the book will be the *warrior tradition* and *ethnocracy*. The warrior tradition in Africa's history

[3]

captured the values of manhood and adulthood, and provided a connecting principle between physical virility and martial valor. Ethnocracy, on the other hand, was primarily a principle of political organization rather than military behavior. Ethnocracy is a distributive system which allocates or divides political power primarily on the basis of ethnicity. The kinship polity is one type of ethnocracy. The kinship polity is normally a monopoly of power by people who see themselves as ethnic kinsmen. If the history of Uganda had hypothetically made it possible for political power to be monopolized by the Baganda almost entirely, Uganda would have become that kind of ethnocracy which is virtually identical with a kinship polity.

On the other hand, a Uganda with an ethnic division of labor, rather than an ethnic monopoly of power, would be a different ethnocracy. At the time of independence there was a Ganda predominance in the civil service, a Nilotic predominance in the armed forces, and an Asian predominance in fundamental parts of the economy. Such a situation was not a monopoly by any one of these three ethno-cultural groups, but a division of power among them.

This book will discuss ethnocratic trends in Uganda's history, and relate them to Amin's policies with regard to both tribal and racial groups in the country. Uganda under Idi Amin has had elements of both ethnic monopoly of power and ethnic division of labor. In some ways Amin's Uganda has been trying to evolve into a kinship polity, but the regime has also sought alternative solutions within the principle of careful ethnic arithmetic.

With the first two chapters let us explore the historical background of these trends, then place them within broader anthropological and cultural contexts, before returning more fully to the central theme of soldiers and kinsmen in Amin's Uganda.

Section I:

Historical Background

Chapter 1

CIVILIAN LEADERSHIP: THE OBOTE YEARS

Leadership in Africa might be said to fall into five major styles: there is first the intimidatory leader; secondly, the patriarchal leader; thirdly, the leader of reconciliation; fourthly, the bureaucratic leader; and fifthly, the leader of mobilization. The terms are largely self-explanatory but may need elaboration.

The intimidatory leader relies primarily on fear and on instruments of coercion to assert his authority. All leaders have to use some degree of force, but the intimidatory leader specializes in it. Military leaders in Africa have tended to drift towards both bureaucratic and intimidatory styles. The patriarchal leader (who may be interventionist or permissive) is the one who commands neo-filial reverence, a real father figure. The permissive patriarchal leader prefers to withdraw from involvement in the affairs of the nation and dominate the scene from a godlike position in the background rather than as a participating politician. There may be occasions when he has to intervene actively in determining the direction of national change, but in general his style is that of delegation to his lesser colleagues who carry out the day-to-day business of guiding the nation. A patriarchal leader with a permissive style intervenes only when his colleagues are unequal to a particular emergency or crisis, or when the "younger" members of his national family are quarreling among themselves. Patriarchal leadership can be profoundly African when it becomes intertwined with African reverence for age and elderly wisdom.

A leader of reconciliation relies for his effectiveness on qualities of tactical accommodation and a capacity to discover areas of compromise between otherwise antagonistic viewpoints. He remains in control for as long as he is successful in the politics of compromise and synthesis. The reconciliation is quite often between antagonistic political interest groups. But in presentday Africa the reconciliation leader may have to perfect also the art of reconciling the military with the civilian sectors of authority. The fifth kind of leader is the mobilization leader. He tends to be activated more by ideological factors than do the other four kinds of leaders. He also needs personal charismatic qualities more than do the other three, though these other kinds of leaders may combine charisma with their other qualities. Indeed, the patriarchal leader—who is a power in the background for invocation in times of national emergency—may often have to rely on massive charismatic presence to maintain his role as the awesome shadow behind day-to-day politics. But certainly the mobilization leader, if he is to succeed in effectively alerting the masses to certain enterprises, needs charismatic qualities either of a personal kind or derived from the mystique of a hallowed position which he occupies.

The bureaucratic style of leadership by contrast, prefers a "low key" approach—efficiency rather than evocation, procedure rather than passion.

COMPARATIVE EAST AFRICAN LEADERSHIP

All five types of leader are present on the African scene but seldom in pure form. The styles of leadership are often mixed; intimidatory elements especially tend to be present in varying degrees. Nevertheless, in East Africa we may say that Mzee Jomo Kenyatta in Kenya is basically a patriarchal leader—the massive presence of national authority, non-interventionist except when really needed, projecting an air of solidity and stability in spite of the cracks and cleavages of day-to-day Kenya politics. The affectionate use of the title, "Mzee," for Kenyatta is itself a manifestation of his patriarchal status and the filial reverence he commands.

Julius Nyerere of Tanzania, originally more of a reconciliation leader, has in the last few years emerged substantially as a leader of mobilization. Nyerere had an ideological viewpoint from the beginning of his political evolution, but early on it leaned more to democratic liberalism than to centralizing socialism. But as Nyerere's ideology has matured, its direction has become more radical with an increasing commitment to broad national interventionist policies in different sectors of the life of the people. There is a feeling that leadership for change is needed at all levels of society—rural and urban, young and old, educated and uneducated. The Arusha Declaration, if it had limited itself merely to the nationalization of industries, need not have been a clarion call for mobilization. But the concept of self-reliance did postulate a more systematic awakening of social commitment in the masses. And effective pursuit of this goal is, by definition, a process of political mobilization. In the end Nyerere has chosen a mobilization style of leadership.

The most dramatic example of the reconciliation leader in East Africa was clearly Apolo Milton Obote of Uganda. In some ways his successes, though less publicized than those of Nyerere and in some respects even of Kenyatta, were personal triumphs in a profound and special sense. Obote took Uganda into independence with few of the advantages which Nyerere and Kenyatta enjoyed, and with far deeper political problems than those which confronted Nyerere at home. Tanganyika had been a society relatively peaceful and substantially homogeneous when compared with its neighbors. The homogeneity, and the relative gentleness of Tanganyika's political culture, greatly facilitated the emergence of a single leader capable of commanding wide popularity. The late George Bennett used to say that the great strength of Tanganyika was the dispersal of its population. Tanganyika had been spared the deeply divisive potentialities of ethnic cleavages partly because it did not have concentrated populations in competition with one another; nor was power and wealth concentrated in the hands of one group. It is significant that although the man who emerged as leader—Julius Nyerere—came from a small tribe of the country, there was no strong resentment of his presence in a society of this kind. In addition, Nyerere had an inherent quality of warmth which captivated the public. Such personal qualities are effective in a society like Tanzania which is not too deeply divided by ethnic considerations.

Kenyatta also had personal charismatic qualities which had considerably augmented his chances of political triumph from the beginning. His platform style was effective—in many ways more effective in Swahili than in English. He had managed to establish a reputation so early in Kenya's history that every young Kenyan who developed any degree of political awareness soon came to know that in the annals of the politics of the country there was a name, Kenyatta, which had assumed significance as far back as the 1930s. In other words, Kenyatta's durability as a political name was itself a great advantage when effective power at last came into his hands. His long detention, the sense of martyrdom at the hands of the colonial authorities, also helped to deepen the mystique surrounding his name. It is true that Kenya had potential ethnic divisions comparable to those which confronted Obote in Uganda, but by the time of Kenya's independence there was no clear rival to Kenyatta's domination of the political scene.

In addition, Kenyatta was Mkikuyu, which gave him an extra credential for leadership on ethnocratic conditions. Had Obote been a Muganda, a parallel with Kenyatta in ethnic terms would have been possible. Obote would then have been a member of the largest tribe in his nation, a tribe which was geographically at the center and near the capital, and a tribe which had had more dealings and tensions with the colonial authorities because of that presence at the heart of power than any of the other tribes. The Kikuyu and the Baganda are comparable at least in the fact that they are both heartland tribes—that is, numerous enough and politically central enough to be at the very heart of their nation's politics. Both lie astride the capitals of their respective countries. Some of the major political issues affecting the nation as a whole take place within close proximity to their homes. Many of the most influential figures in national history and national life have been drawn from them. In some important ways these two heartland tribes have made significant contributions to the very identity of their countries. They have also been a major cause of ethnocratic tendencies in the political systems of their countries.

Since Kenyatta belonged to a heartland tribe, his emergence as the dominant figure in Kenya politics was therefore not surprising. But Obote came from a tribe which had not had a central role in the affairs of the nation during the colonial period. He confronted the centrality of Buganda in the political geography of the nation and the tradition of Baganda pre-eminence in many aspects of national affairs. Obote therefore began with a greater handicap than Kenyatta had done. In fact he had to overcome the great start in national influence that the Baganda had accumulated over several decades of imperial history and even before that. Nor did Obote have the mystique of martyrdom which surrounded Kenyatta. And finally, Obote was less endowed than either Kenyatta or Nyerere with those elusive qualities of personal and political charisma.

Obote's rise had therefore to be based on his political sensibility, his ability to apprehend the right moment for this or that move, his capacity to know what was appropriate at a given moment in time. Faced with a very difficult country, coming from a tribe which had not been specially privileged during the colonial period, battling against a Ganda supremacy which could not be overthrown overnight, bereft of martyrdom in his personal biography, lacking a warm public personality, Milton Obote had to rely on his ability to understand and use the intricacies of tactical and strategic political calculation. It is this ability that creates great reconcilation leaders.

PARLIAMENT AND PARTY LEADERSHIP

Independence was scheduled for October 1962. Obote's initial policy was to retain some link with the inevitabilities of history—to keep some ties with the residual pre-eminence of the Baganda on attainment of independence. To the surprise of some observers, his seemingly more radical Uganda People's Congress (UPC) had concluded an alliance with the seemingly feudalistic Kabaka Yekka Party (KY). Uganda as a whole did not have an international image as a great radical country or even as a militantly pan-Africanist state, but the nearest thing to a radical symbol in Uganda was the Uganda People's

Congress of which Obote was the leader. And here was the party of radicalism associating itself in power with the party of conservatism and traditionalism. Yet that was a concession in the style of political reconciliation, a coming to terms with the continuities of history which in Uganda included the centrality of the Baganda in national affairs. It was a concession to an ethno-cratic heritage.

But the marriage was a rather uneasy one. Obote did support the election of Sir Edward Mutesa as President of the country, while Sir Edward retained his position as Kabaka (king) of the Baganda. Yet this elevation of Sir Edward to the presidency of the nation was perhaps a political move of some shrewdness. Inevitably, it would complicate the loyalties of Sir Edward to entrust him with responsibilities which would force upon him the broader national cause, as well as the narrower one of his own ethnic kingdom. His election to the presidency was indeed part of the price for the continuing alliance between the KY and the UPC—a pact of understanding to share positions of eminence in the new Uganda. Nevertheless, the move had potential value as an instrument either for the conversion of Sir Edward Mutesa to a pan-Uganda vision or as a move towards complicating his perspectives and loyalties deeply enough to make the Ganda challenge to the UPC less formidable.

On attainment of independence in October 1962, the government side of the National Assembly of Uganda consisted of the 44 seats of the UPC and the 24 seats of the KY. In opposition was the Democratic Party with 24 seats.

Before long Obote's party started growing at the expense of the others. Initially its increasing strength owed less to its own appeal than to serious dissensions with the KY movement and the Democratic Party. The party leader and president-general of the Democratic Party was Mr. Benedicto Kiwanuka, who had been premier during the self-government period on the eve of independence. The official parliamentary leader of the opposition, however, was Mr. Basil Bataringaya. Mr. Bataringaya had never commanded enough support within the party to wrest the overall leadership from Mr. Kiwanuka. Bataringaya's position therefore became increasingly untenable. A number of his colleagues in parliament crossed to Obote's party, perhaps partly out of genuine disenchantment with the Democratic Party. On December 31, 1964, Mr. Bataringaya himself crossed the floor and joined the UPC, taking 5 other Democratic Party members with him. Although there were calls that the rest of the party's parliamentary group should also cross, they were resisted. And Mr. Kiwanuka declared a resolute resistance to the apparent tend towards a one-party system in Uganda.[1]

In the meantime Dr. Obote's party had also been gaining at the expense of the Kabaka Yekka. The 24 KY members of the National Assembly had all been indirectly elected—21 by the Lukiiko (Buganda's regional assembly) and

3 by the National Assembly sitting as an electoral college. In its earlier phases
the drift from the KY to the UPC seemed to be a reaction against the way in
which the chiefs and other traditionalists in Buganda had successfully
thwarted any hope of converting the KY movement into a modern political
party or of using its moral assets as a means of bringing about major reforms
within the kingdom itself.

Ideologically, the KY members who joined the UPC appeared to be nearer
to Obote's pragmatic secularism than to the traditionalist conservative forces
grouped around the Kabaka of Buganda. By joining the UPC, KY members
were branded as traitors to the cause of upholding Buganda's traditions. But
though elected by the Lukiiko, they could not be removed by the Lukiiko. In
any case the continuing coalition between the KY and the UPC perhaps
helped to mitigate the sense of betrayal felt by those who had elected the KY
defectors to the National Assembly.

Finally in August 1964 Obote felt strong enough to terminate his alliance
with the Kabaka Yekka. The 14 remaining KY members of parliament
crossed the floor to sit alongside the Democratic Party opposition, though
they apparently made no attempt to enter into any kind of tactical arrangement with them. Obote's sense of timing was remarkable. On the horizon was
an important date—October 8, 1964. That was the date provided for by the
constitution as a moment of decision for the lost counties of Bunyoro.

These counties had been taken away from Bunyoro and handed over to
Buganda quite early in the colonial period as a reward for services rendered
by Buganda to the imperial authority. Through the years the Banyoro had
repeatedly challenged the transfer. And within the counties themselves organized resistance to Buganda hegemony dated back at least to 1921 and
perhaps even further. At the constitutional conference in 1961 in London on
the terms for independence and the fundamental law on which it was to be
based, the two counties of Buyaga and Bugangazi were transferred to the
central government of Uganda, with the requirement that a referendum be
held two years after independence, that is some time after October 8, 1964.
This referendum was to decide what the people of the counties wanted—to
remain part of Buganda or to be transferred to Bunyoro. Ethnocratic factors
were again at play.

Milton Obote, in spite of the risks, decided to hold the referendum at the
earliest opportunity. His tactical moves and his capacity to influence early
defections to his party in parliament had by this time virtually freed him of
the need for Mutesa's support. As the data for the referendum approached,
the atmosphere was tense in the counties themselves, in the capital city, and
in Buganda and Bunyoro generally. Constitutional difficulties were compounded by Sir Edward Mutesa's dual position as Kabaka of Buganda and
President of Uganda. When Obote decided that the central government was to

take over the disputed counties more completely pending the referendum, President Mutesa refused to sign the necessary documents.

The referendum was held as planned on November 4, 1964. The territory's choice was to remain part of Buganda, to become part of Bunyoro, or to be a separate district under the direct administration of the central government. An overwhelming majority voted in favor of reunion with Bunyoro.[2]

Reconciliation leadership often requires a positive demonstration that the leader is still in control. It requires a capacity to prove that certain important promises, affecting one region as against another, are kept. The issue of the lost counties provided Obote with the opportunity to make such a demonstration. In a clear contest of wills with Mutesa, Obote had shown his ability to fulfill the promise which the Ugandan constitution had made to the people of Buyaga and Bugangazi. Reconcilation leadership, like bureaucratic leadership but unlike intimidatory, patriarchal, or mobilization leadership, needs to be especially respectful of procedures which are intended to define the rules of contest between different groups. It may well be that no African government, including Uganda's and Kenya's, had always been scrupulous in following the rules of the political game. But the Uganda situation under Obote had often tended to be particularly responsive to the demands of procedure, to due process of law in some cases, and to the reaffirmation of the rights of groups. Obote's performance in fulfilling the constitutional promise to the people of Buyaga and Bugangazi was in some ways his most important political triumph to that time. It demonstrated his viability as a leader, independent of the residual historical pre-eminence of the Baganda.

Yet, by a curious chance, Obote's overall control within his own party started to decline in the succeeding months. Much of 1965 and the first few weeks of 1966 constituted a period of cumulative dissension and intrigue within the Uganda People's Congress. Was Obote losing his capacity to reconcile warring factions within his own party? Was he about to be overthrown? The two parties in opposition continued to lose some members who crossed the floor to join the UPC, but it was no longer clear that these defections strengthened the UPC.

Then in February 1966 a member of the opposition virtually accused Obote, the Minister of Defense, and Idi Amin, then deputy army commander, of complicity in corrupt practices involving the transfer of gold and ivory from the Congo. The public accusation was itself remarkable. Even more remarkable, as a manifestation of the open acceptance of procedure in Uganda, the accusation was formalized in a motion for the establishment of a commission of inquiry and was openly debated in parliament. And the Uganda parliament agreed, with only one contrary vote, that the commission of inquiry should indeed be set up to investigate the allegations against the head of government and his two prominent colleagues.

FROM CONCILIATION TO CONFRONTATION

What happens when a reconciliation leader is faced with the politics of confrontation? It really did seem that this was the eve of Obote's exit from politics, at any rate from ultimate power. If a motion was so overwhelmingly supported in parliament, it indicated that many of his closest colleagues had taken Daudi Ocheng's allegations sufficiently seriously to feel that a commission of inquiry was justified. Was this the end of Milton Obote? Had he lost his genius for reconciliation? Had he lost his power to lead?

The secret of successful reconciliation is to work from a position of apparent strength. Obote at the time was traveling up north. He took his time to collect his thoughts and then returned to the capital. There he met colleagues and tested to see where his areas of residual strength lay and how much overall support he could count on both among politicians and in the armed forces. He planned his resumption of control—and then started a series of dramatic moves. He suspended the constitution; he arrested five of his ministers in a surprise move as they were at a cabinet meeting; and he relieved the head of state, Sir Edward Mutesa, of his position as President. He appointed himself Provisional Executive President of the nation. To crown it all Obote then proceeded to appoint the very commission of inquiry which parliament had decided upon as a way of investigating allegations about his complicity in corrupt practices. In the politics of confrontation the reconciliation leader has to appear strong. But the continuities of reconciliation demand a speedy return to the politics of procedure. The men that Obote appointed to the commission of inquiry were men over whom he could have no special control—they were *impartial* commissioners: Sir Clement de Lestang of the Court of Appeal of Eastern Africa, Mr. Justice E. Miller, a judge of the High Court of Kenya, and Mr. Justice Augustine Saidi of the High Court of Tanzania. It was a remarkable political performance. Obote had turned the tables on his opponents with aplomb. He had revealed his qualities as a fighter, qualities which are also important for the reconciliation leader. He had utilized tactics that effectively strengthened his position, and also seemed to clear his name in the face of the accusations which had been levelled against him.

Finally, in appointing the commission of inquiry which parliament had asked for, he recognized the place of procedure in the whole task of concilation. Those among the general public who might have been tempted to sympathize with the opposition because of the allegations of corrupt practices were now reassured by the appointment of clearly impartial judges to investigate those allegations. Much of the evidence on the allegations was taken publicly and openly covered by the press; Obote himself gave evidence.

The full report of the commission appeared in 1971, but what was revealed in 1966 was enough to create a sense of confidence in much of the population that the movement of gold and ivory between the Congolese rebels and the Ugandan sympathizers was much more innocent than Daudi Ocheng had intimated.

Meanwhile other procedural formalities continued to be observed by Obote. It was almost as if constitutionalism continued in spite of the suspension of the consitition. A "single day of wrongful arrest" was symbolic of this proceduralism. The warrant for the ex-ministers' arrest was signed on the day *following* their apprehension. This single day of wrongful arrest led the ministers in question to threaten to take action for damages. Their detention had been confirmed by a high court of Uganda, but the single day of wrongful arrest remained in dispute. The Uganda government agreed, by an out-of-court settlement, to pay each minister the sum of five hundred pounds.[3] Again the combination of a posture of power and respect for procedure was a classic example of reconciliation leadership at its best.

The entire bid to embarrass and oust Obote in 1966 was facilitated by the coincidence that the head of Buganda had also been for a while the head of Uganda. As events unrolled in Uganda in 1966, one event led to another, until the ultimate confrontation—the Battle of the Palace—occurred. On May 24, 1966, the national army, on Obote's orders, attacked the Kabaka's residence, and after an exchange with the defenders of the palace, the palace fell. The Kabaka himself escaped and remained in exile until his death in November 1969. But the power of the Baganda seemed at last at an end. In fact with the new constitution and proposals promulgated in 1967 Buganda was split into four districts and denied the distinctive personality that it had legally enjoyed for so long.

The events of 1966 seemed to shake Obote's faith in the viability of institutionalized pluralism in his country. The neo-federal autonomy conceded to Buganda and extended in some measure to one or two other districts had resulted in the institutionalized fragmentation of the country. Obote decided that the gradual elimination of these instruments of fragmentation was essential if unity was to be restored. His first targets were the symbols of regional autonomy, especially the kings.

As a reconciliation leader, Obote's approach to major changes was a piecemeal, step-by-step one. His first task was to prepare public opinion for republicanism, and one way of doing this was to deflate the mystique of monarchy. Kings were surrounded by an air of sanctity and high eminence. After the calculated deflation of monarchical grandeur on radio and television, Obote finally announced proposals for a new constitution for Uganda, one which included the abolition of the monarchies.

Later, in relation to the "move to the left," Obote again adopted the tactic of giving ample warning to the public about major changes to come. But in this case, unlike the earlier abolition of kings, the nature of the change was made explicit from the start. With the issue of republicanism the explicit policy that kings were to be abolished was not declared in advance; it was simply that a prior strategy of royal deflation was adopted. The deflation later culminated in actual concrete proposals abolishing the kings. But in the case of the "move to the left," the intention was more explicitly declared; this was also true of the statement about a forthcoming national service. Indeed a minister for national service was appointed months before the proposals saw the light of day. A piecemeal inauguration of potentially controversial policies is one further attribute of the leader of reconciliation— and Obote often opted for "trial balloons" and careful preparation of public opinion.

TOWARDS THE MILITARIZATION OF THE POLITY

But the confrontation in 1965 and 1966 had long-term repercussions for the style of political activity in Uganda. The trouble with the politics of confrontation is that it can release forces which make the politics of reconciliation more difficult in later years. In 1966 the big issue for Obote was not simply how to keep the system going, but how to survive politically. A reconciliation leader faced with the problem of political survival has to resort to forms of alliance whose purposes are different from those of pure reconciliation. Obote's party had entered into a tactical alliance with the Kabaka Yekka as a way of reconciling otherwise disparate sides by creating a shared political arrangement. But seeking allies in order that the leader himself may remain as leader of the political party is a different matter. There can be little doubt that one of the major precipitating factors of the 1966 events was, quite simply, a plot to oust Obote from the leadership of the Uganda People's Congress. Although the intrigue was to some extent within the UPC itself, it is by no means clear that the plotting was designed to use the methods available for changing the party leader. On the contrary, there is evidence to suggest that extra-procedural tactics were being employed to oust Obote. It would seem that some of Obote's opponents had not ruled out violent means.

The reconciliatory leader is ultimately committed to the maintenance of the system. The survival of a given system of political arrangement on a basis of amicability is in fact the central core of the reconciliation style. But in 1966 it was not clear what was at stake—the survival of the system, the survival of the leader, or the survival of both. When a reconciliation leader is confronted with his own political survival, he may sincerely believe that the survival of his leadership cannot be separated from the survival of the system as a whole. This belief might be encouraged if there is evidence to suggest that his opponents are prepared to resort to extra-constitutional means to oust him. Mutesa had confessed to having explored the possibility of inviting foreign troops—British—to intervene on his behalf should there be a threat to the presidency within the country. On an issue like that did the President (Mutesa) have the constitutional right to negotiate for foreign intervention without the approval of the head of government (Obote)?

It was 1966, much more than January 1964 when the army mutinied for higher pay, which brought to the fore another major area needing reconciliation—that between the military and civilian sectors of authority. During 1965 it had become clear that politicians were vying with each other for the friendship and support of the security forces. The problem was so acute that the commissioner of police had broadcast an appeal to the country to stop trying to divert the police from their normal duties and seeking to implicate them in politics. At the same time he appealed to the police to resist the blandishments of the politicians whose friendships with the police were calculated to achieve political ends. By early 1966 it was evident that the future of civilian authority in Uganda might depend upon who succeeded in winning the confidence of the security forces. A reconciliation between the military and civilian sectors of authority had become critical. The danger of the civilian authorities being eliminated was greater in Uganda than in either Tanzania or Kenya, though a military takeover in Uganda would increase the risk of similar problems in the other two countries.

The end of 1965 and the early months of 1966 called forth from Obote new skills to effect a reconciliation not between one political faction and another, or between one political party and another, but between the soldiers and the politicians, between military force and civilian constitutionalism. It must therefore be counted as one of his most important victories that for five years he succeeded in maintaining civilian authority in the affairs of the nation while retaining the confidence of the army. It was a tightrope and it needed great skill to walk it successfully—but a skill which all great reconciliation leaders have. Had Obote been ousted in 1966 by either his opponents within the UPC or the Mutesa group, or both in alliance, it is almost certain that the surviving civilian government in Uganda would have been precarious sooner. Neither of those two antagonistic groups appeared to have the skills for precisely this kind of reconciliation, and, in the one case, there was the further handicap of representing an ethnic group which had yet to be trusted by large sectors of the armed forces.

But it was precisely this latter factor which complicated the task of reconciliation at the different levels of national life. How many concessions

could Obote make to some of the old Baganda leaders without risking the
viability of the alliance he had made to strengthen him in the confrontation
with those leaders in 1966? Could he create conditions for the repoliticization of the Baganda without increasing the danger of the politicization of
the armed forces? Could he lift the emergency regulations in Buganda
without creating anxieties among some of his allies? These are some of the
dilemmas which Obote then confronted. A move towards reconciling the
Baganda was a move towards repoliticizing the Baganda. And such a move
carried the risk of the politicization of the army, both because of certain
anxieties in the armed forces about the intentions of the Baganda and because
of the risk that a competition between politicians for friends within the
armed forces might again be activated. This in turn carried the danger of
factionalism in the security forces and their division along political lines.

In this web of dilemmas Obote's second phase of reconciliation inevitably
included some intimidation. To keep the Baganda depoliticized could lead to
other forms of activity within Buganda less healthy to the survival of the
polity. These underground activities themselves would in turn increase the
anxieties of those who already distrusted the Baganda. Detention without
trial under the regulations of the state of emergency became recurrent. The
old atmosphere of reconciliation was not entirely absent, and certain moves
were made to try and reactivate the atmosphere of political tolerance. But
elements of intimidation had entered into the style of politics in Uganda
precisely because the web of reconciliation had now become a more complex
pattern of tactical accommodation. The polity had begun to be militarized.

But Obote was genuinely anxious not to let Uganda become either a
militarized polity or a police state. In this atmosphere of uncertainty and
conflicting dilemmas he nevertheless seemed to be groping for areas where
tolerance and public discussion could be allowed, for opportunities for
popular participation in determining the direction of national change.

RESIDUAL CONSTITUTIONALISM UNDER OBOTE

The most dramatic example of this residual freedom was the historic
debate in 1967 on the new constitutional proposals. Obote did want those
proposals thrashed out in the nation within different arenas, with full candor.
And so they were debated, with vigorous bluntness in parliament, with
genuine permissiveness for opposing views in the ruling party's own paper,
The People, and with more academic detachment and analysis at public

sessions on the campus of Makerere University College. There was no doubt that genuine opposition was expressed openly to some key elements in the constitutional proposals, including the dramatic decision to abolish the kingships. Some members of the ruling party were expelled for their opposition, but this was consistent with democratic procedures in the case of fundamental disagreement by individuals with major premises of a party's policy. Such expulsions could have happened anywhere in the liberal world. The magazine *Transition* also carried on a debate within its pages, which, for a time, appeared uninhibited by any security complexes. The groping for residual openness in Uganda's society seemed to have the full backing of Obote.

Even the decision to abolish all the kingships, instead of just the kabakaship, was a venture in reconciliation. There was a feeling that the Baganda would be less ready to accept the abolition of their king alone than the ending of all kingships. Collective republicanism was a more conciliatory gesture than discriminatory republicanism. It is true that the abolition of the other kings made Obote seem to abandon a number of old friends who had stood by him in his confrontation with Ganda pre-eminence and presumption. And yet the abolition of kings in some of the other kingdoms caused a less profound upheaval than the abolition of the kabakaship in Buganda. Discriminatory republicanism, it was calculated, would have alienated the Baganda from the smaller kingdoms in the country.

The issue of republicanism was both defended and condemned in the course of the public discussion. Among the most forthright critics was Abu Mayanja, a former minister in the Kabaka's government who had previously crossed the floor to join the Uganda People's Congress but who was now alienated from that party over the issue of republicanism.

The case of Mayanja illustrated the deep ambivalence in this policy of tolerance. The sincere desire of the government to permit a large degree of free discussion could not be doubted. It was a continuing aspect of the politics of procedure. Yet there were frontiers in the criticism of government policy which could only be crossed at some risk to the critics. Mayanja remained one of the vigorous voices in Uganda's politics for one more year following the approval of the constitutional proposals. But in October 1968 he was detained, along with Rajat Neogy, editor of *Transition* (published in Kampala). The grounds for the detention were never clarified in the case of Mayanja. Was it because of his outspokenness? Or was he guilty of other things behind the scenes, or suspected of such guilt?

The ambivalence was dramatized in the trial of Mayanja and Neogy. The charge was sedition. It was based on a paragraph in *Transition* (No. 37) which ended with the words:

I do not believe the rumor circulating in legal circles for the past year or so that the Judicial Service Commission has made a number of recommendations [in the direction of trying to Africanize Uganda's expatriate High Court] but the appointments have for one reason or another, mostly tribal considerations, not been confirmed. But what is holding up the appointment of Ugandan Africans to the High Court? [4]

Some people interpreted the paragraph to mean that the President had refused to confirm the appointment of qualified judges recommended by the Judicial Service Commission on the grounds that they were Baganda. It was again symptomatic of a reconciliation leader that Obote should have been deeply offended by this insinuation and should have regarded it as dangerous to good order in Uganda. The appearance of conformity with procedure by a reconciliation leader on the basis of rational and impartial criteria had to be safeguarded against innuendos of that kind—hence the decision to take the two people to court for writing and publishing a paragraph which, in the opinion of the prosecution, could amount to the incitement of tribal animosities and therefore constitute a risk to good order.

But the ambivalence about the extent to which freedom should continue to characterize Uganda's style of politics manifested itself in other aspects of the Mayanja-Neogy saga. The very issue of the magazine which was suspected of sedition was nevertheless permitted free circulation and was on sale at newsstands in different parts of the country. The detention of the editor and Mayanja had cast a cloud on the freedom to write in Uganda; yet freedom to *read* what was already written continued. The right of the printed word to circulate in Uganda had seldom been challenged. People were not taken to court for reading certain books, as they were in Kenya, nor were they legally liable for importing certain newspapers, as they were in Tanzania for as long as *The Nation* newspapers were banned. On the contrary, in Uganda Mutesa's book was serialized in the ruling party's own newspaper. There was a sophisticated insistence that Ugandans should be free to read what they wanted, although the right of Ugandans to write what they wanted was nowhere as unrestricted as their freedom to read what was already published. The ambivalence of reconciliation continued to manifest itself in multiple ways under Obote's leadership.

The sedition trial of Mayanja and Neogy ended on February 1, 1969, when the accused were found not guilty of the charges of sedition. They were released with a ringing declaration of the toleration of speech and free expression. It was an impressive demonstration of the freedom of the judiciary in Uganda. The regime in Uganda had profound reservations about the verdict, but no action against the judicial system was contemplated. The two accused were rearrested—but under the emergency regulations. The kind of indignant dismissal of a judge to which Nkrumah descended in 1965 when a verdict against an opponent did not go in the direction of the President's own pleasure was simply not possible in Uganda at that time. The politics of proper procedure continued to exert a profound influence.

In addition to his attempts to maintain areas of political toleration, Obote started to feel his way toward creating a new political order in Uganda. Hence his announcement that Uganda was going to "move to the left." A Ministry of National Service was formed and the nation awaited not only more specific proposals of the form which that the national service would take, but also a broader ideological blueprint.

The blueprint which emerged was the document entitled *The Common Man's Charter* (Kampala: Consolidated Printers, 1969), written by Obote. Yet *The Common Man's Charter* was also an exercise in reconciliation leadership. Obote the man was, on balance, to the left of Obote the leader. If Milton Obote had not been cast in the role of the leader of the political party and had merely been one more member of the Uganda People's Congress, it is likely that his articulated position would have been in the left wing of the party, if not the extreme left wing. But the style of Obote's leadership tended to pull him towards the center of the ideological spectrum, and occasionally to the right of center. While Obote the man would have preferred to be more radical in the changes he put forward for Uganda, Obote the leader had to take into account the disparities and cleavages within his own party, as well as the balance of probable acceptance in the country for any new proposals.

We might therefore say that the title of this momentous document, *The Common Man's Charter,* symbolized the real position of Obote the man. It connoted the respect for commonality and for the average individual. It was a symbol of proletarian solidarity. But the contents of the document stood for Obote the leader, sensitive to the need for conciliation and accommodation, aware of the limitation on radical reforms in Uganda, and prepared to come to terms with certain aspects of those realities. The title promised more radicalism than really existed in the pages inside. If the contents had been designed purely to represent the ideological position of Obote the man, the promise of the title might have been fulfilled. But the contents were one more instance of the supremacy of reconciliation in Obote's style. There was a commitment to greater economic equity and reduction of privilege. But the commitment was not explicit enough to arouse the opposition of the anti-nationalization lobby in Obote's own party. Much of *The Common Man's Charter* was a plea for national unity rather than for socialism.

And yet the earlier priorities in 1969 were perhaps right. The country was seriously divided, and Obote was looking for ways to heal the wounds and achieve greater cohesion. It was not until December 1969 that a shock made him reflect further about how far he should go to change his style of leadership.

THE NEMESIS OF VIOLENCE

On December 19, 1969, there was an attempt on Obote's life as he was leaving the highly successful annual delegates' conference of his party. Who had attempted to kill the President? What lay behind that criminal venture? What did it mean?

Every major figure in a country has his opponents. A major figure in a seriously divided country like Uganda might sometimes have to contend with more than his fair share. There were three conceivable groups of opponents of the President, who, at first sight, might have been implicated in the attempted assassination: first, his ethnic opponents; secondly, his ideological opponents; and thirdly, his rivals for power or those with personal political grievances.

The ethnic opponents of the President were, conceivably, either those who had strong feelings about the President's own tribe or those who felt he had humiliated their own tribe. There were of course a number of theories based on Ganda complicity in the attempted assassination. Was this an effort to restore a Ganda-centered ethnocracy?

The second possible source of the assassination attempt were the ideological opponents of the President, those who had strong reservations about the direction in which Obote was taking the country. Some might be worried about the move to the left and its implications. This worry was linked with a profound suspicion of socialism as an ideology either out of preference for alternate secular ideologies or for reasons of religious inhibition. The idea that socialism was one step nearer Marxism, and "therefore" one step nearer atheism, was not entirely absent from Ugandan public opinion. Others were worried about the future of their own businesses and financial interests should Uganda move too far to the left. All these people could be called ideological opponents. They did not need to belong to tribes hostile to the President, since the main area of hostility to Obote's leadership was in this case ideological rather than ethnic.

A third possible group of opponents were rivals of power or people with personal grievances against Obote. If they were rivals then the cleavage lay at the top of the political structure—an open break in the tense relationships between powerful political peers. If, on the other hand, the issue was a personal political grievance, the person involved could be a political peer or a subordinate. A person whose career had been compromised, for example, might be animated by a sense of political revenge.

There was naturally the fourth possibility—an individual lunatic seeking personal satisfaction or historical immortality by carrying out a crime of national proportions.

If the assassin fell into one of the first three categories, or had been

financed by any one of them, the incident raised important political issues. If
the attempted assassination was by an ethnic opponent of the President, then
the act itself symbolized the simple fact that the task of national survival was
far from complete. Obote's leadership of reconciliation therefore remained
imperative in order to narrow the gaps between the groups.

If, however, the assassination was the work of an ideological opponent, it
could mean that Ugandans were beginning to feel passionately about political
issues above and beyond tribal loyalties, that political violence was moving
from issues of national survival to issues of ideological preference. This new
motivation could have great political meaning. To kill because one hates
socialism is less fundamental than to kill because one hates the tribe of one's
opponent. Tribalistic violence is the violence of identity; ideological violence
is the violence of policy. Violence on policy issues is secondary violence;
violence on identity and national survival is primary violence.

Government authorities must of course try to suppress all forms of
violence, from those associated with robbery to those designed to precipitate
a revolution. But these different forms of violence have varying implications.
And the student of society must try to understand these implications.

If the attempted assassination of the President was tribalistic in origin, one
possible conclusion was that Obote should continue to allow reconciliation to
dominate his style of leadership. The nation was still faced with acute
primary violence. If the attempt on Obote's life was a case of ideological
violence, then it could mean, ironically, that Uganda was a little more ready
for ideological mobilization than it had been on attainment of independence
eight years before. Secondary violence inspired by ideological preference could
mean—though it was still too early to be sure—that the passions of *pure*
tribalism had started on the slow road to extinction. The very attempt on His
Excellency's life might therefore mean that the country was in need of
greater mobilization.

Tribalism in Africa is unlikely to disappear within a single lifetime. But,
pessimistic as it may seem, the first signs of its disappearance might have to
be sought in the changes in the motives of political violence—from primary to
secondary. Much of the violence in developed societies is secondary violence,
less concerned with national survival than with issues of policy preference.
But much of the political violence in Africa remains deeply concerned with
identity, and is therefore primary.

If the difficulties in Uganda were concerned with the tensions of rivalry
for power, this too would be secondary violence. It would indicate that the
President's rivals were sufficiently interested in the central machinery of the
nation to wish to control it themselves. A power struggle for control of the
center is a confirmation that all are interested in the survival of the system.
They simply disagree over who should control it. Violence between political

peers for the control of the center, or violence by subordinates who have political grievances, is therefore normally secondary violence.

In March and April 1970 certain individuals confessed to having participated in the assassination attempt and were sentenced to imprisonment. Who paid them? This point was not firmly established in court. Ethnic opponents of Obote seemed the most likely since the accused were Ganda; but other opponents of the President might conceivably have been implicated as well.

African leaders need to be protected because of the special cleavages in their societies. They in turn have to protect those over whom they exercise authority. They have to protect them from each other and sometimes they have to protect them from the very people who exercise authority. In this special sense, then, the story of Milton Obote of Uganda had important points of contact with the story of independent Africa, in all its dangers and all its opportunities, in all its failings and all its triumphs.

THE QUEST FOR POLITICAL MOBILIZATION

In a deeply divided country, is a reconciliatory style of leadership inadequate for the very purposes it is supposed to serve? Is it indeed inadequate for the task of building a lasting national reconciliation? Is national mobilization ultimately the best approach to national reconciliation?

It is arguable that the publication of *The Common Man's Charter* symbolized an attempt by Dr. Obote to move from being a reconciliation leader to becoming a mobilization leader. It is also arguable that this desire had manifested itself before in Obote's political style. There had been other attempts to arouse in the populace a common moment of national feeling. In years past Obote's occasional quest for a mobilization effect had been astutely calculated in terms of which emotions in a country like Uganda were more likely to be unifying and which divisive. Pure ideological enthusiasm was not in Uganda's style. What then?

Obote seemed to have grasped quite early that the process of nation-building at the psychological level entails the cumulative acquisition of common emotional dispositions and common potential responses to the same stimuli. To be capable of being angry about the same incident is to share an area of fellow feeling.

Social engineering in the new African states has sometimes taken the form of purposeful collectivization of anger in a bid to make the populace share a moment of indignant empathy. The collectivization of anger sometimes results in the nationalization of protest. A capacity for what John Stuart Mill calls "collective pride and humiliation" is a particularly important feature in a sense of shared nationhood. It is precisely because of this that anger as an emotion is so central to the growth of nationhood. After all offended pride gives rise to anger. Collective humiliation is a deeper stage of offended pride. This in turn generates anger, either overtly or in a subdued silent form. Shared moments of collective anger, by being connected with the cumulative acquisition of a capacity for collective pride and collective humiliation, become part of the process of national integration.

Among political leaders in Africa, Obote was particularly aware of the importance of promoting shared emotional dispositions and potential responses to the same stimuli. Faced with a deeply divided country, Obote at times used the devices of collectivizing moments of anger and nationalizing protest.

On February 13, 1965, some Congolese planes bombed the villages of Goli and Paidha in the West Nile District of Uganda. Obote himself was angry that this should have happened. But, more importantly, he saw the moment as one which afforded the opportunity for collective patriotic anger among Ugandans. Anger against the Congolese for violating Uganda's borders in such a violent way afforded some possibilities. Yet Obote perceived that being angry with the Congolese was not adequate. The planes which had crossed the border were American-made, sold or given to Tshombe's regime in the Congo by the United States government. The possibilities of collectivizing Ugandan anger and directing it at the United States, in addition to directing it at Tshombe's regime, were grasped by Obote. The situation did indeed afford possibilities for a sense of wounded pride. In addition, a diplomatic confrontation between Uganda and the United States had all the trappings of a David and Goliath confrontation: the weak, aroused in proud anger, facing the mighty in a posture of defiant protest. Obote said to his countrymen: "We blame the government of the United States. . . . We have been attacked without provocation on our part. I cannot say whether we are going to retaliate. . . . We must all be prepared to throw sand, and sacks of sand, in the eyes of the mighty."[5]

Even then the question arose as to why Obote was dramatizing the bombing incident instead of minimizing it. One reason might have been the obvious one—the desire to take a justifiably indignant stand at having one's frontiers violated. But it also seemed likely that Obote perceived the political function of wounded pride when it is collectivized. After all, an important problem confronting every African government is how to transform the old race-conscious nationalism of the anti-colonial struggle into a new state-conscious patriotism of post-independence days. How could those anti-imperialist protests of transformation of yesteryear be now converted into cumulative dispositions of shared identity?

In the case of the particular incident in Uganda in 1965, there was something very "sovereign" about having to defend one's borders against hostile planes. To be attacked by enemy planes from across the border could almost be a status symbol for a new state. The diplomatic protest which followed had, inevitably, the ring of newly acquired sovereignty. That must have been one reason why Obote felt impelled to remind his countrymen that on October 9, 1962, the country had become *independent*.

If then an African leader like Obote was dedicated to creating a state-conscious patriotism in his people, he had to utilize the sovereign symbolism of a variety of different factors—from flags to airspace. This is what made the "destruction" of a village in the West Nile District of Uganda something which could be used in the construction of a moment of national cohesion. Ugandans in a moment of joint outrage were Ugandans united.

The government therefore arranged popular participation in national anger. A national demonstration was arranged for Tuesday afternoon, February 16, 1965. There were ministerial appeals to employers to release their workers for the great march to the American Embassy and for the rally to follow. At least metaphorically, Ugandans were up in arms—or so the great march was supposed to demonstrate. And even the wounded soldier in the West Nile village was elevated to a symbolic state hero. As Obote put it: "Our one officer has already spilled blood for all of us. It will be our duty to redeem that blood."[6]

The Ugandan government could have protested directly to the Congolese government or to the government of the United States. But this would have been a government-to-government form of protest. Instead, what Obote wished to do was to collectivize anger, and popularize protest as a way of nationalizing it. There were a number of miscalculations in the arrangements and not everything went according to plan in the endeavor to unite Ugandans in shared indignation. But a demonstration did take place. The American Embassy was momentarily besieged and the American flag was burned. Diplomatic protest at the level of government to government was one thing, but Obote was trying to give protest some grassroots, and in so doing to add one more thin layer of experience to this slow cumulative acquisition of a sense of shared pride and shared humiliation among Ugandans. The growth of national identity is inseparable from the process by which prejudices become to some extent homogenized in the population, and emotional dispositions collectivized. Sometimes fear as a source of the behavior of protest is also relevant to this process. The fear of an enemy, the anger arising out of wounded pride, and the ambition to create the foundations of nationhood have often interacted on those occasions of shared protest in a new country.

There were other attempts by Obote to collectivize indignation over a special incident. There was the notorious Tank Hill party, held in Kampala on the eve of Kenya's independence in December 1963. Those attending the party were predominantly European expatriates. It was reported that the occasion was utilized to ridicule and satirize the whole idea of African independence. Games and mimicry, allegedly designed to make fun of the "premature" granting of self-government to African countries, were part of the evening's activities. The party was also a lament for the last days of empire, and a nostalgic cry for the older days of European supremacy. Obote spoke on this party in parliament. He spoke of it in terms which were deliberately calculated to arouse anger against those who had held it. There were even exhibits to show the arrogance and presumption of the merrymakers.

There was a clear danger that excessive dramatization of an incident of this kind could precipitate violent hostility not only toward the expatriates who took part in the celebration but also toward the white community at large in Uganda. Yet, in spite of this risk, the head of government dramatized the incident and sought to arouse the maximum indignation in parliament and in the country at large. Why did Obote do this? He certainly did succeed in arousing fury among fellow parliamentarians. There have been few occasions when the National Assembly of Uganda had ever been as angry. The house reverberated with their speeches demanding revenge. Never was an evening party a more momentous national issue.

There were indeed repercussions in the country, as might have been expected. The house in which the party took place was set on fire. A member of the editorial staff of a leading English-language newspaper, *Uganda Argus,* was "kidnapped" by members of the Youth wing and subjected to minor forms of humiliation, like carrying a bunch of *matoke* (local plantain used as a staple food by the Baganda).

It is likely that a similar speech made in the parliament in Nairobi by Kenyatta would have had more widespread consequences. It was the kind of speech which, in an inflammable racial situation, could lead to riots in the streets. Fortunately, the consequences in Uganda were not very destructive. There was no doubt that many Ugandans were bitterly resentful that such things could still be performed by Europeans in East Africa. But it was clear that Ugandans could not be spontaneously mobilized by a single dramatic speech in parliament. They were significantly less mobilizable in this respect than either Kenyans or Tanzanians.

Was Obote justified in blowing up the Tank Hill party into a national issue? As an incident it perhaps did not deserve that degree of elevation. But Obote's behavior made sense if he was engaged in a long-term attempt to multiply the occasions about which Ugandans could share the same feeling. A people sharing an emotion for however short a time is a nation in the making. A sense of shared nationality presupposes "identity of political antecedents; the possession of a national history and consequent community of recollections; collective pride and humiliation, pleasure and regret, connected with the same incidents in the past."[7]

Obote's attempts to unite Ugandans in anger have to be seen in this context. There is a presumption that when a group of people begins to feel proud about the same things or humiliated by the same things, pleased or saddened collectively by the same incidents, that group of people is acquiring the capacity for collective selfhood.

Yet there was another side to Obote's attempts to make Ugandans angry about the same incidents. At the psychological level Obote's behavior at the time of the bombing of the two villages in West Nile, and in relation to the Tank Hill party, could be seen as a manifestation of a deep longing to use techniques of mobilization. This longstanding psychological longing later came to assume a greater role in his leadership, as Obote's desire to complete his political mission increased. The 1966 revolution may have ended the old order of Buganda pre-eminence—but what new order did it inaugurate? The question was bound to remain unanswered for as long as the Baganda were outside the mainstream of national affairs. The arts of reconciliation are at their most valuable when the crisis facing a nation is one of system maintenance and national survival. But mobilization is needed when the desire becomes one of system *change* and national transformation.

Was Uganda ready to be mobilized in 1969 and 1970? And would Obote have been as successful at mobilization as he had been at reconciliation? We cannot be sure. But there were indications of the conversion of Obote to the view that complete reconciliation in a country like Uganda was not necessarily inseparable from mobilizational techniques. Cutting the Baganda down to size reconciled some groups in the country and enabled Obote to establish greater supremacy as a national leader. In other words, a reconciliation leader has at times to alienate one group as the price for reaching a new basis for accommodation with other groups. Obote had to some extent to alienate the Baganda in pursuit of greater cohesiveness elsewhere. This was the logic of balanced ethnocracy.

CONCLUSION

But no complete national reconciliation was conceivable while the Baganda remained alienated. Milton Obote had won his place in history by ending the old order. But the task of creating a new order had only just begun. And the Baganda had to be full and willing participants in any new order. This desire to create a new order may well have been one of the reasons behind Obote's renewed interest in the techniques of mobilzation. The national service scheme, *The Common Man's Charter,* the partial nationalization of industry in May 1970, and the new one-party system for Uganda were all indications of an Obote who wanted to move from reconciliation to mobilization. They symbolized his ambition to move from issues of national survival to questions of national transformation.

But was Obote equal to the new task? Was the country ready to be led in that style? Before history could provide answers to such questions the military intervened. Some might argue that instead of trying to mobilize the masses, Obote should have sought ways to *demobilize* the military. Yet such glib answers are more easily articulated than implemented. Perhaps Obote's new electoral scheme, which was about to be tested at the polls, was in part an attempt by the man to reverse the process which had been turning Uganda into a militarized polity since 1966. With his new elections Obote was on the verge of strengthening the civilian factor in the nation's political system. But he was too late.[8]

NOTES

1. See *Uganda Argus* (Kampala) and *Daily Nation,* January 2, 1965. Also *East African Standard,* January 11, 1965.
2. 13,602 voted for union with Bunyoro, 3,542 for remaining with Buganda, and 112 for a separate district. See Mazrui, *Violence and Thought: Essays on Social Tensions in Africa* (London & Harlow, 1969), chapters 6 and 7.
3. *Uganda Argus,* March 31, 1966.
4. *Transition,* No. 37, 1968. Later five Ugandan judges were appointed to the High Court by Obote's government.
5. *Uganda Argus,* February 15, 1965.
6. Ibid.
7. John Stuart Mill, *Representative Government* (1861), chapter 16. See also James Mittelman "Plato's *Republic* and Amin's Republic," a paper presented at the annual social science conference of the Universities of Eastern Africa, Dar es Salaam, December 1973.
8. The best analysis of Obote's attempt to control ethnicity so far is by Nelson Michael Kasfir, "Controlling Ethnicity in Ugandan Politics: Departicipation as a Strategy for Political Development in Africa," Ph.D. dissertation, Department of Government, Harvard University (September 1972).

Chapter 2

AMIN'S COUP: ETHNOCRACY AND THE

MILITARY-AGRARIAN COMPLEX

The first successful military coup in the Nile Valley in the modern period took place in Egypt in 1952. Almost twenty years later, at the other end of the White Nile, Uganda became the latest country in the Nile Valley to be captured by its own army. The army which took over power in Egypt in 1952 was described as "solidly Egyptian and rural; its officers were of the rural middle class." General Naguib, who briefly headed the new military government in Egypt, affirmed that the officer corps of the army "was largely composed of the sons of civil servants and soldiers and the grandsons of peasants."[1]

What of the army which took over power at the other end of the Nile in Kampala? Amin's army was even more solidly "rural." If Egyptian soldiers under General Naguib were "the grandsons of peasants," Uganda and Sudanese soldiers under General Amin were the *sons* of peasants. There was no intermediate generation separating the great majority of Ugandan soldiers from the womb of the countryside.

What were the implications of this linkage between peasants and modern warriors? It may be understandable in a developing society that the army should recruit primarily from people with rural roots, but why did the Uganda army consist so disproportionately of Nilotic and Sudanic tribesmen? Did this ethnic division of labor constitute the foundations for a future military ethnocracy in the country? How did political rewards and political allegiances relate to the social and ethnic origins of Ugandan soldiers?

Samuel P. Huntington, in discussing social forces pertinent to relations between the city and the countryside in certain societies, once distinguished between the brains of the intelligentsia, the guns of the military, and the numbers of the peasantry. In Huntington's view, political stability requires a coalition between at least two of these social forces. He sees a coalition of brains and guns against numbers as being rare and basically unstable. A coalition between the intelligentsia and the peasants, on the other hand, was

[30]

potentially the most revolutionary. Such a coalition could destroy an existing system and then create a new and more stable arrangement.

> The third route to stable government is by the coalescence of guns and numbers against brains. . . . Their rural social background often leads military regimes to give high priority to policies which benefit the more numerous elements in the countryside. In Egypt, Iraq, Turkey, Korea, Pakistan, governments born of military coups pushed land reform measures. In Burma and elsewhere military governments gave budget priority to agricultural rather than to urban programs.[2]

How relevant are these precedents for the understanding of what has been happening in Uganda? Is there indeed a military-agrarian complex underlying Uganda's experience with the soldiers?

We have already given a broad outline of Obote's period in the history of independent Uganda. What we propose now to bring out in this chapter is that the Obote years, especially from 1964, were basically years of a coalition between the intelligentsia and the military, between brainpower and gunpower. There was a link with the countryside to the extent that the soldiers were rurally recruited, and also because many of the most powerful members of Obote's government came from some of the least developed areas of the country. But on the whole the basic alliance was between soldiers and a large part of the country's intelligentsia. In this partnership the brains were senior in status. There was genuine civilian supremacy under Milton Obote, but paradoxically that supremacy had to make considerable concessions to the military in order to survive effectively.

One significant implication of the military coup which overthrew Obote in January 1971 was, quite simply, the termination of the supremacy of the intelligentsia. The old alliance between guns and brains, with brains in control, had now been shattered. The stage was set for new alliances.

We propose to argue that there is a military-agrarian complex struggling for survival in Uganda, a fragile alliance between the soldiers and their kinsmen in the countryside. But a major problem confronting the viability of such an alliance is the simple fact that the army has been ethnically unrepresentative, recruited overwhelmingly from Nilotic and Sudanic tribes in a country with a tradition of high ethnic consciousness and ethnocratic tendencies in the political system. The soldiers respond not merely to their rural origins but also to their ethnic origins. The old Egyptian model of a military-agrarian complex, involving dramatic moves toward land reform and the control of the intelligentsia, is struggling in Uganda against the forces of ethnic pluralism. Egypt is ethnically homogeneous; Uganda is painfully heterogeneous. The trend toward a military-agrarian complex in Uganda is struggling against the consequences of an ethnically specialized armed force operating in a country with a highly developed ethnic consciousness. But why were the soldiers of the Ugandan army recruited so selectively from Nilotic and Sudanic communities?

The present tensions in Uganda go back deep into history. And we must turn to history in the search both for explanations and for relevant definitions of critical concepts.

But in order to understand how ethnicity relates to stratification in African conditions, the concept "rural" has itself to be examined. Are there *degrees* of "ruralness"? Were the Nilotic and Sudanic tribes of Uganda particularly rural, and if so, in what sense? It is with the concept of "rural" that we must begin.

LOCATION, FUNCTION, AND STATUS

What, then, is a rural area? From a sociological point of view, three dimensions are particularly important in defining a rural area. These dimensions are *location, function,* and *status.*

An area must be located in the midst of natural greenery short of a dense forest, and must be some minimal distance from major centers of concentrated populations.

As regards function, a rural area earns its livelihood primarily from agriculture, and sometimes forestry and fishing if the requisite resources are near at hand.

From a political point of view, a rural area has also to be seen in terms of status. This is where stratification comes into relevance. In most societies the majority of the inhabitants of rural areas are relatively underprivileged. But there are occasions when the rural elite becomes effectively the national elite. Societies with a landed aristocracy provide such instances in history. But with industrialization and greater urbanization the shift of power has often moved toward the city, and the status of the countryside has declined. The rural folk have often been relegated to a humble role in national affairs.

If location as a dimension of ruralism implies *physical* distance from major centers, status implies *social* distance from urban elites and their influence on national affairs.

Sometimes physical distance is itself a causal factor behind the social distance. In the case of Uganda, the distance separating the north from the capital city of Kampala, and the poor communications which for so long hardened this distance, was a factor behind the relegation of the north to a peripheral role in national affairs. When the country at last had a northern head of government, one of the first priorities undertaken was to improve communications between the capital city of Kampala and the distant areas of Lango and Acholi. Obote converted the highroad from Kampala to Gulu into an all-weather tarmac road. He also provided a bridge to facilitate greater access to West Nile. *The Common Man's Charter,* which Obote issued in 1969 as an ideological blueprint for the new Uganda, reaffirmed the imperative of bridging the gap between the different districts of Uganda, and the necessity to pursue more equitable developmental strategies for the different parts of the country.

When Amin came into power the preoccupation with the imperative of bridging the gap between the north and the more prosperous south continued. His tribe, the Kakwa, had been even more underprivileged than, say, the Acholi. Since Amin came from West Nile, he was himself particularly keen to ensure easy access to West Nile. His interest in having an airport built outside Arua, the main town of West Nile, was in part a quest to reduce the isolation of West Nile. That isolation had a good deal to do with the status of West Nile as a particularly rural area sociologically. Amin employed Israelis to help him build that airport. By the time he expelled the Israelis, the airport was not yet complete. But the ambition to reduce the implications of physical distance, as well as reduce the social distance between the north and the more prosperous south of the country, continued to be a lingering feature of Amin's ambition.

For a while he even entertained the idea of a second university of Uganda, with a campus in Gulu and Arua, but his hopes for considerable support from the French government toward realizing this goal were not fulfilled. The idea of a second university, with special locational preference given to northern areas, was part of Amin's strategy to deruralize the Nilotic and Sudanic areas of the country.

It is certainly clear from Uganda's experience that the dimension of *status* in the definition of a rural area is in turn intimately connected with both location and function. Certainly from a political point of view the status of rural areas in national affairs is what gives rural location and rural function their most salient meaning.

We should now turn more fully to this concept of rural status, explore its ideological implications, and apply it to the analysis of both geographical location and cultural functions in Uganda's historical experience.

A Maoist interpretation of the Third World is that of a global countryside, neglected and sometimes exploited by the city folk of the affluent countries of the world. This approach looks upon the division between the developed and the less developed countries as being basically similar to the division between the city and the rural areas. A pattern of differential development, social and cultural distance, and asymmetrical political and economic interaction between these diverse geographical areas, together find a basis for such a functional definition of city versus country.

A related radical approach uses the categories of center and periphery instead of city and country. The Norwegian scholar, Johan Galtung, has perhaps gone furthest in linking imperialism to the dichotomy between center and periphery, and working out an entire theory of dominance based on that dichotomy.[3]

Applying these concepts to a single society, instead of the world as a whole, could yield important insights of its own. In the history of Uganda the role of Buganda looms large. Using Galtungian terms, Buganda was for so long the center of the society, while northern Uganda was clearly part of the periphery. Using Maoist terms, Buganda was the city writ large, while much of the rest of the country was functionally rural in this special sense of differential development, imbalance in the distribution of industries, and exploitative relationships. The Baganda were at the top of the emerging system of ethnic stratification. They were also at the center of an emerging ethnocracy.

For a while in its history Buganda even entered the role of a sub-imperial power, collaborating with the British in controlling and ruling significant parts of the rest of the country. Buganda provided many of the administrators for British rule assigned to different parts of the country. And through much of the colonial period the Baganda were clearly the heartland community of the country, displaying an impressive responsiveness to the stimulus of the new educational and cultural skills which came with the imperial power and European missionaries. The region became the best developed economically, the best educated, the best integrated through a network of communications, and the most influential politically. As Kampala evolved into the capital city, Buganda developed into the capital region.

As Buganda became more urbanized and consolidated its centrality in national affairs, it also became demilitarized. At the time that the British arrived in this part of the world, the Buganda kingdom had been militarily one of the most powerful in East Africa as a whole. The kingdom had evolved impressive political and social institutions, and had developed systems of collective organization which converted Buganda into an impressive military force.

As we shall indicate more fully in a later chapter, the 1900 agreement concluded between Buganda and Britain inaugurated a new era. The agreement itself put special limitations on numbers and types of arms which the king of the Baganda could acquire or keep for the protection of the palace. But beyond that, the process of demilitarizing the Baganda had got under way. The military profession, which had been one of honor and commitment, began to lose over time some of its luster. We shall show later in the book how the 1900 agreement helped to shift the Baganda from a conception of national autonomy based on military might to a conception of their autonomy based on contractual rights. Over time they learned how to exploit effectively the terms and implications of the 1900 agreement. They learned how to use the courts with sophistication in pursuit of their rights against the British. Militarily they were of course no match for British military technology. The Baganda now realized that their ultimate weapons against the British were legal and political. The profession of arms was now left to "lesser" ethnic communities.

The British themselves had in addition a vested interest in the demilitarization of Buganda. British policies for military recruitment turned to other areas, reinforcing the Baganda's own increasing inclination to look for alternative avenues of honor, income, and achievement.

But if Buganda was becoming a less promising area of recruitment for the King's African Rifles, where else should the British turn for those recruits? There were a large number of alternative areas. The British could have turned to other Bantu areas of the country. To some limited extent the British did do just that. But the Bantu areas were specially susceptible to the demonstration effect of Buganda's ways. Buganda's system of administration and cultural styles were to some extent emulated in the other Bantu areas of the country. Certainly the other areas of the kingdoms of Uganda, all basically Bantu, displayed a marked tendency to use Buganda as a reference point, if not as a model. The demilitarization of Buganda was followed by a demilitarization of the other kingdoms.

Once again the British themselves had a vested interest in helping the demilitarization of the kingdoms. There was in British calculations an assumption that those African societies which were politically organized as states before the British came were a greater military risk once subjugated by the British than those African societies which were segmentary and politically acephalous. Buganda and Bunyoro, as kingdoms which had been particularly strong upon the arrival of the British, were regarded by the British for a while as potential military risks of a specially ominous kind.

The northern tribes of Uganda, to the extent that they were less centralized in their political organization, emerged as safer areas for military recruitment into the colonial armed forces. In reality the British had encountered upon arrival some resistance in parts of the north. And the record of northerners as fighters and warriors was already established. But the nature of northern political organization was such that the societies had collections of individual warriors, rather than units of organized armies. The two factors together increased the attractiveness of the north as a recruiting area for the British colonial armed forces. The *individuals* so recruited were believed to have good martial qualities, but the societies from which they sprang were often not centralized enough to raise the threat of organized armies of resistance under the banner of a single political authority.

The relatively segmentary Nilotic and Sudanic communities of the north were already becoming politically peripheral in Uganda. But their very status as a political periphery made them attractive for military recruitment into the imperial armed forces.

What happened once again was an interplay between political, cultural, and economic factors in converting the rural areas of northern Uganda into a preeminently suitable source of recruits into the Ugandan army. The foundations of a fundamentally different system of ethnic division of labor were being laid.

But behind the historical developments were also some salient cultural differences between ethnic groups. What were originally factors primarily of interest to anthropologists carried implications of long-term consequences. Let us now turn more closely to these cultural variations among Uganda's ethnic groups.

ON CULTURE AND COMBAT

African traditional societies which lacked the structures of state organization had by necessity to develop alternative structures of political and military stability. Many evolved the tradition of "neighborhood defense," based on the principle of constructing settlements in a manner which provided neighborhood self-reliance in military matters.

In addition a number of societies evolved age-grade systems providing for functional specialization. G. P. Murdock may have exaggerated the Cushite derivative nature of age-grade systems, but he was surely right in seeing the system as being designed to compensate for political decentralization. In the words of Murdock:

> The Nilotes unquestionably acquired their age-grade systems through fusion with, or imitation of, the Eastern Cushites. The reason for the spread of these systems must lie in their survival value. They clearly promoted military strength and social integration and thus doubtless served to offset in large measure the disadvantages inherent in a minimal development of political organization.[4]

The special arrangements of settlements, and the age-grade systems, were in turn connected among the Nilotes to pastoralism as a way of life. In both the Sudan and Uganda pastoralism is often a major, and in some cases the dominant, factor in the economic style of the tribes which have produced soldiers for national armies. The tradition of protecting mobile animals, and the quest for new pastures, might have resulted in certain *athletic* qualities pertinent to the military profession. Recruitment into colonial armies sometimes equated athletic qualities with martial qualities. The stamina of the man who walks dozens of miles with his cattle, the stamina of the "long distance runner," could so easily be seen as relevant also for military performance.

In addition pastoralism as an economic way of life produces a world view of its own which encompasses martial values. In this sense one might even distinguish between personal valor and military honor. Personal valor is invoked when the individual herdsman is protecting his own cattle or his own wives and children against raiders. Military honor in this sense comes into play in *collective* combat against a collective external enemy.

Pastoralism may sharpen concepts of personal valor—self-defense in the old sense of the rugged and isolated frontier. Each family had to be its own "army," each man his own warrior.

On the other hand, societies which combine pastoralism with cultivation, but without a tradition of centralized authority structures, may have concepts which are a little nearer to those of collective military honor.

In more elaborate state systems like those of traditional Buganda and Bunyoro, fighting for the king could become an even bigger measure of valor than fighting to protect one's cattle or one's private settlement. Military service was elaborately interlinked with political organization. The contrast between the northern tribes and the kingdoms of Uganda struck the foreign observers quite early, though sometimes they misunderstood the implications of what they were observing. Baker wrote in 1874:

> The order and organization of Unyoro were a great contrast to the want of cohesion of the northern tribes. Every district throughout the [Nyoro] country was governed by a chief, who was responsible to the king for the states of the province. This system was extended to sub-government and a series of lower officials in every district, who were bound to obey the orders of the lord-lieutenant. . . . In the event of war, every governor could appear, together with his contingent of armed men, at short notice. These were the rules of government that had been established for many generations throughout Unyoro.[5]

By the time the British came to Uganda, Bunyoro was beginning to evolve a kind of standing army round the nucleus of the king's, or Mukama's, bodyguard.

Until King Kaberega, Bunyoro did not traditionally have a permanent standing army. In time of war the chiefs sometimes became military leaders, and were responsible for providing a force of ablebodied men under their jurisdiction. Political and military leadership was often completely fused. There were chiefs who gained great national reputation as war leaders—"and crowns (*Makondo*) had been awarded to successful generals."[6] During the reign of Kabarega, the Barusura, or king's bodyguard, developed into an effective military force. Bunyoro was about to institutionalize its warriors and make them a standing army. But the British were at last at hand, and Kabarega's reign signified both the climax of the Bunyoro military organization and the beginning of the demilitarization of Bunyoro.

Ganda political culture also emphasized military honor rather than personal valor. It was also in the course of the nineteenth century that Buganda was developing a special Royal Guard Corps as the basis of a gradually evolving regular army. The bulk of the army was still recruited from peasant militia, but the capacity for mobilizing that army was considerably facilitated by the relative political centralization of the system. As we shall indicate more fully in a later chapter, behind much of Ganda political culture at that time was an ethos of militarism. Once again political and military organization were substantially fused. In the words of Lloyd Fallers:

> Organizationally. . . . warfare represented the clearest working-out of the pattern towards which the whole polity was moving: an institutional system in which positions of honor were open to challenge, in which ability and diligence were quickly rewarded and failure was quickly punished. . . . War was thus the focus of what had perhaps become, in the nineteenth century, the master value in Ganda culture—the aggrandizement of the nation and the king.[7]

These were the organizational factors which made the Bantu kingdom such a striking contrast to the relatively acephalous political arrangements of the northern tribes.

Yet the northern tribes after colonial annexation could still be deemed to produce some of the best *individual* warriors. Just as the British had made assumptions about extra martial prowess among the Gurkhas and Punjabis, so they made assumptions about such prowess among the Nilotic and Sudanic peoples of northern Uganda.

Additional cultural factors included the interplay between food culture and physical anthropology. Eastern and western Nilotes and Sudanic tribes produced a disproportionate number of men who were tall and slim. This particular kind of physique was interpreted in the colonial period as additional evidence of military suitability. The "tall and lean" were regarded as "good drill material."

Food culture over generations could have influenced the emergence of lean physical specimens, especially among communities which were truly pastoral. Reliance on milk and meat as the staple food, with periods when almost nothing else was added to the diet, had its impact on physical anthropology. Millet among other Nilotes was interpreted by the communities themselves as a diet fundamentally more relevant to physical strength than the *matoke* (plantain bananas) of some of the Bantu tribes.

But whatever the relevance of food culture for physique, there is little doubt that the recruitment officers of the imperial power in Uganda came to look at Nilotic and Sudanic communities as being *physically* better "drill material" than most of the people of the Bantu kingdoms. In Ankole the ruling elite was sufficiently pastoral in its origin and culture that specimens of similar physique were available. But as Ankole was a kingdom, and as the new criteria of prestige in colonial Uganda moved away from military symbolism, and since in any case Buganda was an important model for the other kingdoms, Ankole's representation in the Ugandan armed forces was as modest as the representation of the other kingdoms.

An ethnic separation of powers seemed to be underway in Uganda. There was a disproportionate presence of the Bantu in administration and the economy. But there was also developing a disproportionate Nilotic and Sudanic presence within the armed forces of the new Uganda.

Buganda itself remained the most privileged part of the Bantu areas. It was indeed a city writ large. The Nilotic and Sudanic areas were virtually the most peripheral in the new national entity. The soldiers were coming from a part of the country which was rural in location, function, and status. The stage was set for the beginnings of a military-agrarian complex.[8]

THE MILITARIZATION OF THE COUNTRYSIDE

Partly with the disadvantages of physical and social distance, and partly with the presumed advantages of rural culture for military performance, peasant warriors began to join the army in significant numbers. For some villages the army was second only to agriculture as a major source of livelihood and income for the local community. For some peasants a military career was their first introduction to Uganda as a national entity. What was once said of young Turkish farm lads was also true of raw recruits from rural Uganda. These recruits "from isolated villages now suddenly felt themselves to be a part of the larger society. The connection between their private life and public role became vivid to them—and this sense of their new personality they diffused around them when they returned to their villages."[9]

In some important sense the country boys became conscious of their membership in the Ugandan nation. Hundreds acquired some technical training relevant to some aspect of their military functions. Some were helped to become literate. All had to learn or improve their Swahili as a medium of interaction with lads from other ethnic areas. Those areas had indeed become partially militarized when they became converted into major grounds for recruitment into the armed forces. But the recruits themselves also became partially nationalized in their perspectives, though still retaining serious rural handicaps.

The theme of rural status retained a critical relevance. As in many developing societies, the reduced opportunities in the rural areas tended to inflate the value of a military career to many in those areas. In the words of Marion J. Levy:

> Insofar as membership in the armed forces is generally open to members of the society, the vast majority of the members of a given society are likely to be individuals of a single class, and hence if the armed force organizations are large scale, most recruitment is likely to come from people of more or less common origins. This is especially true, of course, of relatively nonmodernized societies. In such societies armed force organizations are frequently elite organizations whose members are likely to come from representatives of a single elite class. If they are not elite organizations and recruitment is open class, the vast majority of individuals concerned are likely to come from agrarian social backgrounds.[10]

In Uganda's experience the military did not recruit from an elite class. On the contrary, it had considerable difficulty in recruiting from the new educated elite. The overwhelming majority of the soldiers were therefore drawn from what Levy called "people of more or less common origins . . . from agrarian social backgrounds."

But were these people in sympathy with their rural origin and peasant compatriots? Their prejudices and predispositions were certainly considerably influenced by their social backgrounds. What Robert Scalapino said of the military rulers of Korea in the early 1960s has also been true to some extent of the majority of the officers and men of the Ugandan army. These were young men "who come from rural backgrounds and who, in many cases, have known poverty at close range. It is natural for these men to have a rural orientation—to feel an empathy with the farmer. Such men must always regard urbanism with a certain ambivalence."[11]

But there is the important difference in Uganda's conditions as compared with either Turkey or Korea. Uganda is a *polyethnic* society, deeply divided along these "primordial lines." Lugbara peasants in the armed forces may have a bond of affinity with Lugbara peasants in the villages, but there is no guarantee that they would have a bond of sympathy with Kakwa or Acholi peasants inside or outside the army. The bonds of shared social origins are sometimes in conflict with the tensions of differing ethnic origins. In such conditions, a military-agrarian complex is seldom either neat or stable. Conflicting loyalties—partly ethnic, partly in terms of social origin, and partly arising from the pulls of occupational allegiance—would periodically shake what might otherwise have been a bond of empathy between soldiers and rural folk.

The concept of a military-agrarian complex implies a *class alliance*. The concept of ethnocracy implies *ethnic power.* Uganda's modern history has been a continuing interplay between the forces which seek class alliances and the forces which seek ethnic power. In a country where ethnic groups are themselves graded and stratified, the issue of where class ends and ethnicity begins is hard to disentangle. The ethnocratic heritage of the country, going back to the days of Ganda-centrism in the political process, has continued to condition the whole process of class formation.

OBOTE'S MILITARY-INTELLECTUAL COMPLEX

But while the army in Uganda was recruiting so overwhelmingly from semi-literate and rustic sectors of the population, politics as a profession was recruiting from the new educated elite. The colonial experience had put a special premium on certain verbal and literary skills. The aspiring politician had to have among his credentials some of the symbols of modern education as defined by the conquering imperial culture. If the legislature was to be the central recruitment mechanism for the new political elite, then entry into the legislature required competence in the English language. Oratory as a political skill at the national level also required an effective utilization of the imperial language. Uganda had to choose its national leaders from among those whc put across their views in the imported language of the European metropole.

As political parties were formed in the late 1950s and the early 1960s, aspiring intellectuals left some of their older professions to join the mainstream of political ambition. Schools especially lost a number of able teachers to the new profession of politics. In the 1961 elections in Uganda the Democratic Party "poached" many a teacher from Catholic schools in different parts of the country to stand as candidates in the parliamentary elections. Obote's own party also "poached" on the schools, but to a lesser degree. What the whole experience did indicate was, quite simply, the need in politics for skills which were also associated with the teaching profession. Although the new educated class was also recruited primarily from rural areas, socialization into the imperial culture had a *deruralizing* effect. The educated were diverted in their perspectives away from peasant ways. In attitude they also turned against rural culture and norms. The imperial culture was interpreted as an urban culture par excellence. Its acquisition was a passport to urban status and its presumed privileges.

The imperial heritage and its prestige, the adoption of the English language as a national language, the requirement of competence in English for parliamentarians in a situation where people learned English from schools and not from the home and marketplace, all prepared the ground for the rise of this new intelligentsia as the dominant force in at least the first few years of Uganda's independence. In the Uganda situation we defined the intelligentsia in educational and occupational terms—a group with at least twelve years of formal education and constituting a white-collar stratum. We shall return in later chapters to the impact of Western education on social stratification in Uganda.

Milton Obote himself was preeminently an intellectual, not only in his education but also in the sense of being someone capable of being fascinated by ideas and with skills for handling those ideas effectively. But at first his alliance was not between the intelligentsia and the military but mainly between the modern intelligentsia under his leadership and the indigenous traditionalists, especially those who followed Kabaka Mutesa II of Buganda. Following the 1962 election, Obote's Uganda People's Congress and Buganda's Kabaka Yekka Party formed a coalition government, with the Democratic Party in opposition. The Democratic Party had always had its own share of Uganda's intellectuals, but before long it began to lose some of its best people in parliament to the Uganda People's Congress.

The basic alliance between the intelligentsia and the traditionalists, especially the traditional aristocracies in the kingdoms of Uganda, came to an end in 1964. That year was also the beginning of a military-intellectual coalition under Obote's leadership. The military mutiny which had taken place in January 1964 had been ended with considerable concessions to the armed forces, and a new basis of partnership was created between Obote's government and what was now increasingly Obote's army. The armed forces on independence had been underestimated as a political force, but by 1964 Milton Obote was determined to maintain a workable alliance with the armed forces against the traditionalist forces of the country. Obote still believed in conciliatory leadership, but this nevertheless required careful alliances.

In 1966, following Obote's military confrontation with the Kabaka of Buganda, another stage was reached in the evolution of the new military-intellectual complex. As head of the army Obote replaced Brigadier Opolot with Brigadier Idi Amin.

The intellectual gulf between Amin and Obote emphasized in symbolic terms the supremacy of the intelligentsia in that partnership. It was indeed to be Obote's brain behind Amin's gun. Idi Amin, grossly underestimated by Obote himself and by many people since then, appeared to be a jovial but ignorant warrior capable of being manipulated in different ways. Many regarded Amin as no more than a buffoon, though potentially a dangerous buffoon. With Obote's astuteness to control and manipulate him, the intelligentsia seemed assured of remaining senior partners in their coalition with the military. The style of leadership was also moving from reconciliation to intimidation.

Obote recruited intellectuals from other parts of the country to his support. Among the Baganda the position was less neat. Ganda intelligentsia were sometimes torn between the demands of traditionalist loyalties within their own ethnic group and the lure of modern reforms as symbolized by the Uganda People's Congress. Had Obote not humiliated the Baganda so continuously from 1966 onward after he defeated their king, he might have recruited many Baganda intellectuals to some of his reforms.

In 1969 there started a new phase in the fortunes of the coalition between the military and Obote's intelligentsia. Milton Obote started his strategy of the "move to the left." He began to define new socialistic goals. He entered the stream of documentary radicalism with his series of documents indicating new political policies and ideological directions.[12] The ideological content of most of the documents of Obote's move to the left implied a concern for the peasantry. The arguments against the injustices of "feudalism," especially in the former kingdoms of Uganda, reaffirmed sympathy with the "oppressed" common folk. The egalitarian theme of the move-to-the-left strategy seemed to be a clarion call for a new partnership between the peasantry and the intelligentsia. Such a partnership between brains and numbers constituted, as Huntington has reminded us, preeminently the catalyst for revolution.

With Obote's Document No. 5, *Proposals for New Methods of Election of Representatives of the People and Parliament,* came the idea of linking the political intelligentsia with peasants in all four corners of the country. A member of parliament could no longer stand for one constituency in one particular area, usually his ethnic home. Document No. 5 required every parliamentary candidate to stand for election simultaneously in four constituencies—one constituency in the north, one in the south, one in the west, and one in the east. Each candidate would therefore have to woo large numbers of ordinary folk in parts of the country distant from his home. And between elections each parliamentarian would have had to nurse constituencies consisting of communities ethnically diverse and regionally disparate. If parliamentarians, including ministers within parliament, constituted the cream of the political intelligentsia, the members of this political elite were now to be nationally interlinked with the voting peasantry in all the four corners of the nation.

Did the army intervene in Uganda in January 1971 in order to prevent this partnership between the peasantry and the political intelligentsia?

The military coup of January 1971 had a number of causes, some personal to the relations between Amin and Obote, others structural to the situation. But if the army did not intervene to stop a partnership between the intelligentsia and the peasantry, it did intervene partly to stop the demotion of the military to a more junior position in its own partnership with the educated elite. In the preceding twelve months Obote had started making decisions about the army without consulting its head or even discussing it with the defense council. Promotions were made behind Amin's back, responsibilities were distributed within the armed forces without the pretense of giving the armed forces an adequate say in determining these matters. There might have been very strong political reasons why Obote had to bypass the normal decision-making machinery for the armed forces in matters like promotion, allocation of duties, and potentially even recruitment; but Obote's increasing tendency to bypass normal channels gave Amin and that part of the army which supported Amin a growing feeling of ominous political demotion.

There is little evidence that Amin feared an alliance between the rural masses and the educated elite under Milton Obote. But he did fear the increasing autonomy of the political intelligentsia, partly signified by Obote's new style of rule, and partly by a concern for the implications of the new elections under Document No. 5 which were scheduled to take place early in 1971. Under the provisions of his Document No. 5 Obote had done nothing to reduce the dominance of the educated class in the political process. All the evidence seemed to suggest that triumphant parliamentarians would be basically drawn from the same stratum of society as in 1961 and 1962, even if they were now ideologically converted to other goals. There was no rethinking about the official language for parliament, if parliament was to continue to be the hub of the nation's political life. If parliamentarians still had to have competence in the English language, and if English was a language obtained through an educational process, a deep-seated preference for the educated class of parliamentarians was bound to remain part of the system.

The linguistic problem could have been handled by shifting the main emphasis of decision-making into the party instead of parliament and making the party more responsive to the pressures of the peasantry. But an alternative way of handling the linguistic problem in a country like Uganda, in a manner which would give greater political influence to people who did not speak English, would have been to choose experimentally two or more African languages as "parliamentary languages" with provision for simultaneous translation. This would have been similar to the experiment conducted in colonial Tanganyika with regard to the role of English and Swahili as parliamentary lauguages.

If a social revolution was what Milton Obote was after, the first alternative of shifting ultimate power from parliament to the *party,* and reorganizing the party in a manner which would increase its responsiveness to the peasantry, would have made greater revolutionary sense. But in reality Obote's move to the left remained basically a game being played by the intellectuals of Uganda. Many intellectuals found a new sense of purpose in this vision, and a new opportunity for verbal enthusiasm. Obote himself was probably sincere, but he did not pursue the logic of his revolutionary ideas. The image which was emerging was not one of a budding partnership between the peasantry and intelligentsia, but one of an increasingly self-righteous and uncompromising group of intellectuals in power in an African country. Obote's military-intellectual complex was cracking without an adequate substitute. Peasants in Obote's revolutionary strategy were still objects; they were not as yet participating subjects in a major social transformation.

On January 15, 1971, Milton Obote fell from power.[13]

AMIN: PANGAS AND PLOUGHSHARES

What sort of changes did Obote's successor, General Idi Amin, seek to introduce? At first it seemed as if this would be another kind of military-intellectual coalition. Amin seemed to have considerable deference towards the educated in his society. He created the most technocratic and best-educated cabinet in the history of Uganda. The style of leadership provided by his government seemed at first to be primarily bureaucratic—rather than either mobilizational or intimidatory. He recruited from the ranks of the highly educated civil service, from the legal profession, and even from Makerere University in Kampala. Amin's original cabinet had a range of expertise which included engineering as well as law, zoology as well as economics. The country seemed to be set on a new approach to that old partnership between guns and brains.

Yet one fundamental difference soon asserted itself. Whereas Obote's military-intellectual complex gave the intelligentsia the status of the senior partner, Amin's temporary partnership with the intelligentsia soon revealed that it was the guns which were enjoying seniority. The technocrats in the cabinet and the civil service responded to the moods of the General himself. There were reports of a minister being physically slapped across the face by the General. There were also reports of cabinet ministers being shouted down and silenced on matters that the General did not want to hear about. An important partnership did indeed exist between these technocrats and the new military government, but the military were now clearly and indisputably the senior partner. The tables had been turned on the intelligentsia.

But would Amin more effectively create a partnership with the peasantry than Milton Obote had done? Would the agrarian social origins of Uganda soldiers establish at least informal links between the barracks and the countryside?

Amin's response to his position in power had a deep agrarian factor from the start. The idea of consulting elders from district to district as a way of getting rural consensus was soon revived by the General. Amin moved from one group of elders to another, from one district to another, vigorously pursuing a primordial system of oral consultation which had already been dying under the weight of political modernization in Uganda. Within the first few months of his rule Amin covered more square miles of Ugandan territory, addressing meetings and listening to elders, than Obote covered in all his eight years in office. Amin converted even Makerere professors into a group of elders, and once came to the university to *listen* rather than to talk. The peripatetic nature of Amin's initial style of rule was itself profoundly influenced by the political culture of rural areas in Uganda. He seemed to be combining special techniques of rustic mobilization with the disciplinary ethos of bureaucratic leadership.

Amin has brought other cultural inputs into the political process in Uganda derived from his peasant origins. His entire style of diplomacy is striking for its lack of middle class "refinements." The world of international relations is dominated in its norm by the values of the middle classes and the international intelligentsia. International law itself was a product of the thinking of European middle and upper classes on how diplomacy was to be conducted and relations between states organized and controlled. There are subtleties and refinements in embassies throughout the world, and in the corridors of international organizations, which are distant from some of the bluntness and relative spontaneity of rural folk. The peasants in all countries of the world are among the least sensitized to international issues. They are often the most obstinately parochial in their view of the universe. And because of this the whole phenomenon of relations between states has remained something shaped, organized, and controlled by the values of the middle and upper classes and their respective intellectual wings.

Idi Amin, like Nikita Khrushchev before him, has brought to the refined diplomatic banquet of the middle and upper classes of the world the rustic embarrassment of inadequate inhibition. Like Russia's Nikita Khrushchev in the 1950s and early 1960s, Idi Amin is today a peasant bull in the china shop of diplomatic manners. In peasant areas one visits friends without being invited. The necessity of an invitation is a middle-class and upper-class phenomenon. Amin came into power and proceeded to treat diplomatic visits with a similar manner. Israel, Britain, and France had claimed to be friends of his regime. He visited each of those on his own initiative. He also visted West Germany with the casualness of one peasant knocking on the door of his rural friend. Of course, in reality arrangements had to be made to receive the President of Uganda, security had to be ensured, major diplomatic banquets had to be held. The refinements of European diplomacy, so dominant in the world as a whole today, had to be extended to this visiting rural dignitary from Uganda. But the spontaneity of going there without invitation had all the bearing of the cumulative rural socialization which Amin and his kind often manifest without thinking.

Most presidents would not give interviews to the press on matters of state wearing nothing but a swimming costume. But Amin has been known to expose himself to the ridicule of international photographic journalism by doing precisely that. Some of the pictures that have hit the international magazines were calculated to portray a naked African in political power.

Most presidents would prepare carefully for their press conferences. Amin has learned to do a little of that more recently, but there is still a wide area of spontaneity in the way in which he addresses the world at large. Almost any idea that occurs to him on the spur of the moment may be given articulation.

Peasants do not normally send telegrams to each other. Amin has learned to use this particular medium but with some rustic bluntness. And his messages have ranged from wishing Richard Nixon a quick recovery from Watergate to a reaffirmation of deep, and even romantic affection, for Julius Nyerere "though your hair is gray."

Some of these tendencies are personal to Amin rather than to his social origins. But the very fact that he lets his personal tendencies have such free play while occupying the top office of his nation might have been influenced by the relative spontaneity of rural upbringing among the Kakwa.

His attitude to the Asians of Uganda was a feeling widely shared among ordinary people in the country. By the time Amin came into power Indophobia, or negative response to people of Indian origin, had become a gut response among peasants in the country.

Indophobia was not unique to the peasants. On the contrary, many members of Obote's ruling intelligentsia were strongly anti-Asian. But Obote's government would never have handled the Asian issue in quite that manner. The normal diplomatic inhibitions that operate in matters affecting other nations would—under Obote—have been allowed to moderate the fate of the Asians.

Even humanitarian arguments quite often are arguments steeped in middle-class assumptions, and are therefore more likely to impress an African intellectual than an African peasant with memories of having been insulted over the years by Asian shopkeepers or Asian employers. The style of Amin's expulsion of the Asians was in this sense an aspect of his peasant origins.

A related factor might well have been derived from the tensions of rural-urban dichotomies. The great majority of the Asians of Uganda were urban people. Those Asians that opened up shop in isolated rural areas often signified an urban presence in the countryside. Much of the resentment of the Asians was racial and economic, but there might also have been a residual symbolic factor signifying rural-urban tensions. These tensions focused on this alien group partly because it could be hated without the complications of cross-cutting kinship ties. But after they were expelled what was to happen? Their shops became available to a wide range of categories of Ugandans. These included Ugandans who would not have stood a chance of moving into this level of economic endeavor in the old days under Obote. Apart from the soldiers themselves, there have been new shopkeepers in Uganda whose origins range from the northern peasantry to the Buganda aristocracy. It is too early to be sure how far this experiment of the indigenization of commerce in Uganda in the wake of the expulsion of the Asians will be successful. But if the experiment does emerge triumphant, it could be interpreted as one of the first steps towards a coalition between the peasant warriors under General Amin and the aspiring masses in both town and country in Uganda.

But one obstacle continues to loom large. The heritage of ethnicity in the country carries its own record of mutual atrocities. Thousands of Acholi, Langi, and members of other rival ethnic groups have died fighting or been murdered under Amin. The ethnocratic heritage has also implied a pull of favoritism, rivalry, and differential rewards. A grand alliance between the soldiers and the peasantry falls short of conclusive consummation in the shadow of the nation's geneological history, in all its ethnic brutality. Amin's own style of leadership is no longer either bureaucratic or conciliatory. It combines intimidatory and mobilizational techniques.

CONCLUSIONS

When Dwight Eisenhower warned his countrymen about the military-*industrial* complex of the United States, he was reminding his countrymen of the political weight of military establishments even in mature liberal democracies. Eisenhower's concern was not with the social origins of members of the military establishment in the United States but with the political consequences of interlocking elites of industry and the armed forces. That section of industry which catered to the hardware of weapons and the whole area of military technology was, by definition, the most intimately related to the military elites. But the interplay between industry and the armed forces in a country like the United States was wider than that, and related especially to the interplay between technology, commerce, and war.

In Uganda, on the other hand, it is precisely the social origins of soldiers that provide the basis of political allegiances. As in other developing countries, the armed forces in Uganda have been recruited overwhelmingly from rural areas. Such a tradition was also present in the history of the United States. The South until recently was disproportionately represented in the American army partly because the South was also relatively underdeveloped.

But not all those who are recruited from rural areas are peasants. On the contrary, in the case of the southern portion of the United States, recruitment was at times from a rural aristocracy and not merely a rural peasantry. Even in Egypt the officer corps under Naguib was from a rural middle class and not from the masses of the countryside.

The distinctive thing about the Ugandan army was the recency of derivation from the rural areas. The soldiers, even those who were trained abroad, were overwhelmingly sons of peasants. Moreover, by being almost untouched by Western education, they remained much more rural in attitude and perspective than the new intellectuals.

An additional factor which entered the scene in Uganda was the sociological dimension defining the rural status of Nilotic and Sudanic tribes. If Buganda was the capital province of the country, the northern districts were the ultimate periphery. Nilotic and Sudanic tribes, by location, function, and status, became available for recruitment into what had become a profession without prestige.

The pattern of military recruitment helped to influence the future history of Uganda after the withdrawal of the British.

By the time of independence the majority of the members of the armed forces had been recruited from the Nilotic and Sudanic tribes of the north of the country. During the Obote years from 1962 to 1971 the size of the army expanded considerably. Recruitment continued to be overwhelmingly from northern communities in Uganda.

And then the army took over power January 1971. Major-General Idi Amin proclaimed a plan to make the armed forces more ethnically representative, and for a while his government started recruitment in other areas. The precise composition of Amin's army two years later had changed considerably. The balance of ethnic groups within the armed forces was no longer a matter of public record. What seemed to continue was an inclination to recruit disproportionately from Nilotic and Sudanic communities. Some Nilotic groups have ceased to feature prominently in the armed forces of Uganda, especially the Langi, Obote's tribe, and the Acholi who were once the military aristocracy of the North. On the other hand, other Nilotic communities have increased in importance, including the Kakwa, Amin's own tribe. The Kakwa are distributed in Uganda, Zaire, and the Sudan. Amin's recruitment has quite often ignored territorial boundaries. Ethnic compatriots have entered the Ugandan armed forces even if their original nationality was non-Ugandan.

It is safe to assume that the Ugandan army would not have remained so disproportionately Nilotic and Sudanic under Obote and Amin had not the original nucleus at the time of independence in 1962 been already disproportionately northern. We enquired earlier into why there was a tendency in the colonial period to recruit from these northern communities. This is where the issue of the army as a *rural force* came into relevance. These soldiers are in an important sense *peasant warriors.* The northern areas became such important recruiting grounds for the King's African Rifles partly because they were supposed to yield good peasant material with warrior values and partly because the north had become comparatively more rural than the south, with a slower pace of urbanization and a lower status politically.

Milton Obote, as a son of the north, started the process of deruralizing the north. Accessibility to these areas from the capital city was improved with new roads, a new bridge was built at Pakwach, and steps were taken to initiate new industries in areas which were previously regarded as being of low priority in development plans.

Again partly because he came from the north, Obote successfully concluded an alliance with an army overwhelmingly recruited from the north. This was the military-intellectual complex which emerged, and which had as its nucleus an alliance between the intellectuals of the northern tribes and the armed forces, but which also extended to encompass other members of the national intelligentsia outside Buganda. When Obote made Amin the head of the army in 1966 he clinched the idea of an alliance between the brains of Uganda and the guns of Uganda, with the brains as the senior partner. Amin's gun was to be manipulated by the calculating intellect of Milton Obote.

Obote's move to the left from 1969 implied for a while a new partnership between the intelligentsia and the peasantry. But Obote failed to push his revolutionary ideas to their logical conclusion. The peasantry remained objects of rhetoric rather than partners in revolution. The army became apprehensive lest their status in the partnership with Obote's educated elite be reduced even further.

Something like a military-agrarian complex seems to be in the making in Uganda. But the process drips in blood partly because of the very nature of Uganda's history. The ethnocratic heritage, going back to the days when Buganda was the powerful province while West Nile was among the poorest of the areas, has left a deep mark on the behavior of the polity. Some of the spontaneity of Ugandan peasantry has a violent theme within it. Just as villagers might spontaneously rise, chase a thief, and beat him to death in response to a hue-and-cry, so the warriors in modern barracks may sometimes brutalize their compatriots in a fit of either insecurity or arrogance. The military-agrarian complex has its costs in a country of many tribal groupings, especially if the military is disproportionately enlisted from only a few of those groupings.

The theme of ethnic rivalry continues to bedevil Uganda under Amin. If Egypt is the most culturally homogeneous of all the countries of the Nile Valley, Uganda might well be the least. It remains to be seen whether rustic warriors in control of a modern state will have greater success in transforming the fortunes of the countryside than alternative coalitions of social forces have had before. If Amin has now planted the seeds of a new partnership between the soldiers and the masses, Uganda is not yet ready to celebrate the harvest. Politics, like nature, takes its time.

NOTES

1. Mohammad Naguib, *Egypt's Destiny* (Garden City: Doubleday, 1955): 14-15. Cited in a related context by Samuel P. Huntington, *Political Order in Changing Societies* (New Haven and London: Yale University Press, 1968): 241-242. Huntington also cites Perlmutter on the army being "solidly Egyptian and rural."

2. Huntington, *ibid.*: 241-242. For related issues consult also Jacques Van Doorn (ed.) *Armed Forces and Society* (The Hague and Paris: Mouton, 1965).

3. See, for example, Johan Galtung, "A Structural Theory of Imperialism," *The African Review*, 1, 4 (April 1972): 93-138.

4. George Peter Murdock, *Africa: Its Peoples and Their Culture History* (1959): 339.

5. S. Baker, *Ismailia*, vol. 2 (London: Macmillian, 1874): 212-213.

6. See John Beattie, *The Nyoro State* (Oxford: Clarendon Press, 1971): 128-129.

7. L. A. Fallers, assisted by F. K. Kamoga and S. B. K. Musoke, "Social Stratification in Traditional Buganda," chapter 2, in L. A. Fallers [ed.], *The King's Men: Leadership and Status in Buganda on the Eve of Independence* (London and Nairobi: Oxford University Press on behalf of the East African Institute of Social Research, 1964): 111-130.

8. For related background issues consult Nelson Kasfir, "Controlling Ethnicity in Ugandan Politics: Departicipation as a Strategy for Political Development," *op. cit.,* (see Chap. 1), chapter 3: 96-135; and William Gutteridge, *The Military in African Politics* (London: Methuen, 1969), and Claude E. Welch, Jr. and Arthur K. Smith, *Military Role and Rule: Perspectives on Civil-Military Relations* (North Scituate, Mass.: Duxbury Press, 1974).

9. See Daniel Lerner and Richard D. Robinson, "Swords and Ploughshares: The Turkish Army as a Modernizing Force," *World Politics* 12 (October 1960): 26-29.

10. Marion J. Levy, Jr., "Armed Force Organizations," *The Military and Modernization,* Henry Biemen [ed.] (Chicago and New York: Aldine, Atherton, 1971): 63.

11. Robert A. Scalapino, "Which Route for Korea?" *Asian Survey,* 2 (September 1962): 11.

12. Documentary radicalism as a strategy of capturing in documents a vision of a new society to be created is discussed more fully in Mazrui, *Cultural Engineering and*

Nation-Building in East Africa (Evanston: Northwestern University Press, 1972), chapter 5. See also Semakula Kiwanuka, *From Colonialism to Independence* (Nairobi and Kampala: East African Literature Bureau, 2973), especially 104-121. Consult also D. L. Cohen and J. Parson, "The Uganda People's Congress Branch and Constituency Elections of 1970," *Journal of Commonwealth Political Studies,* 11, 1, (1973): 46-66.

   13. For related issues consult Selwyn Ryan, "Uganda: Balance Sheet of the Revolution," *Mawazo* 3, 1 (June 1971) and "Electoral Engineering in Uganda," *Mawazo* 2, 4 (December 1970); Yash Tandon, "The Future of the Asians in East Africa," Africa Contemporary Record Current Affairs series (London: Rex Collings, 1973); and Nelson Kasfir, "Controlling Ethnicity in Ugandan Politics," *op. cit.,* especially chapters 4 and 7: 136-172 and 239-269.

Section II:

The Anthropological Context

Chapter 3

THE DECLINE OF THE WARRIOR TRADITION

The new African states started with a borrowed tradition from the West emphasizing civilian supremacy. The arena was therefore open for civilian contenders for national prominence. Those who rose to the commanding heights of the polity were overwhelmingly drawn from the new modernized sector of the population, with a secular education obtained from Western-type educational institutions. Africa definitely approached independence with the signs of being in the process of evolving a meritocracy based on education. The balance of advantages in the new Africa facilitated the emergence of an educated Nkrumah or an intellectual Nyerere as national leader with some charismatic qualities—and completely overshadowed the traditional warrior who had once been a significant contender for hero-worship.

To some extent the situation illustrated a partial demilitarization of African political culture. The virtues of military bravery, the very idea that every young man is a potential soldier in the traditional sense, had been undergoing a process of erosion as a result of the Western impact. Part of the problem may have been connected with Western technological superiority, which to some extent had reduced the meaningfulness of military combat as a stage in one's life. One after another of the African tribes began to lapse in their attachment to military mores.

Jomo Kenyatta of Kenya has told us of the paramount resolution of young Kikuyu boys on being initiated by ancient custom. They used to say in courageous affirmation: "We brandish our spear, which is the symbol of our courageous and fighting spirit, never to retreat or abandon our hope, or run away from our comrades."[1]

The process of demilitarizing African social systems got under way when the invaders came. The demilitarization of African political culture was caused by four major factors. The first concerned Africa's realization of a much superior military technology. In the face of the rifle, the cannon, and later the mechanized battalion, the whole culture of the spear and the bow and arrow became to some extent frivolized. The warrior tradition was driven to the periphery of national life, cowed and humiliated.

In 1941, against a background of the technology of World War II which was then raging, a distinguished friend of Africa reminded Africans of Europe's military might and the role of that might in Europe's expansion. In a book addressed to Africans, Margery Perham said:

> Let it, therefore, be admitted upon both sides that the British Empire, like others, was obtained by force. Even where there was no serious fighting, news of victories nearby, or the fear of stronger weapons, was often enough to persuade tribes to accept the rule of the white strangers. . . . African tribes, backward, disunited, weak, were helpless before Europe, especially since the perfection of the machine gun.[2]

To Margery Perham the imperial experience was nevertheless necessary for Africa's own good. But Africa's conception of her own military humiliation came to feature in the new nationalism which arose after a period of pacification. As Sékou Touré put it once: "It was because of the inferiority of Africa's means of self-defense that it was subjected to foreign domination."[3]

Certainly from the point of view of our own analysis in this chapter, the shock of discovering a vastly superior military technology was a critical factor in the demilitarization of the African peoples under the impact of the colonial confrontation.

A related factor behind the demilitarization was the commitment by the new imperial order to establish and consolidate general pacification.

V. I. Lenin once argued that imperialism was "the monopoly stage of capitalism." What was perhaps more defensible was the thesis that imperialism was the monopoly stage of *warfare.* Nor is this a mere witticism. Implicit in concepts like that of *pax britannica* was the idea that the white races had a duty to disarm the rest of mankind. And so when the champions of imperial rule were at their most articulate in its defense, one argument they advanced was that imperialism had given the African the chance to know what life was like without violence. In 1938 Jomo Kenyatta could therefore complain bitterly in the following terms:

> The European prides himself on having done a great service to the Africans by stopping the "tribal warfares," and says that the Africans ought to thank the strong power that has liberated them from their "constant fear" of being attacked by the neighbouring warlike tribes. But consider the difference between the method and motive employed in the so-called savage tribal warfares and those employed in the modern warfare waged by the "civilized" tribes of Europe, and

in which the Africans who have no part in their quarrels are forced to defend so-called democracy.[4]

Kenyatta here captured both sides of the issue. He captured the presumptuous missionary commitment by the imperial order to "pacify the natives"; but he also captured the issue of Europe's superior military technology, particularly when it was turned against itself, as it was in the two world wars, engulfing at the same time much of the rest of the world.

We have, then, both in the superiority of technology and in Europe's mission to pacify the natives two important factors in the demilitarization of African political cultures.

The third factor was Christianity—the religion of compassion rather than courage, the anti-warrior religion of "turning the other cheek."

The fourth element in Africa's demilitarization was simply a transformation in the techniques of seeking political goods. New territorial entities had been devised necessitating new forms of relations between tribes, and a pattern of imperial authority had now been superimposed over several tribes together. The system of district commissioners, provincial commissioners, and a national Governor led to an entirely new way of articulating interests and processing demands. Later developments culminated in the formation of political parties, in electoral devices and the emergence of the Legislative Council as a school for politicians, and in a transformation of the techniques of bargaining and compromise between groups.

This transformation was itself an additional factor behind the demilitarization of African political cultures. Political alliances were being formed in terms of numerical calculations rather than military organization as such. The need for the spear in order to capture political power seemed to have well and truly receded into the background of African history.

It is with this background of demilitarization that the essence of leadership began to be assessed by different criteria. And the relevant springs of charismatic power were similarly withdrawn from the world of martial qualities.

In this regard the story of the demilitarization of Buganda is particularly illuminating, and it is to this that we should now turn more fully.

When the British arrived in the area late in the nineteenth century the Baganda were among the most martial of all the ethnic polities. They had built a strong state with an effective fighting force. By the time the British left in 1962 the Baganda were no longer warriors. What had happened?

The 1900 Agreement between Buganda and the British was not simply a list of constraints on the Baganda. On the contrary, it had a profound psychological impact on the political identity of the Baganda and helped to shape the style of politics of Uganda as a whole.

THE DEMILITARIZATION OF BUGANDA

The psychological meaning of the 1900 Agreement resulted in what might be called a "treaty complex." The treaty sought to establish a British protectorate in Uganda.

The concept of a treaty complex provides both a point of similarity and a point of difference between the Japanese in the nineteenth century and the Ganda experience. The conclusion of a treaty with a Western power was an act which, in different contexts, helped to precipitate the course of modernization in the two countries. But in the case of Japan, it was the burden of concluding "unequal treaties" which precipitated the kind of nationalism on which the Meiji modernizing revolution rested. In the case of the Baganda the 1900 Agreement became not a symbol of humiliating inequality but a basis of presumed parity of esteem between the imperial power and the Buganda Kingdom. The myth of parity, and the whole tradition of faith in legal instruments and litigation which the Baganda have often displayed, can be traced back to that genesis of the treaty complex of 1900.

The operation of the treaty complex vis-a-vis the Japanese and the Baganda also led to another fundamental divergence of direction. The fact that the 1900 Agreement gave the Baganda a sense of parity of esteem, and generated security for their nationalism independently of military force, resulted in the Ganda abdication from the military. The British did not expect the Baganda to maintain a private army of their own once the 1900 Agreement was concluded. On the contrary, the whole concept of the protectorate rested on military abdication by the Ganda and the entrusting of national Ganda security to the machinery of *pax britannica.*

But the treaty complex in Gandan nationalism and the kind of security it promoted diverted attention from the critical relevance of military power for any long-term effectiveness against competitors. The Baganda, as the treaty complex overwhelmed them and faith in litigation and legal instruments gave them a sense of preeminence in the country, came to despise the profession of arms. They saw themselves as good lawyers and good administrators, even as good farmers. They did not care to see themselves as good soldiers. And the dissipation of military calibre gradually influenced the imperial power itself in its choice of tribal areas of recruitment. The Baganda had been engaged as a subimperial power with the British in conquering parts of Uganda; but the treaty complex gradually relieved them of the tradition of conquest. The Baganda became militarily impotent, with significant consequences for the future politics of Uganda.

In the case of the Japanese, on the other hand, the unequal treaties which they were forced to conclude with foreign agents and foreign powers resulted in the militarization of their nationalism. Indeed, a substantial part of the motivation behind Japanese modernization was military in its roots. It thought in terms of national security, and aspired to consolidate national security through selective westernization in the economy as well as in the military adoption of Western techniques, with a clear commitment to beat the foreigner at his own game. Here lay the germ of the argument that the ultimate security for Japan did not lie in diplomatic agreements with the West (a contractual approach) but in technological competition with the West (a confrontational approach).

Extraterritoriality in Japan did not come to an end until 1899. The Western powers retained, even after that date, the control of fixing customs dues. This further retraction from Japanese jurisdiction did not come to an end until 1911.

The Baganda gave up much more as a result of the 1900 Agreement than the Japanese renounced as a result of the Agreements of Extraterritoriality. And yet, by a curious force of destiny, the Japanese reacted in deep humiliation at the inequalities, whereas the Baganda used the 1900 Agreement as a foundation for vigorous egalitarianism. The modernization of Buganda was a retreat from the warrior tradition.

The identity of Buganda was supposed to have found legal expression in modern history in the 1900 Uganda Agreement concluded between Buganda and Britain, and guaranteeing the region certain rights in exchange for British protection. Out of this understanding gradually grew the treaty complex of the Baganda, whereby major tensions with the Central Government both during the colonial period and in the first few years of independence were somehow referred back to a pre-existent fundamental law. In the case of Buganda's relations with the British colonial authorities, the "fundamental law" was the 1900 Agreement. But in Buganda's relations with the Central Government *after* independence the fundamental law became, for a while, the Independence Constitution of 1962. Both these manifestations of the deep-seated treaty complex in Buganda's style of political manoeuver helped to give rise to and reinforce the region's faith in constitutional and legal arrangements and in the relevance of litigation as a political instrument.

But what is distinctive about the change within the national personality of Buganda concerned the historical switch from a national autonomy based on power to a national autonomy based on contract. Until the foreign powers established themselves in Buganda, the Baganda had been people attached to their ambition of military supremacy. Fallers suggests that the purpose of Ganda warfare is perhaps best indicated by reference to the phrase *kugaba olutalo*—"to wage war"—literally the phrase means "to give war," in a similar way in which a hostess in the English language "gives" a party. "*Kugaba*" means to distribute largesse—and in this lay the whole spirit in which the

Kabaka made war. If, for example, a tributary group failed to pay and the Kabaka decided on war, the war-drum was beaten and all the chiefs went to the palace. The Kabaka then ceremonially and publicly chose one of the chiefs as the "receipient" (*mugabe*) of the war. He became the General and was charged with the task of despoiling the enemy. "This was the greatest benefit which the Kabaka could bestow, for success would bring wealth, promotion and glory."

War was a national commitment. Each chief or official was required to muster as many capable men as he could from his people. In the course of the nineteenth century there did develop a special Royal Guard Corps, which was the nearest thing to a regular army that Buganda had until then. But the bulk of the army continued to consist of peasant militia.

Military glory was greatly emphasized. Military weakness by individuals was a matter for public scorn. There were occasions when cowards were burnt alive or forced to go about dressed in women's clothing. To quote Fallers again:

> War was thus the focus of what had perhaps become, in the nineteenth century, the master value in Ganda culture—the aggrandizement of the nation and the king. That it was a *popular* value which vindicated much of the arbitrary cruelty with which the Kabaka ruled, and not merely an ideology of the elite, is indicated by the acclaim which apparently greeted the brave individual warrior within his own family. There was a special ceremony with which a father might honour his son who covered himself in glory in the national interest. The father roasted a sheep for a feast, thanked the gods for giving him a brave son, and throughout the ceremonial meal waited upon the son as a servant. Organizationally as well, warfare represented the clearest working-out of the pattern towards which the whole polity was moving: an institutional system in which positions of honour were open to challenge, in which ability and diligence were quickly rewarded and failure was quickly punished.[5]

And then the foreigners from far away came, and gradually their presence sought to institutionalize itself. In the case of the Baganda the symbolic instrument of institutionalization became the Uganda Agreement of 1900. At first the Agreement did not seem to be too drastic in the demilitarization of Buganda. Article 13 argued that nothing in the Agreement was to be held as invalidating the pre-existing right of the Kabaka "of Uganda" to call upon every ablebodied male among his subjects for military service in defense of the country. But there were already conditions which were later to assume more critical significance as a process of demilitarizing the Baganda, and affecting profoundly their conception of the ultimate basis of national autonomy:

> Nothing in this Agreement should be held to invalidate the pre-existing right of the Kabaka of Uganda to call upon every able-bodied male among his subjects for

military service in defence of the country; but the Kabaka henceforth will only exercise this right of conscription, or of levying native troops, under the advice of Her Majesty's principal representative in the Protectorate.

Article 13 goes on to say that in times of peace the armed forces, organized by the Uganda administration, would probably be sufficient for all purposes of defense. But if Her Majesty's representative was of the opinion that the force of Uganda needed to be strengthened at any one time, he could call upon the Kabaka to exercise in a full or in a modified degree his claim on the Baganda people for military service. In such an event, the arming and equipping of such a force would be undertaken by the administration of the Uganda Protectorate.

The control of firearms was again at first quite modest by the terms of the Uganda Agreement of 1900. There was indeed a gun tax, just as there was a hut tax. As regards the gun tax, it was held to apply to any person who possessed or made use of "a gun, rifle, pistol, or any weapon discharging a projectile by the aid of gunpowder, dynamite, or compressed air. The possession of any cannon or machine-gun is hereby forbidden to any native of Uganda."

A "native" who paid a gun tax could possess or use as many as five guns. But a separate tax was paid for each gun. As regards exemption from the gun tax, the following was the provision of the Act at that time:

> The Kabaka will be credited with 50 gun licences free, by which he may arm as many as 50 of his household. The Queen Mother will, in like manner, be granted 10 free licences annually, by which she may arm as many as 10 persons of her household; each of the three native Ministers (Katikiro, Native Chief Justice, and Treasurer of the Kabaka's revenue) shall be granted 20 free gun licences annually; by which they may arm 20 persons of their household. Chiefs of counties will be similarly granted 10 annual free gun licences; all other members of the Lukiiko or Native Council, not Chiefs of counties, three annual gun licences, and all landed proprietors in the country, with estates exceeding 500 acres in extent, one free annual gun licence.[6]

But the regulated utilization of firearms, under controlled initiative for war under the supervision of Her Majesty's Government, transformed an important element in the political culture of the Baganda. The theme of military defense, and the idea of manliness as associated with fighting for the Kabaka, fell under the shadow of British overrule.

And yet the Baganda were given enough flexibility, and enough participation in consolidating British administration elsewhere in the country, to retain a feeling of substantial national autonomy. If the old rights to wage war had simply been abolished and then the Kabaka and his people been subject to direct British administration as just another tribe under imperial domination, the psychological turn of events might have been very different.

THE CONTRACTUALIZATION OF BUGANDA

But the Baganda were given a sense of being partners in a "condominium," administering the Protectorate as a whole. The right to bear arms for the Kabaka had been changed and restricted, and yet the sense of autonomous self-reliance had been maintained. The autonomy needed to rest on a different foundation from its previous martial posture. It is this which made the change from an autonomy based on military power to an antonomy based on legal contract.

Recurrently, the treaty complex reared its head in Uganda. One important, and in many ways healthy, impact of the complex on Uganda's political culture had been the belief in legal solutions. The Baganda themselves, it is true, often overestimated the potentialities of litigation. J. M. Lee described Buganda as "inveterately litigious." He regarded this quality as tending towards "legal quibbling" at times: "But at least it shows that the design of the Constitution [of 1962] cannot be ignored in studying Uganda, because the law is one of Buganda's chief weapons. Uganda politics are played in an atmosphere where each side is looking for legal 'loop-holes' to be turned to its own advantage."[7]

The belief in litigation was in fact an important aspect of Buganda's modernizing influence on the political culture of the country. It was certainly an aspect of the modernization of Buganda's own orientation. The move from an autonomy based on military power to an autonomy based on legal contract was in the direction of procedural modernization.

In the history of Europe much of the eruption of modernization was in essence a contractual revolution. Ideas of rights and duties, of constitutionalism and their mode of interpretation, of the social contract as a basis of society, of organized labor and the principle of collective bargaining, of the growth of capitalism and the use of law in the protection of property, of the emergence of socialism and the utilization of agreements for the protection of workers—all had at their center a profound new belief in contract as a basis of modern reciprocity. Indeed, the idea of a contract began to be seen as a move from the principle of hierarchical interdependence to a principle of procedural reciprocity.

One of the ways in which Uganda had become more "modernized" than some of her neighbors lay precisely in this treaty complex which the Baganda had acquired for themselves and then transmitted in time to the country's political culture as a whole.

The occasions in the country's history when the Baganda were prepared to challenge the British on the basis of alleged breaches of agreement are well known. They include parts of the debate which surrounded the exile of the

Kabaka in 1954 by Sir Andrew Cohen, then Governor of Uganda. Had there been a breach of contract? Had the rights of the Baganda, as guaranteed by the 1900 Agreement, been violated?

The Kabaka then returned triumphantly, a hero to the Baganda and indeed to many Ugandans. A confrontation with a British Governor had resulted in a retraction of an earlier decision by the imperial power. A Ugandan king had won the day.

A new contract was devised in the tradition of Buganda's constitutional evolution. This was the 1955 Agreement outlining certain areas of modernized terms as between the imperial power and the Baganda, and seeking to outline a new foundation as Uganda as a whole approached nationhood.

After independence Buganda continued to test the Central Government's powers in relation to formerly agreed documents. Sometimes the Baganda attempted to find loopholes in the Constitution in order to safeguard their own interests, as they tried to do in the case of the future of the lost counties. The Constitution had provided for the possibility of a referendum in the counties to determine whether they wished to remain a part of Buganda or be transferred to Bunyoro. Obote decided to utilize the constitutional provision and hold a referendum in the counties. The Baganda tried to circumvent this provision. And yet even some of their tactics betrayed this profound attachment to the law. There was an attempt to beat the law at its own game.

On February 24, 1966, Prime Minister A. Milton Obote suspended the 1962 Constitution, relieved Sir Edward Mutesa of the Presidency, and took over full power. On March 11, 1966, Sir Edward Mutesa brought a case against the Attorney-General (Civil Suit No. 206 of 1966) in the High Court. Apart from a claim to costs there were nine grounds cited for the action. The three most important were perhaps that the Prime Minister's takeover of full power on February 24, 1966, was null and void; that the 1962 Constitution (with amendments) was still in force in its entirety and had been continually in force; and that, under the 1962 Constitution, Sir Edward Mutesa continued to be President.

No judgment was delivered from the High Court on these charges. This was because the Court procedure allowed the government thirty days to agree to defend the suit and then another thirty days to prepare a case. But before that period was up the situation was transformed when on April 15, 1966, the government introduced a new Constitution which effectively terminated any legal proceedings arising out of the abrogation of the 1962 Constitution. Furthermore, the new Constitution abolished Buganda's special federal status and reduced the power of traditional institutions.

Buganda's treaty complex felt a new outrage. The 1962 Constitution had been the legal expression of the Independence Agreement. It resembled a social contract creating a new society, and the parties to the contract surrendered some of their own "natural" rights for the sake of the compact. Among the natural rights of the Baganda were the rights to the soil of Buganda. Yet, on the basis of the national compact of 1962, Buganda had surrendered her rights to the city of Kampala to the Central Government.

Moreover, when a social contract of this kind was broken, all rights reverted to the original holders, and the logic of the situation required that Buganda should reassert her rights over the city of Kampala. The Lukiiko, or legislature, of Buganda proceeded to issue an ultimatum to the Central Government, demanding that it should leave "Buganda soil" by the end of May. Dr. Obote responded by declaring this an act of high treason. On May 24, 1966, the battle of the Palace took place. The National Army attacked the Kabaka's residence and, in spite of the gallant and ferocious efforts of the Kabaka's defenders, the Palace fell. The Kabaka himself escaped, but Buganda as an autonomous entity seemed at last to have come to an end. The treaty complex of the Baganda, which had played so large a part in giving the country its constitutional style of politics as well as in conditioning its attitude to procedure, had culminated in an upheaval whose long-term consequences are still experienced today in that unhappy polity.

CONCLUSION

The Baganda had become demilitarized as a result of the change in political culture arising out of westernization and the new contractual ethos. Military service, which had been such a great aspect of Ganda national pride before the British came, had declined in prestige in the colonial period among the Baganda. The manifest destiny of the group had sought fulfillment in administrative leadership, political vigor, and general modernization. But the skills of armed combat and the urge to excel in military confrontation have given way to an ethos of litigation and militant proceduralism.

The Baganda, by being the most westernized of all Ugandans, had also retreated furthest away from the warrior tradition.

Western education, Christianity, and a new style of seeking political goods had all conspired to disarm what had once been a major military force in eastern Africa.

Yet even those Ugandans who were not demilitarized in this sense but had been recruited into the colonial army were still stripped of important aspects of the warrior tradition. Africans serving in the King's African Rifles were not as yet warriors: they were military instruments of the imperial power.

The colonial experience had included a commitment to demasculate the subjugated peoples. In the wake of that demasculation the warrior tradition in Africa went into retirement. The question at issue since independence is whether that retirement need be permanent.

NOTES

1. Jomo Kenyatta, *Facing Mount Kenya* (first published in 1938) (London: Secker and Warburg, 1939): 199. The initiation ceremonies have been simplified since then.

2. Margery Perham, *Africans and British Rule* (London: Oxford University Press, 1941): 53-54, 60.

3. Conakry Home Broadcasting Service, June 7, 1965. See BBC Monitoring Service Records of Broadcasts in non-Arab Africa.

4. *Facing Mount Kenya, op. cit.*: 212.

5. L. A. Fallers, assisted by F. K. Kamoga and S. B. K. Musoke, "Social Stratification in Traditional Buganda," chapter 2, in L. A. Fallers [ed.] *The King's Men: Leadership and Status in Buganda on the Eve of Independence* (London and Nairobi: Oxford University Press on behalf of the East African Institute of Social Research, 1964): 111-113.

6. For the text of the Uganda Agreement of 1900 see appendix 2 in D. Anthony Low and R. Cranford Pratt, *Buganda and British Overrule* (London and Nairobi: Oxford University Press on behalf of the East African Institute of Social Research, 1960): 350-366.

7. J. M. Lee, "Buganda's Position in Federal Uganda," *Journal of Commonwealth Political Studies* 3, 3 (November 1965): 175-76. This point is also discussed in G. F. Engholm and Ali A. Mazrui, "Violent Constitutionalism in Uganda," *Government and Opposition* 2, 4 (July-October 1967). The article is reprinted as chapter 7 in Mazrui, *Violence and Thought: Essays on Social Tensions in Africa* (London: Longmans, 1969): 152-153, 158-161.

Chapter 4

THE PERSISTENCE OF ETHNOCRACY

While the warrior tradition declined in Africa, ethnicity was stronger than ever. Ethnocracy is basically a political system based on kinship, real or presumed. It could take the form of an ethnically exclusive state, in which citizenship is basically governed by biological descent. Alternatively, a political system could be ethnocratic if it is based on an ethnic division of labor—with, say, Baganda for adminstrators and Nilotes as soldiers. Thirdly, a system could be ethnocratic if it is based on quantified ethnic balance—so many Nilotes in the civil service to balance so many Baganda in the same service.

When the British arrived in Uganda, they found a number of societies some of which had state structures. Among the more developed, and certainly one which developed even further under colonial rule, was Buganda. Bunyoro was also a highly structured polity. The concept of citizenship in these societies was inseparable from the concept of kinship. All the Baganda together were deemed to be descended from a single ancestor. The state rested on a principle of political consanguinity, a presumed descent from a shared forefather. The polity was ethnocratic.[1]

At its most literal, consanguinity implies a blood tie, but in fact there were other ties connected either with marriage and adoption or with cultural assimilation.

New citizens of an African society did not become full citizens until they mixed their blood with the original members of that society or adopted more fully the language and culture of that society. Biological intermingling and cultural assimilation were the most effective ways by which foreigners could enter the mainstream of African citizenship.[2] President Amin's response to the cultural and sexual exclusiveness of the Asians of Uganda rested in part upon a primordial African conception of true citizenship. The Asians, by being distant culturally and by being reluctant to mingle their blood with black Ugandans, remained alien by this criterion. They could no more become Ugandans than an Acholi who refused to intermarry with the

[66]

Baganda and resisted the adoption of the Ganda cultural ways could ever be deemed to be a Muganda.

Among communities to the north, both on the Sudanese and the Ugandan sides of the border, political ideas sometimes went to the extent of regarding all those who were not kinsmen as basically potential enemies. The distinction between a foreigner and an enemy could be very thin indeed. This did not necessarily mean that the groups automatically attacked strangers and foreigners who came in contact with them. But it did mean that they regarded them with the kind of reserve and deep suspicion usually accorded to traditional enemies.

It is possible to be adopted as a kinsman fictionally, or be given protection in terms of presumed kinship, but the stranger is then expected to behave like a kinsman, permitting himself to be assimilated into the system of rights and duties of that society. In the words of Evans-Pritchard in his study of the Nuer:

> If you wish to live among the Nuer you must do so on their terms, which means that you must treat them as a kind of kinsman and they will then treat you as a kind of kinsman. Rights, privileges and obligations are determined by kinship. Either a man is a kinsman, actually or by fiction, or he is a person to whom you have no reciprocal obligations and whom you treat as a potential enemy.[3]

East Africa as a whole betrays some ethnocratic tendencies which go back to these primordial conceptions of citizenship. What should be remembered is that ethnocracy in East Africa has colonial antecedents as well as precolonial.

The colonial antecedents of ethnocratic tendencies include the consequences of racial and sometimes tribal stratification under British rule.

In the days of the legislative councils in colonial Kenya, Tanganyika, Zanzibar, and to a lesser extent Uganda, the most important cleavages in the electoral process were ultimately *racial* rather than "tribal." Kenya especially had a heavy European presence in the political and economic system and a significant Indo-Pakistani presence in the economy. Representation in the legislature was apportioned by race—European, Asian (Indian and "Muslim"), Arab, and African. Tanganyika and Zanzibar each also had an elaborate system of representation by races. Uganda combined the racial principle of representation with the beginnings of ethnic tensions among Africans themselves.

To the extent that the entire colonization process was tied in with issues of race and ethnicity, the colonial legislative council was a school for ethnic politics from the start. As independence approached, the nature of ethnic politics began to shift away from "race" as the ultimate line of cleavage to "tribe" and region. (We use "ethnicity" in this chapter to refer to both "racial" and "tribal" identities.) Kenya and mainland Tanzania gradually ceased to be described as multiracial societies—even though the numerical inferiority of the few non-Africans was for a while disguised by their economic and political power. But with the expansion of the franchise and the coming of African majority rule, the nature of the political system became primarily multitribal rather than multiracial. The colonial legislative councils matured into the sovereign national assemblies. But the tradition of ethnic pluralism as a fundamental factor of electoral behavior now characterized the black majority itself and remained a major political variable in the life of independent East Africa. It had all the potential of ethnocratic evolution.

Both Kenya and Uganda have heartland tribes. We define a "heartland tribe" as a community located relatively near the capital city, large numerically, politically active, and historically important. The heartland tribe of Kenya is the Kikuyu; the heartland tribe of Uganda is the Baganda, and the territory they occupy is Buganda.

The Baganda were privileged during the colonial period. By the terms of the 1900 Agreement the British gave the Baganda considerable autonomy under the rule of their king, the Kabaka. The Baganda also responded well to the stimulus of acculturation and became among the best educated and most affluent of all East African communities. They increased their political preeminence over other communities. Their status sometimes resulted in an ethnic division of labor in Uganda, as they performed the more prestigious functions of the colonial polity. Later on the legacy was to result in a system of quantified restoration of ethnic balance.

The privileged position of Buganda remained one of the major bones of contention throughout the 1950s and most of the 1960s. The non-Baganda were hostile to Bagandan preeminence, and the Baganda were defensive in response. Electoral politics and legislative behavior in the critical initial years of independence were substantially concerned with how much autonomy and status the Buganda political unit should continue to enjoy. Even Buganda's members of Parliament were indirectly elected by the region's own legislature acting as an electoral college rather than popularly elected as were the rest of the M.P.'s.

By contrast, Kenya's heartland tribe, the Kikuyu, were *not* a privileged group in the colonial period. On the contrary, the Kikuyu, because of their nearness to the white settlers and their plantations, were among those who suffered most from the arrogance and exploitation of colonizers. The Mau Mau insurrection was one consequence of this predicament.

Yet the first African nonofficial member of the colonial Kenya legislative council, Eliud Mathu, was an Mkikuyu. The stage was set for the gradual rise of the Kikuyu to political prominence in Kenya. After independence Kenya had a Kikuyu President, Jomo Kenyatta, and a Kikuyu-dominated civil service. But the cabinet and Parliament maintained substantial representational balance among all tribes.

As for Tanzania, her strength has in part been her lack of a heartland tribe. The ethnic groups are relatively small and dispersed. The ethnic origins of the President are not a significant political issue; his group is small and distant from the capital. If anything, regionalism in Tanzania is a stronger force than ethnicity. Some regions feel "neglected," but they do not attribute their grievances to ethnic discrimination. Since 1972 the government has attempted to give the regions greater say in policy-making, without fear of rising ethnic tensions.

But once again we have to see the Ugandan experience in a larger historical and theoretical context. We have to see Uganda as an illustration of larger trends in human history.[4]

KINSHIP AND NATIONHOOD

If the aggregation of families in history led to the first pre-political societies, the aggregation of small societies gradually led to the emergence of nations. In 1875 Henry Maine argued that the development of nationhood was in fact a transition from kinship to territoriality. At least in the earlier versions of his theory, Maine saw kinship in patriarchal terms. The bond of union within the group started by being a belief or fiction of common descent, and the myth of origin sacralized a common ancestor. The transition first from family, to tribe, and then to nation was, in the words of Maine, "a system of concentric circles which have gradually expanded from the same point."[5]

Maine then discussed the transition from bonds of kinship to the boundaries of territory:

> We may bring home to ourselves the transformation of the idea in another way. England was once the country which Englishmen habited. Englishmen are now the people who inhabit England. The descendants of our forefathers keep up the tradition of kinship by calling themselves men of English race, but they tend steadily to become Americans and Australians. I do not say that the notion of consanguinity is absolutely lost; but it is extremely diluted, and quite subordinated to the newer view of the territorial constitution of nations.[6]

Although Maine's general theory was stimulating and has to a substantial extent been vindicated by history, he grossly underestimated the continuing residual political power of kinship. Territory has not replaced kinship as a basis of allegiance; it has simply introduced a new way of defining kinship. Territoriality is an extension of the old methods by which new members of a society were absorbed by an allocation of artificial kinship status and sometimes kinship roles. Territoriality provides a broader definition of kinship but by no means supplants it.

In England kinship, real or imaginary, is still a major factor behind attitudes to policies on both immigration and emigration. The Commonwealth Immigration Act of 1968 drew a sharp distinction between citizens who could successfully claim kinship ties with people in England and those who could not. The Act was intended to regulate the flow of British Asians from East Africa, as these individuals sought to claim what would otherwise have been a natural right of access to England as the country of their citizenship. But the British concept of citizenship was premodern at least in the sense of clinging substantially to presumed descent as a basis for the right of access to Britain. The concept of a first-class citizen in Britain continues to bear heavy ethnocratic implications.

Nor is this merely a question of skin color, though color played a large part in the events which led to the Commonwealth Immigration Act of 1968. In 1972, with Britain's impending entry into the European Common Market, a related issue of kinship arose. Would Italians and Germans as citizens of fellow members of the European Economic Community have easier access to Britain than New Zealanders and Australians? An initial draft put before Parliament by Edward Heath's government carried implications which made Australians and New Zealanders less favored in terms of access to Britain than citizens of the members of the European Economic Community. The debate culminated in a defeat of the government in Parliament, to the surprise of many observers. Edward Heath's government retreated from the original formulation of the legislation, and proceeded to revise it in a manner which would restore the rights of British "kith and kin"—now citizens of other countries—to have access to Britain on special considerations. The revised Act even made it difficult for the governments of Australia and New Zealand, since it discriminated by implication between Australians and New Zealanders who were of British origin and those who were not. Both governments in the antipodes expressed some anxiety about this differential treatment of their own citizenry in terms of access to Britain. But for the time being the residual pull of kinship considerations seemed to have triumphed in England. The evidence would seem to suggest that Sir Henry Maine was a little premature in seeing kinship as an anachronistic factor in political allegiance. On the contrary, political phenomena which range from racism to regional integration have continued to be influenced by considerations of shared descent. Continental movements like the European Economic Community, on one side, and the British reluctance to use arms in overcoming Ian Smith in Rhodesia, on the other side, have all included various degrees of presumed kinship ties.[7]

When nationality is defined in "racial" terms, the issue of presumed consanguinity asserts its immediacy. Movements in Europe like Pan-Germanism and Pan-Slavism encompassed theories of nationhood based on shared *blood*. In Africa, the whole theory of *apartheid* rests partly on considerations of "kith and kin" and partly on the rationalization of cultural differentiation. In Uganda, General Idi Amin has sought to create a nation of black Ugandans, partly on the grounds that black peoples are in a sense which is more than just metaphorical what the General would call "my brothers and sisters." And in the Middle East a whole new state was created in 1948 on the basis of shared descent from ancient Hebrews. The creation of Israel was once again an event deeply related to the interaction between kinship and nationhood.[8]

President Idi Amin of Uganda seems to have a general theory to the effect that people who are not prepared to mingle blood are not prepared to form a shared political community. The sexual exclusiveness of the Asians in Uganda prior to their expulsion led Amin to the conclusion that since Asians were not prepared to mingle blood with black Ugandans, they were by that very reluctance unprepared to share nationhood with Ugandans. There is considerable evidence to indicate that Amin adheres to this interpretation and has by his own example encouraged transethnic marriages within the country. But there have been occasions when even he has been reported as being suspicious of Eurafricans and Eurasians. In February 1973 *The Times* of London reported that there were signs of "a new clampdown beginning on Eurafrican and Eurasian Ugandans, whom General Amin recently described as 'even bigger crooks than the Asians.' "[9]

The link between citizenship and readiness to engage in joint military self-defense has certainly continued onto the national scale of the growth of the polity. There was a time when citizenship itself could never be described as complete unless it included eligibility for military service:

> In the primitive nation as exhibited to us by its earliest records in Greece and Rome, and in the German tribes so far as they have a common permanent head, we find political functions distributed among three differently constituted organs—the king or supreme chief, a council of subordinate chiefs or elders, and the assembly of fully qualified citizens which is . . . a martial muster of the freemen in arms.[10]

In the growth of the Islamic Empire the ultimate differentiating characteristic between fully absorbed citizens and conquered peoples was that the citizens were eligible for military service.

In Israel today the Arabs who are Israeli citizens fall short of being full citizens again by the yardstick of eligibility for military conscription. All Jewish Israelis are liable to military conscription, but not Arab Israelis. In a curious way the Arabs are second-class citizens partly because the nature of a racially purist state like Israel is such that the non-Jew cannot be called upon for that ultimate sacrifice in war. Some countries have second-class citizens by reducing the rights of the less privileged group; but both Israel today and Islamic states in the past had second-class citizens by reducing the *obligations* of the less privileged groups.

Of all the countries in the world, perhaps the United States comes nearest to fulfilling Sir Henry Maine's criteria of territoriality as against kinship as the basis of nationhood. The mixture of nationalities and races in the composition of the population of the United States has certainly transformed the concept of "American" into a territorial concept par excellence. Territoriality as a basis of nationhood is even stronger in America than it is in those other immigrant countries like Australia and New Zealand. The greater mixture in the United States has oriented the history of the country precisely towards illustrating Sir Henry Maine's precept.

Even the duty to do military service in the American situation has been distinctive in being distributed not only among first-class citizens, nor indeed only among citizens in lower classes, but also among resident aliens. The laws of the United States until recently allowed for the conscription of those who were territorially located in the United States even if they had not as yet been granted citizenship nor indeed applied for it. Even foreign students studying in the United States at the peak of the Vietnam war were sometimes threatened with conscription by American authorities on the basis of the laws as they then existed.

But although the United States has perhaps gone furthest in the move from kinship to territoriality, it has still retained kinship factors as a force within its political system. Again issues of race and ethnicity, taboos of intermarriage and principles governing racial descent, have all had their ultimate roots in the dominant kinship culture of white Anglo-Saxon Protestants. The impact of Anglo-Saxon kinship on other groups has ranged from a desire by Italians or Jews to shed their names in preference for Anglo-Saxon names to the whole problem of racial disparities between black and white within the American society. Sir Henry Maine has not had it all his way in the United States.

KINSHIP AND STATEHOOD

There is a good deal of overlap between the evolution of the polity as nation and the polity as state. And both do link up with Eugene Victor Walter's concept of a chiefdom. In some parts of the world the principle of primogeniture in the family did help to consolidate the principle of hereditary succession in the chieftainship or kingship. Primogeniture sometimes implied the right of the eldest son to inherit *the family*. Primogeniture in Japanese society certainly tended in this direction, though the system in England narrowed itself more to the right of the eldest son to inherit the title and the lands of his father. The question of how far Japanese and British principles of monarchical succession were conditioned by the broader doctrine of primogeniture in the wider society has remained one of the more intriguing issues in the political anthropology of monarchical institutions.

But apart from the impact of the wider kinship system on monarchical principles, there was also the political role of the monarch's relatives and the role of leading aristocratic families in societies like Japan and England. The polity in Japan and England has at times been indeed a family affair, at least to the extent that elite recruitment has drawn so disproportionately from a number of distinguished upper-class and upper middle-class families. The polity as an extended family in such situations is almost literal, in spite of the enlarged scale of political organization in a nation of fifty million and more.

The behavior of the monarch's relatives and the leading families in Japan and England bears a strong resemblance to the style of politics in chiefdoms in traditional Africa. Certainly the history of the British monarchy until this century, when the monarchy became powerless, was the history of an institution subject to the pulls of relatives and distinguished families within the realm, and therefore similar in important respects to experience in chiefly polities in Africa. In the words of Schapera:

> Tribal politics is in fact made up to a considerable extent of quarrels between the chief and his near relatives, and of their intrigues against one another to command his favor.... They are entitled by custom to advise and assist him in his conduct of public affairs, and they actively resent any failure on his part to give them what they regard as their due.[11]

The interplay between politics and militarism continues both at the level of chiefly polities and on the larger scale of imperial monarchical systems like that of Japan and Great Britain before World War II. Sons from distinguished families entered the military profession, thus partly consolidating the hold which their families already had over the political sector of the power structure in the land. The officer corps in such armies drew disproportionately from the illustrious kinship systems.

When statehood included imperial ambitions the interplay between politics and militarism was particularly strong. Again both Britain and Japan qualify in this regard. But so does Ashanti in Ghana's history. Fortes comments:

> The Ashanti state was created and maintained by war, and a military ideology remained a central feature of its structure to the end. Guns and gold were its trading foundations. As imported firearms spread among the populace, the

chiefdom which could muster the largest supplies of guns and ammunition had
every chance, if ably led, to triumph in the intertribal wars.[12]

That old link between economic survival and military survival had become
in Ashanti a link between gold and guns by the nineteenth century. Statehood and imperial ambitions reinforced the military factor in the foundations
of the Ashanti polity. It is here that we come back to the centrality of the
concept of *force* in the very definition of statehood.[13]

Eugene Walter's own definition of the state mentioned earlier is Weberian—since Walter sees the chief difference between a state and a chiefdom as
lying in the nature and means of coercion authorized within the system and
exercised in the political community. To Walter the head of state does claim
"the legitimate monopoly of force and commands a special body of men
organized to use it."[14]

Radcliffe-Brown, Fortes, and Evans-Pritchard take the link even further
and assert that the control and manipulation of force is what all political
organization is about, and not just what statehood is about: "The political
organization of a society is that aspect of the total organization which is
concerned with the control and regulation of the use of physical force."[15]

British social anthropologists, by venturing into political anthropology,
have helped political scientists to refine some of their concepts. And yet this
should not blind us to the fact that the social anthropologists themselves
betray a residual difficulty in distinguishing between statehood and a political
system. Radcliffe-Brown invoked the principle of territoriality not only as
part of a definition of a state but as part of a definition of political authority.
To Radcliffe-Brown political authority is concerned with "the maintenance
or establishment of social order, within a territorial framework, by the
organized exercise of coercive authority through the use, or the possibility of
use, of physical force."[16]

Another major British anthropologist, John Beattie, has also embraced the
principle of territoriality as part of the definition of "political authority."
But Beattie goes on further and uses territoriality as a way of distinguishing
political authority from authority in a family:

> I take authority to be "political" only when its applicability depends upon,
> among other things, the occupation of a certain territory by the persons who
> acknowledge it and are subject to it. . . . This is not the case with the, for
> example, domestic authority; a man's acknowledgement of his father's authority
> over him depends not, or not primarily, on where he is, but on what he is, that is,
> a son.[17]

Beattie is awakening us to the limits of regarding the polity as an extended
family. While important kinship factors were still at play for a monarch like
the Mukama of the Nyoro state, the nature of the Mukama's authority went

beyond mere kinship. What Beattie does not fully grasp is that this is because the Mukama's authority was the authority of a head of state and not merely because it was political authority. While territoriality remains pertinent to the very concept of statehood, it is not necessary as a basis for certain levels of political authority, nor does it necessarily replace the principle of kinship.

The issue of organization of physical force is more difficult to handle if we are to regard the state also as an extended family. Are the bonds which keep a family together ultimately definable in terms of the organization of physical force? Weber himself reminded us that "the most varied institutions— beginning with the sib—had known the use of physical force as quite normal." But although coercion is a factor which can condition the sib as a system of relationships, it is not a factor important for the sib's definition.

We are back now to the distinction between economic survival and military survival. The sib or family cooperates primarily for economic survival, at least in the sense of eking out a living and having bread to share. Statehood, on the other hand, has so far been the final consummation of that marriage between politicization and militarization. Is the state an extended family? The answer must be negative for as long as the ultimate impulse behind the state is the manipulation of force for public ends. The instincts of companionship and economic solidarity so basic to the survival of a primordial family are not the same as the impulses of organized coercion within a state as a militarized polity.

And yet the twentieth century has seen a closing of the gap between the ethos of an extended family and the ethos of modern statehood. A gradual transition, still incomplete, has started, from a warfare state to a welfare state. The emergence of the welfare state indicates a return to the principle of a shared family budget, and the principle of responsibility for the aged, the economically unproductive, and the infirm.

For the time being the welfare state coexists with the warfare state. Indeed, they are often fused in one. Principles of shared economic survival and policies of presumed military survival are conducted simultaneously. But the very emergence of the welfare state in the twentieth century signifies a reinforcement of the ethos of kinship in this particular kind of polity. The welfare tribe, with all its kinship obligations, begins to influence the morality of the welfare state.

CONCLUSION

In his book, *Primitive Society,* Robert H. Lowie emphasized the role of associations as "potential agencies for the creation of a state by uniting the population within a circumscribed area into an aggregate that functions as a definite unit irrespective of any other social affiliations of the inhabitants."[18]

In a later article on the origin of the state Lowie went on to say that "associations invariably weaken the prepotency of blood ties by establishing novel ties regardless of kinship; and they may indirectly establish a positive union of all the occupants of a given area."[19]

But Lowie came to have second thoughts before long on the issue of the autonomy of associations in relation to kinship within political processes.

> Further study leads to serious modification of this view. Undoubtedly the claims set forth for the destructive efficacy of associations hold: by the very fact of their existence they have created novel bonds bound to encroach upon the omnip-otence of kinship ties. But their positive achievement is more doubtful: it is only when supplementary factors of unification supervene that they achieve the solidarity of the entire local group. In itself, in other words, associational activity is not less separatistic than the segmentation of society into groups of kindred.[20]

Lowie sees the need for supplementary factors to give associational activity the driving integrative force. What he does not adequately work out is the impact of kinship itself as a factor behind the integrative functions of association. When political integration is an aggregation of subsocieties, it is quite often also an aggregation of kinship fields, real or fictitious.

The politicization of society had its origins less in economics than in combat. We have sought to illustrate in an earlier chapter that the growth of the polity in the direction of statehood was in part a process of militarization.

The polity continues to be, in an important and more than metaphorical sense, one type of extended family. When intertwining with nationalism and territoriality, the language of mother country and fatherland have exerted a symbolic influence on the imaginations of men and women in otherwise diverse societies. Perhaps this is not surprising after all. Even political man was once born and reared as a child. Has not William Wordsworth reminded us that "the child is the father of the man?"

General Amin is in some respects deeply primordial in his attitudes and presuppositions. His demands on the Asians echoed some of these anthropological findings about traditional political societies in Africa. Amin has been primordial in his demand for cultural identification and biological intermingling; he has also been primordial in his tendency to regard complete aliens as basically potential enemies; and thirdly, he has been primordial in his distrust of private choice in matters of public concern.

African societies within themselves are an impressive cluster of mutual obligations and responsibilities, an impressive system of fellowship based on the solidarity of kinship. That is why President Julius Nyerere virtually equated the English word *socialism* with the Swahili word *Ujamaa*. The latter is a term denoting the bonds of kinship, the obligation of young people to look after the old, and of the old to care for the young, the readiness to extend hospitality, the presumed duty of whoever is better off among kinsmen to look after those who are not quite as well off. Nyerere saw in *Ujamaa* the roots of socialism.

By contrast, Amin saw in *Ujamaa* the roots of citizenship. Just as Nyerere moved on from tribal solidarity to the solidarity of socialistic fellowship, so Amin sought to move from the bonds of the clan to membership of the nation-state.

Amin could see this easily enough where all the groups were black in color. Racial identification permits the psychological leap from tribal pride to black ethnicity.

Soon after assuming power Amin emerged as someone within the classical tradition of viewing the nation as a family writ large. His adoption of the name Dada, patriarch, confirmed his image of the role of the President as being in some fundamental sense a father-figure. His view of marriage as a device of tribal intermingling was also in a classical tradition of its own. Intermarriage becomes part of the foundation of national integration, simply because kinship was part of the foundation of citizenship. The General himself began to take pride in having one wife drawn from the Lugbara, one from the Basoga, one from the Langi, and later one from the Baganda. From this point of view, in his approach to social integration General Amin was indeed profoundly African from the start although not all his own marriages have survived.

But there is always a problem when, in the context of modern sensibilities, a head of state sees himself as the father of the nation. The logical problem in terminology arises when he is unable to refer to his fellow citizens as "my children." If he had been a very old figure, like Mzee Kenyatta, the term "my children" could have aroused an indulgent response from the population. Mzee Kenyatta is after all a real "Mzee"—an old man, an aged elder, enjoying widespread, though not universal, reverence among Kenyans.

But General Amin is relatively young as a head of state. In his role as a Dada, or patriarch, he must at the same time refrain from the condescension of treating his fellow citizens as children.

And yet the General still likes to think of Uganda as in some sense a Kakwa family writ large, and all Ugandans as being to some extent his kinsmen. And so, although the General himself is a father, he calls his children "my brothers and sisters." By calling his children "brothers and sisters" he maintains an egalitarian relationship with them, at least in vocabulary and tone.

It is like those Westerners who now permit their children to call the parents by their first names and have abolished the term "daddy" and "mummy" from the vocabulary of the family. The philosophy behind this Western innovation is an attempt to establish a kind of parity of esteem between children and their parents from an early age and prepare the ground for a relationship of equality. Similarly, General Idi Amin Dada, while viewing himself as the head of the family, prefers to use the vocabulary of fraternity rather than of filial relationship.

The General can see himself as a father figure for all black Ugandans. But he has great psychological problems in seeing himself as a father figure for brown Ugandans or white Ugandans. The racial exclusiveness of the Asians aggravated the General's incapacity to see the Asians in kinship terms.

And yet in the ultimate analysis Africa must move away from conceptions of citizenship based on kinship to conceptions of citizenship which, though retaining some link with descent, also allow for contractual rights and obligations. The modern nation-state has in fact to respect even more the citizen who is a citizen by act of will, as compared with the citizen who is a citizen by biological accident.

On attainment of independence in Uganda the Asians had in effect three choices. They could become British, adopt Ugandan citizenship, or return to the Indian subcontinent. A similar choice confronted the Asians of Kenya and less clearly the Asians of Tanzania.

The majority of Asians in East Africa chose to invest in British citizenship. But those Asians who had adopted local citizenship were, from the point of view of the modern rational basis of social arrangements, greater East Africans precisely because they had a choice to be something else—and yet decided to commit themselves to the soil of their adoption.

Very few indigenous East Africans had any choice in their citizenship. To some extent their predicament was classical in African terms, as it was derived from the biological accident of descent. Of course these ought to retain full rights as citizens. The modern state ought not to move in the direction of victimizing indigenous citizens simply because in their case they had no choice. But it is especially important to protect the rights of these contractual citizens—those Asians in East Africa who looked at that ominous question mark hanging over the continent at independence and decided by a conscious act of will that they would throw in their lot with the social groups among whom they lived.

And when they were ordered in Uganda in August 1972 to go and stand in queues to confirm what they thought was already confirmed, they responded with impressive conformity. I know of Uganda Asians who accidentally happened to be abroad thousands of miles away when they were required to report at the Kampala Immigration Office to confirm their citizenship. Some traversed half the globe in order to join those queues. Because the notice was so short, the queues outside the Immigration Office used to assemble from the previous night, sleeping on the pavement, waiting for the offices to open at 8 o'clock the following morning. I know personally of a family that joined those queues outside the Immigration Office at midnight the previous night. I also heard of families that started to stand on the pavement at about 8 p.m. the previous evening, soon after their supper.

And then these groups, when they got to the counter the following noon, perhaps stood there anxiously awaiting the verdict. A little irregularity, a wrong numbering here, and an unclear signature there, or a birth certificate of one's grandfather long lost, was sometimes enough to lead to cancellation of citizenship. This is quite apart from those who renounced British citizenship after the ninety-day deadline.

Citizenship in the modern sense has often as strong a moral content as kinship solidarity. Administrative or legalistic irregularities should indeed necessitate further scrutiny of individual cases, carefully considered with a readiness to give the benefit of the doubt to the person who is a citizen. Only concrete proof of fraud could justify the cancellation of citizenship. The discovery of administrative delays, or wrong pagination, or unclear official stamps, or clerical delays from the London end of renunciation, may justify further thought on the matter but on no account do they justify a frivolous game with people's moral commitments.

The General's decision not to expel Asian citizens after all was a decision of political courage considering that he had pronounced otherwise before. But the meaningfulness of the decision required a seriousness of purpose further down below in the administrative hierarchy to prevent technicalities and irregularities being invoked as a mode of trivializing solemn contractual obligations.

In historical terms, there was more at stake in Amin's adventure than the fate of a few thousand Asians. What was at stake was Uganda's capacity to modernize herself and move efficiently from a world of pure kinsmen to a world of compatriots, from a morality of clan to a legality of contract, from primordial ethnicity to modern nationhood.

What was also in question was Uganda's capacity to transcend her ethnocratic heritage and provide a new basis for the quality of *belonging.*

NOTES

1. Consult Eugene Victor Walter, *Terror and Resistance: A Study of Political Violence, with Case Studies of Some Primitive African Communities* (London and New York: Oxford University Press, 1969): 57-58. Walter was adapting E. R. Service, *Primitive Social Organization* (New York, 1962).

2. Walter, Ibid., p. 59.

3. E. E. Evans-Pritchard, *The Nuer* (Oxford: Clarendon Press, 1940): 183.

4. Some of these issues are discussed in a wider international context in a book by the same author provisionally entitled *A World Federation of Cultures,* sponsored by the Institute for World Order, New York, and the Carnegie Endowment for International Peace.

5. Maine, *Ancient Law,* chapters 5 and 7.

6. Sir Henry Maine, *Lectures on the Early History of Institutions* (New York, 1875).

7. For a recent discussion of the supposed anachronism of kinship in British identity, consult Jerome Caminada, "Kith and Kin: A Myth Wearing Thin?" *The Times* (London), December 2, 1972.

8. For a more extensive comparison between Israel and Amin's Uganda see chapter 10. For issues of nationhood in relation to race in Kenya, consult Donald Rothchild, "Kenya's Minorities and the African Crisis over Citizenship," *Race* (London) 9, 4. (April 1968): 421-437. See also the companion piece by Rothchild, "Citizenship and National Integration: The Non-African Crisis in Kenya," Studies in Race and Nations, Center on International Race Relations, Graduate School of International Studies, University of Denver, vol. 1, study 3 (1969-1970), 1970.

9. *The Times,* February 2, 1973. The General had presumably just been irritated by particular individuals, conceivably of mixed racial extraction, and was responding to the mood of the moment rather than to his interest in seeing black men mingle their blood with others as a form of black assertiveness.

10. Henry Sidgwick, *The Development of European Polity* (London: Macmillan, 1920): 57.

11. I. Schapera, "The Political Organization of the Ngwato of Bechuanaland Protectorate," in M. Fortes and E. E. Evans-Pritchard (eds.) *African Political Systems* (London and New York: Oxford University Press on behalf of the International African Institute, 1940, 1950 edition): 79.

12. M. Fortes, *Kinship and the Social Order* (Chicago: Aldine, 1963): 140.

13. See Max Weber, "Politics as a Vocation," in H. H. Gerth and C. Wright Mills, *From Max Weber: Essays in Sociology* (Routledge and Kegan Paul, 1957): 78. Also Mazrui, *Cultural Engineering and Nation-Building in East Africa* (Evanston: Northwestern University Press, 1972): 247-275.

14. Walter, *Terror and Resistance, op. cit.:* 59.

15. Fortes and Evans-Pritchard, *African Political Systems,* op. cit.: xxiii, 14.

16. A. R. Radcliffe-Brown, Preface to Fortes and Evans-Pritchard, *African Political Systems,* ibid.: xi-xxi.

17. John Beattie, *The Nyoro State* (Oxford: Clarendon Press, 1971): 4-5.

18. Robert H. Lowie, *Primitive Society* (1920) pp. 394-396.

19. Robert H. Lowie, "The Origin of the State," *The Freeman* 5, July 19 and 26, 1922: 440-442, 465-467.

20. Robert H. Lowie, *The Origin of the State* (New York: Harcourt, Brace, 1927): 107-108.

Section III:

Violence and Social Change

Chapter 5

THE DEMILITARIZATION OF VIOLENCE

In this chapter we start from the assumption that general attitudes to violence in the wider society affect the behavior of soldiers not only on the battlefield but also in their relations with civilians. A society with a high incidence of violence among civilians themselves in the streets is a society vulnerable to brutalization by its own soldiers and policemen. Was Uganda a violent political system well before the soldiers took over power?

In this connection we must distinguish between four forms of violence— political, civic, military, and deviant.

Political violence is concerned with disputes about the control of political institutions, the determination of political goals, the allocation of collective resources, or the definition of the political community itself. Acts of political violence in Uganda have ranged from the "disappearance" and murder of Chief Justice Kiwanuka in 1972 to the racial riots by Makerere Univeristy students four years previously.

Civic violence arises when private citizens, out of a sense of outraged civic conscience, take the law into their own hands and inflict punishment on suspected criminals or moral transgressors. The whole tradition of vigilantism in the United States, the ugliness of lynching, the tradition of hue and cry in Uganda, the recurrent cases of outraged villagers beating suspects to death—all these are instances of civic violence at work in society.

Military violence involves actual war or collective engagement akin to warfare proper but includes violent individual acts to promote military aims. Not all violence involving soldiers is military. In Uganda there has been a good deal of violence by soldiers which cannot be described as military in this sense. When a soldier beats up the bartender, or kills his wife's lover in a fit of jealousy, the violence perpetrated has little to do with the soldier's role in

AUTHOR'S NOTE: This chapter could not have been written without the assistance of my students at Makerere. Special thanks are due to Mr. Jack Mpiima and Mr. S.A.K. Oporia-Ekwaro. But responsibility for the interpretations is mine.

society. Violence by soldiers in pursuit of personal satisfaction is usually
deviant violence. On the other hand, violence by soldiers against, say, a
nation's Chief Justice would probably be political violence. It is only when
soldiers unleash violence in pursuit of war aims, or in pursuit of something
very similar to the collective goals of armed combat, that the violence could
be deemed military in our sense.

As for *deviant violence,* these are acts of an individual transgressing the
values of the society in pursuit of personal advantage. Armed robbery,
individual murders, drunken brawls culminating in physical mutilations, are
usually all instances of deviant violence in our sense.

In this chapter we are addressing ourselves to the non-military forms of
violence in Uganda. We shall examine civic violence as a response to deviant
violence, and also political violence and its relationship to nationhood.

FROM THE WARRIOR TO THE VIGILANTE

The decline of the warrior tradition in Uganda did not result in the
elimination of violence but only in its partial demilitarization. Warfare in the
old days was often concerned with economic goods—with defending one's
cattle, or one's land, against raiders and marauders from rival tribes. Sometimes counter-raids were needed to increase the cattle-wealth of one's own
tribe, or strengthen the labor force with new captives, or capture women as
wealth with which to reward the gallant.

British colonial rule drastically reduced the incidence of such raids except
in a few isolated areas, but the tradition of being on the alert against
"cattle-raiders" took new forms, including the form of vigilantism. The
warrior tradition as a system of collectively defending the community's
economic goods gave way to a system of collective "hue and cry" against
individual thieves in otherwise very modern urban centers.

The colonial impact had resulted in increased urbanization and greater
residential intermingling of ethnic groups. A thief coming from a different
tribe in an otherwise homogeneous community is sometimes regarded as an
"enemy" in almost the old military sense of a cattle-raider from a rival
community. But even in urban situations involving considerable ethnic intermingling at close quarters, the idea of a thief as an "aggressor" against the
community as a whole is remarkably resilient in Uganda. The cry "thief"
becomes indeed a battle-cry almost literally—as collective vengeance descends
on the miserable suspect. The warrior tradition might have been demilitarized

by the British, but it finds some fulfillment in the ethos of alertness against the new "cattle-raiders" of modern cities—the sneak thief and the criminal gang. This is what civic violence is all about.

As a residue of the warrior tradition, this kind of private alertness against "cattle-raiders" bears strong resemblance to the frontier tradition in the history of the United States. It might enrich this analysis of the Uganda situation if we pursued this comparison with the United States more fully. Both the warrior tradition in Uganda and the frontier tradition in the United States have had consequences for the quality of life of those countries today—sometimes for the better, sometimes for the worse.

Both Uganda and the United States have a record of varied forms of violence. Both countries have deep internal cleavages, with some propensity towards a substantial tradition of rustic self-reliance and a readiness on the part of simple folk to make arrangements for their own protection

It is in the context of this mixture of social phenomena that civic, deviant, and political violence interact.

A major thesis of this chapter is that civic violence is at its most prevalent in situations of fragile *statehood,* while political violence is at its most dangerous in situations of fragile *nationhood.* The experience of Uganda merges with the experience of the United States in a joint illumination of this area of social reality.

The concept of statehood that is at stake here has points of contact with the Weberian definition. Weber asserted that, sociologically, the state could not be defined in terms of its ends. Maintenance of law and order, preservation of society, promotion of the well-being of the community, control or suppression of deviant behavior, may all be very central to the purposes of a state. And yet Weber's point is that there is scarcely any task that some political association has not taken in hand, and there is no task that one could say has always been exclusive and peculiar to those associations which are designated as political ones. We shall return to Weber's concept of the state in later chapters. To Weber the modern state could be defined sociologically only in terms of the specific means peculiar to it, namely, the use of physical force.

Weber goes on to quote Trotsky's belief that "every state is founded on force." Weber concedes that force is not the normal nor the only means of the state, but he regards it as a means specific to the state.

Today the relation between the state and violence is an especially intimate one. In the past, the most varied institutions—beginning with the sib—have known the use of physical force as quite normal. Today, however, we have to say that a state is a human community that (successfully) claims the *monopoly of the legitimate use of physical force* within a given territory. Specifically, at the present time, the right to use physical force is ascribed to other institutions or to individuals only to the extent to which the state permits it. The state is considered the sole source of the "right" to use violence.[1]

Weber's definition of the state has elements of ethnocentricism. But in its basic outlines it has significant analytical utility. Societies which have a widespread incidence of civic violence, in the sense of citizens taking the law into their own hands and inflicting punishment, are societies in which statehood has not as yet consolidated itself. Even now statehood in the United States has fractures of fragility, and the incidence of civic violence has by no means been eliminated. But in the case of the American experience one of the major reasons why civic violence has been retreating is the simple fact that political violence has been advancing. The upsurge of the civil rights revolution and black militancy, the readiness of black people to take risks in retaliation against acts perpetrated on their fellows, has been one of the last disincentives against the tradition of racial lynching in the United States. The rise of new forms of political violence, while manifesting a deep crisis of identity in the nation, has at the same time helped to eliminate one of the uglier forms of civic violence in the American tradition.

The vigilante tradition in the United States goes back as far as 1767. It persisted in America as a major factor in extra-legal organization until well into the twentieth century.

Vigilantism in the United States arose as a response to a problem not too unfamiliar to some villagers in Uganda—the absence or inadequacy of an effective law-and-order infrastructure in areas away from major concentrations of populations. In the case of America, the frontier played an important role in the evolution of the vigilante tradition. The normal foundations of an evolved society were as yet inadequately laid in a frontier region. The sheriffs were sometimes there, and attempts were made in some places to observe due process as far as possible. But the whole machinery for enforcing the law was often painfully inadequate, and a good deal had to depend on the civic readiness of the citizenry if society as a whole was to be protected from outlaws.

In October 1969 four men were fatally burned and another was slashed to death at Buseta in Budaka, Bugwere, Bukedi. A group of people who described themselves as "999" (Nine-Nine-Nine) vigilantes surrounded a house where they claimed a group of thieves was hiding. They set the house on fire. Four of the five men inside were burned to death. The fifth managed to escape, after sustaining serious burns. One of the 999 men was slashed to death when he was mistaken for a thief in the course of the same evening.[2]

The eruption of militant vigilantism in Bukedi and Bugisu in Uganda in 1969 had ideological connections with an earlier movement in 1960. This was a taxpayers' rebellion centered especially in Bugerere. It was a manifestation of profound dissatisfaction with the services rendered to the community in return for the taxes they paid. The tax-collector began to look dangerously like a "cattle-raider".

When we analyze American vigilantism we see an intimate connection between it and the whole ethos of American liberalism. Approval of private initiative and rugged individual self-reliance lay both in the vigilante tradition and in the stream of American liberal thought.

Curiously enough, while vigilantism in American history is thus connected with individualism, vigilantism in Uganda is more closely connected to collectivism. The same activity, consisting of the initiative of citizens to punish criminals themselves, could thus be a manifestation of two widely divergent cultural ideologies. In the American case the distinctive characteristic of the activity is the readiness to take action privately where the machinery of the state is inadequate. There were indeed occasions when vigilantism was a parallel structure of law enforcement and not simply a compensatory device for the inadequacies of the more formal structures. Where vigilantism in America was a parallel structure, the motives were again sometimes connected with an old basic tenet of American liberalism—a distrust of excessive taxation as part of the American distrust of government power. Taxpayers in local communities sometimes devised voluntary ways of law enforcement as a contribution to the security of society which did not entail any further financial strengthening of institutionalized authority.

But the tradition of responding to the cry of "thief" in Ugandan villages, and joining the multitude to chase a suspect, and participating in inflicting punishment, was a tradition within the stream of primordial collectivism rather than liberal individualism. In the Ugandan instance the same impulse which makes a neighbor help another in building his house leads the neighbor to help in punishing him who has broken into the house. The paramount animating value in the Ugandan situation is not the value of private initiative but the value of *collective security*. We are back here to the essence of the warrior tradition in indigenous African political systems.

ON LIFE AND PROPERTY

Another traditional factor to be borne in mind in the Ugandan situation as compared with the American is the comparative worth of life and property. In the United States the Lockean ideological tradition has indeed often related life closely to property. Locke himself sometimes used the word "property" comprehensively to include life as a possession. Security of life, security of property, and security of liberty were to Locke intimately interdependent. This relationship profoundly influenced the evolving ideology of the American colonists. In the words of Karl J. Friedrich and Robert C. McCloskey:

> Locke stresses the preservation of property as a very essential feature both of self-preservation and happiness. When Jefferson in drafting the Declaration of Independence came to pen the famous triad of "life, liberty and the pursuit of happiness" (in lieu of life, liberty and property as well as happiness, as the Virginia Bill of Rights June 12, 1776 had it), he did not make as much of a change from Locke as is sometimes supposed. In Locke the lines between happiness and property are fluid.[3]

Friedrich and McCloskey go on to remind us that when Jefferson wrote the Declaration of Independence he referred to no book, not even to Locke's *Second Treatise*. But, according to Friedrich and McCloskey, this only goes to show how deeply influenced by the book Jefferson and his contemporaries had been. The ideas and even the phrases of John Locke had become so well embedded in the thinking of educated Americans of the period that "they came to mind unbidden":

> Even Jefferson's use of "the pursuit of happiness" as the third term in the triumvirate of basic rights instead of Locke's term "estate" was not ... necessarily a departure in meaning. Stylistically, "pursuit of happiness" is unquestionably better, and it may have been no more than an instinct for a graceful phrase that caused the substitution.[4]

Nevertheless, in the evolution of American jurisprudence, life increasingly assumed greater value than property. Murder was a more serious crime than theft. And a life was seldom demanded by the law for a crime which was less than the taking of another life.

The curious thing about the evolution of judicial ideas traditionally in Uganda is the extent to which the sanctity of property seems quite often to overshadow the sanctity of life. The Lockean tradition in the United States may have subsumed life under property and may, at times, even have equated life with property. And yet in spite of the fact that the United States is more deeply committed ideologically to private ownership than Uganda, and has a more profound attachment to the doctrine of maximizing returns and responding to the profit motive, it remains true that ordinary villagers in Uganda rise in more ferocious defense of property than is normally experienced these days in the United States. The items stolen are sometimes staggeringly modest. Here are a few examples picked out almost at random from the record of civic retribution in Uganda.

.In December 1968 Lebaleba, aged about 60, was beaten to death by villagers of Kabulamuliro. The allegation was that he was caught stealing a chicken at night. In the same month in Busoga a man was allegedly caught stealing a radio, was beaten by villagers, and later died at Kamuli Dispensary. In September 1969 a man who was accused of stealing three shillings from a passenger at Tororo Bus Park was chased by a mob of people and beaten to death.

There are occasions when the ferocity of the villagers is connected with the symbolism of the item stolen. In February 1969 a man was beaten when he was found with a stolen *empalu*, a circumcision drum. It was alleged that Augustine Gutaka was caught with the drum by villagers in Bugisu and beaten up severely. He was later taken to the Muluka Chief where he died.[5]

Why do the villagers seem to take life so lightly? Or is it because they take property so seriously? Do the villagers regard a thief, in his violation of the right of property, as someone who has forfeited the right to live? Is the attitude similar to that which a soldier has in a confrontation with the "enemy" on the battlefield?

Sometimes the sense of retribution against thieves in Uganda is in response to the violence of the thieves themselves. Burglars and robbers in the country have been known to be singularly indifferent to life. Old women have been robbed of a few shillings and then slashed to death. Whole families have on occasion suffered heavy brutalization in the course of surrendering a few items of property in their homes. The *kondos* (robbers with violence) have struck terror in many a community.

Successive Uganda governments, bewildered by the callous disregard by such robbers, have groped for legal and penal solutions. There is a temptation in a country which has limited resources to seek an answer in the severity of punishment. It is not always remembered that the certainty of punishment, arising out of an efficient law enforcement infrastructure, is often a greater deterrent than mere severity in a situation where only a few get caught. Nevertheless, it is not very difficult to understand why in 1968 the Uganda government felt it had to raise the punishment for robbery with violence from mere imprisonment to a capital offense.

Voices did protest, arguing that by making robbery with violence a capital offense the thief would be more tempted than ever to destroy all witnesses after he had stolen. Having threatened first in order to get the loot and having thereby exposed himself to capital punishment, the kondo might then feel more secure if he murdered those whom he had already robbed.

It is still not clear whether the government's decision helped to increase the incidence of murder rather than decrease the incidence of robbery with violence. It is conceivable that the measure has had both effects. For a while there might have been fewer robberies as a result of the new law, but also more murders of those who had been robbed.[6]

But if each Central Government in Uganda has felt this sense of desperation, so have the villagers now and again. In April 1969 a number of people were killed and many others wounded in the villages of Kibuzi, Bugadu, and Busana in Bugerere County, East Mengo District, when villagers carried out an organized search for people who were suspected of being kondos. This had been preceded by several robberies in the area which had terrorized the villagers. A number of villagers, unable to bear the torment of fear in the area, migrated to other villages. But then the tension mounted too high, and the villagers broke loose on those they suspected as kondos and proceeded to wreak vengeance.[7]

Both the violence of the kondo and the counter-violence of village retribution might be related in their causes. They might be connected with the whole universe involving attitudes to war and to death. The people of such areas are a cultural world apart from societies which are more deeply shocked by such events. It is not that the villagers in such districts of Uganda necessarily value human life less than others; it is more likely that they view the whole issue of human death differently. The sharp finality with which death is associated in Western thought is not necessarily shared by villagers in Bugerere. It is true that even in Western thought, whenever the influence of Christianity remains relevant, the soul lives on even after the body has decomposed. But this is a spiritual continuity, taking the deceased away from his relatives even if he does continue to inhabit some heaven beyond.

But the whole concept of the *living dead* in African traditional religions reduces the sharp differentiation between the here and the hereafter, between the living and the dead, between relatives alive and relatives deceased.[8]

A related aspect of traditional perspective operating in the behavior of Uganda villagers is in fact neo-Lockean. Locke's definition of a "state of war" is not far removed from the interpretation which villagers give to major intrusions into the rights of the local people. Thomas Hobbes had argued before Locke that in a state of nature, prior to the formation of society and government, the prevailing condition was one of a state of war. Every man was for himself, and every man had to be his own policeman in order to safeguard that which was his. Locke, answering Hobbes, argued that a state of nature was not to be equated with a state of war. To Locke you could have a state of war in civil society and you could have social peace in a state of nature.

When does a state of war in civil society arise? One situation would be when a thief breaks into your house. Thus, in Locke's terms, the thief's action would be a declaration of war on the owner of the house. One would have a right even to kill the thief if one feared the thief's intentions. In the case of the villagers, the thief is regarded as having broken not into the single house of an individual but into the collective home of the village community.[9] It is the village which is burgled, rather than the individual hut or chicken compound. The thief is then interpreted to have declared war on the village itself by the mere act of breaching its security. In a state of war collective vengeance becomes legitimate. The cry of "thief" becomes, in fact, a war cry. Its analogies include the trumpet proclaiming a collective crisis, or the siren demanding a coordinated collective response to a shared danger. The fact that traditional warfare was characterized by raids for cattle and other forms of wealth re-emphasized the links between theft and war. Robbing and raiding become indistinguishable.

But the phenomenon of civic violence in Uganda is not simply a residue of ancestral ways of military defense and law enforcement. It is sometimes a manifestation of fragile faith in the state as a competent instrument for this kind of undertaking. Of course, residual traditionalism is indeed connected with a distrust of the modern state, but such skepticism may have found additional reasons and causes for its existence. It is a mixture of factors conditioning attitudes and determining general civic behavior.

THE COSTS OF POLITICAL CENTRALIZATION

Sometimes what has happened in certain parts of Uganda is an actual relapse. Reliance on formal state structures for law enforcement had begun to consolidate itself. The Baganda as a tribe seemed to be experimenting with new ways of dealing with deviants and lawbreakers—ways which were intermediate between traditional and modern methods. Sometimes they were simply ways of averting actual violence against a thief, but in exchange for his disappearance from the community. This was some kind of deportation, from one district to another. Killing had become illegal, but induced expulsion from a community could still be undertaken short of infringing the law of the land.

It is sometimes argued that severity and oppression do not themselves deter thieves. The discussion here hinges on the issue of whether those who are already inclined to deviate from the norms of the society are necessarily deterred from that course by the prospect of punishment. Is it conceivable that the criminal inclination is not only indifferent to the sanctity of norms but also to the prospect of penalty? Can punishment therefore ever be a deterrent?

This whole line of reasoning looks at the deviant in order to judge the impact of punishment on *him*. But in a situation where respect for authority has yet to be consolidated, the issue is not simply what sort of authoritative decisions are likely to impress the deviant but also what type of authoritative decisions are likely to influence the population as a whole. Popular faith in the official law enforcement structures becomes as important as the issue of inculcating fear in the lawbreakers. The task of inculcating respect for the law among ordinary villagers assumes, in some ways, a significance which is even more fundamental than the task of inspiring fear in the lawbreaker.

Even if the oppressive nature of law enforcement in autonomous Buganda served little purpose in the task of deterring thieves from stealing, it might at least have served a purpose in deterring some local communities from handling every thief themselves. Some thieves were indeed beaten up even in the regionally autonomous Buganda, but there is a suspicion that the nationalization of law enforcement structures has, for the time being, resulted in a greater incidence of civic violence by the villagers themselves in local communities. The figures are inconclusive, but the climate of opinion in relation to attitudes to the police seems to indicate an erosion of faith in the official structures.

The centralization of the structures of law enforcement has helped to aggravate two areas of skepticism among the villagers in relation to modern judicial and penal methods. One area concerns the rules of evidence; the other concerns the nature of punishment. The rules of evidence have a rigidity which precludes even the presentation of hearsay evidence. This deprives important members of the village of opportunities to relate aspects of the case which they may have been informed about. In societies which put a high premium on oral tradition, and where the concept of *news* is a constant process of oral transmission, a rigid exclusion of hearsay from court proceedings has at times created the impression among villagers that the courts were not doing all they could to ascertain the guilt of a suspect. The villagers argue that the police are all too keen to induce villagers to give evidence against themselves when a thief has been beaten up, but they are not keen to solicit evidence against a thief or even a murderer if what is offered seems to be "hearsay." In the words of one local man interviewed by a research assistant, "Our police are more inquisitive about what surrounds the death of a thief when killed by the people than about the circumstances in which an innocent person has been killed by the thieves."

This is clearly a distortion of police behavior. But it does signify a profound dissatisfaction and sense of frustration among those who think they can testify against suspected thieves, and who find themselves precluded by modern procedures.

A high-ranking officer in the department of the Solicitor-General in Uganda once expressed privately the need for more concessions to hearsay evidence, partly as a method of giving villagers greater participation in contributing to the trial of a suspect, and therefore averting the temptation on their part to circumvent the official procedures for dealing with suspects.

The other area of rural distrust of modern methods of law enforcement concerns the nature of punishment. The sentences imposed are seen as much too short. Some witnesses who are in fact permitted to give evidence, while appreciating the opportunity to testify, become worried about the imminence of the thief's emergence from jail. Vengeance on isolated witnesses is inflicted by newly released thieves.

In some areas any kind of stealing, no matter how small the article, is regarded as extremely serious. We have already drawn attention to the brutal punishment sometimes inflicted on people who steal what seem to be insignificant items. The police, when handling such cases, appear to the villagers to be incapable of dealing with petty thieves—who in the eyes of the villagers are violent thieves in the making or indulging in a momentary pastime prior to a bigger job. The police appear not to take seriously the case of somebody caught with a stolen egg or hen. At the most the police may arrange that the man so caught should do a bit of digging for the owner of the egg or hen as punishment.

Villagers often regard this as constituting an incentive to steal rather than a deterrent. Someone would venture to steal a hen knowing that if he were caught he would be handled peacefully and, at the most, be asked to do a bit of digging for the day. This would amount to telling a thief that he was free to steal a chicken but, if caught, he would have to pay the price for that chicken.

A fourth factor in this erosion of trust in official methods of law enforcement concerns the suspicion of nepotism and corruption among the police. There is a belief in some quarters that the centralization of the structures of law enforcement has increased the danger of nepotism. Policemen work in tribal areas other than their own. Far from decreasing the incidence of nepotism, this brings it about more sharply. The people of the policeman's own tribe are thus in a minority in a given area, and there are temptations in the policeman to protect a person from his home area in this semi-foreign part of the country. One man related the story of thieves attacking his old mother, beating her up and stealing her belongings, including two hundred shillings in cash. She recognized two of them, or thought she did, and told her son the next morning. The son went to the *muluka* chief who asked him to report the matter to the police. The police arrested the men and took the son with them to the police station.

> As we entered the office, one of the men sighed and spoke a few words in his language—Ateso. Immediately one of the officers started to speak to this man in Ateso and continued for nearly ten minutes. He later had a word with two other policemen. They then told me [the old woman's son] to go back and that I would be called later. The next day the men were released and I have never been called. It is now over a year later.[10]

The nature of nepotism in this case arose out of the minority status of the community to which the policeman belonged and the pressures for solidarity in a situation of minority vulnerability. But where the policemen were recruited from the dominant community of the area, the pressures for this kind of special solidarity did not apply. Deviants from tribal norms were dealt with with a mixture of firmness and understanding. People drawn from other communities who were in a minority were also dealt with firmly, and not necessarily unjustly, by the local police. It was when the police felt they had to protect fellow tribesmen in contexts of minority status far from home that the temptations for nepotistic solidarity were at their height.

As for bribery as another form of corruption, it is not clear that this is aggravated by centralization. But there is enough suspicion among villagers that the police would accept with impunity a bribe from thieves that the sense of distrust of the official methods of law enforcement finds additional vindication. It becomes more tempting than ever to deal with the thief on the spot instead of handing him over to the police with all the risk of easy release.

These, then, are among the factors which have aggravated the incidence of civic violence in Uganda. Residual traditional attitudes to questions of self-defense, warriorhood, and law enforcement have interacted with new forms of distrust of official structures. The centralization of law enforcement in Uganda, the formal rigidity of rules of evidence, the seemingly inadequate severity of punishment, and the incidence of nepotism and corruption among the police have all made a contribution to the difficulties of consolidating these aspects of statehood in Uganda. A relapse back to the warrior tradition has in part been caused by a disenchantment with more modern forms of protection and defense.

In the United States the distrust of the judicial system has not disappeared by any means, but the nature of the distrust has changed from the old frontier days. In the earlier days there were insufficient jails and those that existed were often not strong enough to prevent criminals from escaping. Then there was corruption in the American police, in many ways far more elaborate and extensive than anything as yet experienced in Uganda. The juries, too, were corruptible and sometimes capable of being intimidated:

> The system presented numerous opportunities for manipulation by outlaws who could often command some measure of local support. Whenever possible outlaws would obtain false witnesses on their behalf, pack juries, bribe officials, and, in extreme cases, intimidate the entire system: judges, juries, and law enforcement officials. Such deficiencies in the judicial system were the sources of repeated complaints by frontiersmen.[11]

In America, as in Uganda, there has persisted to the present day the common grievance that the administration of justice has favored the accused rather than the society. In the case of the American system, the elaborateness of methods of appeal, the layers of jurisdiction in a federal system, the complex nature of constitutional rights for the individual—all have seemed to afford the guilty ones multiple loopholes for the evasion of punishment. In

Uganda the system is far less complicated, but it looks complicated enough to disgruntled villagers unsure of their security and it tempts them toward their own collective retribution as a substitute for official arrests, trial, and only possible conviction.

CONCLUSION

We have attempted in this chapter to throw new light on civic violence by comparing countries which are otherwise very different from each other— Uganda and the United States. We have compared the tradition of vigilantism in America with hue and cry in Uganda villages and the recurrent phenomenon of rural people beating up suspected thieves, sometimes to death. We have suggested that the comparison is in part between the American frontier tradition and the warrior tradition of ancestral Africa.

In the United States vigilantism was in part connected with the ethos of rugged self-reliance and the need for citizens to make provision for their own protection. Ideologically vigilantism in the United States was also connected with the whole doctrine of individualism and private initiative. American liberalism, American capitalism, the ruggged self-reliance of the frontier, and the tradition of private violence for civic ends have all been interconnected in the American ethos.

In Uganda, on the other hand, civic violence is animated more by collective ideals than by an ethic of individualism. The same phenomenon, that of citizens taking the law into their own hands, seems to be inspired by very different cultural and ideological factors. In Uganda the ultimate motivation behind the hue-and-cry phenomenon is not the virtue of private initiative but the virtue of collective security.

We have discussed the relative esteem given to life as against property within the two societies. Although American capitalism seems to put a special premium on property, the behavior of citizens in defense of property in the United States is more restrained than the behavior of citizens in similar situations in Uganda. Men kill thieves more easily, and receive the approval of their community more readily, in Uganda than in the United States. Is it because Ugandans value property more than Americans do? Is it because Americans value life more than Ugandans do?

The difference may include divergent conceptions of the meaning of what is aggression and what is death. Another difference may concern the brutality of Ugandan thieves themselves. It is true that American thieves are often as trigger-happy as the kondos in Uganda are panga-happy. Yet organized crime in the United States has for its targets those who are relatively well-to-do. In Uganda the phenomenon of poor people stealing from poor people somehow accentuates the levels of vengeance. Marxist analysis sometimes assumes that *inter*-class clashes have more power for mutual brutalization than *intra*-class antagonisms. The nature of civic violence in Uganda as contrasted with the United States in recent times would not necessarily support this. American violence is more inter-class. The relatively underprivileged, often from the ghettos, organize themselves for the extraction of high returns from the ranks of their own class. But the balance of crime in the United States is of the kind which makes the privileged the more obvious targets of assault. The under-privileged produce the largest numbers of criminals.

In Uganda much of the activity of groups like the kondos hits the people who are basically within their own stratum of society. A few shillings here, a few chickens there, a cow or two, accompanied quite often by the brutal-ization of witnesses—such is the phenomenon of violent crime in Uganda.

In the course of the late 1960s and early 1970s there seemed to be progressing a certain modernization of crime in Uganda, and the moderni-zation of crime was in the direction of inter-class confrontations. The use of sophisticated firearms, which appeared to be gaining ascendancy in the second half of the 1960s, made it increasingly possible for criminals to aim for high stakes. In addition to burgling the house of a relatively poor widow, as was the case in the 1950s, gangs of criminals were also aiming for bank trucks on pay day, overcoming at times armed guards, and in one or two cases machine-gunning the proprietor or manager in charge of funds on a particular day. The modernization of crime in Uganda has in fact meant its extension beyond the poor and more systematically against the well-to-do. But this modernization of crime has not always been accompanied by a modernized response. Primordial notions of alertness against "cattle-raiders" have condi-tioned the response of private citizens to thieves in modern cities.

In these big cities burgling residential houses of Europeans, Asians, and other affluent individuals is an older phenomenon in Uganda. The moderni-zation of this kind of crime takes the form of more modern weapons and organization rather than the trans-class extension which was already there.

It is not always clear why intra-class brutality in rural Uganda should be higher with regard to theft than inter-class brutality in the same field in the United States. Beating thieves to death is an almost daily affair somewhere in Uganda; it seldom happens in the United States. An individual American may shoot a burglar dead. But the idea of the community as a whole joining together in order to inflict fatal vengeance on a suspected thief is very rare in the current experience of Americans.

What should be remembered is that both Uganda and the United States illustrate how the quality of the wider society can affect the behavior of those in uniform. Uganda soldiers are among the most violent in Africa;

American policemen are among the most brutal in the West. Both the Ugandan army and the American police have themselves been affected by attitudes to violence in the wider society. Americans are fortunate that they have so far had to deal only with their police and not—as yet—with their soldiers in the streets of Chicago.

The struggle for both nationhood and statehood continues in both Uganda and the United States. Both have yet to forge different ethnic groups into newly integrated communities. And behind that struggle are the different functions of non-military violence in social change. These functions range from exposing fragile statehood and inchoate national identity to revealing the impact of ancestral beliefs on current behavior. Out of such honest confrontation with aspects of national and cultural fragility may emerge a social system which would withstand cleavage, consolidate authority, and still permit creative interaction among people.

NOTES

1. Max Weber, "Politics as a Vocation," originally a speech at Munich University, 1918. See H. H. Gerth and C. Wright Mills, *From Max Weber: Essays in Sociology* (London: Routledge and Kegan Paul, 1957: 78.

2. *Uganda Argus* (Kampala), October 29, 1969.

3. Karl J. Friedrich and Robert C. McCloskey, *From the Declaration of Independence to the Constitution: The Roots of American Constitutionalism* (New York: Liberal Arts Press, 1954): xi.

4. Ibid: xxxix.

5. For press reports of these incidents consult *Uganda Argus,* December 17, 20, 27 and 30, 1968; September 22, 1969, February 5, 1969.

6. The Kenya government was also briefly tempted to resort to a similar solution of capitalizing robbery with violence. Such a proposal was seriously considered and debated, but that government then decided to retreat from this kind of solution. For an earlier analysis of such violence in the continent consult Colin Leys, "Violence in Africa," *Transition* 21 (1965): 17-20

7. *Uganda Argus,* April 17, 1969.

8. For a selection of Western concepts of death see Jacques Choron, *Death and Western Thought* (London: Collier-Macmillan, 1963). For the concept of the living dead in Africa consult John S. Mbiti, *African Religions and Philosophy* (London: Heinemann, 1969).

9. See Locke's *Second Treatise* (1690). Also Hobbes, *The Leviathan* (1651).

10. This oral evidence was obtained by a research assistant. The precise locality cannot be released for reasons of protecting the source.

11. Brown, "The American Vigilante Tradition," chapter 5 in *Violence in America: Historical and Comparative Perspectives,* a report to the National Commission on the causes and prevention of violence, June 1969, prepared under the direction and authorship of Hugh Davis Graham and Ted Robert Gurr for the President's Commission (New York: New American Library, 1969): 166-67.

Chapter 6

THE REGIONALIZATION OF VIOLENCE

While some forms of violence did thus get demilitarized in the wake of the colonial impact, other forms of conflict and tension were regionalized. The artificial territorial boundaries created by the colonizers carried the seeds of conflict not only within individual countries but also across state boundaries. Ethnic, cultural, and pre-colonial historical links have often regionalized what would otherwise have been domestic national conflicts.

Uganda is a link between two regional political complexes—East Africa and the Nile Valley. Until General Amin's coup of 1971 it was violence along the Nile Valley which was regionalized. But since the coup violence in Uganda has also affected Tanzania and Kenya. Let us examine the Nile Valley and then link it to East Africa.

When President Nasser of Egypt died in September 1970, President Obote of Uganda cancelled the independence celebrations scheduled to take place in Uganda on October 9, 1970. The reason which Milton Obote gave for such a cancellation was Uganda's desire to pay solemn homage to that great African leader at the other end of the River Nile.

But there was reason to believe that Obote's decision to cancel the independence celebrations was as much motivated by internal domestic considerations in Uganda as by anything else. Independence celebrations in the First Republic of Uganda had already established a military tradition. Uganda displayed her military might as part of celebrating her sovereignty. Yet in 1970 there were tensions within the armed forces and between the President and his army commander. This made it somewhat inadvisable to arrange a full military display at that particular moment in Obote's political career. The death of Nasser at one end of the Nile, and even the question of who was to represent Uganda at the funeral, became intertwined with domestic political tensions within Uganda.

THE VALLEY OF VIOLENCE

The major premise of this chapter is that violence and economic interaction are the two most effective agencies of penetration in the politics of
regional state systems. Economic interaction between Egypt and the Sudan is
of long standing, and the Sudan has always had an economic value for Egypt's
expansionist ambitions. But economic interaction between the Sudan and
Uganda, or Uganda and Egypt, or Ethiopia and the Sudan has been relatively
negligible. In this chapter we shall pay attention to the Valley of the White
Nile from Jinja to the Mediterranean, and ignore for the purposes of this
particular analysis the case of Ethiopia. In other words, our concern in this
part of the chapter is with Uganda, the Sudan, and Egypt. And one question
we are raising is whether this Valley of the White Nile is, because of the
penetrative power of social conflict and social violence within each of these
countries, destined to become an international political system in its own
right in the days ahead.

It is not always remembered that conflict and even violence do play this
integrative role in both national and regional processes of development. Let
us first examine the *intra-* state functions of violence before we address
ourselves more broadly to *inter*-state relations. At one level of argument it
may indeed be true that internal conflict within a country is inherently
disintegrative. Yet paradoxically no national integration is possible without
internal conflict. The paradox arises because while conflict itself has a
capacity to force a dissolution, the *resolution* of conflict is an essential
mechanism of integration. As I have stated before, the whole experience of
jointly looking for a way out of a crisis, of seeing one's own mutual hostility
subside to a level of mutual tolerance, of being intensely conscious of each
other's positions and yet sensing the need to bridge the gulf—these are
experiences which, over a period of time, should help two groups of people
move forward into a relationship of deeper integration. Conflict resolution
might not be a sufficient condition for national integration, but it is certainly
a necessary one.

If we look at the Nile Valley as an emerging political system, we see the
interpenetration between domestic politics in the Sudan and the Egyptian
presence to the north on certain issues. The Uganda presence to the south of
the Sudan has, with regard to other issues, also become increasingly manifest.

In the case of Egypt and the Sudan some of the initial areas of interaction
were indeed economic—in addition to the all-powerful factor of the Nile
passing through the Sudan before it enters Egypt to give Egypt its life. But
preeminent among the forces of interpenetration in recent years has remained
the phenomenon of conflict and violence. Aid in military situations, diplo-

matic support in moments of political wrangles, have all contributed to deepening a shared political experience between Egypt and the Sudan in the years of independence.

Further south, a civil war raged for seventeen years in southern Sudan. And that civil war again opened up opportunities for penetration by others into Sudanese affairs. While in domestic politics it is not conflict but conflict *resolution* which promotes national integration, in regional integration conflict itself could, by being penetrative, also sometimes be integrative. The Valley of the Nile might be converted into a regional political system not simply by the flow of its waters but also by the flow of blood.

A military coup is itself a moment of violence. We might therefore say that in the modern period the warning bell of violent penetration and interpenetration in the Nile Valley was rung by the Egyptian Revolution. In many ways the Egyptian coup was an exceptionally non-violent one. Farouk was spared and deported, most of the high-powered aristocrats and main opponents were cut down to size socially rather than physically. And Nasser maintained the principle that a revolution which starts in violence runs the risk of ending in violence.

Curiously enough the military junta which came into power in Egypt was the first government ever to allow for the complete separation of the Sudan from Egypt since the nineteenth century. The Sudan had been influenced by Egyptians since the days of the Pharaohs, but it was Mohammed Ali in the nineteenth century who annexed the Sudan to the Egyptian Empire. It was also the Mahdi who fought against Egyptian imperialism. And it was finally the British and Egyptians together who re-established some kind of Egyptian suzerainty over the Sudan and declared the area a condominium under Anglo-Egyptian rule. On the eve of the Egyptian coup the civilian government in Egypt virtually abrogated the condominium agreement and proceeded to regard the Sudan as effectively Egyptian. But it was the soldiers who seemed to be cutting the links of regional integration between Egypt and the Sudan by conceding to the Sudanese the right of complete separation from Egypt. On November 2, 1952, four months after the Egyptian Revolution, the Egyptian government delivered to the British government a note concerning the issue of Sudanese self-determination. For the first time in all the negotiations with Britain over the decades, Egypt declared that "the Egyptian Government believes firmly in the right of the Sudanese to decide their destiny."

What we have therefore is a situation where, on the one hand, Egyptian soldiers initiate what becomes a tradition of military coups along the Nile Valley; and yet, on the other hand, the same soldiers proceed diplomatically to loosen the bonds between Egypt and the Sudan by accepting the idea of an autonomous Sudan. Egyptian soldiers had a strong vested interest in protecting the flow of the Nile. It was in fact an Egyptian army colonel who had said way back in 1948, in the year of the creation of Israel:

> Egypt gets its waters from the Nile, which flows in the heart of the Sudan. The Nile to Egypt is a matter of life or death. If the waters of this river were discontinued or were controlled by a hostile state or a state that could become hostile, Egypt's life is over.[1]

That, as we indicated, was the year of the formation of Israel—the birth of a state that was destined to become clearly Egypt's number one enemy. In the words of the Egyptian colonel once again: "If the waters of this river were discontinued or were controlled by a hostile state or a state that could become hostile, Egypt's life is over."

The succeeding decades opened up new eras of interaction between the Sudan and Egypt. We might here again remind ourselves that the Egyptian coup of July 1952 was the first in post-colonial Africa. On July 23, 1952, Brigadier Mohammed Naguib, leader of the dissident army officers, marched on Cairo at the head of a few battalions of troops. He captured the city and its administration with little resistance and little bloodshed. A few days later the government was dismissed, King Farouk was forced to abdicate and leave the country, and plans were afoot for certain reforms.

There were voices even then that the king should, like his French predecessor in the eighteenth century, be executed. Those who urged this policy were apprehensive lest the king should become the focus of counter-revolutionary forces and help to give strength and hope to a resistance movement. There was a feeling among some of the dissident soldiers that the best insurance for a coup lay in the physical elimination of the prospective symbol of resistance, i.e., the former head of state. By killing the former head of state, it was argued, counter-revolutionary forces would be denied a rallying point.

Among those who took a position against this kind of reasoning was an obscure officer in the group, Lt. Colonel Gamal Abdul Nasser. Nasser argued that a revolution which started in blood would end in blood. The killing of the king would make a martyr out of him and a dead Farouk might well prove to be a more symbolic rallying point than a living, fat, pleasure-loving, and nauseating ex-king.

In fact the Egyptian coup was not completely bloodless. An army colonel was sentenced to death on a charge of inciting officers to mutiny against the new regime. And eleven months after the coup a number of prominent personalities including former politicians were imprisoned and several were hanged for treason. A cloud of violence did indeed hang over even that first military coup of post-colonial Africa, the Egyptian coup. But there was a studied attempt by the officers to keep violence to a minimum. Egypt, after all, was not a new nation in the sense in which Uganda is. It may be an under-developed nation, but it is also ancient and deeply rooted. A bloody convulsion in an integrated nation might set the clock back several centuries and create cleavages among Egyptians which their long history as a political entity had already helped to mitigate.

This counsel of magnanimity in the Egyptian coup prevailed. There was even the brief gesture of regarding Farouk's infant son as king with a regency council to exercise the prerogatives of the monarch until he attained maturity. But the period of the regency turned out to be a brief interlude to get the people used to the idea of deposing kings. Before long "Bey" and "Pasha" were abolished. A republic status was ultimately reached.

Nasser replaced Naguib as the real ruler of Egypt. He came to hold power from 1953 until his death in September 1970. Upon his death at one end of the Nile, the atmosphere of an impending coup hung like an ominous cloud over Lake Victoria at the other end. And Milton Obote used the death of Nasser as an excuse for postponing his day of reckoning with his army commander and indeed with the dissident section of the Ugandan armed forces at large.

The situation in its trans-Nilotic significance was pregnant with historical memories. The death of a military leader at one end of the Nile, the attendance at his funeral by a military leader from the other end of the Nile, and the tensions struggling to surface across the entire span of the Nile seemed to amount to a new formulation of that historic doctrine of the Unity of the Nile Valley.

PAN-NILOTISM: ETHNIC AND IDEOLOGICAL

Historians differ as to the practical significance of the doctrine of the Unity of the Nile Valley in British colonial policy, but the balance of evidence, as I have had occasion to argue before, is probably on the side of those who regard the doctrine as an important conditioning factor on British attitudes. Two British historians, Robinson and Gallagher, remind us that "the idea that the security of Egypt depended upon the defense of the Upper Nile was as old as the Pyramids."[2] The historians point out its effect on Lord Salisbury, who in 1889-90 decided that if Britain was to hold on to Egypt, she could not afford to let any other European power obtain a hold over any other part of the Nile Valley. The historians go on to assert that, in so doing, Salisbury took what was perhaps the critical decision for the partition of

Africa: "Henceforward, almost everything in Africa north of the Zambesi River was to hinge upon it."[3] The doctrine of the Unity of the Nile Valley tended to exclude the Blue Nile of Ethiopia as being of secondary relevance to this particular policy.

Under Salisbury's successors the doctrine of the Unity of the Nile Valley helped to seal the fate of Uganda. As Robinson and Gallagher put it with reference to Rosebury's vision, "the Cabinet quarrels over Uganda were really quarrels over Egypt."[4]

And so the snowball of imperial annexation proceeded. Egypt was important for Britain's whole Middle Eastern strategy, and so Egypt had to remain occupied. But Egypt depended much on the Nile, and the Nile passed through the Sudan. So the loose Egyptian suzerainty over the Sudan had to be converted into a strong British sovereignty. But the unity of the Nile Valley was not complete until its very source was controlled by the same power. So Uganda had to be under British control. And the way to the lakes from the important port of Mombasa was through what came to be known as Kenya. So Kenya had to be annexed too. The forceful torrent of British expansionism shared a valley with the River Nile—and overflowed into other areas of the East African land surface as well.[5]

In the course of the colonial period the doctrine of the Unity of the Nile Valley continued to influence events and policies along the route of the great river. The Sudan gradually became what was called a condominium, a territory whose sovereignty ostensibly resided in both Britain and Egypt. Southern Sudan in turn was, in a sense but not in name, a "condominium" with authority exercised by Britain and northern Sudan. But the British attempted to keep Egyptian influence in northern Sudan to a minimum in spite of the condominium status; and the British attempted to keep northern Sudanese influence in the south also to a minimum, in spite of the infusion of southern territories into the body politic of the Sudan as a whole. The status of southern Sudan was, to all intents and purposes, a condominium within a condominium. And these ambiguities had long-term consequences for the whole issue of the identity of the south.

That issue in turn touched the fortunes of Uganda. The ethnic overlap across the boundary between southern Sudan and Uganda made the boundary itself uncertain for a while. There was even a school of thought which quite early played with the idea of integrating southern Sudan with Uganda. There was yet another school which believed in uniting the Nilotic peoples of Uganda with those of the Sudan which were also Nilotic and creating a state separate from both Uganda and the Sudan. Among the more articulate of Nilotic irredentists earlier in the century were spokesmen for Acholi in Uganda. The Nilotes in Uganda felt underprivileged in relation to the Baganda and other Bantu; and the Nilotes in the Sudan felt underprivileged in relation to the Arabic-speaking north. The beginnings of Pan-Nilotism were at hand, but the movement did not gather enough momentum.

The fortunes of the Nilotes within Uganda began to change as independence approached. The Baganda were still preeminent, but the sons of the north had voices which were beginning to be heard. From Lango came Apolo Milton Obote, who was later to control the fortunes of the country as a whole for a number of years. But Pan-Nilotism even within Uganda was itself fragile. Briefly it was engendered by a shared opposition to the Baganda. From 1966 the armed forces, recruited mainly from the north, derived a sense of national purpose from the very policy of keeping Buganda under a state of emergency and keeping the Baganda strictly subject to northern restraints.

Pan-Nilotism within southern Sudan did not fare much better, as internecine squabbles among the separatist movements reduced southern resistance to a deeply fragmented if still vital force.

But before the coup of January 25, 1971 in Uganda, an important phenomenon was taking place. The word "Nilotic" refers both to a particular family of tribes in black Africa and to the Nile as a whole. Ethnic Pan-Nilotism envisaged the unity of a particular group of tribes in black Africa, some of whom may no longer be along the Nile Valley. The Luo of Kenya as western Nilotes, the Masai as eastern Nilotes (formerly known as Nilo-Hamites) are no longer inhabitants of the banks of the Nile but they belong to the family of tribes bearing that name.

There is, however, an older sense of the word "Nilotic." The word is of Greek derivation, and according to the Oxford dictionary it means quite simply "of the Nile."

We may therefore have here another sense of Pan-Nilotism—not an ethnic sense denoting a community of black tribes but an ideological sense denoting commitment to the old doctrine of the Unity of the Nile Valley.

If the Acholi in Uganda had once taken the lead in recommending Pan-Nilotism in the sense of a separate state for that family of black tribes, the Langi came later to take the leadership in championing an ideological Pan-Nilotism in the sense of a shared movement of sympathy along the Nile Valley from the lake to the Mediterranean. The Langi who seemed to be exploring the possibility of ideological Pan-Nilotism were none other than Milton Obote himself, as President of Uganda, and his cousin Akena Adoko, a fellow traveler on the seas of radicalism. A major factor in the whole story of ideological Pan-Nilotism in the independence period was the burst of socialism along the Nile Valley. And the first socialist ruler along the Nile Valley was Gamal Abdul Nasser. Nasser started more as an Arab nationalist than as an Arab socialist. His career in the army included a sense of humiliation at the defeat of the Arabs by Israel in 1948, and the cynical corruption of the palace and politicians in Egypt. But in that very sense of nationalism and its causes were the seeds of radicalization towards socialism. This radicalization was certainly fostered by Western suspicion of Egypt's quest for new links with the Communist world. The Western suspicion culminated in the fiasco of the Suez adventure of 1956, when France, Britain, and Israel jointly attacked Egypt in a bid to create a situation which would result in the fall of Nasser. Nasser survived that, and emerged a martyr and a hero with a fame that reached far beyond both Africa and the Middle East. The beginnings of Nasser's stature as a world figure are ultimately to be sought in the Suez adventure of 1956. Nasser was militarily defeated but he was politically triumphant. It was again one of those occasions when victory goes to the vanquished, and the man who has been knocked out in the ring rises to have his fist raised by the world referee as the hero of the day.

What had precipitated the Suez attack was a measure basically motivated by nationalism yet often associated with socialism. This was the nationalization of the Suez Canal. When the World Bank refused to grant Nasser a loan, and Britain and the United States used that as a reason for similarly withdrawing the tentative offers of aid they had once made, Nasser made the most dramatic move of his career—he nationalized a canal which had once been primarily foreign-owned. The move was a manifestation of Nasser's nationalism in the sense that he was reacting to a rebuff from foreigners, but the act of nationalization itself is often associated with the postulates of socialism and the underlying doctrine of state control.

Nasser's ideology got increasingly radicalized. He had already embraced the idea of an Egyptian revolution and later regarded Egypt as the springboard for further revolution in the Arab world. He also made up his mind from the very beginning to keep Egypt moving within the African circle of her geographical destiny, as well as within the Arab and Muslim circles.

Further up the Nile Valley in the Sudan there was indeed a strongly pro-Egyptian sector of opinion, and soon after the Egyptian revolution Nasser was optimistic about a possible union between the Sudan and Egypt. The old condominium status could form the genesis of a big federation down the Nile Valley.

But Sudanese opinion also included a strong anti-Egyptian component, including some of the most traditionalist and some of the most radical of the Sudanese. Indeed, among the least Nasserite of Sudanese were often the most socialistic. Nasser's dual symbolism of being at once both a nationalist and a socialist resulted in a divergence of opinion farther up the Nile. The Sudanese Communist Party, the largest in Africa and one of the oldest, had often supported Nasser in his anti-imperialist stands, but it was deeply afraid of any close links between Egypt and the Sudan. The Sudanese Communists had enjoyed the benefits of a relatively open society in the Sudan and did themselves let their communism wear a human face. The Sudanese Communists were among the most moderate and humane in the whole Communist world. But they could see across the border in Egypt the suppression of Communists by Nasser, and they were apprehensive about the consequences of union with Egypt for their own survival as a distinct sociological group. Their fears were to assume profoundly tragic shape in the month of July 1971.

Still further up the Nile, in the southern provinces of the Sudan, there was little scientific socialism to be found. On the contrary, the profound impact of the missionaries on the educated class created, at least for a while, a strong anti-Communist inclination among southern Sudanese intellectuals. And as the Arabs to the north began to have closer relations with the Soviet Union, black anti-communism in southern Sudan became more sharply manifest. Many of the religious groups which poured money from the Western world into the southern movement were as much influenced by anti-communism as by any solidarity with Christians. At least one distinguished academic at Makerere from the Western world found it appropriate and compatible with his job at Makerere to involve himself financially and materially not only in the welfare aspects of the resistance movement of the south, but also in the military aspects of that movement. Small committees or cabals of western intellectuals within Uganda, partly influenced by liberal concerns, partly inspired by Christian solidarity, and partly animated by the fear of communism in Africa, conspired in the corridors to play their part in the southern separatist movement.

Within Uganda itself there was a long history of near-McCarthyism, or the utilization of the bogey of communism in the denunciation of political opponents. Milton Obote spent much of his political career trying to combat two accusations against the Uganda People's Congress—that it was a Protestant party and that it was also an ungodly and "fellow-traveling" party. The latter epithet was connected once again with the fear of communism transmitted by the white missionaries to local African opinion. It was in 1968 that Milton Obote started talking about the "move to the left," though he characteristically remained vague for a while, partly to assess reaction to his trial balloons.

But before Milton Obote actually took the steps leftwards the soldiers in the Sudan marched ahead. The revolution of May 1969 in the Sudan was indeed a decisive move to the left by Khartoum. The soldiers worked out an alliance with the Sudanese Communists, and the policies of the Sudanese government reached a point of radicalism never before reached in that country. A number of foreign enterprises came to be nationalized. There were purges in some important institutions and an operation to remove elements of opinion that were not regarded as adequately leftist. The Communists in the

Sudan had at last come to share the commanding heights of both the economy and the polity. There was still anxiety about too close an integration with Egypt under Nasser, but there were areas of collaboration in foreign policy against imperialism and Israel. Moreover, the Nile Valley was now under socialist control from the Mediterranean to the borders of Uganda. But would the bug of radicalism affect the body politic of Uganda as well? A good deal depended upon one Nilotic figure from Lango, Apolo Milton Obote. In the course of 1970 what was beginning to take shape as an idea was the possibility of an ideological unity of the Nile Valley, from the waters of Jinja to the shores of the Mediterranean. The precedent of Nasser in inaugurating a local brand of socialism and establishing the era of nationalism and state control with the historic act of the takeover of the Suez Canal in 1956, was not finding echoes of solidarity from the vibrating stadium walls of Lugogo and Nakivubo in Uganda.

May 1969 had given the Sudan its move to the left. October 1969 gave Obote's Uganda *The Common Man's Charter.* For the first time since independence there was indeed the possibility of socialistic solidarity along the whole course of the Nile Valley.

And then, on January 25, 1971, a military coup overthrew Obote in Uganda.

MILITARY COUPS: RIVALRY AND REFORM

We may here distinguish between two broad categories of military coups. These are coups of rivalry for power and coups which are, at least partly, motivated by the quest for reform.

Quite often the two ingredients of *power rivalry* and *political reform* are both present. The big issue is which is more pronounced as a motivating factor behind the sudden change.

The Egyptian coup of 1952 was ultimately a reform coup. There had indeed been discontent, in the armed forces especially, with the Palace. The element of power rivalry was by no means unimportant in the tensions which were building up at that time. At the beginning of July 1952 the Prime Minister made a move to appease the army by asking King Farouk to approve the nomination of Brigadier Mohammed Naguib, leader of the dissident army officers in the Egyptian armed forces, as Minister of War. The King not only refused; he then proceeded to appoint one of his relatives instead. The Prime Minister resigned.

A successor Prime Minister was appointed, but before he really assumed control, Naguib marched on Cairo on July 23, 1952, at the head of a few battalions. He took over the city, dismissed the government, forced the King to abdicate, established a Regency Council for Farouk's infant son, and made arrangements for a new government.

So far the events seemed consistent with the concept of a rivalry coup. The army wanted much greater say in the formulation of at least those policies which had a bearing on the military, and the name of Naguib as War Minister was nominated partly with the view to giving the army this extra voice. When a relative of the King was appointed in place of Naguib, one additional grievance was added to the long list of items of military discontent within the forces.

But before long the reform component of the Egyptian coup began to manifest itself:

> It soon became apparent that Naguib and his junta of young army officers had not only achieved a successful coup, but were aiming at a social revolution. The titles "bey" and "pasha" were abolished. A land reform decree was issued. A purge of corrupt officials was put in hand. In all these measures the army, acting through the civil government, provided the motive power and very often the means of execution.[6]

Other reforms which were soon pressing for attention included questions of land reform and redistribution of the big estates, expansion of irrigation, expansion of industry, and resolution of the Anglo-Egyptian dispute concerning the canal base. The reform component of the Egyptian coup became even more pronounced when Abdul Nasser replaced Naguib as the head of the new government and consolidated military control without pretence at civilian participation in the leadership of the country.

The first coup of the Sudan, on November 17, 1958, was primarily for rivalry rather than reform. Of course, every military coup seeks to legitimate itself by pronouncing on the inefficiencies of the regime it is replacing and by an explicit or implicit promise to initiate reforms. Such declarations were not of course absent when General Abboud took over power in the Sudan in November 1958. But in reality there was no firm commitment to major reforms. The coup was a rivalry coup between the armed forces and the politicians, complicated by sectarian considerations.

Only a few months earlier Sudan had had its first general election since independence. It was on balance a smooth election—perhaps the smoothest in Africa until that time. A successful coalition emerged, consisting of the Umma Party and the People's Democratic Party. The National Unionist Party of Sayed Ismail el-Azahry, which favoured closer affiliation with Egypt and aspired to divorce politics from religious sectarianism, made much less of a showing that it had hoped. It won 45 seats instead of the 80 seats that some of the more optimistic calculators in the ranks thought it might win in the north alone. In 1958 the swing was definitely towards conservatism in Sudanese politics, but the election as a whole had been so peaceful that commentators began to discern at least amongst northern Sudanese "a natural democratic instinct."

When the army took over power there was no real evidence that the parliamentary system had in fact failed. As *The Economist* argued a year after the coup:

> The army first came to power a year ago at a time when one coalition was collapsing and another was about to be formed. The new one Umma, the political expression of the Mahdi's tribal following, and the National Unionist Party led by a former Prime Minister, Ismail el-Azahry, was likely to give a stability which the old coalition had failed to provide. Instead, the generals took over, and the pad of parliament, which softened the blows of sudden change, was lost.[7]

The years of Abboud were years of benevolent dictatorship. Some changes did take place, and there was an attempt by Abboud to improve communications between the south and the north. The endeavor to add a railway route to the traditionalist Nile route was a case in point. But on balance Abboud's regime was not a regime of militant social reform.

Abboud fell from power in 1964 following agitation from students, judges, and other professional people. It was one of the few occasions when popular agitation against a military regime in Africa has led to the fall of that regime. Abboud's fall was facilitated once again by divisions within his own army and by a clear reluctance of Sudanese soldiers to fire too readily at civilians.

It was not really until May 1969 that the Sudan had a coup of genuine radical reform. This was Numeiry's coup, in alliance with Communists both within the armed forces and among the civilian population. The Sudan took a sharp turn to the left, and soldier and socialist jointly exerted their influence on the nation's destiny.

Numeiry's alliance with the Communists turned out to be an uneasy one. Perhaps from the start it had been a marriage of convenience. At the beginning the main opposition came from the right-wing Umma Party led by the Mahdi. Partly to cope with this threat from the right, Numeiry forged strong links with the Communists and included some Communist leaders in his cabinet. Although political parties had been banned on May 25, 1969, Numeiry shut a blind eye to the resistance of the Sudanese Communist party. It was not until early in 1971 that the rift between the Communists and Numeiry's government assumed proportions of national risk. In February 1971 Numeiry gradually declared war on the Communist Party. After days of meetings in Khartoum, he came out at last in the open. He reminded the nation that political parties in the Sudan had been banned on May 25, 1969.

The ban, he argued, included the Communist Party, and yet that party was still in force: "Destroy anyone who claims there is a Sudanese Communist Party. Destroy this alleged party."[8]

This was the culmination of months of simmering discord. The Communists had not only sought to exert their full influence at cabinet level, but had systematically attempted to infiltrate the army and the civil service and to put pressure for the removal of those suspected of "anti-socialist tendencies." For a while Numeiry played the game in a manner which sought to retain Communist support. Then in 1970 the Sudanese army smashed the Mahdi's forces on the island of Aba on the Nile. With the brutal defeat of the Mahdi, one of the major platforms of alliance between Numeiry and the Communists was at last made redundant. The discord between him and the Communists became more and more manifest.

On the day he at last formally declared war on the Communist Party, Numeiry accused the Communists of having committed sabotage, opposing Sudan's participation in the Four Power Alliance with Egypt, Libya, and Syria, organizing boycotts of visiting heads of state, making fun of the army, and opposing "the revolution step by step."

In July 1971 the Communists attempted a coup. At first it appeared to be the swiftest and least painful coup almost anywhere. It was a coup which was largely executed in much less than an hour, although the planning had taken months. But the Communists' coup in the Sudan turned out to be a very brief phenomenon. With a startling suddenness, forces loyal to Numeiry reasserted themselves, and the three-day wonder of Communist control came dramatically to an end. Numeiry was back in power, the leaders of the coup were given swift "trials," sentenced—and executed. More than a dozen and a half of the leading socialists of the Sudan, including the southerner Joseph Garang, were put to death by the restored Numeiry regime.

Were the coup and the counter-coup of the Sudan of July 1971 coups of rivalry or of reform? The factors here were particularly compounded. But it seems almost certain that the Communist coup included a high ambition to push the country further leftward. To that extent the Communist coup was reformist, with important dimensions of rivalry.

The Numeiry coup, to the extent that it was restorative, was basically an exercise in power rivalry.

What of the Uganda coup of January 25, 1971? This was clearly a coup of rivalry rather than of reform. In fact we might here touch upon the related distinction between a *politically inspired military coup* and a *militarily inspired military coup*. A politically inspired military coup is one where issues of rivalry or reform are connected with wider issues of policy concerning the political system, and principles of government as they impinge upon relations between participants. A militarily inspired military coup, on the other hand, is concerned with questions of internal military organization or relations between those concerned with military policy and decision-making. A politically inspired military coup tends to include an ideological component even if the dominant motives are concerned with the rival for power. A militarily inspired military coup is more likely to be concerned with issues of who makes military decisions on recruitment, strategy, or deployment. The Ugandan coup was vehemently militarily inspired. It concerned ultimately relations between the Commander-in-Chief of the armed forces, the President himself, and the head of his army, Major-General Amin. There have been a variety of theories and accounts of how the Ugandan coup took place. What is clear in all the versions is that a supreme game of sheer survival had been in motion between President Obote and Major-General Amin. Amin had been under a political cloud for some months before the coup. On January 25, 1971, he turned the tables on his rivals.

Because the Ugandan coup was a militarily inspired military coup, it managed at the beginning to be politically magnanimous even if militarily tough. There was fighting and revenge between soldiers. There was also fighting and revenge between civilians, especially in Buganda. But there was little fighting and revenge between soldiers on one side and civilians on the other.

Amin started off with an air of "let us forgive and forget and start afresh to tend our wounds and recover our health as a society." Although at the heart of the coup itself there had been a bitter rivalry for survival between Amin and Obote, Amin was conciliatory. In his first press conference Amin said that the former President was not a bad man but had been badly advised by those he trusted. Amin insisted that Obote's memory in the history of the country would remain honored. He was indeed going to have portraits of the late Sir Edward Mutesa at last exhibited in his own country, but alongside portraits of Dr. Milton Obote. Amin assured the country that he would not approve of the removal of Obote's medallion from beneath the entrance to Parliamentary Buildings. He said: "To do so would be attempting to re-write history."

He said in the first press conference that the only ministers who were in detention were those detained by Obote in 1966 and afterwards. Obote's own ministers were scheduled to meet Amin. Many of them were not hiding in bushes, nor languishing in prison, but had sought refuge in Uganda's most expensive and most luxurious hotel, the Apolo Hotel. There was little doubt that vengeance on politicians was not part of the grand design of the Ugandan coup of January 25, 1971.

This contrasted sharply with the Nigerian coup of January 1966 when the Federal Prime Minister was killed, two regional Premiers were butchered, and a large number of politicians as well as soldiers were bayonetted or shot. The

Nigerian coup was certainly not a purely militarily inspired military coup. It was vengeful and bloodthirsty from the start, and set the pattern for counter-revenge in less than a few months.

The Ghanaian coup of February 1966 was not as bloodthirsty, but a lot of people were locked up who had once been leading politicians. Six hundred or so of Nkrumah's detainees emerged from prison; six hundred other detainees went in instead. Even Nkrumah's Foreign Minister, Alex Quaison-Sackey, in spite of having deserted Nkrumah from Peking and flown directly home after the coup, was nevertheless promptly put behind bars by the new regime. His desertion from the Osagyefo did not constitute enough credentials to earn him the status of a free man on his return home after the coup.

By contrast, the leaders of Obote's regime were left free, and from Uganda went out the call:

> Let word go forth from this time and place that all those Ugandans who accompanied the former President to Singapore are welcome back home. Those in the Public Service are to report for duty by next Wednesday at 8 o'clock in the morning. Dr. Obote is also welcome back as a son of Uganda—but strictly as a private citizen.

Many did come back and resume their positions. The most startling of all those early returns was that of Henry Kyemba, who had been Obote's principal private secretary, enjoying a nearness to the former President that gave him a distinctive status among those who served Obote. Kyemba had accompanied the former President to Singapore and was waiting with him in Dar-es-Salaam when the summons from Kampala went forth. Kyemba took Amin at his word, and arrived back home. He was promptly promoted to secretary to the cabinet.

Chris Ntende, another permanent secretary who had apparently been important as a messenger to Singapore to alert Obote about the plotting that was going on in Uganda, not only retained his freedom but also retained a position in the civil service as permanent secretary of the new Department of Religion in the Second Republic of Uganda.

It can almost be said that for the first two weeks or so of the coup the arch-enemy of the coup was not Obote's government as a whole, it was not even Obote himself personally, it was ultimately the head of intelligence, Akena Adoko. The eighteen points of legitimation enumerated by the soldiers were themselves brilliantly conceived. So well done and so well conceived were those eighteen points that they included grievances against Obote which could have been held only by the Acholi. And so some people, including some Acholi themselves, believed the coup of January 25, 1971, was primarily an Acholi coup against Obote. The eighteen points did not even attempt to isolate all the Langi. It sought to isolate only Obote's own home county, Akokoro.

These factors and the later air of magnanimity which characterized the atmosphere of the coup did help to give the Ugandan coup the image of one of the least vengeful and least brutal coups in the history of the Third World.

One question which arises in retrospect was whether the political magnanimity was a mistake. Was the attempt to focus hostility on the persons of Akena Adoko, and later Obote, fraught with the risk of ethnic tensions from the start?

UGANDA AS A CRISIS FOR TANZANIA

Obote was important both to Lango, his place of birth, and to Tanzania, his place of political exile. The two political factors interacted.

In my estimation, four factors went toward aggravating ethnic tensions following the coup, and one of those four factors was the political magnanimity which characterized the first few days and weeks of the Second Republic. The first factor which fostered potential tensions included quite simply those prior tensions within the armed forces, focusing quite often more on the Acholi than on the Langi. The Acholi in the armed forces have been the largest single group, going upward to one-third of the soldiers. A tradition of good military performance had created certain forms of self-confidence among the Acholi, which might have on occasion been mistaken for military arrogance. It is sometimes assumed that sharing life together in the barracks helps to give armed forces in Africa opportunities for ethnic intermingling. That may be taken for granted. But there is a further assumption that ethnic intermingling does itself reduce ethnic tensions and animosity. It is this latter assumption which is not always borne out by events. Ethnic intermingling first results in increasing tension before it finally reaches a plateau of normalization and ultimate ethnic integration. Social scientists often underestimate the tension-generating effects of premature integration. Inter-tribal animosities within the Uganda army were taking shape well before the coup of January 25, 1971.

The second factor which aggravated the potentialities of an ethnic eruption was what I called Amin's great blunder. This was his account of why the coup took place. Until Amin had his press conference, much of Acholi was available for possible recruitment to his side. As indicated, the eighteen points mentioned on the first day of the coup made the statement itself almost of Acholi authorship. The eighteen points played up the issue of the Lango Development Master Plan written in 1967, ostensibly urging that all key positions in Uganda's political, commercial, military, and industrial life were to be occupied and controlled by Akokoro County, Lango District. In the words of the soldiers' eighteen points, ". . . the same master plan decided that nothing of importance must be done for other districts, especially Acholi District."[9]

But then Amin gave his press conference to explain how the coup took place. He said that former President Obote had sent a directive to certain army officers in Kampala instructing them to arm Acholi and Lango tribesmen within the army and disarm and arrest other army units, consisting of different tribesmen. Amin said that on the weekend in question he had been at Karuma Falls, and on returning home Sunday evening he found a tank and a personnel carrier outside his residence. In the carrier, the General said, was an injured soldier.

The soldier told the General that Lt. Colonel Akwanga, Commanding Officer of the Mechanized Battalion, had been instructing Lango and Acholi soldiers to go to the armory to obtain weapons and ammunition. The soldier, realizing that something was amiss, had alerted some of his own colleagues and tribesmen and attempted to obtain weapons for himself for self-defense. In the attempt to procure the weapons he had been wounded. The other soldiers had realized by then that Amin was not one of the selected ones and had gone to the General to warn him and help in protecting him. The General, after making sure that the wounded man received medical treatment, took control of the situation.

This was Amin's account of the coup. Should he have revealed such an account? Should he not instead either have suppressed the account, or have fundamentally distorted it in an attempt to eliminate the heavy tribal dimension implicit in it? By this account Obote had intended to trust only the Langi and the Acholi, and had intended to arm them, possibly at the expense of other tribesmen in the army. The whole account of the coup rested on an ethnic dimension. If it was a correct account, it should deliberately have been made less correct for the sake of national survival. If it was an incorrect account from the start, the errors in it were disastrous. Amin later promised to have the whole thing written out in detail and published, but wiser counsel within the government of the Second Republic prevailed. But the ethnic dimension had already set the tone, tragically. The Acholi, who had been available for possible mobilization to the side of the coup, were now rendered insecure by the very account which Amin had brought forth. Many Acholi in the army might indeed have been wary from the start, but civilian Acholi had enough grievances against Obote's regime to have been potential allies of Amin and his Second Republic. And those Langi who might have been ready to dissociate themselves from Obote with a little persuasion and patronage retreated after Amin's press conference into a new sense of defensive insecurity. Meanwhile, the non-Langi and non-Acholi tribesmen within the armed forces, who need never have known in detail some of those plans to disarm them at the expense of Acholi and Langi had Amin acted in a manner which sought to reduce ethnic tensions within the armed forces, now found an additional deep grievance against their comrades-in-arms from the two northern districts. After all, these two groups had retained Obote's trust and were on the verge of being armed in a posture of combat against the rest of the armed forces.

The third aggravating factor behind the later ethnic eruptions in Uganda was Obote's decision to fight back. If Obote had behaved like old Farouk of Egypt, or General Abboud of the Sudan, and retreated into oblivion after being overthrown, the atmosphere in Uganda might have retained its air of at least political magnanimity for a little longer. But Obote's own first press conference was a fighting press conference. He was not only claiming that he was still President of Uganda, but he was making charges against Amin from a neighboring capital and seeking to rally pan-African forces against the new republic in Uganda. Obote's travels in different capitals in a bid for diplomatic, and conceivably military, support began to assume an air of militant endeavor to make a comeback. Nyerere's diplomatic support for Obote, and the massive utilization of Tanzania's diplomatic and journalistic influence to discredit the new regime in Uganda, were also important contributory factors toward the climate of tension within Uganda itself. Violence began to be regionalized in the East African Community and beyond. The politics of the Organization of African Unity and the wrangle about credentials, culminating in Obote's minister Sam Odaka's trip to Addis Ababa as a rival delegation to Amin's, could not but induce cracks in the whole aura of magnanimity which had characterized the coup from the beginning. One after another of the former gestures of conciliation toward Obote were withdrawn. Symbolic of the whole shift in direction was the decision to do what Amin had promised not to do—re-write history. Obote's photographs were banned, the grand medallion outside Parliament was brought down, and a reward of a million shillings was proclaimed for the person of Obote delivered alive to the new Uganda government.

At the beginning it was Amin who was cool and collected, while Obote, Nyerere, and the Tanzanian press were hysterical in their response to the event of January 1971. The calculated measures of Tanzania to snub the new regime of Uganda, humiliate her diplomatically, and finally refuse to recognize the government's appointees to the East African Community, all contributed toward aggravating the atmosphere and sharpening the postures of combat. Uganda's tensions were being regionalized both along the Nile and in East Africa. Tanzania's hysteria ultimately generated counter-hysteria from Uganda. The shrill cries of war on the border, guerrilla intrusion into Uganda, mobilization of forces, closure of borders, banning of Tanzania's Minister Malecela from Uganda, withdrawing working rights to Amin's namesake, Idi

Simba, Governor of East African Development Bank, refusing to ratify the
Appropriations Bill of the East African Community, pirating the helicopters
intended for Tanzania—all these amounted to a posture of counter-aggression
against Tanzania, clearly generated by the sense of frustration and humiliation which Tanzania's initial hysteria had sought to impose on the infant
Second Republic of Uganda. It was not realistic to expect a military regime to
remain magnanimous and forgiving toward Obote and his supporters while
Obote and Tanzania pursued a policy of militant denunciation. The bad
atmosphere created by Tanzania's and Obote's reaction to the coup had
ethnic repercussions. There was a genuine fear of the recruitment of Langi
and Acholi to fight for Obote. And many Langi and Acholi, uneasy and
insecure within the armed forces, found the strategy of disappearance as
much the best part of valor. The fact that they were gone itself reinforced
suspicions that they had vanished in order to rally—and fight again.

There is probably also enough reason to believe that some of these men
did organize themselves into units for possible sabotage. The attempts at
penetrating ammunition depots reinforced further the new Republic's fear of
subversion and guerrilla attack. It was a classic case of a vicious circle—
suspicions leading to the realization of those suspicions. It was a classic case
of self-fulfilling prophecies, as the fear of an underground movement made
the Second Republic aggressive toward potential Obote supporters within the
tribal areas, and these supporters became in turn insecure and sought protection in the shadows of concealed existence and fearfully disguised intrigue.

The whole enterprise culminated in the invasion of Uganda by Obote's
supporters from Tanzania in September 1972, clearly with the connivance of
the government of Tanzania. The invasion was President Nyerere's "Bay of
Pigs." The invaders were decisively defeated. And relations between Uganda
and Tanzania dropped to an all-time low. Bukoba was bombed by Ugandan
planes. The two countries were on the brink of an all-out war.

The Nile Valley was nearly involved when President Numeiry prevented a
contingent of Libyan troops from flying over Khartoum to go and help Amin.
Somalia meanwhile entered into determined attempts to prevent the regionalization of violence, especially between Tanzania and Uganda, from getting
worse.

The fourth factor behind the aggravation of ethnic tensions was the initial
magnanimity which characterized Amin's coup. That magnanimity had
sought to narrow the focus of hostility within Uganda to two individuals,
Akena Adoko and Milton Obote. Unfortunately, both those people were
Langi. In the current phases of African politics a focus on unique personalities tends to expand and include their tribal origins. To blame a catastrophe
on an individual who happens to be a Langi exposes not merely the individual
himself but also the ethnic roots from which he springs. The villain is often
regarded as a villain partly in relation to his tribe.

We are already familiar with a situation where individuals sometimes suffer because they are deemed to belong to the wrong tribe. Under Obote a particular Muganda might sometimes be discriminated against because he was a Muganda. In Kenya a particular Luo applying for a job in either the private or public sectors might be discriminated against because he was a Luo. These are situations where the individual suffers because of hostility to his tribe.

But we have also a reverse phenomenon at times. This is when a tribe suffers because of hostility to the individual. The classic illustration of this second phenomenon is the case of the Langi in relation to Milton Obote. The villain of the piece initially was not Lango District as such. The villains were Akena and Obote. But because they were both Langi, and once powerful and influential Langi at that, their fall from eminence had adverse consequences for their tribe. The relentless interaction in Africa between ethnic factors and personal factors had found yet another arena of performance in the very magnanimity which characterized the Ugandan coup.

Had the vengeance of the coup been directed at the government of Obote as a whole, it would have had to be directed at people from almost every corner of Uganda. The ministers were multi-ethnic, drawn from West Nile, Lango, Acholi, Kigezi, Ankole, Buganda, Bunyoro, Teso, and elsewhere. If the blame for the first errors of the Republic were to be well and truly laid on Obote's regime as a whole and not simply on Obote himself, the tribal repercussions would have had to be virtually national. If not every tribe, certainly every district, was compromised in having participated in the First Republic. If the revenge against the First Republic had been based on a denunciation of the regime as a whole, and its performance and its scale of values, such revenge would probably have had less potentiality for degenerating into pure ethnicity than the attempt to pin the blame on two Langi, and on those two alone.

The phenomenon has deep roots in the whole tradition of collective responsibility among kinsmen in African societies. The collective responsibility has been known to take a variety of forms, ranging from finding a job for an unemployed kinsman in Kampala who has just arrived from the home village to joint participation in an inter-clan feud. The collective responsibility may be among fellows of the same clan, members of the same age group, inhabitants of the same village, or even speakers of the same language, depending upon circumstance and the groups concerned.

Murder in African society is sometimes a question of collective guilt and collective obligation. Murder across the tribal line certainly often involves inter-tribal accountability, and in some cases could result in inter-tribal conflict.

It is considerations such as these which can convert physical animosity directed against one individual into animosity against his tribe as a whole. General Idi Amin in Uganda repeatedly sounded a warning after the coup, addressed to Dr. Obote, advising him that a continuing militancy by Obote against the regime could have adverse consequences on his kinsmen and his tribe. The magnanimity of the Ugandan coup in the intial stages, to the extent that it basically tolerated all the former ministers of Obote's government with the exception of Basil Bataringaya, Minister of Internal Affairs, was, while it lasted, a major gesture in humanitarianism. What we have sought to demonstrate is that even such gestures do sometimes have certain costs. In the Ugandan situation the cost of Amin's decision to be magnanimous was the phenomenon of ethnically focused political blame. By blaming Obote and Akena alone, the Langi became extra-vulnerable. By forgiving almost all other ministers, the rest of the country was able to withhold responsibility for the excesses of the First Republic of Uganda. The blame was narrowed—and the barometer of ethnic tensions rose.

With the eruption of these further tensions, violence once again played its role as a penetrative agency. And the Nile Valley took one more step toward becoming a valley of political blood as well as the waters of an eternal river.

THE NILE VALLEY AND THE MIDDLE EAST

But is the Nile Valley really emerging as a regional political system because of this phenomenon of violent interpenetration?

If we take the Valley of the White Nile from Jinja to the Mediterranean it does provide evidence of an international subsystem *in the making.* It also provides a classic illustration of an interpenetration of domestic politics and interstate relations. Indeed, we might say that the Nile Valley has become a situation where interstate relations arise almost as a direct result of the overspilling of domestic politics. Sadat in Egypt sought to strengthen his domestic position partly through concepts of pan-Arab solidarity with Libya, Syria, and the Sudan. Then we have Egypt's entry into the politics of northern Sudan. Upwards of 10,000 Egyptian troops moved into northern Sudan. An Egyptian academy for military training was established in northern Sudan. The survival of General Numeiry as the ruler of the Sudan was for a while consolidated through the utilization of an Egyptian presence in the Sudan. The Egyptian presence in turn enabled the Sudan to spare more troops for the war in the south without risking the survival of the regime in the north

There was increasing evidence that the war in the south in turn was supported militarily and financially by Israel. Arms, vehicles, and medical supplies were all part of Israel's strategy to keep the war in the south of the Sudan alive.

But what was Israel to use as the base from which to support the war in southern Sudan? Again, there was increasing evidence that this support came in part through Uganda, with or without the blessing of the regime in power.

When Milton Obote was overthrown from power in Uganda in January 1971, we did expect the coup to be partly attributed to external forces. But the leading candidate in people's expectations for these accusations was Britain. After all, Obote had just returned from Singapore where he was the leading African spokesman against Edward Heath's proposal to resume British arms' sales to South Africa. Obote in Singapore had been passionately critical of British intentions. The world limelight had focused on him, and he had been interviewed for a variety of newspapers and television stations serving populations from London to Melbourne. There was no doubt that following the Singapore denunciations the British government was more alienated from Obote than ever. Then, less than a week before the coup in Uganda, about seven hundred British troops had arrived in Kenya. What were they there for? Was it in readiness to protect British lives should there be violence against the resumption of arms' sales to South Africa? Was it simply, as the official explanation claimed, a case of joint exercises between Kenya soldiers and British soldiers? Or was there a foreknowledge in London about the coup in Uganda? Were the troops there should something go seriously wrong with the planned coup in Uganda?

These were questions which occurred to observers, and many expected Obote to lay the blame for the coup firmly at the feet of British machinations. But that in fact was not what Obote did. He did indeed invoke the charge of external participation in the coup. But his candidate for the charge was not Britain but Israel.

But what would Israel stand to gain by intervening to help overthrow Obote's regime? A critical factor to be borne in mind was that it was in Israel's strategic interest to keep the third largest army in the Arab world busy with an internal civil war in the south of the Sudan. The paramount interests of Israel were not in obtaining autonomy or independence for southern Sudan, but in maintaining a state of affairs serious enough to tie down a substantial part of the Sudanese army to a civil war in the south. There was also the calculation that this diversion of the Sudanese army to a southern war might in turn necessitate the diversion of part of the Egyptian army to northern Sudan. As we have indicated, this is precisely what did in fact happen. Thousands of Egyptian troops moved to northern Sudan as thousands of northern Sudanese troops fought in the south.

But why should Israel have a vested interest in overthrowing Obote? After all it was Obote who had brought Israelis into Uganda as trainers of his air force and advisers on other aspects of Uganda's military needs. This is true. But Obote had, in the twenty months prior to his fall, become increasingly uneasy about his links with Israel. The pressures on Obote, which resulted in a gradual rethinking of his policy on the Middle East, may have begun with the June war between Israel and the Arabs in 1967. When the question was brought before the United Nations General Assembly, Uganda voted in favor of a motion demanding Israeli withdrawal from Arab territory. For some reason Israel was surprised by Uganda's vote. For many months after the incident itself Obote was being asked to explain why he voted the way he did—virtually against Israel. Obote protested that he had cast his vote in a direction no different from the direction of the vote of Her Majesty's Government in London, though there had been no collusion whatsoever between the two governments. And yet, although no one questioned Britain's decision to vote for Israeli withdrawal from Arab territory, it appeared as if Israel questioned Uganda's decision to vote in the same direction. In an address to the Makerere Institute in Diplomacy, delivered in the Main Hall at Makerere on August 30, 1968, Obote said:

> Up to now we are being requested to explain why we voted that way. . . . I am very doubtful whether repeated requests for us to explain why we voted in a particular manner is [sic] being also put to Her Majesty the Queen's government in London. Uganda, however, voted for Israeli withdrawal not to favour the Arab countries but as a matter of principle and in the circumstances of the state of affairs in Southern Africa today. We cannot rule out the possibility of the Union of South Africa either alone or together with Rhodesia invading or over-running Zambia. The first thing that Uganda would do if such a situation arises, would be to call for a withdrawal of the invading troops from Zambian territory. . . . We do not see any difference between possible invasion and occupation of Zambian territory by hostile troops, or part of Uganda being invaded by foreign troops on the one hand, and on the other, the Israeli occupation of Arab territories.[10]

Milton Obote continued to tell the African trainee-diplomats at Makerere in 1968 that "for the people of Uganda the June war of 1967 was very close to them." There had been political and geographical considerations which "brought the 1967 June war not just to Uganda's borders but right into Entebbe and on the Presidential desk."[11]

But what was going on in southern Sudan? Obote was all too aware of certain areas of injustice in the policies pursued by the government of Khartoum against the south. He also warned both northern Sudanese and southern Sudanese against the temptation of carrying the war into Uganda. He offered his services to help resolve the conflict.

Obote was also aware of the propaganda dimension involved in the situation. Voices tried to persuade him that the real motive behind the northern Sudanese thrust into the south was to exterminate the black population there, so that the displaced Palestinians could settle in the south of the Sudan and create a new Palestine of their own. It was in a way a circular inversion of the whole story of the creation of Israel. Distant Jews trekked from Europe and the Americas and other parts of the world, created an Israel in Palestine, and displaced thousands of Arabs. Then across the Red Sea a war took place between Arab northern Sudanese and African southern Sudanese—ostensibly with the view to preparing the way for the settlement of the displaced Palestinian Arabs in the south of the Sudan.

It is not clear who put these stories into the ears of Obote, but it may be presumed that among the voices he heard were voices from outside Africa. To use Obote's own words in his address to the diplomats at Makerere: "You will observe that in talking about Uganda's neighbours, I travelled by way of Jerusalem."[12]

But Obote wanted to keep out of other people's quarrels by the curious, yet fundamental, argument that Uganda itself was constantly on the brink of her own internal quarrels. He assumed that until Uganda maintained her own national cohesion, she could not afford to be involved in other people's adventures. His statement was correct as a moral assertion, but it was unsound as a political proposition. Obote argued:

> Uganda's foreign policy can only be a reflection of Uganda. If Uganda is divided into tribal, religious or ethnic factions, no Government of Uganda will be in a position to project any other image except the image of a country dissected by tribal, religious, ethnic and other considerations. For the people of Uganda it is academic and dishonest for them to aspire to influence international relations ahead of their being able to bury their sectional interests. After all, Uganda in international relations presupposes that Uganda itself has an identity—that is, one image—but . . . Uganda is amorphous.[13]

In the political assumptions of his analysis Milton Obote was wrong. It is precisely in situations of amorphous national identity and imminent social violence that quarrels of one country spill over into another; transnational interpenetration is facilitated by intra-national cleavages. The fluid identities of both the Sudan and Uganda have been part of the process by which the two countries have profoundly affected each other.

There have been occasions of concern lest there be a Ugandan factor in the Sudanese civil war. Obote himself kept repeatedly reassuring the Sudanese that in spite of ethnic ties he did not intend to make Uganda a base for the liberation movements. At times Obote fulfilled this promise; at other times he fell short of upholding it. A Ugandan factor was never entirely absent in the Sudanese civil war.

The question which was arising as the 1970s entered the scene was whether there would be a Sudanese factor within Uganda's own power struggles. After all, if the border tribes traversed the two nations, it was not simply a question of the Ugandan sector of a tribe helping the Sudanese sector; there was also the question of whether the Sudanese sector of the tribe would help the Ugandan sector in potentially similar circumstances. Are there southern Sudanese in the Ugandan army? After all, there are still Ugandans in the Kenya police, and Tanzanians in the Ugandan police (if by that we mean people born in one country, and later finding employment in another). Has there been an interpenetration between southern Sudan and Uganda in their respective fighting forces?

Colin Legum, in one of his reports in *The Observer* (London) about the Ugandan situation, claimed that certain southern Sudanese had been rapidly promoted not long after the coup. The Ugandan government of the Second Republic corrected the excesses of Legum's report, pointing out that the only officer of Sudanese extraction who had been promoted had in fact been in the Ugandan army for a number of years. The new government repudiated the innuendo that southern Sudanese had assumed critical areas of decision-making in the Ugandan armed forces. But for the purposes of this particular paper all we need examine is whether there is a Sudanese factor, however modest, which has now become significant in the balance of forces within Uganda.

Then there is the case of the white mercenary, Steiner. Steiner was a West German who had fought for money in Zaire under Tshombe, and in Biafra, and later in southern Sudan. In this latter enterprise there seems to be some evidence that he was in fact paid by the Israelis to advise the southern Sudanese insurrectionists.

Steiner was arrested in Uganda in 1970. Obote was confronted with an OAU resolution recommending that white mercenaries arrested in one African country ought to be repatriated to the African country in which they had last been operating as mischief-makers. Obote hesitated about sending Steiner to Khartoum. In December 1970 this resolution was re-affirmed by the OAU. In January 1971 Obote's regime at last decided to hand over the mercenary to Khartoum. Was the fate of Steiner symbolic of a great shift in Obote's policy, away both from tacit sympathy with the southern Sudanese insurrectionists, away also from responsiveness to Israeli advice on Middle Eastern, Sudanese, and military affairs? Did the Israelis regard the fate of Steiner as symbolic of the end of the honeymoon with Obote's regime?

Further questions arose following the coup itself. Perhaps prematurely, the Israelis were conspicuous in some of the initial ceremonies which took place after the coup. These included the colossal public gathering which assembled at Kololo airstrip to witness the release of those who had been detained under Obote's rule. Significantly or not, a token Israeli presence, in uniform, was noticed. Not long after this, the Israeli Ambassador, Mr. Aron Ofri, took his leave. There was speculation in Kampala as to whether the Israelis working in Uganda at Obote's invitation had in fact been divided over the issue of how much Israeli participation in Uganda's internal affairs was legitimate. The civilian side of the Israeli diplomatic presence had opted for a conventional approach in diplomacy—that is, to refrain from being identified with any faction in an internal cleavage. But the military and paramilitary section of the Israeli presence in Uganda was more prepared to manifest its sympathies for General Amin and his point of view. Was Ambassador Ofri gifted but conventional in his diplomatic approach? Was he outwitted by his military compatriots? Did he have to leave Uganda earlier than he might have done? In short, was he leaving because the hawks within the Israeli team in Uganda had won—in the face of reservations from the Ambassador? These are questions yet to be adequately answered. But the speculations originally emanated from usually very well-informed sources on Ugandan affairs in Kampala.

Then General Amin made his first trip outside the country. It was a risky undertaking considering that he had overthrown his immediate predecessor while the latter was absent abroad. Was Amin taking a gamble by going abroad while the situation in Uganda was still unsettled?

He was in fact taking a gamble. His first stop was Israel, where he met the Ministers of Defense and Foreign Affairs, and the Prime Minister, Mrs. Golda Meir. He then proceeded to Britain, lunched with the Queen and had discussions with Prime Minister Heath and Foreign Minister Sir Alec Douglas-Home.

On his way back General Amin stopped once again in Israel. A new military agreement was to be finalized between Uganda and Israel. Before Amin's departure from Israel the government-controlled television broadcasting had in fact said explicitly that Amin was going to Israel to negotiate the withdrawal of Israeli technicians and military advisers from Uganda. But on his arrival in Israel General Amin categorically denied that that was the purpose of his visit. On the contrary he was there to negotiate a more comprehensive agreement for Israeli military assistance to Uganda.

Was Israeli military support tilting the balance of effectiveness in the power struggle within Uganda? Was it also affecting the power struggle in southern Sudan? And then in northern Sudan we had drawn attention to the Egyptian presence. On balance were we witnessing the Egyptianization of Sudanese politics concurrently with the Israelization of Uganda politics on the border issues with southern Sudan?

If so, violence was once again playing its penetrative game. Violent conflict and tensions within northern Sudan loosened resistance to Egyptian influence and gradually opened the gates for a significant Egyptian military presence. The violent insurrection in southern Sudan brought in vested interests. And then more violent confrontations within the politics of Uganda in turn made the country more responsive to external participation in domestic power struggles. The regionalization of violence was taking Uganda into the vortex of the Middle Eastern crisis.

If there was an Israelization of Uganda politics, history once again indulged her ironic sense of humor. At the beginning of this century Joseph Chamberlain offered "Uganda" to the Zionist movement as a home for the Jews. Chamberlain's offer to the Zionists was probably not entirely of Uganda but also of the Highlands of Kenya, parts of which were at that time sometimes included within the territory designated as "Uganda." But Uganda's name has remained more prominent in the historical recollections of Zionism. We shall return to this more fully in a later chapter.

Had Zionism evolved a new "manifest destiny" to supplement its original raison d'être? The original one was to bring Jews from all corners of the world to a country they could call their own. The new manifest destiny was to distribute Jews to all corners of the *Third* World as harbingers of change and development.

As Milton Obote listened to some of the representations made to him by his Israeli friends following the war of June 1967, he might himself have thought of Joseph Chamberlain and the plan to create an Israel within Uganda. He might also have been weighing the Israeli claims that southern Sudan was for seventeen years being systematically depopulated for the sake of creating a home for those Arabs who have been displaced by the creation of Israel in Palestine. A Jewish home in Uganda, and a Palestinian home in southern Sudan, an Egyptian presence in northern Sudan, a Jewish presence in Eastern Egypt and the Canal Zone—the politics of the Nile Valley as an international sub-system did indeed seem destined to merge into the politics of the Middle East. And violence as a penetrative agency for regional integration seemed once again to be asserting its omnipresence.

If we turn our eyes to East Africa and the East African Community, we see a different kind of regionalized tension. On the one hand, the experience of regional integration under the British increased the capacity of each member-country to empathize with the others. On the other hand, that very regional integration increased national consciousness in each constituent national entity. We find, for example, that few things contributed more to Ugandan national consciousness than Uganda's competitive relationship with its own immediate neighbors.

Within the East African Community itself, the habit had grown of encouraging territorial competition for a share of the economic cake of the region as a whole. The awareness of conflicting interests had been deepened. Each country had not only grown more protective of its own interests as *opposed* to the interests of the others; it had sometimes developed a more enduring psychological complex and suspicion of the motives of others. It was this consideration which could convert regional economic cooperation as a stage of compromise into a breeding ground for economic nationalism within each member state in certain circumstances. But the degree of nationalism varied with each nation state. And usually it varied in relation to the benefits which each derived from the cooperation. Sometimes it was a case of the greatest beneficiary being the least defensive and the least militant in its economic nationalism. Within the East African Community Kenya therefore tended to be less defensively nationalistic in economic matters than either Uganda or Tanzania.

East Africans have for quite a while now had dreams about merging into a single federal state. Among the experiences which have given them that idea is precisely the experience of having shared an economic community for a while. And yet it is meaningful to ask whether the spirit of economic rivalry fostered between the constituent members of the East African Economic Community has itself harmed the cause of an East African federation. The competitive habits and protective militancy which were nourished by the existence of an economic union might conceivably have pushed the federal cause further away from realization for the time being. What this means is that a period of compromise relationships has generated enough tensions to push East African relations backward toward mere contact rather than forward toward real regional coalescence. The compromise relationships may indeed later generate enough integrative momentum to cross the boundary at last into coalescence. But in the initial phases the tensions of compromise relations are of such a kind that they pull a regional entity backward toward bare contact and then forward again. It is almost like Lenin's concept, duly inverted, concerning two steps forward and one step backward. Occasionally it becomes indeed two steps backward and one step forward. But if the compromise relationships survive over a sufficiently long period, the momentum of habit may gradually push the region past the difficult barrier that separates compromise from coalescence.

Perhaps even Tanzania's overreaction to the Ugandan coup was itself a measure of empathy with the Ugandan people. The tensions of Uganda became the tensions of Tanzania. In a strange and paradoxical kind of way, violence was once again serving painful integrative functions on a regional scale.

NOTES

1. Abdul Rahman Zaki, *Al-Sharq Al-Awsat* (Cairo: Egyptian Rennaisance Bookshop, 1948): 63-64. Cited by Tareq Y. Ismael, *The U.A.R. in Africa: Egypt's Policy under Nasser* (Evanston: Northwestern University Press, 1971): 163-164.

2. Robinson and John Gallagher with Alice Denny, *Africa and the Victorians* (New York: St. Martins Press, 1961): 283.

3. Ibid.

4. Ibid: 320.

5. This part of the paper borrows extensively from two previous papers. These are the author's inaugural lecture, *Ancient Greece in African Political Thought* (Nairobi: East African Publishing House, 1967) and the author's subsequent paper "The Indian Ocean and the Nile Valley: The View from East Africa" (mimeographed), 1971.

6. Sir Reader Bullard (ed.), *The Middle East: A Political and Economic Survey,* issued under the auspices of the Royal Institute of International Affairs (London: Oxford University Press, 1958): 190-191.

7. See "Sudan's Divided Army," *Economist,* November 14, 1959: 637; also issues of March 15 and November 22, 1958.

8. See Joel Balloch, "Sudan Declares War on Communism," *The Daily Telegraph,* February 13, 1971: 5.

9. *Uganda Argus,* January 26, 1971.

10. Makerere Institute in Diplomacy, Speech by H.E. the President of Uganda, Dr. A. Milton Obote, on 30 August 1968 (mimeographed): 20-21.

11. Ibid., pp. 23-24.

12. Ibid.: 27.

13. Ibid.: 28.

Chapter 7

THE RISE OF THE LUMPEN MILITARIAT

How much of a revolution in Africa's political experience do military coups signify? This chapter starts from the premise that, however conservative Major-General Amin might have been in January 1971, the very fact that a soldier had captured political power constituted a basic revolution in Uganda. Changes of a profound political and psychological significance have arisen out of the modernization of military skills in Africa and out of the impact of these skills on society. The case of Uganda is to be seen in this wider perspective.

From the point of view of political sociology, the most important consequences of the emergence of modern armies in Africa are reducible to two areas of impact. The first area concerns the consolidation of statehood and the second area concerns the diversification of the class structure.

We hope to indicate in this chapter that the emergence of the modern army in African countries is a critical variable toward the centralization of power in the polity and, therefore, an important stage toward the emergence of state structures of authority. This is our first hypothesis. Our second hypothesis is that the emergence of the modern army in African countries has broken the correlation between political power and Western education by interrupting the trend toward the dictatorship of the educated class in modern African history.

The lumpen proletariat is a mass of disorganized workers and ghetto dwellers in the developed world; but the *lumpen militariat* is that class of semi-organized, rugged, and semi-literate soldiery which has begun to claim a share of power and influence in what would otherwise have become a heavily privileged meritocracy of the educated.

AUTHOR'S NOTE: This chapter borrows heavily from the author's previous book, *Cultural Engineering and Nation-Building in East Africa* (Evanston: Northwestern University Press, 1972) and the author's article, "The Lumpen Proletariat and the Lumpen Militariat: African Soldiers as a New Political Class," *Political Studies* 21, 1 (March 1973): 1-12.

Related to this second hypothesis of this chapter is the third hypothesis
that the history of modernization in independent Africa might well be a
gradual transition from a political supremacy of those who hold the means of
destruction, as might be the trend in the first two or three decades of
independence, to a future political supremacy of those who control the
means of production. The initial methods of technological development in a
relatively backward society, to the extent that they are applied both to
military and civilian areas of life, tend to widen the gap of power between the
unarmed citizenry, on the one side, and those who hold control over the new
means of war, on the other. It is only after the society has become more
technologically complex, and factories and laboratories have generated their
own power-holders, that the means of production become critical enough to
the survival of national systems to provide a countervailing balance to the
power exercised by the military.

Those who control the means of production—workers, managers and
owners—are at their most powerful in relation to the soldiers in situations of
technological complexity. They are at their weakest in relation to the soldiers
in situations of rudimentary technology, manifested both in the new cotton
mill situated in the midst of rural backwardness, as weel as symbolized by the
machinegun in a society which still experiences cattle raids with spears.

Let us take each of these three hypotheses in turn. If we can establish
these, we shall have established that General Amin's assumption of power was
a revolutionary event irrespective of his own ideological position. We shall
then discuss the *embourgeoisement* which awaits his men.

TECHNOLOGY AND CENTRALIZATION OF VIOLENCE

The first hypothesis, that the emergence of the modern army is a step
toward the consolidation of statehood in African countries, derives its concept of statehood partly from the implications of Weber's definition.[1]

Uganda has been the first East African country to experience a military
coup. And yet it can hardly be stated that Uganda has, in Weberian terms,
concentrated a "monopoly" of the "use of physical force" in the hands of
the institutions of the state. On the contrary, one of the staggering aspects of
the Uganda scene is precisely the phenomenon of decentralized violence. The
country per capita has one of the highest rates of homicide in the world. Nor,
as shown in Chapter Two, is the violence perpetrated only by deviants and
antisocial criminals.[2]

When the army took over Uganda on January 25, 1971, *kondoism,* or robbery with violence, had already reached high proportions in Uganda. We have already discussed how Obote's government, in desperation, had even made robbery with violence a capital offense—to the consternation of those who feared that this would not reduce the violence but increase murder as a way of eliminating all witnesses to a robbery.

Following the coup, in the wake of instability and uncertainty about the survival of legitimate authority, kondoism rose even more sharply. There was also a suspicion that some members of the intelligence department of the Obote regime, stripped of power and disgraced following the coup, used the firearms they had acquired from the previous regime for new purposes. Old informers became new kondos as they took to gangsterism and armed thuggery.

But what is even more significant from the point of view of this analysis is the style by which the military regime then sought to claim a "monopoly of the legitimate use of physical force" (again in the Weberian sense).

On the night of March 18, 1971, the government issued two decrees giving powers to the armed forces to search houses and other buildings, vehicles and aircraft, and to take possession of vehicles, stolen property, and dangerous weapons. The campaign was designed, in the words of the Attorney General, to "stamp out the scourge of *Kondoism.*" The Armed Forces (Powers of Arrest) Decree gave members of the armed forces and prison officers power to arrest persons for an offense against public order, or an offense against other persons, or an offense relating to property.

> In simple terms the offenses listed are the sort of offenses committed by kondos. For example, armed robbery and armed attacks on defenseless members of the community. Members of the armed forces and prison officers are given power to search houses and other buildings and motor cars and aircraft if they have reason to believe that a person who is to be arrested is in any of those places or anything stolen may be found in such places. They may also take possession of vehicles, stolen property and dangerous weapons. . . . The Decree will remain in force for twelve months. It is hoped that before that time has expired kondoism will have been banished from Uganda.[3]

Even before this Decree, soldiers were already being used to patrol certain streets of Kampala, following repeated burglaries. There was also a vigorous attempt to prevent armed political victimization of supporters of the former Obote regime by other civilians.

In general, what the new military regime was doing in trying to centralize power and monopolize violence was what was to be expected of any central government in such a situation. The relevance of military technology to this phenomenon arises out of the real gap which modern weapons create between the army and armed civilians in African conditions. There are parts of East

Africa where military skills are still assessed in terms of prowess in handling spears and in the use of the bow and arrow. The centralization of power and the consolidation of authority in Uganda would have been even more difficult if the armed forces were not equipped both with relatively modern weapons and with relatively rapid technological mobility.

Even the emergence of the metal spear was a significant variable in the process of emerging kingdoms in Africa. The use of metal was a leap toward statehood to some extent, at least as compared with a combat culture based on the bow and arrow. In the words of Jack Goody:

> The bow and arrow is essentially a democratic weapon; every man knows how to construct one; the materials are readily available, the techniques uncomplicated, the missiles easy to replace (though more difficult with the introduction of iron that affected even hunting people like the Hadza of Tanzania and the Bushmen of the Kalahari). With the technologies of the bow and stone-tipped arrow any kind of centralization is almost impossible. But with the introduction of metals, kingdoms are on the cards.[4]

In the case of the original kingdoms it was, according to Goody, the uneven distribution of raw materials which involved systems of exchange and often long-distance trade which therefore necessitated systems of control and security. Secondly, the processes of manufacturing the metal weapons were relatively complicated.

> In some areas of West Africa we find special kin-guilds of blacksmiths who hand down their traditions among their members; and in centralized groups such as Mossi the members of the guilds often have a special relationship with royalty, who are often their major patrons. But elsewhere (among the acephalous Lo-Dagaa, for example) smiths are not restricted. Even here, however, such individuals have a special role to play in the maintenance of peace, perhaps to counter-balance their role as manufacturers of arms.[5]

With the coming of the rifle in colonial Africa, and the tank in independent Africa, military elitism assumed an even sharper differentiation. The old days of military democracy, when everyone passed through the warrior-stage and the weapons were the simple ones capable of being manufactured by the warrior himself, were now replaced by the era of military professional specialists, with weapons requiring high technological skill to manufacture, and some specialized training to use. The Ugandan army might not have a monopoly of the legitimate use of armed force; it has even lost a monopoly of certain types of firearms partly because of theft from the armories themselves. But in the totality of concentrated technological power of destruction, the armed forces in an African country like Uganda are in a position to assert special rights of primacy.

Moreover, there is a built-in inclination on the part of the national army to engage in active prevention of separatism. It is true that there have been civil wars in Africa which have included the defection of important sectors of the armed forces to support regional or ethnic separatism. But even those civil wars themselves illustrate the compelling urge within the system either to save the territorial integrity of the country or to share its center of power to prevent a successful bid to secede. In the absense of external warfare and preparation for distant military adventures, national armed forces in Africa very often find a special sense of mission in seeking to keep intact the territories inherited. And, given the fact that Africa was in an age of post-spear combat, the capacity of national armies to maintain national integrity has been much enhanced by modest improvements in weaponry and military carriers.

Even as between different segments of the armed forces, slight differences in technological capability can be critical and decisive in affecting the fortunes of a coup. For example, the coup in Uganda was a victory of the mechanized batallion in control of armored vehicles, as against numerically more preponderant soldiers from Acholi and Lango in possession of less mobile weaponry. A minority segment of the armed forces in Uganda succeeded in outwitting the rest of the army, and in ejecting Milton Obote after eight years of power, simply because that relatively small segment had acquired technological superiority by preempting the control of armored vehicles.

But in Uganda, too, the political intervention of the armed forces has generated as a consequence separatist tendencies in areas that are insecure. Nevertheless, the propensity of the central army to maintain territorial integrity remains as effectively illustrated in Uganda's experience as elsewhere. And the technological superiority enjoyed by the forces of the center retains a critical relevance in the slow evolution of structures which seek to monopolize violence and centralize power.

ON SOLDIERS AND SOCIAL STRATIFICATION

But precisely because military technology puts such a substantial power differential on the side of the soldiers, the phenomenon has a profound relevance for the diversification of the class structure in independent Africa.

We must again emphasize that Africa approached independence with considerable evidence that it was evolving a power elite based on education. Some societies may have evolved an oligarchy based on birth and ascription, as indeed some African traditional societies have done. Other societies might have developed oligarchical systems based on wealth differentials, with the rich exercising power because they were rich. What seemed to be happening in Africa was the emergence of a class assuming critical areas of influence and prestige because it had acquired the skills of modern education.

The elite started by being, in part, the bureaucratic elite—as major positions in the civil service were rapidly Africanized, and the criteria for such Africanization included a high premium on modern Western education. But the emergence of an educated bureaucratic elite was accompanied by a slightly less educated political elite. The triumph of anti-colonial movements had thrust leaders into the forefront of affairs, but leaders who would not have attained such preeminence but for at least some basic exposure to modern schools. Indeed, many of the modern successful leaders, and certainly a high proportion of the politicians, were drawn from the schools where they had previously served as teachers. The modern educational system had served the cause of politics by contributing some of its pioneer African teachers to politics as a profession.

In East Africa the most prominent of these pioneers who were contributed to politics by the schools is President Julius Nyerere of Tanzania. Indeed, the President still carries the name *"Mwalimu,"* signifying teacher or mentor.

In a country like Uganda, the necessity of educational credentials for national politics was partly derived from the issue of language. Where political power was acquired through communication and interaction with a wide variety of groups, a lingua franca was necessary. The one which attained the status of a national language in Uganda gradually became the English language. A person could become a party official in the local constituency without a command of English. But he could not become a member of Parliament without a command of English. Moreover, the English language in Uganda was not normally acquired in the streets and the markets, but had to be acquired, in the majority of cases, through exposure to formal education.

It is true that one could reach the heights of political power without a high level of education. But there was no escaping the minimum command of the metropolitan language, and a certain flair for appearing to be educated. In brief, those African countries which did not have an indigenous language widely understood across different ethnic communities were indeed developing a system based on the primacy of the educated class.

It was in this kind of situation that Milton Obote, as President of Uganda, began to lament the inequalities which were evolving in the country and aspired to raise the mystique of the common man. In relation to the English language he was all too aware of its positive functions in some areas of national life. But he was also aware of its propensity toward conferring certain privileges on those who had acquired an adequate command of it. Obote noted that in the colonial period English was the language of the central administration in Uganda. Many Ugandans learned the English language in order to serve in the administration. That was in the days of imperial supremacy.

> It would appear that we are doing exactly the same; our policy to teach more English could in the long run just develop more power in the hands of those who speak English, and better economic status for those who know English. We say this because we do not see any possibility of our being able to get English known by half the population of Uganda within the next fifteen years. English, therefore, remains the national language in Uganda when at the same time it is a language that the minority of our people can use for political purposes to improve their own political positions. Some of our people can use it in order to improve their economic status.[6]

But, as we have indicated, there was one section of the population in Uganda, inter-ethnic in composition, which was not using English as the primary qualification for professional ascent. This section was the armed forces of Uganda. It was in the armed forces that Swahili played virtually its only official role in independent Uganda. The commanding heights of the military profession, unlike any other major profession in Uganda, did not require any special fluency in the English language. Skills of weaponry, courage and efficient military behavior, loyalty and discipline, counted for more than a command of the metropolitan language. And so the man who came to command the armed forces of Uganda rose to the rank of Major-General, and to the title of Commander of the Armed Forces, with little formal academic education behind him and limited eloquence in the English language. If Obote was looking for a model of social mobility which did not require a command of the metropolitan language, he had it right there in the barracks of his armed forces in Uganda.

Yet for a while the implications of this situation escaped the attention of President Obote, in spite of his commitment to the mystique of the common man. Obote was aware that education and Western culture continued to widen the gaps between certain sectors of Uganda's population. In his *Common Man's Charter,* Obote elaborated upon Benjamin Disraeli's concept of the "Two Nations." Disraeli had been concerned about the trend toward polarization in British society, as the nation continued to be divided into two essentially antagonistic "nations within the nation"—the poor versus the rich.

Obote's *Common Man's Charter* took the Disraeli analysis a stage further and related it to the local Ugandan situation. The worry in Uganda was not simply that of a division between the rich and the poor, but also a cultural division between those who had been exposed to Western culture and those who had retained traditional ways. Both forms of fragmentation needed to be arrested while the going was good.

> We cannot afford to build two nations within the territorial boundaries of Uganda: one rich, educated, African in appearance but mentally foreign, and the other, which constitutes the majority of the population, poor and illiterate.... We are convinced that from the standpoint of our history, not only our educational system inherited from pre-Independence days, but also the attitudes to modern commerce and industry and the position of a person in authority, in or outside Government, are creating a gap between the well-to-do on the one hand and the mass of people on the other. As the years go by, this gap will become wider and wider. The Move to the Left Strategy of this Charter aims at bridging the gap and arresting this development.[7]

In some societies some families were rich to begin with and through their wealth they became politically powerful, and through their power as well as their wealth they were able to provide their children with the best education available. But in Africa the trend of causation was reversed. It was through education, at least at certain levels, that some figures managed to enter Parliament and organize political parties; it was as a result of capturing political power that they, in turn, proceeded to make themselves rich. In this case, wealth came at the tail-end of the career afforded by political power; instead of political power emerging out of the support of wealth.

John F. Kennedy succeeded in being elected on a relatively simple and small majority partly because he had wealth in his family behind him. A poverty-stricken Irish Catholic family would not have stood a chance of riding to that presidential preeminence, regardless of the Harvard education which John F. Kennedy had had.

Milton Obote, on the other hand, or Kwame Nkrumah before him, started first by having at least a modest exposure to Western education before they could succeed in capturing national power. And it was, at best, only after capturing national power that they could consolidate their economic positions. In fact, Obote himself seemed to have done far less in consolidating his economic position than some of his colleagues in the Cabinet. But the main point to be grasped here is simply the reversal of the chain of causation. Economic achievement in Africa's first decade of independence is the fruit of political power rather than the seed from which it springs.

But Obote himself fell short of controlling his colleagues in their propensity to consume economically. His *Communication from the Chair* in April 1970 did attempt to curb the special privileges of the civil service. But the civil service was even better educated than the majority of the politicians. And the civil servants' morale could not be reassured if they were made to make sacrifices while ministers and other politicians continued to reap the rewards of their own political positions.

A song of the common man in Uganda continued to be sung in spite of these paradoxes and ironies. And then on January 25, 1971, a modestly educated Lugbara voice haltingly read out to the nation eighteen reasons why the army had taken over power. From a linguistic point of view, that voice which came across radio Uganda was indeed the authentic voice of the common man—probably coming from a peasant family in West Nile, with limited exposure to Westernism and formal education, and retaining his deep roots within the indigenous soil.

Not long afterwards a more educated voice, that of Chief Inspector Oryema of Police, announced that power had been taken over by the armed forces, the police concurred, and the man in charge was going to be Major-General Idi Amin. Again, from a linguistic point of view and in relation to standard of education, General Idi Amin sounded much more like a common man than ever Obote did. And from a cultural point of view he was more authentically African than the people whom the *Common Man's Charter* dismisses as "educated, African in appearance but mentally foreign."

In a sense which was at once glorious and tragic, Obote's song in honor of the common man had at last come to haunt him: that Lugbara voice on Radio Uganda enumerating the eighteen charges against the prophet of the common man, and then a new President for Uganda emerging from the womb of the countryside far from the capital, equipped with less than full primary education, and self-educated to some extent. The *lumpen militariat* had indeed staged their revolution.

FROM REBELLIOUS SOLDIERS TO
REVOLUTIONARY STRIKERS

This is what brings us to the third hypothesis in this discussion of military power and political efficacy. Marx has assumed that the common man or, to use his terms, the proletarian, would derive his revolutionary power from his position within the processes of production. Technology would be on the side of the workers in industrialized societies, though indirectly. The capitalists would have a special vested interest in improving the methods of production and enhancing their levels of profit. The factories and workshops, "the material forces of production," would therefore be undergoing improvement all the time. But in the very process of improving their technological efficiency the capitalists would be digging their own graves.

> The bourgeoisie cannot exist without constantly revolutionizing the instruments of production, and thereby the relations of production, and with them the whole relations of society. . . . The bourgeoisie, during its rule of scarce one hundred years, has created massive and more colossal productive forces than have all preceding generations together. Subjection of nature's forces to man, machinery, application of chemistry to industry and agriculture, steam navigation, railways, electric telegraphs, clearing of whole continents for cultivation, canalization of rivers, whole populations conjured out of the ground—what earlier century had even a presentiment that such productive forces slumbered in the lap of social labor?[8]

Technological change outstrips changes in relations between classes and between individuals engaged in the process of production. What Marx and Engels describe as "the epidemic of overproduction" begins to create revolutionary conditions. The revolutionary forces are, in fact, the productive forces, now too vast and extended to serve merely the interests of bourgeois property. The stage is set for an economic civil war.

> The weapons with which the bourgeoisie felled feudalism to the ground are now turned against the bourgeoisie itself. But not only had the bourgeoisie forged the weapons that bring death to itself; it has also called into existence the men who are to wield those weapons—the modern working class—the proletarians.[9]

In this Marxian picture of the emergence of the common man to supremacy there is, then, the insistence that ultimate power lies in the control of the forces of production. The forces are initially controlled through ownership, since the law gives the means of production to the bourgeoisie as their property. But gradually the means of production fall under the de facto control of socialized labor rather than legal ownership. The ownership principle is then challenged, and a domestic economic war seeks to resolve the disequilibrium which has taken place between technological progress and the lethargy of antiquated social relations.

It was Georges Sorel more than half a century later who made explicit the weapon of the general strike as the appropriate mode of the proletarian revolution. Sorel's theory of purposeful violence through industrial action was worked out with a conscious analogy to more conventional warfare. To Sorel the road to revolution is not through the control of the army, for the army is there to protect the state and the state to exploit the masses. As a Syndicalist he sees salvation through, first, a technological revolution strong enough to make capitalism vulnerable, and secondly, industrial action which seeks to bring a technological civilization to a halt.

Sorel then goes on to ridicule military writers who discuss the new methods of war which have been necessitated by the employment of troops "infinitely more numerous than those of Napoleon, equipped with arms much more deadly than those of this time"—and yet those same military writers do not imagine that wars could be decided in any other way than that of the Napoleonic battle. Nevertheless, those writers do have a point when they look at every battle and every skirmish as a preparation for a more decisive international confrontation.

> The revolutionary Syndicates argue about Socialist action exactly in the same manner as military writers argue about war; they restrict the whole of Socialism to the general strike; they look upon every combination as one that should culminate in this catastrophe; they see in each strike a reduced facsimile, an essay, a preparation for the great final upheaval.[10]

But Sorel, like Marx before him, is all too keenly aware of the precondition of technological advancement before industrial action can become a true revolutionary weapon. Until that happens it is not the control of the means of production which can be used to transform the balance of power in a particular society; it is the control of the means of destruction. It is, therefore, fitting that the gradual ideological legitimation of the skills of *war,* as against the skills of *work,* came to be undertaken by Marxists from less developed societies. The whole collection of schools of guerrilla warfare and radical organization for military purposes derives its inspiration precisely from the ambition to manipulate the skills of military combat against those who hold and wield the power. The range of such ideological positions in relatively underdeveloped countries is from the position taken by Mao Tse-Tung that power comes from the barrel of the gun to the views of Ernesto Che Guevara and his vision concerning the guerrilla genesis of the Cuban revolution.

In East Africa the nearest thing to a people's revolution so far has been the Zanzibar revolution. Again, control over the forces of destruction was a critical variable in the situation. The importance of technological advantage on a modest scale was grotesquely illustrated on that Isle of Cloves. John Okello, who spearheaded the revolution, had an army of his own. And yet, by Okello's account, his army did not come into possession of a single "modern weapon" until the attack on the government was initiated. The group skillfully approached the principal armory at Ziwani in Zanzibar. Okello claims that until he personally seized the rifle from the sentry guarding the armory, his soldiers were equipped with only bows and arrows, spears, and pangas. The armory made all the difference to the success of the confrontation with this age-old sultanate. The attackers had primordial weapons of bows and arrows; the government had a modern armory in readiness. The technological imbalance had to be either tilted or reduced before the attack could stand a chance.

The strategy for the tilting of the balance depended on *surprise*. When the little group had then overcome the guards at the armory, in a swift surprise move they proceeded to distribute arms and ammunition among the revolutionaries. "Thus, when dawn broke on Sunday morning [January 12, 1964], and reporters on the scene caught their first glimpse of the revolutionaries, they saw a fairly well equipped soldiery."[11]

Okello was later eased out of the power structure of the Zanzibar revolution and suffered indignity and detention in all three countries of East Africa. But the legacy of the barrel of the gun as the ultimate source of revolution was not forgotten in Zanzibar. Sheikh Abeid Karume, the leader of the Afro-Shirazi Party and the first Vice-President of the union between Zanzibar and Tanganyika, kept on reaffirming this. As we have mentioned elsewhere, Sheikh Karume often emphasized that it was through a violent confrontation that the people of Zanzibar and Pemba had won back their rights as human beings. "It is through the barrel of the gun that those rights will be upheld."[12]

The Zanzibar revolution itself had a demonstration effect on the mainland which culminated in the armed mutinies of 1964. But mutinies themselves were the first challenge of this kind from people who in other circumstances were regarded as drawn from the non-elite.

And then, on January 25, 1971, at last an army coup on the East African mainland took place. The successful combatants were, by comparison with the civilians they had overthrown, only modestly educated and indubitably non-Westernized. As we have indicated, they were, in relation to the whole movement of meritocracy in colonial and post-colonial Africa, people drawn from the semi-literate countryside rather than from the polished sophisticated Westernized elite. The barrel of the gun had once again asserted supremacy in a situation of technological underdevelopment.

THE EMBOURGEOISEMENT OF THE LUMPEN MILITARIAT

But the lumpen militariat is by definition an army which is under-professionalized. An internalization of professional norms, an adherence to a professional ethic, a readiness to submit with pride to a professional discipline—these are qualities still underdeveloped. In such a situation the assumption of political power carries the risk of the further deprofessionalization of the army.

As an ideal type, the professional politician needs the foundation of *popularity;* the professional soldier in combat needs to arouse *fear*. When soldiers become politicians, a conflict takes place between the demands of *political popularity* and the demands of *military awe*. In that very conflict lie special hazards.

Africa has had neither ideal types of political regimes nor ideal types of military regimes. But the theoretical issue posed between the claims of popularity and the claims of awe has been as central in Africa's political history recently as it was to Machiavelli in his advice to his Prince nearly five hundred years ago. Machiavelli had attempted a reconciliation between popularity and awe, but he preferred ultimately the techniques of fear. He said: "It is better and more secure . . . to be feared than beloved. . . . Yet a prince is to render himself awful in such sort that, if he gains not his subjects' love, he may escape their hatred; for to be feared and not hated are compatible enough."[13]

Machiavelli's preference for awe rested on its relative certainty, as contrasted with the fluctuations of popularity. The ways of winning the love of the populace are much less certain and psychologically more complicated than the means of arousing their fear. In the ultimate analysis, fear is a more basic and more primeval emotional condition than love. The ruler should, in the ultimate analysis, base his survival on techniques of fear rather than on those of popular acclaim.

Many an African politician after independence became Machiavellian at least to that extent. Many an African politician also instinctively operationalized Machiavelli's grand strategy of moralistic appearance and righteous image-building. As Machiavelli put it:

> It is not essential that a Prince should have all the good qualities . . . but it is most essential that he should seem to have them. Nay, I will venture to affirm that if he has them and practices them all, they are hurtful, whereas the appearance of having them is useful. Thus, it is well to seem merciful, faithful, human, religious and upright, and also to be so; but the mind should remain so balanced that were it needful not to be so, you should be able and know how to change to the contrary.[14]

Yet the emphasis which Machiavelli and African politicians have put on techniques of fear have constituted a borrowing from the world of military organization and warfare itself. It was Milton Obote, not Idi Amin, who began the militarization of Uganda's political system. Obote did this partly by treating the Baganda as a *conquered people* in a clearly military sense. He also did this by expanding the domain of fear as a strategy of political persuasion, complete with an elaborate system of internal informers and with a readiness to display military might as a method of silencing dissent. Baganda university students, wanting to march barefoot to the tombs of their kings in traditional mourning upon the death of Mutesa in 1969, were prevented from leaving the campus by a display of mechanized military might outside the main gate of

Makerere University. That small incident captured both the policy of treating the Baganda as a conquered people and the increasing tendency to use terror and insecurity as methods of silencing dissent. It was in this manner that Milton Obote initiated the militarization of Uganda's political system.

Nevertheless, the coup of January 1971 did change further the ratio between techniques of fear and techniques of popular persuasion. Obote as a politician had made his mark by starting from an ethos of popular persuasion; Amin as a soldier had started from an ethos of fear. Obote began to move from popular persuasion to the manipulation of fear. Would Amin move from the manipulation of fear to a quest for popularity?

The very first manifestations that a coup had taken place in January 25, 1971, lay in the soldiers' attitude to civilians. Kampala had echoed with firing through much of the preceding night and the following morning. Was all the shooting a coup in the making? Or was it a mutiny being suppressed? The first suspicion I had that the firing we had been hearing meant a coup came when a student arrived at my house from town. He was a non-resident student. Had he risked traveling through Kampala with all that firing? He said: "Yes. And what's more the soldiers are very nice to civilians. They are our friends."

I began to suspect that the army was about to assume supreme authority. Until January 25, 1971, the soldiers of Uganda had physical power and sometimes used that power strongly. They used it in 1966 in the confrontation with the Baganda; and they used it in December 1969 following the attempted assassination of President Obote. But at that time the army had power without accountability. They were trained in the techniques of maiming and killing, but not in the techniques of seeking acclamation. And since Uganda had not been involved in any war since independence, there had been few opportunities of winning popular acclamation as *military heroes*.

For many Ugandan soldiers the coup was their first moment of national heroism. But a coup is not a *system* of acclamation. It is an event. Once the event receded into history, the soldiers had once again to face the issue that their training had been for manipulating fear rather than manipulating love. Is there a way out?

In fact the slow experience of being held accountable may, in the long run, introduce new inhibitions in the behavior of soldiers. One good thing which may emerge out of Africa's agony of militarism might well be the moral socialization of African soldiers through the experience of public accountability.

But concurrently with that very experience is the gradual embourgeoisement of African soldiers as they acquire new life styles and new economic ambitions. Political analysts so far have focused on the *politicization* of African armies. What needs to be observed from now on is the *economicization* of those armies. The consequences of soldiers becoming political animals are different from the consequences of their becoming significant economic agents.

The idea of warriors acquiring the spoils of war is as old as war itself. In Africa the interaction between waging war and acquiring economic goods is still deeply embedded in the political cultures of some ethnic communities. Every year the Kenya government and the Uganda government examine afresh methods of controlling the border raids between the Turkana of Kenya and the Karamojong of Uganda for cattle.

To this extent, the idea of an African warrior being at the same time an economic agent is primordial. Its origins are indeed lost in the mists of antiquity.

And yet we must distinguish here between a vertical and a horizontal relationship between militarism and economics. A vertical relationship is a relationship of means and ends. The Turkana wage war *in order* to acquire cattle. Sometimes the "spoils" are only one of the reasons behind a war—and the spoils could as easily be colonies to rule as cattle to herd. In such cases the relationship between militarism and economics continues to be vertical—a relationship of means and ends, basically sequential.

A horizontal relationship, on the other hand, is a relationship of *parallel roles* rather than of functional sequence. In this relationship a soldier becomes at the same time a businessman, for example. His role as a soldier and his role as an entrepreneur are technically distinct, but in practice the two roles carry implications for each other. Unlike parallel lines in geometry, parallel social roles do not have to wait for infinity in order to establish some form of contact. When African soldiers become businessmen, an important dual process is initiated. It is this particular form of the economicization of African soldiers, which constitutes the gradual embourgeoisement of the old lumpen militariat.

The phenomenon is bound to have implications for the political system. In Uganda not all the implications of the expulsion of Asians are as yet calculable, but it seems almost certain that one important consequence of the de-Indianization of Uganda will be the rapid embourgeoisement of a significant section of the armed forces. The availability of easy terms for the acquisition of some of the Indian shops and industries has attracted not only African civilians but also African soldiers. Some soldiers may leave the army completely and try their luck in business. But more important for the political system will be those soldiers who remain soldiers and become shareholders or owners of businesses as a "sideline."

Will this further aggravate the crisis of professionalism in the Ugandan army? That is indeed one possibility. But at least as arguable is the reverse proposition. The entrepreneurial values in favor of stability and careful calculation could gradually help the process of reprofessionalizing the Ugandan army. Soldiers who themselves own shops will be more responsive to considerations of commercial stability than soldiers who see themselves in a relationship of "economic warfare" with alien or otherwise differentiated shopkeepers. The other entrepreneurial habits of thinking about profit and loss, the advantages and disadvantages of each successive venture, could in turn reintroduce into the military ethos the counterpart habits of strategy, tactic, and discipline. If the politicization of an African army aggravates the crisis of professionalism, the economicization of that same army could gradually help to restore the balance. As soldiers become part of the bourgeoisie, the control of the means of destruction becomes co-extensive with participation in the means of production.

But the Waswahili have a saying: *Jengo lilosimamishwa kwa mwezi, hwenda likalazwa mchana mmoja!"* (A structure which took a month to raise may be put to sleep in a day!). It does indeed take less time to destroy than to build. The negative consequences of politicizing the lumpen militariat in Africa may indeed need the balming influence of embourgeoisement—but treatment is a slower process than terror.

CONCLUSION

We began this chapter with a number of hypotheses. But the linking hypothesis might well be the assertion that the control over the means of destruction, the guns and the armored cars, was more decisive in a situation of technical underdevelopment than was the control over the means of production.

The final hypothesis we advanced was that the embourgeoisement of the militariat could help to restabilize the political system in a technologically underdeveloped country, partly by helping to reprofessionalize the armed forces, and partly by bridging that very dichotomy between the means of destruction and the means of production.

Marx has been at once vindicated and contradicted by Africa's experience. He has been vindicated in his assumption that the relevance of the means of production as a weapon for revolutionary efficacy comes when industrial sophistication has been achieved as a result of continuing investment in technical improvement. Marx has been contradicted in Africa by the emergent primacy of the military factor as a basis of power, overshadowing the economic domain in this regard.

It is, of course, arguable that both industrial action and the utilization of the machinegun are means of destruction. The former, bringing to a standstill technological civilization, was destructive of the ultimate purposes of productive capacity. The latter, by using gunpowder or nuclear power, was physically destructive of life and property. But both modes of revolutionary action were, in their ultimate animation, counter-creative.

And yet this equation overlooks the important distinction between withholding productivity, on the one hand, and unleashing destructiveness on the other. Industrial action and manipulation of economic power, as a form of political sabotage, is basically a case of withholding productivity, or jamming the processes of economic creativeness. But destroying a factory with cannon-fire, or throwing a grenade into a restaurant, or bringing a post office and a radio station under army control are different utilizations of power. They do entail a display of destructive power, rather than a display of productive power capable of being withheld at enormous costs.

George Sorel's ideas provided the intermediate link between these two forms of counter-creativeness. By looking upon the general strike as a mode of purposeful proletarian violence, Sorel was indeed seeking to obliterate the distinction between revolutionary efficacy based on the control of the means of production and revolutionary assertion springing from the powers of destructiveness. But even his attempt at obliterating this distinction has always had to presuppose a high degree of industrial sophistication.

> The Marxian theory of revolution supposes that capitalism while it is still in full swing, will be struck to the heart, when—having attained complete industrial efficiency—it has finally achieved its historical mission, and whilst the economic system is still a progressive one. . . . It is very important always to lay stress on the high degree of prosperity which industry must possess in order that the realization of Socialism may be possible. . . . The dependence of the revolution on the constant and rapid progress of industry must be demonstrated in a striking manner.[15]

But in a country like Uganda, the peasantry could not be expected to seize power. The urban workers proved to be no less vulnerable to the power of the state. They were increasingly bullied into discipline by the Obote regime, their Labour College for industrial training was abolished with ease, and they were compelled to enter into a consolidated trade union movement by a mere pronouncement from the Ministry of Labour. Neither the proletariat nor the peasantry in Uganda could use their economic roles as ways of forcing their wishes on the rest of the population or on the government. After all, subsistence agriculture in the countryside is not the kind of labor which could be wielded against the power structure. And the utilization of industrial countervailing power, so characteristic of the rise of collective bargaining in industrial Western countries, was distant from the political realities of a country like Uganda. Once again the common man had to resort to the barrel of the gun if he was to challenge the ultimate heights of power in a technologically backward country.[16]

Was the success of the lumpen militariat a change for the better? In one sense, socialists ought to applaud the victory of those who were once underprivileged. This is the aspect of socialism which judges a regime not by its performance but by the social origins from which the members of the regime are predominantly drawn.[17]

Yet the most painful of all leftist paradoxes will come when the performance of Africa's lumpen militariat is gradually improved through the stabilizing influence of its own embourgeoisement.

NOTES

1. See Chapter 5, pp. 85-86.
2. These issues are discussed more fully in Chapter 5 on the demilitarization of violence.
3. Statement by the Attorney General, *Uganda Argus,* March 19, 1971.
4. Jack Goody, *Technology, Tradition and the State in Africa* (London: Oxford University Press, 1971): 43-46.
5. Ibid.: 46.
6. Milton Obote, "Language and National Identification." Opening address delivered before a seminar on "Mass Media and Linguistic Communications in East Africa" held in Kampala from March 31 to April 3, 1967. The speech was published in *East Africa Journal,* 4, (April 1967).
7. Articles 21 and 22 of *The Common Man's Charter.*
8. Karl Marx and Friedrich Engels, *The Manifesto of the Communist Party.* The edition consulted is that edited by Lewis Feuer, *Marx and Engels: Basic Writings on Politics and Philosophy* (New York: Anchor Books, Doubleday, 1959): 10-12.
9. Ibid.: 13.
10. See Georges Sorel, *Reflections on Violence,* trans. by T. E. Hulme, with an introduction by Edward A. Shils (New York: Collier Books, 1967): 114, 119-120.
11. See Michael F. Lofchie, "Was Okello's Revolution a Conspiracy?" *Transition* 33 (October-November 1967): 37. See also John Okello, *Revolution in Zanzibar* (Nairobi: East African Publishing House, 1967): 30-34.
12. Reported in the *Uganda Argus,* February 7, 1968.
13. Consult chapters 7 and 8 of Niccolo Machiavelli, *The Prince* (1513).
14. Ibid.
15. Sorel, op. cit.: 92, 137.
16. Morris Janowitz discusses suggestively the relationship between technological innovation and military conservatism in the history of the armed forces in the West. See Janowitz, *The Professional Soldier: A Social and Political Portrait* (New York: Free Press of Glencoe, 1960): 24-35. In less developed countries Janowitz was once more optimistic about the innovative potential of the military. Consult Janowitz, *The Military in the Political Development of New Nations* (Chicago: University of Chicago Press, 1964).
17. For socialists a more congenial interpretation of Uganda events may be Michael Lofchie's "The Uganda Coup: Class Action by the Military," *Journal of Modern African Studies* 10, 1 (1972). Lofchie argues that the soldiers overthrew Obote because they were afraid of his socialism.

Section IV:

Leadership and Political Change

Chapter 8

THE MILITARIZATION OF CHARISMA

It has been noted quite often that Max Weber took the concept of *charisma* from the world of spiritual and religious experience and attempted to operationalize it within the domain of political leadership. The two central areas of experience associated with charisma have tended to be the world of religion and the world of politics.

And yet there is a third domain, quite obvious in its own way, which is also pertinent to charismatic phenomena. This is the world of warfare. Indeed, I hope to illustrate here that the military dimension, either direct or derivative, is at times the most fundamental aspect of charisma. The readiness of a people to follow in special situations, the hunger for deliverance from a real or imaginary "enemy," the impact of insecurity on the imaginations of people and the resultant responsiveness to a particular leader, are all intimately linked to an atmosphere of *combat*.

Yet, apart from passing references to the military factor in the charisma of such figures as Charles de Gaulle and Gamal Abdel Nasser, this dimension has received less attention than it deserves. There may be many more charismatic figures who are actual soldiers than the literature of the social sciences would seem to indicate. One major reason why the soldiers have not come to the fore and become conspicuous is the whole European tradition of civilian supremacy in politics. This tradition is indeed relatively new, but it has coincided with the periods of scholarly interest in charismatic leadership.

The European tradition of civilian supremacy in politics created a curtain between the populace and the charismatic leader. Civilian politics favors the non-military contender for national prominence. The qualities which were permitted to reveal themselves in the open political arena were military only

AUTHOR'S NOTE: The first draft of this paper was written at Makerere University, Kampala, under the stimulation of a number of colleagues whose own work included a special interest in political leadership. I am especially indebted to colleague D. L. Cohen for his unrelenting but stimulating criticism of my approach to the study of leadership.

[147]

in a derivative sense. The strong man who captures the imagination of the electorate, or of the city mob, still owes part of his success to the entire imagery of combat. But the civilian leader with this kind of style is a political warrior rather than a directly military one.

What might need to be investigated more thoroughly is the possibility of considerable charismatic impact within the armed forces themselves. There may be soldiers whose command on the loyalties and imagination of their men is derived from qualities which we would recognize in the civilian domain as clearly charismatic. But because of the Western conspiracy of civilian supremacy, militarized charisma in the literal sense has not always captured the attention of observers.

POLITICAL MASCULINITY AND CHARISMA

As an example of a charismatic figure drawn from the world of the new military organizations in Africa, and symbolizing a resurgence of the warrior tradition in African political culture, we are focusing here on General Idi Amin of Uganda. The choice may surprise some readers since Amin is still one of the most underrated leaders of Africa and one whose behavior has often been least understood.

A factor to bear in mind in the case of Amin is both the *cumulativeness* of charisma and its *perishability*. It is not always remembered that charisma, like power itself, is a matter of degrees. Just as leaders may have more or less power, they have more or less charisma. What is also too often forgotten is that charisma increases as well as declines. Since charisma is not simply a quality in a leader but also a particular relationship between the leader and his followers, situational factors could either enhance or diminish the leader's impact on his charismatic constituency.

A. R. and D. Willner may have carried the argument too far when they suggested that almost all leadership which elicits deference through personal impact is charismatic, but at least they grappled with the issue of degrees of charisma, even if not the issue of charismatic accumulation. Shils, on the other hand, handled aspects of the latter more effectively.[1]

Giovanni Sartori has warned us against conceptual "stretching" or "straining" in the study of comparative politics. And D. L. Cohen has made Sartori's warning more specific in relation to the concept of "charisma." Illustrating with David E. Apter's evaluation of Nkrumah from one scholarly work to the next, Cohen concluded as follows:

What we have seen in Apter's work on Ghana is a scholar, originally using a meaningful and theoretically interesting concept of charisma, borrowed directly from Weber, being driven, over time, to stretch the concept to such an extent that it loses any connotative specificity and becomes meaninglessly vague. From this usage there is little distance left before we reach the journalistic habit of using charisma to describe . . . any politician who manages to get one percent more of the vote than his opponent as a charismatic leader unless he is noticeably ugly, inarticulate or ill-mannered.[2]

As a general warning Sartori's and Cohen's criticism of conceptual stretching and straining in political science is well-taken. But an equally serious danger is *conceptual shrinkage*—an excessive preoccupation with "connotative specificity" which, if taken seriously, would impoverish rather than enrich the language of comparative politics and make comparison itself virtually impossible. There are more political figures with *some* degree of charisma than scholars like Cohen assume, though such scholars are right in warning us against charismatic proliferation.

When we relate charisma to the warrior tradition in Africa, there is one quality which demands particular attention. We call this quality *political masculinity.*

As a personal quality political masculinity is a powerful image of manliness in a political leader, which tends to affect his style of leadership and his impact on his followers. In February 1972 I visited Elmina Castle in Ghana—a castle built in 1482 by the Portuguese near Cape Coast. I was shown round the castle by a tall and broad policeman, who had learned a good deal about the history of the castle. In the course of the tour the policeman said to me: "You say you come from Uganda? I really like your General Amin. He is a real man."

What struck me was that across the continent in Ghana the manly image of the General, already evident within Uganda, had been perceived by an unknown policeman in Elmina Castle.

The political masculinity of the General does not lie merely in his size, though he is impressively tall and broad. Nor does it lie merely in his insistence that he fears no one but God. Yet these factors are part of the story, combined with the additional factor that an affirmation of fearlessness and an athletic build have indeed been part of the total picture of martial values within African political cultures.

The whole concept of manliness does indeed have points of contact with questions of self-defense and fearlessness. The dignity of the individual male citizen is sometimes conceived in militaristic terms in societies otherwise vastly different from each other. For many societies there has been something rather effeminate or infantile in being defenseless. Manliness has postulated a capacity to defend oneself physically. We note Jomo Kenyatta's reference to the paramount resolution of the young Kikuyu boys on initiation, as they affirmed their "courageous and fighting spirit, never to retreat or abandon our hope, or run away from our comrades."[3] In fact, the equation of manliness with a capacity to defend oneself physically brings the Constitution of the United States into a relationship of shared values with the Kikuyu. After all, the Second Amendment of the American Constitution guarantees "the right of the people to keep and bear arms."

Max Weber by no means overlooked the component of masculinity within charisma, but he did not push the analysis in this regard. Indeed, his sensitivity to this particular issue is virtually an aside as he discusses the routinization of charisma. Charisma has to be awakened or tested though it cannot be learned or taught. When a new person is to succeed a charismatic leader, the manliness of the successor has to be tested. Weber refers to "the magical and warrior asceticism of the men's house with initiation ceremonies and age groups." Weber goes on to note than an individual who has not "successfully gone through the initiation, remains a woman; that is, is excluded from the charismatic group." Weber also saw the relevance of military heroism for certain types of charismatic figures.[4]

In Africa the concept of initiation itself with regard to boys has included notions of manliness. Those African societies which have practiced circumcision ceremonies traditionally, or have adopted circumcision as a result of conversion to Islam, have often tended to transform the ceremony itself into a great test of masculinity.

In the case of General Amin, even his official polygamy helped to consolidate the image of manliness. General Amin was the first head of state in East Africa to be officially married to more than one woman and have all his four wives participate openly on ceremonial occasions of state. What was startling was not that Amin was an openly and officially polygamous President within his own region of the world, but that he was the only one. After all, polygamy is a widely accepted institution among the overwhelming majority of African societies. It is true that Christianity has resulted in a system by which the wife married in church becomes in effect the official wife. But even there it is possible to find important public figures with "unofficial" wives, sanctioned by customary law. But the heads of state continue to be sparing in their matrimonial adventures. A residual influence of the Christian missionary impact is precisely the type of political atmosphere which regards polygamous relationships as a political stigma. Even leaders like Kenyatta of Kenya—though traditionalist in some respects—have preferred to leave their matrimonial pluralism unofficial.

What General Amin did was to engage in a transvaluation of this particular value. Indeed, he even went as far at to make a nationalistic virtue of the four wives, asserting that they indicated how completely nontribalistic he was in his vision of the universe. After all, he had taken one wife from busoga, one from Lango, one from among the Lugbara, and a fourth wife from Buganda. Polygamy has been used as an instrument for national integration, as General Amin has scattered his Maker's image among the different ethnic groups of Uganda.

What seems to have emerged from Amin's official and sanctified promiscuity has been a strengthening, among the ordinary people, of his stature as a political he-man.

The image of prowess has been reinforced by Amin's sporting background, with special reference to his achievements in the ring as a boxing champion in Uganda. Boxing as a game is itself preeminently masculine, and a heavyweight champion acquired the extra impact of stature and build.

From quite early Amin evolved a charismatic hold on the loyalties of a sizable section of the Ugandan army, and this hold came to have great political consequences for the country as a whole. It has been so important partly because Amin's influence within the armed forces made President Obote delay for too long the question of whether or not General Amin should remain Chief of the General Staff. The other significant aspect has concerned Amin's preoccupation with the paramount necessity to maintain his image as a *man*. This preoccupation echoed Franklin D. Roosevelt's and John F. Kennedy's shared refrain that the only thing which Americans had to fear was fear itself. The worst thing which Idi Amin came to fear was perhaps truly fear—though he formulated his own fear of being afraid in terms of fearing no one but God.

THE DREAD OF COWARDICE

In December 1969 there was an attempt to assassinate President Obote as he emerged from a successful party conference at Lugogo Stadium in Kampala. Major-General Idi Amin was not present at this particular function of the party. When a number of his soldiers went to report the attempted assassination to him, and Amin from within saw them coming to his house, he mistook their intentions. He reportedly scrambled out of his residence, through a fence, and ran. Like Julius Nyerere when his army mutinied in 1964, Idi Amin decided discretion was the better part of valor. And just as Nyerere had been deeply disturbed by the experience of the mutinies and the need to go into hiding, so Amin was psychologically disturbed by that experience of having to run for his life. In the case of Amin, the greater was the humiliation because the men who were coming were, in fact, not coming to harm him but had come to get him to do his duty as commander of Uganda's army.

In the absence of adequate leadership immediately after the attempted assassination, Ugandan soldiers went about Kampala brutalizing the population. It took the action of the second-in-command, Brigadier Okoya, to finally restore the reins on the soldiers and get the bulk of them to return to the barracks. Apparently at considerable peril to himself, Okoya personally moved around the streets of Kampala in a bid to restore discipline among the soldiers.

When Okoya later discovered that Amin had actually gone into hiding, Okoya made sarcastic remarks concerning Amin's manliness. It appeared that Amin's image was badly damaged, or could be badly damaged, if large numbers of his own men accepted the story of his flight when a messenger came to report that a crisis had hit the country.

Was Amin afraid of being mistaken for a coward? Did this seal the fate of Brigadier Okoya? On January 25, 1970, Brigadier Okoya and his wife were murdered in the small town of Gulu in Northern Uganda. Who was responsible for the murder? Was it connected with the attempted assassination of Milton Obote the previous month?

My last conversation with Obote's head of intelligence, Akena Adoko, was in Mulago Hospital in Kampala. Akena had telephoned me from Mulago asking me to go and visit him at the hospital. He said he was slightly indisposed and wanted to have a chat with me.

In his room in the hospital, surrounded by work files of different kinds, Akena Adoko and I talked about a variety of issues. I then inquired about the rumor surrounding the name of General Amin.

Akena Adoko thought for a while and then decided to be communicative. He said they had arrested a number of Baganda "plotters" and some of these were clearly implicated in the murder of Brigadier Okoya. The allegation that was emerging from these suspects was that Amin in turn had been implicated in the Brigadier's assassination. The Baganda "plotters" asserted that they did the job after being given to understand that the murder had the backing of Major-General Amin. Akena admitted that no direct link apart from suspects' allegations had as yet been established, either between the murder and Amin, or indeed between the Baganda suspects and Amin. Who had employed those Baganda? Was there evidence that Amin had had any communication with them? Akena admitted to me in that conversation at Mulago Hospital that they had not yet found the missing link necessary to compromise Amin.

President Obote summoned Amin. He explained the allegations which had been made by those Baganda. Amin listened carefully, and then retorted, approximately in these terms:

"But sir, I have very well-trained men of my own capable of doing a job of this kind neatly and efficiently with no risk of discovery. Why should I go to the streets of Mengo (the capital of the former kingdom of Buganda) to look for Baganda to do the job? The Baganda's motives for such a job could not possibly be the same as mine. Their loyalty to me could not be assured. Why should I go and pick ordinary Baganda cut-throats for a job of this kind, when I have well-trained men of my own whose loyalty is to me and to no other extraneous considerations?"

Then Amin challenged Obote to produce the evidence. Amin said to his President that if he could produce evidence really incriminating Amin in the murder of Brigadier Okoya, he, Amin, would walk voluntarily on his own to Luzira Prison in Kampala and take the punishment which was due to him.

Akena Adoko admitted in that conversation with me that no further evidence of a persuasive kind had as yet emerged to implicate Amin. Akena was then silent for a minute or two, and I did not intrude into his thoughts. I just waited. Then he said softly, perhaps more to himself than to me: "Some people think they can control the army. They are wrong. The balance in the army is of such a kind that only Obote himself can control it."

And yet not even Obote felt confident enough to give Idi Amin the treatment he had given to Amin's predecessor as head of the army, Brigadier Opolot. Opolot had been removed from his position on suspicion of being implicated in a conspiracy with civilian groups directed against the President. Opolot came to spend five years in Luzira Prison. His removal from the headship of the army appeared to be neat and quick, and then he retreated into oblivion behind bars until General Amin released him after the Ugandan coup of January 1971.

If Opolot had been removed with such ease, why did Obote hesitate for a whole year when confronted with similar suspicions surrounding Idi Amin? In terms of the ethnic basis of the two soldiers within the armed forces, Opolot as an Atesot had in fact a more substantial ethnic following within the army than Amin as a Kakwa could claim to have at that time. Obote had been receiving from a variety of sources warnings concerning the loyalties of Amin. Growing doubts seemed to be entering into the calculations of Obote's intelligence service with regard to Amin's dependability. And yet, although Obote managed to remove Brigadier Opolot with such ease, Obote hesitated over the issue of getting rid of Amin until it was too late.

Indeed, as Amin then sought to restore his image as a fearless man, he started openly entering areas of national life which before were not regarded as proper for him. He started affirming the proposition "I fear no one but God"—clearly implying that he did not fear President Obote either. Amin also began to fraternize with that section of the Muslims of Uganda which had been under a political cloud for a while. Obote had succeeded in pushing into prominence a different group of the Muslims of Uganda and had managed to put into the leadership of that group, N.A.A.M., his own cousin Adoko Nekyon. The other side of this inter-Muslim controversy was known by the name of the Uganda Muslim Community, led by Prince Badru Kakungulu, an uncle of the late King of Buganda. Amin began to socialize and fraternize with the latter group openly, at times making speeches which were verging on the political.

It soon began to appear that a supreme game of survival was being played between General Amin and his commander-in-chief, President Obote. Why did Obote continue to hesitate? There is little doubt that Obote had a considerable following within the armed forces and retained substantive power behind the principle of civilian supremacy. Obote had certainly begun to take certain courses of action, reducing the areas of command that Amin had previously controlled and promoting certain individuals without consulting Amin. Amin, on the other hand, continued in what appeared to be an independent line.

Was Amin for a while put under house arrest by Obote? The facts are unclear on this, but there were certainly a lot of rumors in Uganda. Yet at a ceremony at Makerere University the soldier turned up (quite unexpectedly) to the applause of the students assembled there waiting for President Obote. Amin's strategy of restrained independence was beginning to capture the imagination of a civilian following as well as repairing the damaged image of fearlessness within the armed forces.

The question persists as to why Obote continued in fatal hesitation. It would be naive to suggest that Amin's survival in this contest between him and the President was entirely due to the loyalty which Amin could command through his charismatic influence within the armed forces. But it seems impossible to explain Amin's command of those loyalties during that period under Obote without taking Amin's simple charisma into account. The Uganda army was underprofessionalized. Loyalty was quite often either ethnic or charismatic. During this period there was no doubt that Obote had the power, in the sense of being able to exercise his authority and command obedience from the bulk of those under him. The ethnic composition of the army favored Obote more than Amin. But if power in this sense of ethnic support is to be contrasted with charisma, the contrast between Amin and Obote was, in part, a contest between Amin's charisma and Obote's wider ethnic base in the army. In addition, Obote was still President and had what Weber would call "legal-rational" power. Amin had a charismatic hold over a dangerously significant part of the army—and powerful Obote, in spite of ethnic and constitutional advantages, hesitated for too long. On January 25, 1971, while Milton Obote was attending a Commonwealth heads-of-government conference in Singapore, he was overthrown in Uganda, and Major-General Idi Amin assumed power as the new head of state. Uganda for the first time in the modern period acquired a charismatic head of state.

The first head of state after the departure of the British Governor-General was Sir Edward Mutesa. Mutesa had no personal charisma, though his office as king of the Baganda was an office steeped in routinized charisma. Obote, a brilliant tactician and one of the most gifted politicians modern Africa has produced, had achieved his political successes in spite of his lack of charismatic influence rather than because of it. But at last came Idi Amin, a national leader with the potentiality for personal magnetism, an immense personal presence, an embodiment of rugged, peasant, and masculine charisma.[5]

POLITICAL FRENZY AND THE HEROIC FANATIC

What should also be borne in mind is that charismatic leadership is often a process of interaction between the intellectual imbalance of the leader himself and the mental distress of the followers. The term "intellectual imbalance" is preferred to the term "mental imbalance" for the simple reason that the latter tends to connote a pathological state of mind, whereas an intellectual imbalance simply signifies a lack of proportion in certain perspectives and certain values embraced by the leader. At its most positive, intellectual imbalance is sometimes approved of as a state of "singlemindedness." But the distinction between being singleminded and being fanatically attached to a certain interpretation of reality is a nebulous one.

Robert C. Tucker has reminded us certainly of this tendency towards singlemindedness in charismatic leadership. He traces this singlemindedness to a peculiar sense of mission on the part of the leaders, combining a belief in a certain direction of change and in themselves as the leaders and instruments of that change.

> Needless to say, in the lives of most of these leaders—even those who do achieve success—there are moments of discouragement and despair when they and their cause seem to display such feelings in public. Rather, they show a stubborn self-confidence and faith in the movement's prospects of victory and success.[6]

Tucker goes on to suggest that this particular quality may be central to an understanding of charisma and its impact. The singlemindedness sometimes explains the extreme devotion and loyalty which such leaders often inspire in large numbers of their followers.

But why should this be so? This is what brings us to the second element in the interaction—the element of mental distress in the followers as they interact with the intellectual imbalance of the leader. Charismatic leadership thrives in situations of crisis and despair among large numbers of people.

Weber was again sensitive to this dimension of the environment for charismatic leaders. He traces their greatest success "in time of psychic, physical, economic, ethnical, religious, political distress"—and the charismatic figure helps to inspire "a devotion borne of distress and enthusiasm."[7]

Other writers have concretized this analysis with specific examples. Tucker himself speaks of Lenin's faith in his mission and in his role as an instrument of history, and the degree to which this faith was itself part of his hold over the hopes and emotions of others. Hadley Cantril has also explored the meaning of Hitler to the Germans in the 1930s.

> The message of Hitler, his own belief in the righteousness of his programme, his sincerity, and his faith in himself made an indelible impression on those who heard him. In a period of doubt and uncertainty, here was a speaker who did not argue the pros and cons of policies but who was fanatically self-confident.[8]

Mussolini was another example of a fanatic who captured the imagination of his people.

> In 1922, to a population that had lost sight of its aims and wills, that lacked faith in itself and was affected by a mass inferiority complex, that suffered from both real and imaginary ills, the idea of a saviour capable of bringing well-being to all by the sheer force of his will was not only appealing, it was a last hope. And Mussolini, saviour and superman, promised law and order, a full appreciation of victory and its worth, and Italy cured of poverty, restored to its worth, resuming its place among the great nations of Europe, and governed by youth and youthful energy.[9]

What we have in these examples is the critical interaction between the unbalanced intellect of the leader and the mental distress of the followers.

But the trouble with leaders that succeed quite early in capturing ultimate power is that there is, at least for a while, a period of bungling, of revised programs, or even of a volte-face or two. The leader could gradually stabilize his policies and help to consolidate his position. But there are moments when fanatical fervor combined with changeable ad hoc policies becomes an exercise in self-negation. This is a situation which could lead to diminution of charisma unless there are significant compensating payoffs.

A striking example in recent African experience was the fate of John Okello, the Ugandan from Lango who spearheaded the revolution in Zanzibar which overthrew the Arab Sultanate in January 1964. John Okello was a charismatic leader for a couple of weeks, before he retreated into oblivion. Okello was closer to Weber's conception of the charismatic leader than other Africans who have been attributed with those qualities. This is because charisma in Weberian terms does carry a strong element of irrationality about it. The charismatic leader tends to be messianic—and the compulsion of his personality on his followers is often psychic.

The issue with regard to leaders like Julius Nyerere of Tanzania and Kwame Nkrumah of Ghana had been whether civilian leaders such as they were capable of drawing from their stock of charisma the necessary power to command obedience from their soldiers. But with self-styled Field Marshal John Okello the issue was already beginning to be posed in Africa on how far this charismatic *warrior* could command the obedience of the civilian population at large.

How much of an impact did John Okello make on the masses of Zanzibar? It seems reasonable to suppose Okello was effective with the masses in Zanzibar for a while because, first, it was believed he had been *the* military instrument of the coup which overthrew the Sultan's regime; second, because he filled a kind of pan-African void among those island people; and thirdly, because his colorful character and rugged enthusiasm appealed to the masses.

Yet John Okello was later ousted with relative ease by Abeid Karume. Okello became persona non grata in mainland Tanzania, in Kenya, and even served periods of detention in Uganda. No revolutionary leader in contemporary African history fell so quickly into disrepute and then into total oblivion.

Why had Okello's charismatic frenzy evaporated so quickly? One reason might have been that people had begun to be afraid of John Okello. It is true that there have been leaders in history who have managed to command admiration as weel as inspire fear. Indeed, what is "awe" but a blend of reverence and timidity? Here then was John Okello—perhaps an adventurer in disguise, perhaps a visionary among pan-Africanists with a confused mission of racialistic socialism, but he came to be dreaded on the island he ostensibly liberated.

Why should such dread have neutralized charismatic authority? Because John Okello was feared not because of his strength but because of his weird unpredictability. In other words, he was too eccentric even for a messianic character—and it had become difficult to be a consistent admirer of his. The eccentric fluctuations of positions clashed with the original image of singleminded fanaticism. When excessive changeability seems to coexist with persistent fanaticism, the question must arise as to whether the leader shows symptoms of intellectual imbalance or the more pathological mental imbalance.[10]

Idi Amin, like John Okello, has shown signs of rugged enthusiasm and simple commitment. Idi Amin has lasted much longer in power and has controlled a more substantial country than John Okello managed to do. On some matters it is clear that Amin has a consistent perspective. Among these is a vision of a devout society, influenced ultimately by a fear of God. Amin's preoccupation with religious affairs has taken forms which range from establishing a special Department of Religious Affairs under a permanent secretary to organizing public conferences with bishops, archbishops, and Muslim leaders. The theme "I fear no one but God" became an aspect both of his fear of fear and of his genuine interest in God.

His preoccupation with the Asian question in Uganda has also been a fairly consistent theme in its broad outlines, though later there have been fluctuating policies on how to deal with it. People of Indian extraction had lived in Uganda for several generations and had become socially conspicuous in the professions and among executives in the world of commerce. Quite early in his reign President Amin began to discuss the Asian question. He was concerned about their social exclusiveness and inability to mix with other races very easily, just as he was concerned about their disproportionate share of economic power in Uganda. The theme of his preoccupation continued until the final crisis of August 1972 when he decided on a plan to de-Indianize Uganda. On the Asian question the combination between an underlying fanatic obstinacy, on the one hand, and fluctuating policy decisions, on the other, was well illustrated. There was little doubt about his stubborn desire to de-Indianize Uganda. But on what scale and at what pace? His first decision was that all the estimated 83,000 people descended from the Indian subcontinent were to go. These in fact included an estimated 23,000 who had taken out Ugandan citizenship.

A later clarification specified that all non-Ugandan Asians were to go. These were citizens of the United Kingdom, Pakistan, India, and Bangla Desh. Then a further clarification exempted a number of professional categories, ranging from managers of banks to doctors, teachers and lawyers. But then there appeared to be a reversal of this latter policy of exempting professionals with a decision that all non-citizen Asians were to go after all.

Yet the policy of expulsion came, fortunately, to be reversed within a few days for some. By Tuesday, August 22, 1972, General Amin had decided that those Asians who were Ugandan citizens could remain after all. But special precautions would be taken to ensure that those whose papers were defective, even if only technically and through an administrative oversight, would be liable to lose their citizenship.

What was consistent throughout much of that momentous month of decisions in Kampala in August 1972 was the underlying Indophobia. But the actual policies fluctuated with bewildering rapidity.

General Amin's charismatic hold on the population, even among simple and less sophisticated people, was endangered more by the changeability than by the fanaticism. As we indicated, charisma is not a permanent resource. A number of writers, starting from Weber himself, have referred to this perishable quality of charisma. In the words of Weber:

> By its very nature, the existence of charismatic authority is specifically unstable. The holder may forego his charisma; he may fall "forsaken by his God," as Jesus did on the cross; he may prove to his followers that "virtue is gone out of him." It is then that his mission in extinguished, and hope waits and searches for a new holder of charisma.[11]

David E. Apter, in discussing Nkrumah's charisma, has also referred to the perishability of this resource and gone on to add that declining charisma could result in rising despotism. In the words of Apter: "When charisma declines, the leader characteristically becomes a despotic, uneasy, and certainly undemocratic strong man.[12]

If tenacity is such an important aspect of charismatic authority, the leader who changes too rapidly could by that very process accelerate the erosion of his own charismatic impact.

"Frailty, thy name is woman!" Hamlet referred not simply to feminine weakness but also to a presumed feminine fickleness. If fickleness is a feminine attribute par excellence, a leader who values the image of masculinity cannot afford to betray too often a tendency to be fickle. The ladies may change their fashions and foibles, the length of dresses may fluctuate when permitted to do so, and the right of the woman to change her mind may even be institutionalized in at least some areas of domestic life. But if masculinity includes a premium on rugged tenacity, a military charismatic leader like General Idi Amin has more than just fear to be afraid of. It may even be that a charismatic figure of his kind has to be on guard against fickleness, frailty, as well as fear.

THE EXTERNALIZATION OF TERROR

What may for a while consolidate charisma is, paradoxically, a display of toughness and even ruthlessness. Amin's policy on the Asians within his ninety-day deadline showed elements of both fluidity and toughness in the face of mounting international protest. Amin would appear to be at one stage under the influence of the President of Zaire as the latter sought to persuade him to extend the deadline of expulsion. But before long Amin would disavow publicly any intention of extending the deadline and deny any such agreement. By the time the deadline ended and the last trickle of Uganda's alien Asian population found its way out of the country, the General assumed a new stature. His concept of "fearlessness" had been pushed to the extent of "taking on the world." On the Asian question he had pulled off an act of massive diplomatic daring.

But here one must distinguish between two aspects of Amin's behavior since he assumed power. One must distinguish between Amin's strategy of political survival, on the one hand, and Amin's image of the new Uganda, on the other. His image of the new Uganda took a little while to find shape and coherence. As a soldier under the British and later under Milton Obote he might not have had the inclination to determine the proper social and political directions for his country. Soldiers of his relatively limited formal education are not normally ideological animals. When Amin assumed power, it was probably with only a very rudimentary sense of what he wanted to do with that power in national terms.

The religious factor entered the scene quite early, and he evolved a relatively coherent approach towards creating an ecumenical state in which Protestants, Catholics, Muslims, and followers of African traditional religions could at least coexist as citizens of Uganda without some of the tensions which had previously torn them apart. As we indicated, Amin created a special department under the President's office for religious affairs and took concrete steps to end some of the more passionate divisions within the Protestant community and within the Muslim community. But apart from this commitment to religious unity as a solemn and simple concept, the soldier did not have a broad ideological sense of direction for his country.

His image of the new Uganda emerged partly through religion and partly through race. In his own rustic way, Amin was opposed to ethnic stratification in the Sudan, with the Arabs reigning supreme and the black Sudanese relatively underprivileged. Gradually Amin's dissatisfaction with ethnic stratification redirected itself at the Ugandan situation. His basic distrust of Asian traders and merchants had been there before he ever became the most powerful man in his country. But when he did have the power, he suddenly realized he was in a position to do something about that old prejudice. The prejudice was not devoid of a concrete objective base—it was indeed true that the Asians had a disproportionate share of important sectors of the Ugandan economy. It was even arguable that racial stratification in Uganda had persisted into independence, with the Asians constituting a disproportionate segment of the privileged classes. Amin acted upon this combination of prejudice and principle—and gave the ultimatum which led to the de-Indianization of Uganda.[13]

The normative universe of Idi Amin in the political sphere therefore borrowed from basic issues of race, ethnicity, and religion. Drawing from these elemental sensibilities, "Idi-ology," or the political beliefs of Idi Amin, gradually acquired coherence. The General wanted to go down in history as a man who helped Ugandans to become economic masters in their own house. It is not clear if Amin has the kind of skills needed to take these goals beyond the initial points of his own attempts. Certainly in the religious domain the General, partly because of his own limitations and partly because of the cumulative impact of the history of sectarianism in Uganda, may prove unequal to the task of consolidating religious amity. But at least the ambition has been an aspect of "Idi-ology" from the outset, even if the dreamer turns out to be unequal to the religious task he has imposed upon himself.

On the ambition to make Ugandans masters of their own economic destiny, this too can never be completed under his presidency even assuming he remains consistent and maintains power for quite a while. But there are elements in the situation created by him which, though initially painful and unjust, may in the long run provide part of the foundation of indigenous self-reliance in Uganda.[14] But while Amin's image of the new Uganda is at least defensible, Amin's strategy of political survival constitutes an externalization of his fear of fear. Amin has used terror in different forms as part of his claim to political survival. Preeminent among the techniques used under his regime is the technique of *disappearance.* Opponents and critics, real or presumed, have been known to disappear. These include Chief Justice Benedicto Kiwanuka, who was once Uganda's first Premier, was later President-General of the opposition party under Obote's government, was detained by Obote, released by Amin, and made Chief Justice by Amin. Kiwanuka was one of the most courageous, if not always prudent, individuals produced by modern Uganda. On a writ of habeas corpus in August 1972 he had ordered the release of a British national detained by the military—and went on to add that the soldiers had no right to detain individuals arbitrarily. With that courageous decision in his capacity as the judicial conscience of Uganda, Kiwanuka probably passed sentence of death on himself. The following month he was picked up from his own court, humiliated in the presence of his colleagues and staff, dragged out of the building and taken away in a car—never to be seen again.

Amin ordered a search and an investigation, disclaiming all knowledge of the whereabouts of Kiwanuka and claiming that he was in fact a victim of Obote's guerrillas who had infiltrated Uganda in order to embarrass the successor regime.

The technique of disappearance has certain advantages for Amin. The government can claim complete ignorance and blame the enemies of the state. Some ordinary citizens might believe the disclaimers, others might be terrorized. It is often the more sophisticated and better educated individuals that have disappeared in this manner. It is precisely these intellectuals and bureaucrats that the military regime would like to discipline and intimidate into adequate compliance. The better educated would know that the disappearances had meant death for those who were not seen any longer. The technique would therefore serve to keep the better educated quiet. On the other hand, the lesser educated may be confused and not always realize what was happening. Their loyalties towards the regime could also be consolidated by the possibility that the worst had indeed happened to the presumed enemies of that regime.

Amin's religious orientation, his belief both in Allah and in magic, has helped to condition his own self-image as a superman. No ordinary man has power over both life and death; a brutal man could have power at least to terminate life, though never to restore it. Disappearance creates an atmosphere of uncertaintly, an intermediacy between life and death because of that uncertainty. Is the victim alive or dead? The very fact that the question cannot conclusively be answered by the populace provides a lingering image of real power over life and death in the General himself. The rumors and speculations about whether particular individuals are in hiding or in their graves, including a number of the former ministers of the previous regime, help to deepen the mystery.

Can we be sure of the charismatic hold of General Amin in the face of such violence and intimidation? We can never be absolutely sure, but we should remember that such tactics have often been preeminently the tactics of charismatic leaders. Charisma flourishes best in situations of institutional fluidity and general uncertainty. Precisely because of that absence of adequate social anchorage, the populace is tempted to look to a superman. And the superman is in turn tempted to ensure that he remains in power by fair means or foul. James C. Davies captured the interaction between charisma and intimidation when he said:

> Charisma seems most likely to occur during periods when the force of neither tradition nor reason appears to be adequate to cope with mounting political crises. . . . The tendency of strongly charismatic leaders to seek power by the use of violence, intimidation, and fraud indicates their deep-seated reluctance to rely even primarily on persuasion and their recognition, perhaps, that in no society at any time can enough people be trusted to believe in the infallibility of any one man.[15]

In his own rustic ways Amin builds himself up into a superman both by continuous reference to being in direct communication with God and by the utilization of intimidation. Both the invocation of supernatural forces and the technique of intimidation—though not uniquely techniques of charismatic leaders—have often interacted with charismatic behavior.

> The tyrants in the Greek city states, Alexander the Great, and the succession of Roman Emperors starting with Augustus, were to some extent dependent on charisma for their rule. Augustus appears to have tolerated and unofficially encouraged the building of his popular image as a superhuman. Three centuries later the Emperor Aurelian had medals of himself struck with the inscription "Lord" and "God."[16]

Davies refers to more recent charismatic rulers, including Napoleon and Hitler, and again draws attention to the tendency to build up superhuman images as well as to utilize terror and intimidation.

In the case of Amin, the claims of being in communication with divine inspiration came into the open earlier than the full impact of his strategies of intimidation. In fact, at the time of the coup Amin acted with impressive magnanimity. Of course, all that shooting which went on from the night before the coup was announced until the afternoon of Amin's final triumph meant a good deal of fighting and killing between the soldiers themselves, between those who were loyal to Obote and those who were trying to assume authority. But, as we indicated in Chapter Six, the new regime's attitude to its *civilian* opponents was initially one of conciliation. Instead of killing some of the members of the previous government, as was done in the Nigerian coup of January 1966, or imprisoning the members of the previous government, as was done in the coup of Ghana in February 1966, Amin permitted many of the former ministers to stay in the most expensive and luxurious hotel in the country, known at the time as the Apolo Hotel, Kampala. He organized a well-publicized meeting with the ministers, more for a benign lecture at them than for humiliating or brutalizing them. He invited those who had accompanied the previous President, Milton Obote, to the conference in Singapore on the eve of the coup to return to Uganda and resume their jobs where appropriate. A number of administrators returned, some of them were even promoted. Obote himself was invited back as a private citizen if he wished. He did not respond to the offer.

Vice Chancellor Kalimuzo of Makerere University had been elevated to that position by Milton Obote a few months before the military coup. The appointment was primarily political. Now that the coup had taken place, there were forces within the Ugandan government which wanted the Vice-Chancellor sacked from his job or at least transferred to another position outside Makerere. Amin at that time resisted these pressures, arguing that there was to be no victimization. There was some victimization by civilian Baganda against civilian Baganda as retribution descended on those Baganda who had supported the previous regime. But even there the armed forces often intervened to save the supporters of the previous regime.

And then that great day when Obote's political detainees, some of whom had been in detention for five years or longer, were at last released in a public ceremony attended by thousands of enthusiastic and sometimes weeping Ugandans. There was little doubt that the strategy of Amin at the beginning of the coup, either by conviction or as a matter of Machiavellian calculation, was one of magnanimity and conciliation.

The argument that he was simply biding his time assumes that Amin had a coherent plan well in advance. It is easier to believe that Amin at the time had no long-term strategy, and that magnanimity was genuinely accepted by him as the best policy in his dealings with civilians. However, his ruthlessness toward his *military* opponents, former colleagues in the Army, was soon to reveal itself.

Clearly the Amin that allowed ministers of the government he had over-thrown to live luxuriously in January and February 1971 was not the same Amin that permitted them to be kidnapped and murdered in the second half of 1972. The Amin that had resisted ministerial pressures within his own government to sack Vice-Chancellor Frank Kalimuzo in February 1971 was not the Amin that denounced him as a spy for another country in August 1972 and then permitted Kalimuzo's abduction from his home on campus in September 1972, probably to his death. It remains as true as ever that Amin's military coup was characterized by a spirit of magnanimous conciliation toward potential civilian opponents. But the qualities of the coup are not necessarily the qualities of the second republic of Uganda. A coup is an *event,* a way of bringing someone to power. An election is an event, also a way of bringing someone into power. To say that an election is clean is not to say that the regime so elected will also remain clean. Even if it were demonstrated that Hitler captured power in a clean election in 1933, this would by no means demonstrate that his rule after he was in power was bound to be clean and constitutional.

In the case of Amin, he continued to be haunted by a sense of insecurity. He has combined at once a deep desire to be the ultimate symbol of valor in his country and a fear that he might be put to a humiliating fate if compromised. Like other charismatic figures before him, he seemed bedeviled by both ambition and insecurity. His fear of being mistaken for a coward resulted in flamboyant appearances in public without adequate protection against assassination. But in addition, he proved himself by deciding the fates of others. Amin demonstrated that he was fearless partly by making others fearful. He asserted himself as a symbol of valor—partly by sowing the seeds of cowardice in the rest of the population.

And yet in an important sense the man still remains a little bigger than life, a symbol of something important not only in Uganda's history but in Africa's. The colonial experience, as we indicated, had reduced Africa's capacity for manliness. The warrior tradition had been softened by a religion of turning the other cheek. A new atmosphere of intellectual and moral dependency had been created by a well-meaning conspiracy between the missionaries, the teachers in the new schools, and the colonial administrator. The demilitarization of Africa was in some respects also a demasculation of Africa.

In his own rough and brutal ways Idi Amin symbolizes a partial resurrection of the warrior tradition in African political culture. That tradition has its costs in humanitarian terms, but it also has its promise in terms of African rebellion against dependency and excessive orientation towards the West as a reference point.

Is Amin's charisma cumulative or perishable? It is certainly subject to both possibilities. If he maintains his symbolic meaning as a personification of rebirth of the warrior tradition in African political culture and perseveres in some of the policies he has initiated, the charismatic mystique might indeed find additional layers. On the other hand, if he returns to the fluctuations of his earlier period in office, or if he pushes the weapons of intimidation and brutality too far, his charismatic hold on the imaginations not only of Ugandans but also of other Africans elsewhere might diminish.

His fear of fear and his love for Africa are legitimate emotions and could be potentially creative. But they may need to be tamed, perhaps even softened, by an interest in humanity—without necessarily abandoning the warrior tradition.

CONCLUSION

We have attempted to remind ourselves in this paper that charisma is not merely rooted in man's religious and political experience. It also has a central affinity with martial values. Even those charismatic figures that are primarily civilian owe part of their power over the imagination of others to martial attributes and to an image of fitness for combat against hostile forces, real or imaginary. Charismatic leaders have indeed often also betrayed some signs of a persecution complex, all too prone to suspect conspiracy. The charismatic leader seeks to arouse a generally defensive mood among his followers, urging alertness against the evil forces of hostility and ill intention. The combination of conspiratorial, martial, and masculine values adds up to this whole process of the militarization of charisma.

We focused in this paper on an African case study, using General Idi Amin as a particularly fascinating example in this regard. But in the African situation there is the additional theme that the coming of military coups is itself a process by which African societies are getting remilitarized, though in fundamentally different ways. Before colonial rule many African societies included in their modes of education and patterns of authority a special focus on the warrior. Then the coming of colonial rule helped to demilitarize Africa. The superior technology of the imperial powers raised fundamental issues about the meaningfulness of being a spear-holding warrior in the old sense; the colonial powers were themselves committed to policies of general pacification; and the imperial system helped to inaugurate new patterns and styles of politics divorced from direct martial considerations.

The African meaning of Idi Amin may lie in his being a symbol of the rebirth of the warrior tradition. Relevant in Amin's case is the factor of *rugged* charisma, implying the harsh simplicity of peasant stock as well as the harsh discipline of a military career.

A certain earthiness entered the commanding heights of the polity in Uganda with the assumption of power by General Amin. The fear of fear sometimes interacted with a rugged acceptance of the ups and downs of sexual life. Prominent members of government and the armed forces were sometimes reprimanded openly and by name for seducing each other's wives and asked to be more disciplined in future. In a public meeting with thousands of university students at the main center of the city, the students were reprimanded by the President for the high incidence of venereal disease among them. He had seen a medical report indicating that a good number of Makerere students suffered from V.D.: "How can you then advise the youngsters and the elders if you yourselves are not clean? I want you to stop this habit."[17]

He then proceeded to advise the students to go for medical checkups lest they infect the whole population with gonorrhea.

The General also sometimes wondered whether the reports he received from some of his citizens against other citizens were not on occasion influenced by sexual jealousies between individuals. He has been known to tell an audience that some evil people informed wrongly against others. Maybe, the General said, a girl had rejected them, so they said she was keeping kondos in her house. "This is not good. I want only fact reports. If a girl refuses you—go to another girl!"[18]

This earthiness has been known to enter even his diplomatic style and has been known to interact with his fear of fear. In an elaborate telegram he sent to President Julius Nyerere of Tanzania, in response to Nyerere's public criticism of Amin's Asian policies, Amin taunted Nyerere for the day the latter had to go into hiding in the face of a military mutiny in Tanzania. This, as we indicated earlier, took place in 1964 when the soldiers mutinied for better terms of service and Nyerere had to hide. Amin claimed that Nyerere had hidden in the American Embassy while this went on.

Amin proceeded to suggest not only that Nyerere was a coward but that he aroused in Amin affectionate feelings of the kind a real man sometimes senses when confronted with a woman. In an incredibly earthy and startling statement, perhaps unprecedented in recent times as a remark from a President of one sovereign country to another, President Amin said to President Nyerere in that telegram.

> I want to assure you that I love you very much and if you had been a woman, I would have considered marrying you although your head is full of grey hair, but as you are a man that possibility does not arise.[19]

What all this does imply is this recurrent interplay of different factors of masculinity in Amin's rugged style of leadership. His fear of fear has at times found external manifestations in his will to terrorize others. It has intruded in affairs ranging from political abductions to recurrent claims about impending invasions from his neighbors. He doth bestride Uganda's narrow world like a colossus. Amin as a political he-man has, in that very fusion of masculine and martial values, captured the essence of rugged and militarized charisma. A Weberian warrior has cast his massive shadow across a point of the equator, and could only be adequately understood by a re-evaluation of the very concept of charismatic presence.[20]

NOTES

1. See A. R. and D. Willner, "The Rise and Role of Charismatic Leaders," *Annals of the American Academy of Political and Social Science* (1965): 77-88; E. A. Shils, "The Concentration and Dispersion of Charisma: Their Bearings on Economic Policy in Underdeveloped Countries," *World Politics* 1958.
2. D. L. Cohen, "The Concept of Charisma and the Analysis of Leadership," *Political Studies* 20, 3 (September 1972): 304. Apter's works cited by Cohen are *Ghana in Transition* (New York: Atheneum, 1963): 108, 218; *The Politics of Modernization* (Chicago: University of Chicago Press, 1965): 408; and "Nkrumah, Charisma and the Coup," *Daedalus* (Summer 1968). For a different interpretation see also L. Tiger, "Bureaucracy and Charisma in Ghana," *Journal of Asian and African Studies* 1 (1965): 14.26. Giovanni Sartori's strictures occur in his "Concept Misinformation in Comparative Politics," *American Political Science Review* (December 1970): 1033-53.
3. Jomo Kenyatta, *Facing Mount Kenya* (first published in 1938) (London: Secker and Warburg, 1939). The initiation ceremonies have been simplified since then.
4. Weber, *The Theory of Social and Economic Organization* (trans. by A. M.

Henderson and Talcott Parsons; ed. Talcott Parsons) (Oxford University Press, 1947): 364-73. Mattei Dogan refers to de Gaulle's military background in discussing his charisma. See Dogan's essay, "Charisma and the Breakdown of Traditional Alignments" in M. Dogan and R. Rose, *European Politics* (Boston: Little, Brown, 1971).

5. Dennis L. Cohen disputes the claim that Idi Amin has been a charismatic figure. But then Cohen's definition of charisma is so narrow that even Hitler has a hard time qualifying. See Cohen, "The Concept of Charisma and the Analysis of Leadership," op. cit.: 304-05.

6. The quotation from Tucker is from his paper "The Theory of Charismatic Leadership," published in *Daedalus: Journal of the American Academy of Arts and Sciences* 97, 3 (Summer 1968): 749. See also J. T. Marcus, "Transcendence and Charisma," *Western Political Quarterly* (March 1961): 236-42.

7. For Weber's definition of the charismatic situation, see *From Max Weber: Essays in Sociology*, trans. by H. H. Gerth and C. Wright Mills (New York, 1946): 245, 9. Gerth and Mills later elaborated on this definition by describing charismatic leaders as "self-appointed leaders who are followed by those who are in distress and who need to follow the leader because they believe him to be extraordinarily qualified." See *Daedalus*, ibid.: 52.

8. Hadley Cantril, *The Psychology of Social Movements* (New York, 1963): 235. I am indebted to Robert Tucker for bibliographical guidance on this theme. See also P. Berger, "Charisma and Religious Innovation: The Social Location of Israelite Prophecy," *American Sociological Review* (December 1963): 940-50.

9. Laura Fermi, *Mussolini* (Chicago, 1966): pp. 214-15. See also Peter Worsley, *The Trumpet Shall Sound* (Shocken Books, 1968).

10. For a discussion of John Okello in a similar context consult Donald Rothchild and Ali A. Mazrui, "The Soldier and the State in East Africa: Some Theoretical Conclusions on the Army Mutinies of 1964," *Western Political Quarterly* 20, 1 (March 1967) and reprinted as a chapter in Mazrui's book, *Violence and Thought: Essays on Social Tensions in Africa* (London: Longmans, 1969): 14-17.

11. *From Max Weber* op. cit., p. 248.

12. Apter, "Nkrumah, Charisma, and the Coup," *Daedalus*, op. cit., p. 764.

13. Consult Justin O'Brien, "General Amin and the Uganda Asians," *The Round Table* (London), January 1973; Jack D. Parson, "Africanizing Trade in Uganda: The Final Solution," *Africa Today* (Denver) 20, 1 (Winter 1973): 59-72; Yash Tandon, "The Crisis of the Jews of East Africa," Paper No. 124, Eighth Annual Conference, East African Universities Social Science Council, University of Nairobi, December 19-23, 1972; Ali A. Mazrui, "The De-Indianization of Uganda: Does It Now Require an Educational Revolution?" Eighth Annual Conference, East African Universities Social Science Council. For an older analysis of the predicament of the Asians of Kenya, and of some of the comparable issues of principle involved, consult Donald Rothchild, "Kenya's Minorities and the African Crisis over Citizenship," *Race* 19, 4 (1968): 421-437.

14. For my reservations concerning self-reliance when it is too strictly defined in racial terms see "Nation-Building and Race Building: Israel and Amin's Uganda as Racially Purist States," paper presented on the panel on "Economy and Culture in the Politics of Nation-Building," Ninth World Congress, International Political Science Association, Montreal, August 19-25, 1973.

15. James C. Davies, "Charisma in the 1952 Campaign," *American Political Science Review* 48 (December 1954): 1083-1086.

16. Ibid.

17. See *Uganda Argus,* August 22, 1972.

18. This formulation is cited in the *Sunday Times* (London), August 13, 1972, in an article entitled "Profile of Idi Amin, Uganda's Unpredictable Ruler: A Natural Sergeant."

19. See *Uganda Argus,* August 23, 1972.

20. Also worth consulting as theoretical formulations of charisma in African contexts are the following works: Thomas E. Dow, Jr., "The Role of Charisma in Modern African Development," *Social Forces* 46 (March 1968): 328-338; also Dow, "The Theory of Charisma," *Sociological Quarterly* 10 (Summer 1969): 306-318; W. E. Runciman, "Charismatic Legitimacy and One-Party Rule in Ghana," *Archives Européennes de Sociologie* 4 (1963): 148-165; Irving L. Horowitz, "Party Charisma: Political Practices and Principles," *Three Worlds of Development* (London: Oxford University Press, 1966): 225-246; Edward Shils, "Charisma, Order and Status," *American Sociological Review* 30 (April 1965): 199-213.

Chapter 9

THE TRANSFORMATION OF THE PRESIDENCY

The first President of Uganda, Sir Edward Mutesa, was a king. The third President, General Idi Amin, was a common man from the womb of the countryside. In between these two was President A. Milton Obote, descended from a chiefly family in Lango, educated at Makerere, and basically a member of the middle class. In the history of the presidency in Uganda so far we have, therefore, a process of structural democratization, starting with a king-President, then a President drawn from the middle classes and a chiefly house in Lango, and finally a President drawn from more humble origins.

We might here distinguish two forms of democratization—electoral democracy and structural democracy. Electoral democracy, as its name implies, entails the exercise of the vote and an expanding franchise. Sir Edward Mutesa was the first elected head of state in the history of Uganda, and so far the only one freely elected. He was, of course, elected by Parliament rather than directly by the population. Nevertheless, his was the only presidency which emerged out of a real interplay of political forces, competing for the highest office, and culminating in the choice of Mutesa as head of state. Before him was the Govenor-General, representative of the Queen and by definition, in this context, in non-elective office. After Mutesa was Obote, initially self-appointed as President following the Daudi Ocheng parliamentary motion of February 1966, but later confirmed by his hold over what remained of the Uganda People's Congress, and by the support he enjoyed at the time within the armed forces. We shall return to the Ocheng motion.

General Amin's presidency was born out of a military coup and therefore was again non-elective. If we define democracy by the yardstick of the electoral process we must, for the time being, regard the presidency of Mutesa as the most democratic in Uganda's history so far.

And yet we are faced with the paradox that this was the presidency of a king, descended from a line of kings of the Baganda, acquiring power and influence through hereditary privilege. Was the electoral process an adequate system of democratizing the presidency of Uganda? Should not the top man in the country be more typical of the population as a whole?

Here, then, we have two senses of being representative of the people. One sense is again the electoral sense whereby someone is chosen by the people and acquires his representativeness from the declared will of the people, either directly or through the elected representatives. In the case of Mutesa it was the elected representatives in Parliament who voted for him as President. This is the electoral sense of "representativeness."

But there is a structural sense of representativeness—not in the sense of a man elected by the people but in the sense of a man more typical of the rest of his country. This is what I call the structural sense of representativeness. The criteria are based on the structural composition of the society as a whole, and the leadership is considered representative if it reflects that structural composition of the society.

Nikita Khrushchev, in a campaign speech in a Soviet election in 1958, applied the structural criteria to the composition of the Congress of the United States and thereby managed to reveal that the composition was not democratic in the structural sense, even if it was highly democratic in the electoral sense. This is what Khrushchev said:

> Take the present composition of the United States Congress. Of the 531 Congressmen, more than half are lawyers and one quarter are employers and bankers. All of them are representatives of Big Business. How many workers are members of the United States Congress? There are no real workers in the American Congress. Or let us see how many ordinary farmers are members of the American Congress. There are no farmers either. Seventeen and a half million Negroes, or ten point four percent of the country's entire population, are citizens of the United States. How many Negroes have been elected to Congress? According to American sources, there are three Negroes in the United States Congress, or 0.56% of the total number of Congressmen. Or let us see how many women are members of the United States Congress. In all, seventeen women have been elected to Congress, or only 3%.[1]

What Khrushchev was saying was that the American Congress was not really representative of the composition of the American people. From a structural point of view, the composition of the American Congress needed to be really democratized.

If we now turn our eyes towards Uganda we find that the history of the presidency consists of a transition from electoral democracy to structural democracy. The transition has not been a conscious design, but the structural transformation is nevertheless real.

What should be remembered is that democratization in a structural sense has in turn been along three dimensions. One dimension concerns a change from ascription and hereditary succession to secular and competitive credentials for power. Mutesa became President of Uganda partly because he had inherited the throne of Buganda. He was elected by Parliament as President from a number of candidates, all of whom were traditional or neo-traditional rulers. As king of the Baganda, Mutesa's qualifications for the headship of state were therefore in part ascriptive and hereditary. Amin, on the other hand, became President of Uganda through a triumphant manipulation of military and political skills. The structural change in the presidency was from mystical credentials to naked cunning.

Another level of structural democratization involved a change from an educated President to a semi-literate one. Mutesa was a product of Cambridge University; Amin had hardly completed primary education. Mutesa was suave, sophisticated, and cosmopolitan, Amin came from the ranks of the barely literate.

The third level of structural democratization was *geo-ethnic*. Mutesa came from the heartland tribe of Uganda, the largest and most prosperous community; Amin came from a peripheral ethnic group on the outer borders with the Sudan and Zaire.

By a curious destiny, it was the military profession which narrowed the cultural gap between these two historically significant Ugandans. Let us therefore first turn briefly to their historical backgrounds before relating those backgrounds to the wider issues of social change in Uganda.

HISTORY IN UNIFORM

The first president of Uganda, Sir Edward Mutesa, was a soldier by honorary affiliation, by training, and by romantic aspiration. The third President of Uganda, General Idi Amin, is a soldier by training, experience, and lifelong profession.

It was in 1939 that Mutesa went through the initial ceremonies of coronation upon his father's death. When he later returned to Budo he had a new possession—the first rifle he ever owned. It was presented to him by the British resident, Tom Cox. Mutesa kept it in working order until the fateful year of 1966 in Uganda.

Mutesa's father was a captain under the British monarch—Captain Sir Daudi Chwa II. Amin's father is also reported to have had a military background. He was apparently a member of the King's African Rifles for a while and rose quite high during those difficult days. It was at about the age of 20 that Idi Amin himself joined the King's African Rifles as a private, with little formal education behind him. But he had qualities of leadership and sheer physical presence, great enough to win him rapid promotion to lance corporal, then to corporal, and then to sergeant.

In 1959 Idi Amin was promoted from sergeant-major to effendi, a rank which had been resurrected to provide new promotion opportunities for outstanding African soldiers.

Amin was then commissioned second-lieutenant in 1961, on the eve of Uganda's independence. With independence he became captain.

Captain was also a title which Mutesa acquired, but through a different career. Mutesa's finest military skill was his marksmanship. He was not using the rifle for military purposes, but he was acquiring proficiency in handling it. It was in 1945 that he left Makerere to go to Cambridge in England. His greatest success at Magdalene was, in fact, with the rifle. In his second year at the College he won the shooting cup for Magdalene with the best individual score.

He joined the Cambridge Officers' Corps soon after arrival at the University and became an officer. His enthusiasm for shooting practice was tested in the severe winter of 1946-47. Mutesa insisted on going to practice at the range and won a revolver shooting competition.

He then formally applied to join the army, specifying the Grenadier Guards as his first choice. He was interviewed by a lieutenant-colonel and then was accepted. It was King George VI who, as a personal gesture of good-will, suggested that Mutesa be made a captain. Mutesa went to Buckingham Palace for the ceremony.

> Though I had been kindly given my rank, I had now to earn it. This I proceeded to do at the Victoria Barracks, at Windsor, and at Caterham and at Warminster. My liking for uniforms and pleasure in being smartly turned out were an asset. My unpunctuality was, temporarily, cured. At Windsor we were on parade at 8 a.m., when we were drilled. Then it was our turn to shout orders, which is harder work still. If your voice did not reach what the drill sergeant considered sufficient volume, he would tell your squad to carry on even if they were heading for a brick wall and therefore total chaos. The rest of this course, which was specially designed for training young officers, consisted mainly of weapon training and a knowledge of such things as first-aid.[2]

While Amin had later claimed service experience in Burma, Mutesa seriously considered the possibility of going to Malaya with the 3rd Battalion of the Grenadier Guards. But Mutesa's commanding officer summoned him and told him that the choice was between Mutesa returning home to his people or electing there and then to remain in the army. Of course, although Mutesa later spent many years unwillingly away from his people, there was no question of actually electing a military career instead of the kabakaship. Nevertheless, Mutesa did sometimes wish it were otherwise. As he came to put it twenty years later: "If it had been possible, I think I should have been a soldier. Certainly I had enjoyed these months as much as any."[3]

The outbreak of World War II took place in the same year as the coronation of Mutesa. But before he died Sir Daudi Chwa had issued a proclamation allowing the Baganda to volunteer for war service. Other Ugandans also participated. Mutesa was himself keen to join up, but his Regents and the Governor would not entertain the possibility. A division of the King's African Rifles was sent to Burma. Was Idi Amin among them? Certainly Lincoln Nddaula, the Kabaka's brother, was.[4]

Two decades later Uganda was independent, and by 1963 Mutesa was commander-in-chief of the armed forces of independent Uganda. This was the year that Idi Amin was promoted to the rank of major. The following year witnessed the mutinies in East Africa, followed by the replacement of British officers which thus accelerated promotions for Ugandans. Idi Amin became Colonel Amin and held the post of deputy commander. Then began the rather uncanny series of "25th Januarys" in the history of independent Uganda.

In was on January 25, 1964, that British troops disarmed the mutineers at the Jinja armory, and restored civilian supremacy in Uganda. It was on January 25, 1966, that Daudi Ocheng began to elaborate on his charges of corruption against members of the Uganda government, implicating Idi Amin, and later Obote and Ministers Onama and Nekyon. The UPC Parliamentary group met on January 31 and decided to reject Ocheng's motion, recommending the suspension of Idi Amin pending an investigation. The fateful motion, which later encompassed the head of government himself, did not come before Parliament until February 4, 1966. But what needs to be noted here for the time being is the simple fact that the January 25, 1966, fell within the stream of accusations which culminated in the Ocheng charges in Parliament accusing Amin and Obote of corruption and misappropriation for personal use of gold and ivory from Zaire (then the Congo). This in turn precipitated the entire Uganda crisis of 1966.

Then came January 25, 1970, when Brigadier Ocoya was murdered on that day in Gulu together with his wife. He was the second highest ranking officer after Amin by that time.

Finally came January 25, 1971, when the armed forces of Uganda at last terminated the rule of Milton Obote and established a military government in Uganda with a technocratic cabinet.

It was, of course, the 1966 crisis which led to the detention of the former commander of the army, Brigadier Opolot, and the assumption of the army command by Amin. Until then Amin had been deputy commander. As deputy commander he had comparatively limited contact with President Mutesa. Mutesa himself believed that Obote had specifically asked Amin never to approach Mutesa, although the latter was, in fact, his commander-in-chief. If a meeting was necessary between Colonel Amin and President Mutesa, only Prime Minister Obote could determine that necessity. Amin, in other words, was to have no dealings with Mutesa without the express permission of Obote.

On the lighter side of their relationship, Amin had made an impact on Mutesa when he had been to the Palace informally and Mutesa had watched him box. Way back in his Cambridge days in the 1940s Mutesa had himself boxed for his college, Magdalene, at Cambridge. Amin's interests in other sports also appealed to the aristocratic instincts of Mutesa. Amin was an accomplished Rugby player, a game of great significance in the history of British public schools and in its effect on the British ruling elite. In his youthful days in England Mutesa had found that games were his first source of friends. His interest in boxing, shooting, and riding prepared him to appreciate the sporty side of Amin; in Mutesa's own words: "Amin was a comparatively simple, tough character. He had been to the Palace, and I had watched him box, which he did efficiently."[5]

Already the difference between the king and the boxing champion was a difference between hereditary status and acquired rank. But then came 1966, and the ultimate confrontation at the Palace between Obote's forces and the Kabaka's guards. Did Amin command the attack on the Palace? Mutesa's answer went thus: "I did not see Colonel Amin, but I expect he was in command. Obote remained well away from the scene."[6]

What Mutesa was suggesting was that Obote, having ordered Amin to attack the Palace, then allowed himself to enjoy the relative security of distance from the battle-ground. Mutesa conceded that Amin as a soldier under civilian authority had to obey commands. He was in the same position as those soldiers in Kenya during the Mau-Mau insurrection who obeyed the command of the colonial authorities to control or suppress the rebellion in Kikuyuland.

If Mutesa himself had been allowed to go to Malaya as a soldier after the end of World War II, he might have had to shoot Malay Communists. What did a Muganda have to do with a left-wing insurrection in Malaya? Very little—except that he who joins an army accepts to carry out the orders of his superior officers as far as is honorably possible. There is no doubt that the third President of Uganda had participated in the ouster of the first.

But even those who continued to feel that Amin should not have participated in the attack on King Mutesa's palace, the Lubiri, had to bear in mind that nation-building required a capacity to be selective in what one remembered. It was the French philosopher Ernest Renan who in 1882 wrote an essay entitled "What is a Nation?", and then proceeded to observe that one essential factor in the making of a nation is "to get one's history wrong." In an exaggerated way Renan was making a basic point not only about successful nationhood but also about successful marriage. The secret of successful marriage over a long span of time is to know what old quarrel to forget.

Such considerations are indeed at play in nation-building and in relations between groups generally. Accord between those groups necessitates a cultivated ability to emphasize the positive aspects of their relationship and try to control and underplay the negative aspects.

There are a number of things in Buganda's relations with her neighbors which need to be forgotten. There is a history of arrogance and cruelty by the Baganda and among the Baganda. There is also a history of aggression and cruelty against the Baganda. It can indeed be argued persuasively that Uganda is an impossible country to govern with the support of the Baganda, but it is also impossible to govern effectively without the support of the Baganda. There are, in other words, seeds of profound discord between Buganda and some of her neighbors. And yet the process of nation-building in Uganda cannot really start without recognizing the importance of this central cleavage. The first major destination in the process of national integration in Uganda must therefore be a struggle to make it no longer true that Uganda is ungovernable with or without the Baganda.

So far the military regime which has come into being since January 25, 1971, has attempted to keep the balance between, on the one hand, conciliating the Baganda and, on the other, stopping short of giving them their greatest desire of all. Although now no longer publicly discussed, the biggest ambition among the Baganda is probably still the restoration of the monarchy, and the military government has continued to resist pressures in this direction. There are clear dangers of alienating other parts of the country if this particular wish of the Baganda were to be too hastily granted. The military government would, by such restoration, ensure that it had the support of the Baganda but at the serious risk of losing support elsewhere. On the other hand, Uganda is equally ungovernable without the Baganda, and so any denial of passionate requests from the Baganda has to be done in a conciliatory move. Concessions of a significant kind have to be given. Sometimes the concessions may be little more than granting certain ceremonial rights to the Baganda. But even more dramatic was Amin's concession to bring the body of Sir Edward Mutesa back to Uganda from its burial place in England.

History very often has its surprises. The life history of Sir Edward was itself a game in surprises. After the attack on his Palace in 1966, many thought he had died. *The Daily Express* in London carried the headline "King Freddy is dead." As Mutesa himself was struggling through the bushes to safety before he left Buganda, he was often afraid of being mistaken for a ghost by his own supporters, leading to screams which might result in his being discovered.

In 1966 when they expected him to have died, Mutesa had lived. In 1969 when they expected him to live, he had died.

Mutesa died in London after making plans for the celebration of his birthday the following day. His sense of order was again striking. It was on November 22, 1939, that the Katikiro of Buganda announced: "The fire of Buganda is extinguished. Our beloved Kabaka, His Highness, Sir Daudi Chwa, released his hold on the shield at seven o'clock this morning."

Exactly thirty years later to the day, November 22, 1969, Mutesa symbolically released his own hold on the shield in England. That uncanny habit of Uganda's historical dates to play games of coincidence was once again at work.

Yet the very place of his death was symbolic when seen in the total circumstances of Mutesa's life. Mutesa came to have one funeral in London and another in Kampala and Mengo. Two funerals for one man. Between England and Buganda Mutesa had shared his life. And then between England and Uganda he came to share his death. This duality of Mutesa's cultural affiliation brings us to the second dimension of structural democratization in Uganda—the transition from a suave and highly Westernized President, on the one hand, to a semi-literate head of state, on the other.

In Mutesa we had a trans-cultural man, a figure of cultural continuity. He represented the forging of two national cultures in one person. In this case the man is symbolic of Africa's predicament, in the sense of intermingling between indigenous traditions and the imported British heritage.

There is no doubt that Mutesa was a man of two worlds in this sense. Even his eligibility for the kabakaship presupposed his being sufficiently anglicized to be able to talk in terms of equality with the British and protect the autonomy of Buganda. The choice of the Kabaka was to be made by the Lukiiko. We know that the Kabaka did not need to be the eldest son of the king he succeeded. Certainly Mutesa was not. Nor did the Kabaka need to be a legitimate son of his father's, though Mutesa was indeed legitimate. The father's own preference before his death did count for a lot, and Mutesa's father had indicated his preference for Mutesa. But an English education, either given locally in Uganda or administered in England, was deemed, by the time of Mutesa's succession, to be an important precondition for the effective discharge of the Kabaka's duties. Mutesa himself in his book

Desecration of My Kingdom assures us that, important as an English education was, it was not "conclusive":

> During his life a Kabaka may hint as subtly or blatantly as he wishes as to whom he personally favours, and such hints may well carry weight, but he cannot will the Kabakaship as you will a possession. I think my father did drop such hints, and it is true that I had an English tutor, as he had done, but this was by no means conclusive—my eldest brother, for example, was educated in England.[7]

In an important sense the kabakaship had already become an Anglo-African institution, and the English language as a precondition for effective kabakaship was an important element in this trend towards biculturalism.

The English language became important also for membership of the Ugandan Parliament as independence approached and was in any case a major factor in the political culture of Uganda as a whole. Milton Obote lamented when he was President about the impact of the English language on Uganda as a society, pointing out that it tended to stratify society into those who spoke the language well and therefore had access to certain advantages, and those who did not speak it well and were thereby handicapped. Mastery of the English language had become a basis for a new form of aristocratic privilege—until the army coup of January 25, 1971. English will remain important in independent Uganda both in politics and outside politics. But one of the consequences of the army coup lay in destroying the myth that a high political position could not be effectively held without the command of a foreign language. There are other qualities for leadership apart from linguistic versatility and very often those others might be much more important.

Both in Uganda and elsewhere in East Africa Muslims have lagged behind in education. One of the major reasons was simply the massive role which Christian missionaries played in education in East Africa. Many Muslim parents were afraid of sending their children to missionary schools, out of understandable fears that the ultimate purpose of Christian missionary activity was to Christianize Africans. The Kakwa as a tribe have large numbers of Muslims, like my own Swahili people in Mombasa. All African Muslims were profoundly suspicious of missionary schools, and their educational and linguistic qualifications have been affected by that.

In Buganda Mutesa had also noticed this lag and had become aware that there were fewer Muslims with a good command of the metropolitan language than either Protestants or Catholics. It was against the background of this simple fact that the king and I first met.

It was early in the 1950s that the late Kabaka Mutesa II of Buganda paid a visit to the Mombasa Institute of Muslim Education in Kenya. He arrived there after sunset with his entourage, but without notice to the institution.

No special arrangements had been made to receive him and his group. I received a phone call from his host in town indicating that the group was coming to the Institute. The Institute, built in Arabian style in the immediate suburbs of Mombasa, constituted at the time one of the show places of the town. My own position in it then was that of boarding supervisor, a position somewhat comparable to that of a warden in a hall of residence. I was, therefore, available at night when the Kabaka and his group came to visit the Institute. I showed them round some of the major sections of the educational institution, and then tried to entertain them to some non-alcoholic Muslim refreshments in my modest apartment.

Many years later I discovered that one of the things which had impressed the Kabaka's group was the phenomenon of a young Muslim speaking English so "fluently." Apparently the Kabaka on his return to Buganda recounted this episode. More than ten years after the event I was myself a resident in Uganda and was introduced to one of the Muslim members of the Buganda royal house. This was Prince Badru Kakungulu, a leader of the Muslim community and an uncle of Mutesa. When it was explained to the Prince who I was, complete with my family background, his eyes brightened up. He remembered so late in the day the comments made by the Kabaka and his group about a young Muslim in Mombasa who spoke English fairly fluently. The Prince himself had been a member of that group at the Mombasa Institute of Muslim Education.[8]

But it was not, of course, merely the command of the English language which made Mutesa a trans-national figure; otherwise large numbers of educated Africans might have to be fitted into that category. Mutesa did not simply have a command of the English language; he was in addition profoundly anglicized. The special tutoring he had in English ways, the long contacts with members of the British upper class, even the additional attention he received at King's College Budo and at Makerere College all contributed towards the foundation of Mutesa's deep acculturation.

Both his education and his political career came to add further dimensions to his trans-nationality. His education at Makerere was interrupted to make it possible for him to go to Cambridge. This decision was taken partly by Oxford Englishmen—the Governor, Sir John Hall, and George Turner, the principal of Makerere College at the time. The British old-boy network played its part.

Ernest Haddon, a friend of my father's and a lifelong friend of mine, was returning to live at Cambridge, as he still does, and George Turner had a brother who was a don at Magdalene and subsequently my tutor. These were, I think, the deciding factors [behind the choice of Cambridge].[9]

Again the continued contacts with the British upper classes deepened this exposure further. A particularly memorable occasion for him was when George VI suggested to the Grenadier Guards that Mutesa be made a Captain of the Guards. Mutesa went along to Buckingham Palace for the ceremony. Mutesa was a little nervous but he had been well briefed. He held his cap properly under his arm, saluted the King at the right moment and, "a nice point of etiquette in which I had been instructed, when we were talking afterwards I accepted a cigarette the King offered me. To refuse, I had been told, might seem hypocritical, as I was a known smoker. I almost finished it when he recalled his own visit to Uganda as Duke of York and memories of my father.[10]

But it was not merely his education, including an exposure to some military training, which linked Mutesa to England. Politics also came to play their part. He was exiled twice to England, first in 1953 in a confrontation with the British Governor, Sir Andrew Cohen. The confrontation was, in part, connected with questions of Buganda's autonomy in relation to the British, and also Uganda's autonomy in relation to Kenya settlers. The precipitating factor had been a speech by the Colonial Secretary which seemed to recommend the formation of an East African federation which, in the circumstances of the day, would have meant greater settler say in Ugandan affairs. Buganda reacted sharply to this speech, and before long there was a fusion between the issue of Buganda's rights as against the Governor and Uganda's rights as against white settler dreams of an East African federation.

Sir Andrew Cohen sent him into exile, ostensibly forever. Mutesa lived in England, partly in comfortable respite and partly in continuing agitation for his return to his people. His first year was very unhappy, but it was also deepening his love for England. By the time he was being recalled to return to his people, he knew what he would miss. He recalled:

> It can never be pleasant to be an exile. My first year was miserable, though I was living a life that must have looked easy and luxurious from a distance. As the certainty that I should return grew, however, my love for England was able to struggle with my pain at being forced away from Uganda.[11]

It was also partly because of this experience that he began to feel very much like what he called himself—a "liaison" between England and Uganda.

The capacity of the Baganda to be deeply anglicized and at the same time profoundly traditionalist remains one of the fascinating aspects of these people. Sometimes it is the Africans who have completely abandoned their roots who become particularly hostile to foreign influences and Western ways. Their own abandonment of their roots creates a sense of insecurity, and a struggle starts to recapture a little of the mystique of the past. Some of us turn to a dress which is clearly less Western in trying to reassure ourselves that we are indeed different and more than black Europeans. Others use alternative gimmicks, like libation in Ghana at the ceremony which is otherwise Western, or an extramural lecture denouncing Western cultural imperialism. Many of these elements ranging from the wearing of Kitenge shirts to writing *Song of Lawino* are indications of a cultural complex—westernized African intellectuals not yet completely at peace with themselves. But many Baganda have been different. They have shown no great evidence of anglo-phobia nor ritualistic rejection of British ways. On the contrary, their taste in dress is sometimes singularly British. The Kabaka or king wore a kanzu at times, the Nabagareka or queen wore a basuti at times. They could wear their own national dress with elegance, while they were also capable of wearing Western dress with striking fastidiousness. It was Professor Lloyd A. Fallers, former director of the East African Institute of Social Research and later Professor at the University of Chicago, who once wrote:

> One of the striking characteristics of the Baganda is their ability to wear western clothing with a real feeling for style. Over much of Africa, western clothing is worn like an uncomfortable ill fitting uniform, but Baganda men and women have penetrated sufficiently into the inner recesses of western style that many of them can wear Western clothes with real taste. . . . The Kabaka himself is an elegantly-tailored, Cambridge-educated young gentleman who speaks flawless English.[12]

What should be remembered is that Westernization differentiated Amin not only from Mutesa but also from Obote. It is to this stage in the democratization process that we must now turn.

THE COMING OF THE COMMON MAN

The voice which most consistently sang the song of the common man was the voice of Apolo Milton Obote, the middle-class President from a chiefly family in Lango District. Contrary to certain assumptions, Obote did not start speaking about the common man on the eve of his "move to the left." He was using the imagery of structural democracy from his earliest days in Parliament. In the initial phases he thought electoral democracy could result in structural democracy, that by giving the vote to the common man one could produce the kind of government that was democratic in terms of being typical of the people. In March 1960, while Obote was aiming for universal adult franchise, he betrayed this unconscious equation between electoral democracy and structural democracy. He said in Parliament: "Mr. Speaker, whatever we may be in life, whatever we may be in Government, however proud we may be of being Ministers in Central Government, however much we may feel proud of being Members of Legislative Council, the man who is important is the common man."[13]

There were interruptions in the course of Obote's delivery; he then proceeded to make his point more explicit. He rejected criteria of education as the basis of political power and influence; he rejected the criteria of wealth.

> We cannot be bullied about that because somebody has got a university degree, therefore he is much more important. He is not important in Uganda. We cannot be bullied that, because someone has got thousands of pounds in his pocket, therefore he is considered important enough for an extended franchise. He is not important. The man who is important is the common man who must have a vote.[14]

Obote himself had passed through Makerere College as a student. His intellectual orientation included literary anglophilia. He adopted the first name "Milton" in honor of the author of *Paradise Lost*. And while a student at Makerere Milton Obote had prophetically played Caesar in a college production of Shakespeare's *Julius Caesar*. Yet Obote did show egalitarian leanings from quite early.

Later in life much of Obote's utilization of the concept of the common man was connected with his opposition to aristocratic privilege, and connected further with his republicanism. He did indeed form an alliance of convenience with Kabaka Yekka, which he broke later. He also cooperated in facilitating Mutesa's election to the presidency of Uganda. But there did remain in Obote a hankering for structural democracy, both in the sense of having some kind of tribal representativeness in positions of authority and fair distribution of power among the different parts of Uganda, and also in the leftist sense of giving the ordinary man a greater say in the affairs of the nation. Obote's republicanism may also have been connected with his Lango origins. Though descended from a chiefly family, Obote knew that he belonged to a relatively egalitarian culture. Privilege among the Lango was far less hierarchial than among the Baganda.

But Obote was not consistent in his policies, nor was he tough enough with his ministers. His own ascent to the presidency was in the direction of greater structural democratization, at least to the extent that he was not a king. But the nature of his ascent, including his blatant endeavor to save his political career in February 1966 regardless of the consequences, was seriously anti-democratic in the electoral and constitutional sense.

Then in 1968 he started talking about a move to the left, and finally in 1969 he emerged with *The Common Man's Charter*. The same concept which he had used in that parliamentary speech in the Legislative Council way back in 1960, when he was asking for universal adult franchise, now became the cornerstone of his socialistic creed. In 1960 the idea of the common man was still very much in the liberal tradition in Obote's mind, implying electoral power universally extended. But by 1969 his ideas were getting more purely structural, in the sense of wanting power to devolve to those who were really typical of the composition of society.

Obote declared in *The Common Man's Charter* an opposition not only to a division of society between the rich and the poor but also to a division between the educated and the uneducated. He was all too aware that formal education, and the English language as a political and economic asset, conferred on those who had received them certain privileges. Parliament itself was inaccessible to those who did not have an adequate command of the English language. *The Common Man's Charter* denounced those who were "educated, African in appearance but mentally foreign."

And then, on January 25, 1971, a voice was heard on Radio Uganda. The voice had a Lugbara accent, speaking halting English, seemingly educated only modestly. In a fundamental sense it was a voice from the hinterland of Uganda, the voice of a common man in the sense which Obote himself would, in different circumstances, have emphatically conceded. That modestly educated Lugbara voice on Radio Uganda enumerated eighteen points against Milton Obote, the author of *The Common Man's Charter*. Before long we knew that our new President was Major-General Idi Amin, with less than full formal primary education, though self-educated in other spheres. He was not the son of a chiefly family, as Obote had been. He was not a product of Makerere College, as Obote had been. He was not an intellectual, as Obote had been.

Colin Legum, a friend of Obote's and Commonwealth correspondent of *The Observer*, was deeply distressed by the coup. His initial reports in *The Observer* indicated the complete acceptance of Obote's version not only of the causes of the coup but also of what was happening in Uganda. It was almost as if Colin Legum had suspended his better judgment in instinctive revulsion against the overthrow of Obote.

But what is significant from the point of view of this analysis is what Legum had to say about Idi Amin in an article written for the British socialist publication *Venture*. One would have thought that in such an egalitarian publication, committed to some of the oldest values of the Fabian Society, the significance of Amin's commonality would have occurred to Legum. He denounced Amin—"this rough-hewn, self-made soldier"—and then proceeded to castigate Amin for —"having always preferred the company of his non-commissioned officers to his modern corps of officers." Legum saw this as further evidence of an inner antagonism in Amin to educated and sophisticated people. The article was published after Amin had already shown his readiness to appoint a carefully selected council of ministers, with a wealth of administrative and organizational experience, and included among them no less an educated person than a university professor. The council of ministers reflected the continuing participation of the educated middle class in policy-making, but the top man in Uganda was no longer necessarily drawn from that class. The structural democratization of the commanding heights of the polity had at last come full circle.[15]

ON REVOLUTION AND THE MARGINAL MAN

The third dimension of structural democratization is the *geo-ethnic* one. This involves the role of the marginal man in history.

The first coup in post-colonial Africa was the overthrow of King Farouk in Egypt in 1952. To lend respectability to the coup and reassure the population of the rationality behind it, the soldiers entrusted leadership to General Mohammed Naguib. In ancestry General Naguib was a trans-national man, in the sense that his mother's side originated in the Sudan while his father's was Egyptian. In this sense he was a marginal man.

The first military coup started with the assassination of Togo's President Sylvanus Olympio. In order to lend respectability to the coup and reassure the population that the country was in responsible hands, the soldiers formed a provisional government and entrusted the presidency to Mr. Nicolas Grunitzky. Mr. Grunitzky was a marginal trans-national figure in almost the same sense as General Naguib. Mr. Grunitzky was born of a Polish father and a Togolese mother in the town of Atakpame in Western Togo in 1913.

The first social revolution which took place in East Africa was the Zanzibar revolution of January 1964. The leader of the Zanzibar revolution was a marginal figure in a different sense from either Naguib or Grunitzky. John Okello was a trans-national figure in the sense that he was a Ugandan who had led a revolution in Zanzibar. He was someone drawn from another society but cast in the role of initiator of fundamental change in a country of later adoption. "Field-Marshal" John Okello was later eased out of power and was succeeded in Zanzibar by the towering figure of Sheikh Abeid Karume.

Sheikh Karume, too, was a trans-national marginal figure. His father was from Nyasaland (now Malawi) and some accounts of his life place his own entry into Zanzibar at the age of 10. Prior to one of the elections of pre-revolutionary Zanzibar Abeid Karume's citizenship was challenged in a court of law. Did he have a right to lead a political party in Zanzibar? Did he have a right to stand for election in a Zanzibari legislature? It was the Nationalist Party, later overthrown by the Zanzibar revolution, which was challenging Abeid Karume's credentials for political leadership in Zanzibar. Karume won the case. He was, after all, a citizen, even if he had previously been of Nyasaland extraction. Nevertheless, from the point of view of our analysis in this essay, Karume was yet another instance of the trans-national marginal man in major movements of change in Africa.

The Zanzibar revolution was a revolution primarily arising out of popular discontent and the challenge of armed civilians rather than from any professional army. The Zanzibar experience cannot therefore be described as a military coup.

The first military coup in anglophone East Africa must therefore be deemed to be the Ugandan coup of January, 1971. The soldiers handed over power to Major-General Idi Amin. Major-General Idi Amin was a marginal figure in a third sense, different both from the category of Naguib and Grunitzky and the category of Okello and Karume. In General Amin we have a trans-national figure connected with a more fundamental aspect of the African scene. This is the aspect concerned with the division of ethnic communities across official territorial boundaries. Amin's father was born in what is now the Sudan. The border with Uganda was moved, and what was previously administered as part of Uganda was transferred to the jurisdiction of the Khartoum government. It might, therefore, be said that Amin's father was born a Ugandan, but the borders of Uganda have contracted since then.

In any case the Kakwa tribe continues to be divided between Uganda and the Sudan, with some Kakwa also in the Congo (now Zaire).

Thus the marginality of Amin is an ethnic marginality rather than a personal one. He belongs to a small community which extends over more than one territorial entity. The marginality of Naguib and Grunitzky, on the other hand, was a personal trans-nationality. They themselves were of mixed parentage, trans-national in dimension.

The marginality of John Okello and Abeid Karume was also basically personal in the sense that it was they themselves who were previously of foreign ancestry and yet came to play a leading role in a country of adoption.

The question which arises is, what elucidation does this throw on the role of the marginal man in major movements of transformation in Africa? Obviously certain distinctions would need to be made. In the case of Naguib and Grunitzky the trans-national figures did not themselves symbolize great revolutionary fervor. On the contrary, they were chosen because of the air of solidity and calm respectability which their names would lend to the coups which had taken place in their countries. Their personal careers had a good deal to do with the air of respectability that they had acquired. But even in their case it might be said that they derived part of their capacity to inspire confidence from their status as marginal men. There are occasions when distance from the major contending families in a particular country, or from the heart of the web of kinship in relation to political power, could itself be a worthy qualification in moments which need national reconciliation. It is like looking for somebody from a small tribe as a way of averting rivalries between big tribes.

Comparable considerations are sometimes at play in African countries when a Vice-President has to be chosen. In a country with, say, two major tribes, when the President is drawn from one of them, is it safe that the Vice-President should be from the second? Would this create certain temptations in the political process? Would the problem of succession be compounded precisely by the ethnic balance which had sought to manifest itself too immediately in a kind of institutional balance? Kenya had to confront this situation when the time came to choose a Vice-President, especially after the fall of Oginga Odinga. In terms of sheer political dynamism, and in terms of his record during the colonial struggle for liberation, Tom Mboya was, in many ways, an obvious man to be second in command to Jomo Kenyatta. But precisely because Mboya had such charismatic claims to be heir presumptive to the presidency, and also because he came from the second biggest tribe in Kenya, a tribe which was now increasingly competitive, Mboya was not in the running for the vice-presidency. The choice for the new Vice-President in Kenya's history fell on a trans-national figure in almost Grunitzky's sense. This was Joseph Murumbi, the son of a Masai mother and a Goan father. There was an element of marginality of Murumbi's background which made him suitable to be both a major figure in politics and yet not too serious a complication to issues of balance of power between sizable contenders.[16]

In the case of John Okello, his role in the Zanzibari convulsion was not in lending respectability to it but in actually initiating it. John Okello and his band of fighters captured the armory at Ziwani in Zanzibar, distributed the new weapons to these raw political challengers, and inaugurated the most convulsive revolution in the region.

Why was a Ugandan successful in launching a revolution outside his own country? In terms of roots on the island, John Okello was more of a foreigner in Zanzibar than the Sultan he overthrew. The Sultan was born a Zanzibari, so was his father, his grandfather, and his grandfather's father. Sultan Jamshid was indubitably much more Zanzibari than John Okello; but he was definitely less African than John Okello. In terms of nationality John Okello was a marginal man, coming from Lango to initiate a violent eruption in Zanzibar. But in terms of ethnic identity it was the Sultan who was the marginal man, part-Arab, part-African, more fully Zanzibari than the man who overthrew him but less purely African than his enemies.

For a delirious few weeks John Okello might indeed have derived his mystique from his distance. The local Africans in Zanzibar had interpenetrated with the Arabs, either culturally, religiously, or biologically. Islam was the religion of the great majority of Africans, as well as of the Arabs. Swahili was the language of both groups, and Swahili as a culture, born of both Arab and African traditions, was dominant over the population as a whole. There was no doubt that the local Africans shared a large number of attributes with the Arabs that they were now challenging.

But precisely because the challenge was against the Arabs, it made sense that its chief articulator in the initial stages should be distant enough to symbolize the purity of the African challenge. The bonds in this case were not the bonds of culture, or of religion, or even of intermarriage. In many ways the majority of Zanzibari Africans had more in common with the majority of Zanzibari Arabs than they had with this Langi revolutionary from Uganda. But what was at stake in that revolution was racial sovereignty rather than national sovereignty. By the tenets of national sovereignty, as I have indicated, Sheikh Ali Muhsin, the leader of the Zanzibari Nationalist Party which was overthrown, as well as the Sultan himself, were more Zanzibari than John Okello. But by the criteria of racial sovereignty, it was the fact that John Okello was an African in a purer sense than either Muhsin or the Sultan which really mattered. And a Langi on the Isle of Cloves was a symbol of pure Africanity.

As we indicated, John Okello, having served his purpose and being basically an unpredictable if charismatic personality, was eased out of office. And Abeid Karume, another trans-national man, assumed supreme authority.

In the April of the same year of the revolution, Zanzibar and Tanganyika were united to form what came to be known as the United Republic of Tanzania. Revolutionary leadership in Tanzania came to be firmly held by Julius Nyerere. But the first major challenge to the stability of Nyerere and even to his status as a revolutionary came to be articulated by yet another trans-national man.

This time it was Oscar Kambona, who was born in 1928, the son of a Nyasaland Anglican priest who had crossed the border to live and serve in southern Tanganyika. Kambona himself insists that this is a misinterpretation of his family background. Certainly it is defensible to see his case as very similar to that of General Idi Amin, a trans-national figure because the community to which he belonged defied artificial territorial definitions. And yet in a sense, the situation was enough to give Nyerere's government an excuse to withdraw Kambona's citizenship. Kambona heard of this withdrawal from an official of the Tanzanian High Commission in London. The grounds were ostensibly connected with his alleged extra-Tanzanian origins. In many ways Kambona is much more of a Tanganyikan than Abeid Karume is a Zanzibari, since Oscar was at least born in Tanganyika and his community had branches across both sides of the border between Tanganyika and Malawi. Karume's community, on the other hand, is not really trans-national in that sense. Karume's father was decidedly an immigrant, and so was Karume himself.

The tradition of trans-national figures playing dominant roles in great movements of change is by no means peculiar to Africa. Napoleon from Corsica and even Hitler from Austria spring to mind. Nor is the tradition in Africa peculiar to this century. We started by mentioning Naguib in Egypt. But in fact the great initiator of modernization in Egypt was Mahomet Ali, the modernizing Ottoman ruler of nineteenth century Egypt. That Kakwa boy from Uganda's border with the Sudan, Idi Amin, lies in a tradition at once old and momentous.

It is partly this peripheral background of Amin which brings us back firmly to the issue of structural democracy. Was Amin's assumption of power an instance of the periphery taking over the center? Was it a case of the countryside taking over the capital city? Was it a case of the common man assuming supreme authority? If Amin is placed once again alongside Mutesa, the evolution towards this structural democracy becomes clearer. Mutesa was a king, Protestant, and privileged. Amin was a commoner, Muslim, and poor. Mutesa came from the region of the capital city, in the full glare of national centrality. Amin came from the periphery of the country, descended from a small tribe. Mutesa was Cambridge-educated, a friend of African and British upper classes, a host as well as a guest of kings and princes. Amin was a rough and ready soldier, sometimes accused by his critics like Colin Legum of preferring "the company of his non-commissioned officers to his modern corps of officers." In short, Mutesa was a king; Amin was a peasant warrior.

Yet these two figures were destined to share a moment of national reconciliation. The rough boxer from Arua became suddenly a commanding figure of presidential dignity in 1971, showing signs of warmth and magnanimity. General Idi Amin might well emerge as the first really charismatic national leader that Uganda has had. He seems to have a certain personal magnetism, which Mutesa found only because he was Kabaka with all the mystique of kingship, and which Obote never found. And this peasant boy from the borders of Uganda and the Sudan, descended from a tribe which was not uniquely Ugandan but split across the frontier, became the instrument for ensuring that the king of the heartland tribe of Uganda, the Baganda, did in fact fulfill in death what he had promised in life—"In the end I shall return to the land of my fathers and to my people."[17]

WESTERNISM AND THE MILITARY

In the final analysis it was the military profession which helped to breech the cultural gap between General Amin and Sir Edward Mutesa. Mutesa, by being the king of the heartland tribe, was geographically central in Uganda. But by being anglicized to the extent that he was, Mutesa was culturally marginal in Uganda.

Amin, on the other hand, was the exact reverse. By being a member of a tribe of the very borders of Uganda, Amin was geographically marginal. But by being drawn from the womb of the countryside, and by being highly indigenous and non-Westernized in many of his inclinations, Amin was culturally central.

But the military profession was the bridge between the cultural world of Edward Mutesa and that of Idi Amin. In its own specialized way, a military career in the Ugandan army was a semi-Westernizing process for Amin. The rituals of the military in Uganda, from the drill to the ceremonial music, are overwhelmingly British derived.

A member of the British delegation to the funeral of Sir Edward Mutesa exclaimed to me in private how British Uganda had appeared to him in the five days he spent here. I told him that although the British influence was still significant in Uganda, the particular five days of his stay had been especially anglocentric. I argued that there were three reasons why the entire atmosphere of the funeral had included this heavy British dimension. The first reason concerned the fact that the funeral was designed to be with full military honors. And military honors and all military ceremonies in all the armies of English-speaking Africa remained firmly within the British tradition. There had been less inclination to change the rituals of the military than there had been with regard to the Westminister model of political arrangements. The music, therefore, which accompanied the coffin at the Kololo airstrip had a singularly Britannic tone.

The second reason why the five days were so anglocentric concerned the simple fact that the funeral had to have important Christian rites. Among African countries Uganda is particularly religious. Religion in Uganda has tended to affect politics much more than it has done in most other parts of the African continent. Moreover, the cleavage between Catholics and Protestants has in part resulted in a purist approach to ritual and ceremony in both denominations. There were therefore fewer changes in Ugandan Christianity at large when compared with its European counterparts than might have been the case without this tendency toward purity. The ceremony at Namirembe Cathedral, very moving in its simplicity, was nevertheless something indistinguishable from similar ceremonies in that other St. Paul's Cathedral 4,000 miles away.

The third reason why those days of Mutesa's funeral were so anglocentric would bring us back to the Baganda and their own capacity to imbibe so much which was British and at the same time remain so deeply African in their traditions. Again few people have put it better than Lloyd Fallers in his introduction to the symposium entitled *The King's Men.* Fallers has this to say:

> Baganda are, in many ways, extremely "acculturated" and the leading members of society are the most acculturated of all. There are here no culturally conservative, traditional chiefs pitted against a group of young, western educated commoner politicians. Baganda do not see or practice politics in these terms, as so many African peoples do, rather, Ganda society has acculturated, as it were, from the top down, and hence the new culture tends to have universal legitimacy. Indeed, from the point of view of the Baganda, this new culture, which includes many Western ideas of government, Western education, Anglican and Roman Catholic Christianity, the motivations appropriate to a money economy—all this has been *their* culture in a fundamental way. They have, so to say, "naturalized" the foreign elements and thus kept a sense of cultural integrity and "wholeness" through a period of radical change.[18]

It was the convergence of these three factors—anglicized military rituals, anglicized Christianity, and anglicized Ganda styles—which gave those five days of the funeral of Sir Edward Mutesa that highly anglocentric personality.

As they sounded the last post at the ancestral quadrangle of the Kasubi tombs, and President Amin stood to attention under the blazing sun of Kampala in the full splendor of a Britannic military tradition, the two soldier Presidents of Uganda were suddenly culturally close.

There had been a last post in the first burial of Mutesa in London in 1969. On that occasion the military component of the burial was handled by the British Grenadier Guards. Now the Grenadier Guards were only part of the ceremony. The bulk of the military component was the Ugandan army. And yet the universe of discourse between that trumpet in London in 1969 and the trumpet at the Kasubi tombs in Uganda in 1971 was indeed a shared universe.

Two funerals for one man. Yes, between England and Uganda Mutesa had shared his life. Yes, between England and Uganda he had come to share his death.

The peasant warrior from West Nile, now head of state, lay a wreath at the coffin in a concluding farewell gesture. Then the remains of the late Sir Edward Mutesa received a final presidential salute. The coffin was handed over by the Uganda army to the Baganda elders. And five hundred years of a piece of African history came to an end.

Or did it? Were peasant warriors to be forever supreme from now on? Was the principle of kingship in Uganda forever dead?

TOWARDS THE FUTURE

What of the future? The future must be a quest for some meeting point between structural democracy and electoral democracy in Uganda. There has to be a return to civilian politics to resurrect electoral democracy, and there have to be policies which increase social mobility and expand opportunities for that mysterious individual about whom Obote sang so much—the Common Man of Uganda.

In the issue of marrying structural democracy with electoral democracy the issue of kingship itself comes into play. My own position on the matter has been clear. As I indicated to an interviewer of the *Sunday Nation* (Kenya) in February 1971, I am not a "republican fanatic." I do not believe that kingship is wrong in its own right, nor do I share the automatic aversion to feudalism that some of my colleagues and friends have. If someone had asked me in 1966 whether the kingships in Uganda should be abolished, my answer would have been no.

But now that they have been abolished and Uganda has been without them for a number of years, my own feeling is that a restoration would be dangerous. My arguments again are not identical with those of people who see the kingdoms as divisive elements.

I have never been convinced that in February 1966 the system of government in Uganda as such had failed. On the contrary, my view has been that in February 1966 it was not the whole survival of Uganda as a nation which was at stake; it was the survival of Milton Obote as head of government. The Daudi Ocheng motion in Parliament, and the kind of massive support it received, with only one dissenting voice from John Kakonge, implied that it was possible to ease Obote out of office through new realignments of political forces in Uganda. It had by then dawned upon the Baganda that they could not hope to have an effective share in national affairs without seeking allies beyond their own regional borders. The Daudi Ocheng motion signified such a quest for alliances. And all politics is in some fundamental sense a persistent realignment of forces in pursuit of changing aims and interests. The Ocheng motion was the nearest thing to a vote of no confidence that Obote as head of government had ever had to face. The appointment of a commission of inquiry by Parliament in the full awareness that Obote was not in favor of such an inquiry was again a dramatic assertion that it might be possible to ease Obote out of power without resorting to extra-constitutional means. Some extra-constitutional means were indeed envisaged, including some by people such as Mutesa himself. But the parliamentary vote indicated that the aim of changing the leadership of the UPC could, in fact, be realized short of a resort to extra-constitutionality.

But Obote returned from his trip to the north, suspended the constitution, relieved Mutesa of the presidency, declared himself executive President, and put in detention five of his cabinet colleagues. What Obote had done in February must, therefore, be regarded as a case of political self-preservation rather than national self-preservation. What Obote had to do in *May* 1966 was more clearly a national endeavor, as the wrangles which his own action in February had released were now endangering the integrity of the country itself.

Were the kingships fundamentally divisive? We ought not to look at 1966 for the evidence, for the evidence is not really there. What we had at the beginning of that year was a situation where a major king in the country, the Kabaka, was being forced to establish new alignments with others in order to achieve the ouster of his political opponents. This is a classical political game, inevitable in any society which permits politics, and is no indication whatsoever of the viability of the nation concerned.

But although I would not have been in favor of the abolition of kings in 1966, I am more uneasy about their restoration later. Too many people outside Buganda have by now assumed that the disappearance of the kings was itself an indication that the different regions of Uganda had now achieved equality. The kings of Uganda were not a sign of disunity, as many have argued; but they could have been symbols of inequality. The Baganda especially had, because of the peculiar circumstances of the colonial period and the privileged status they enjoyed, evolved into something like a caste. The Baganda were the Brahmins of Uganda in a loose sense. And part of the luster and glitter of being a Brahmin at that time was connected with the monarchy in Buganda. Many Ugandans outside Buganda were sometimes tempted to imitate certain elements of Buganda political culture. Even Ganda administrative institutions were objects of emulation. Yes, the Baganda were the Brahmins of Uganda—and the kabakaship symbolized their status.

Then Obote, in a confrontation of power, succeeded in doing certain things which were unhealthy for the country; but at the same time he accomplished the task of cutting down the Baganda to size. He at any rate made it easier for future governments of Uganda to establish parity of esteem and equality of treatment between the Baganda and the other regions.

But need the restoration of the monarchy imply a privileged status reactivated? After all, the other kings in Uganda were not as powerful as the Kabaka and did not in reality imply greater privilege for the regions concerned. This is true. Yet equality sometimes must not only be accomplished; it must also be seen to have been accomplished. Restoration of the monarchy could imply, wrongly or correctly, a restoration of the privileged Brahminism of the Baganda.

And yet finally there is one argument which the Baganda might be forgiven for advancing. The issue of whether there should be kings or no kings in Uganda should, in the opinion of some of the more sophisticated Baganda, be a matter to be decided in the normal electoral and political process rather than a matter for a decree. Amin is justified in saying that he has no intention of restoring the kings; after all, a military government should be no more than a caretaker government. Should not the issue of restoring kingship be left to the processes of civilian politics when these are restored? If the Baganda can convince the rest of their countrymen in Uganda that there is a case for resurrecting some of the traditional institutions without the power they enjoyed, would not the kingships then have been restored through democratic means?

I have not myself fully resolved the ethics of this position. It is true that questions of this kind are at the heart of constitutional problems; and the kind of constitution which Uganda is to have one day should be a matter to be resolved when civilian politics are restored. Why should not the issue of kingship be resolved as part of the total constitutional arrangements?

It may well be that the Baganda would fail to convince the rest of Ugandans that kings need to be restored. If that is the case, then the Baganda would have to accept the verdict of the nation as a whole. The issue would have been postponed for resolution in the free political battlefield of a free country. If the Baganda lost in their bid to persuade their compatriots that kingships should be restored, electoral democracy would itself have pronounced a verdict in favor of structural democracy. That would be the highest point of fusion between the liberty which is yielded by the electoral process and the parity which emerges out of structural democratization. Let a national vote of Uganda decide whether any particular part of the country is to have a constitutional monarch. And, if the national vote decides negatively, parity and liberty in Uganda might at last find a point of symbolic integration.

The presidency itself, while remaining accessible to a peasant warrior, would no longer be available for a royal contender. Such an electoral verdict could be another major stage in the history of Uganda as a plural society.

In the sense of renunciation of hereditary leadership, democratization would be consolidated. In the sense of partial demotion of the educated class, democratization would be enhanced. And in the sense of expanding opportunities for previously peripheral tribes and regions, democratization would at last be truly underway.

NOTES

1. Khrushchev, "Speech at Meeting of Electors of Kalinin Constituency, Moscow, March 14, 1958," in N. S. Khrushchev, *For Victory in the Peaceful Competition with Capitalism* (Moscow: Foreign Languages Publishing House, 1959): 155-158.

2. The Kabaka of Buganda, *Desecration of my Kingdom* (Constable, 1967): 98-99.

3. Ibid.: 101.

4. Ibid.: 88. There is disagreement about whether Amin served in Burma.

5. Ibid.: 185.

6. Ibid.: 192.

7. Ibid.: 76.

8. This incident is discussed in a related context in my paper "Islam and the English language in East and West Africa," chapter 9, *Language Use and Social Change,* ed. by W. H. Whiteley (London: Oxford University Press on behalf of the International African Institute, 1971): 181-186. For a more detailed account of the incident and its sociological significance consult also "The King, the King's English and I," *Transition* 38 (1971).

9. *Desecration of My Kingdom,* op. cit.: 91.

10. Ibid.: 98.

11. Ibid.: 139.

12. Fallers, "Ideology and Culture in Uganda Nationalism" *American Anthropologist* 63 (1961): 677-686.

13. Debate on the Constitutional Committee Report, *Parliamentary Debates,* 40th Session, 7th March, 1960, *Hansard:* 374 ff.

14. Ibid., p. 376.

15. Legum's conception of Idi Amin in the terms quoted above occurs in his article "Uganda after Obote," *Venture* 23, 3 (March 1971): 20.

16. On his resignation to enter a business career Murumbi was succeeded as Vice-President by Daniel Arap Moi, drawn from a minority tribe of Kenya.

17. *Desecration of My Kingdom,* op. cit., p. 194.

18. L. A. Fallers (ed.), *The King's Men: Leadership and Status in Buganda on the Eve of Independence* (London: Oxford University Press, 1964): 9.

Chapter 10

THE RESURRECTION OF THE WARRIOR

TRADITION IN AFRICAN POLITICAL CULTURE:

FROM SHAKA THE ZULU TO AMIN THE KAKWA

Partly as a result of stimulation provided by the Dar-es-Salaam School of African History, increased attention has recently been paid to the phase of "primary resistance" when Africa first had to confront Western intrusion. The argument of scholars like Terrence Ranger for eastern Africa and Michael Crowder for western Africa identify those early armed challenges by Africans against colonial rule as the very origins of modern nationalism in the continent. By this argument Tanzania's ruling party and its function as a liberating force has for its ancestry both Maji Maji and pre-Maji Maji rebellions against German rule from the 1880s onward. African struggles against colonial rule did not begin with modern political parties and Western-trained intellectuals, but originated in those early "primary resisters" with their spears poised against Western military technology.[1]

This author is basically in sympathy with the Dar-es-Salaam School of African historiography, but with one important difference. While the Dar-es-Salaam historiography regards the Nkrumahs and Nyereres of modern Africa as the true heirs of those primary resisters, we believe that it is some military regimes in independent Africa and the liberation fighters in southern Africa that really carry the mantle of the original primary resisters. By our calculation it is General Idi Amin rather than Dr. Milton Obote who is the true successor to those early warriors in Bunyoro, Acholi, as well as West Nile, who reached for their spears to strike a blow, however weak, against European imperialism.

But the warrior tradition in Africa was not born on the day the white man landed. It was not a technique invented on the spur of the moment to meet a foreign challenge. On the contrary, it was deeply interlinked with the totality of the cultures of most African societies before the white man came. Our account here therefore must choose for its starting point not a famous resister against European intrusion but a warrior who did not as yet have to fight the white man as such. Hence our choice of Shaka as a point of departure. This chapter will start with Shaka as a symbol of the warrior tradition in Africa prior to large-scale colonization, and then proceed to General Idi Amin as a symbol of the beginning of a new warrior tradition, or perhaps a partial resurrection of what had once been the meeting point between the discipline of combat and the diffuseness of culture in Africa's social experience. As we have indicated, colonialism and Christianity not only demilitarized Africa but demasculated Africa. To many Africans, Shaka became at the most a symbol of nostalgia rather than a model of current emulation. Much of Africa retreated from the hard virtues of the warrior tradition, and embraced instead a set of imported values for the time being.

Let us first explore more fully the elements of the warrior tradition, and then relate the whole issue to the significance of both Shaka and Amin in African history.

THE WARRIOR IN SOCIETY

African societies have differed in their modes of self-defense and security arrangements, and certainly in their conceptions of the rights and duties of the warrior. But certain themes have persisted in cultures within the African continent which are otherwise very different from each other. This is partly because the concept of the warrior captures some quite fundamental aspects of human organization and human symbolism. Pre-eminent among the more obvious shared aspects is, firstly, the link between the warrior and idea of *adulthood;* and secondly, the link between the warrior and the concept of *manhood.* These are quite fundamental linkages and carry a variety of implications.

Adulthood is related to notions of self-reliance. The adult is he who has a capacity to earn his own living and maintain his own homestead. But adults are sometimes to be differentiated from elders. In this sense, while children are pre-adults, elders are post-adults, no longer at the peak of their physical powers though hopefully much enhanced in their mental powers. African languages differ in the way they handle the distinction between relatively young adults with warrior duties, on the one hand, and elders, on the other.

But even if we use the term adult in its usual sense in the English language to indicate those who are no longer children, the basic point remains that it is from the ranks of adults that full warriors are recruited. One became a warrior when one was presumed to be capable of protecting cattle, or defending land, or collectively fighting to protect the clan. A heavy element of self-reliance was thus built into the concept of warriorhood because of its link with the concept of adulthood.

In many African societies the process of initiation carried implications of this presumed stage of self-reliance. The generations are separated for a while. The young adults are separated from their elders. In this respect there is sometimes a closer bond between the third generation and the first, between the elders and the children, than there is between the elders and the young adults. Many African societies encourage newly grown boys to live separately in a lodge after puberty.

> The removal of the boy from parental care is a matter of separation of the generations. The boy is developing into a man, a new generation has come into being within the family. This is on an individual level. Seclusion of the whole group of initiands in their own lodge, and their reluctance to give the fathers, i.e. the parental generation, access to the lodge, also points to the separation of adjacent generations, but on a *group* level. The "oneness" of the circumcised in the lodge would seem to express the solidarity of a new adult generation.[2]

The gulf between the parental generation and the generation of the new adult has its own tensions. Alnaes tells us about Konzo fathers who are reluctant to have their sons circumcised "too soon." This is because the circumcision ceremony converts a son in some sense into a rival in adulthood. Among the Konzo a boy eager to cross the line into adulthood might in desperation go to a Muslim to be circumcised without going through the traditional Konzo ritual. But this is a last resort. A better strategy in the face of a reluctant father is to run away and be circumcised in the traditional manner before the father manages to intervene. "A fair number of boys run away to be circumcised in the traditional manner and they usually manage to have the operation before the father arrives on the scene. . . . The traditional circumcision is a symbolic transition from childhood to manhood."[3]

African societies with age-grade systems have more complex stages of social progression. The Nandi of Kenya have seven age-grades, each with a name of its own and all operating on the basis of a recurring cycle. Every fifteen years the fighting age hands over to the age next below it. And members of that succeeding age would have been preparing themselves for the previous fifteen years to qualify for warriorhood after circumcision. The retiring age-grade moves up to become elders.[4]

The theme of mature independence again links adulthood with warriorhood. The initiation ceremonies, both those involving circumcision and those which do not, share certain important characteristics. S. N. Eisenstadt has summarized the descriptions of these ceremonies as they abound in the literature. We might use here Eisenstadt's summary, but relate it more explicitly to the theme of self-reliance and mature independence which initiation implies:

(a) In these ceremonies the pre-adult adolescents are transformed into full adult members of the tribe, the transformation being effected through
(b) a series of rites in which the adolescents are symbolically divested of the characteristics of youth and invested with those of adulthood from a sexual and social point of view. This symbolic investment, which has deep emotional significance, may have various concrete manifestations, bodily mutilation, circumcision, taking on of a new name, symbolic rebirth, etc.;
(c) the complete symbolic separation of the adolescents from the world of their youth, and especially from their close status attachments to their mothers; i.e., their complete "male" independence and autonomous male image are articulated (the opposite usually holds true of girls' initiations);
(d) dramatization of the encounter between the different generations, a dramatization which may take the form of a fight, competition, etc., and in which the basic complementariness—whether of a continuous or discontinuous type—is stressed; thus, in all initiation rites the members of different generations must act together, the ones as teachers, the others as "students." The elders sometimes assume frightening forms and stress that without them the adolescents cannot become adults. Quite often the discontinuity between adolescence and adulthood is symbolically expressed in the "rebirth" of the adolescent—in their symbolic death as children and rebirth as adults.[5]

Those communities in Africa which have had age-set systems have usually done so in relation to the military organization of the tribe. But even among the Nuer, where the age-set system is less directly militaristic, the link between adulthood, manhood, and warrior remains explicit. In Eisenstadt's words:

When a boy passes into the grade of manhood his domestic duties and privileges are radically altered. From being everybody's servant and an inferior, he becomes an independent adult. This change of status is epitomized in the taboo on milking through which he becomes separated from women, with whom he was identified as a boy—a taboo which begins at his initiation and remains in effect throughout his life.... At initiation the youth receives a spear from his father or uncle and becomes a warrior.... He becomes a true "man" when he has fought in war (battle) and has not run away, has duelled with his age mate, has cultivated his garden and has married.

We hope to demonstrate later that the theme of self-reliance involved in this warrior tradition is antithetical to the dependency complex which many Africans later acquired under the impact of colonial rule. We hope also to illustrate that the struggle against dependency as exemplified by General Idi Amin at his best is, in an important sense, a reactivation of the ancestral assertiveness of warrior culture.

What should not be overlooked is the sexual dimension of the warrior culture. As we indicated, an initiation ceremony was simultaneously a moment of confirmation as an adult and graduation as a man. Adulthood and manhood were sometimes indistinguishable for the male line of the tribe.

But there is also a primeval link between manhood and warriorhood. In societies otherwise vastly different from each other one factor remains constant—it was a man who fought for the society on the battlefield. Virtues like courage, endurance, even ruthlessness, were regarded as hard masculine virtues. The statement "he is a real man" could mean either he is sexually virile or he is tough and valiant. Virility and valor were interlinked as masculine attributes.

In some African societies special sexual rites were accorded to warriors. Among the Nandi, warriors enjoyed considerable sexual privileges, especially legitimate access to uninitiated girls who could thus be adopted as sweethearts for the warriors. A warrior did not have to marry his sweetheart, but could continue keeping her in that role even after he had married someone else, provided he also remained within the warrior set. Upon retirement from warriorhood the men had to limit themselves to their wives. It was partly because of this that problems sometimes arose at the time when a warrior was due to relinquish his status within the fighting grade and move up into the level of elder. Many a warrior among the Nandi was reluctant to be promoted to elder if this reduced his sexual privileges.

Among the Nuer the newly initiated enjoyed considerable sexual license.[7]

As we shall later indicate, there are African cultures which demand on the part of the warrior sexual abstinence rather than according him sexual privileges. But even in these cultures that demand of the warrior such patience the assumption is that the promise of later sexual advantages would help increase current martial commitment. The knight or crusader is promised a sexual paradise when the fighting is all over.

THE MYSTIQUE OF VIOLENCE

Because manhood was thus linked not only to sexual virility but also to valor in war, violence itself became in some sense a masculine attribute. Capacity to take ruthless decisions, or inflict brutal damage when this was "required," became associated with hard-headed manliness.

This kind of equation is not of course uniquely African. Western culture to the present day allocates fighting roles disproportionately to men. The people who dropped bombs from B-52 planes in Viet-Nam were American men. The thousands who were sent to the front lines throughout Indo-China from the United States were overwhelmingly men. Those who died in those distant lands for what American Presidents regarded as American national interests, as well as those who were taken prisoner and spent years in bondage and deprivation away from their homes, were again men. But in addition there were those who committed acts of brutality against the enemy in Indo-China, or authorized the destruction of villages, or facilitated the destruction of vegetation and food supplies for peasants—and found themselves vindicated by a sense of ruthless manliness in conditions of war.

In African history the equation between masculinity and warriorhood sometimes links matrimonial eligibility with martial prowess. There were African societies where a man could not marry unless he proved himself either in a major hunting exercise or in a major battle. The idea of either killing a lion or killing brave warriors from another tribe as part of the process of qualifying for the role of husband survived in some African societies into the twentieth century. Bravery itself was sometimes defined as the capacity for ruthless actions when this was necessary.

Chinua Achebe, Africa's leading novelist in the English language, captures some elements of this theme in his first novel, *Things Fall Apart*. Okonkwo, the leading character in the novel, is above all fearful of being mistaken as weak. His father had been a relatively weak man, in some ways lazy, and Okonkwo's main ambition in life was a perpetual quest for vindication as a brave man. He was in fact brave, but in addition he imposed on himself a sense of eternal vigilance against even momentary weakness. When circumstances demanded that his adopted son, Ikemefuna, should die because the tribal oracle had so decreed, he not only permitted that ritual killing to take place; he even participated in it. Okonkwo loved the boy, and above all would have wished to see him live. But if the ancestors wanted his death and the community had to kill him, Okonkwo was determined not to betray his affection for the boy lest it be mistaken for weakness. Okonkwo killed someone he loved out of fear of being mistaken for a coward.[8]

Given the link between manliness and warfare there could also be an easy link between violence and sexuality. A man taunted as weak in a sexual sense could seek vindication in martial prowess. In this regard the story of Shaka emerges as profoundly symbolic.

Shaka created the Zulu state at its most powerful. He took over from Dingiswayo, who ruled from 1808 to 1818. Dingiswayo had laid the foundation of the Zulu kingdom. Shaka's own period of power overlapped with that of Dingiswayo, taking partial control in 1816, consolidating in 1818, and expanding from then onward until 1828 when Shaka was assassinated. Among the rulers of this remarkable kingdom of the Zulus, Shaka has remained a powerful memory.

Shaka stands out as the greatest of them all—both Romulus and Napoleon to the Zulu people—and his legend has captured the imagination of both European and African writers, inspiring novels, biographies, and historical studies in several tongues. As a violent autocrat he is both admired and condemned: admired by those who love conquerors, condemned by those who hate despots.[9]

Shaka's capacity for brutality remains one of the wonders of world history. He liquidated his enemies with remarkable vengeance while at the same time integrating others into a new Zulu empire. Communities not previously designated as Zulu became eligible for assimilation, while some recalcitrant Zulus were annihilated. European observers of Shaka's behavior sometimes exaggerated his brutality, but even allowing for that exaggeration there was indeed a substantial degree of wanton violence and cruelty.

Time and again, for no discernible reason, Shaka, with a flick of his hand and no further attention, ordered the execution of some member of his entourage. It was a phenomenon that was noted on every occasion on which a European paid a visit to the royal kraal, and despite the initial impression that Shaka merely wished to impress his visitors with his absolute powers, it gradually sank in that the executions were a normal part of Zulu court life and that Shaka gave as little heed to the impression left on his visitors as he did to that he made on the victims or their families. The power was indeed absolute, and it had reached the ultimate corruption.[10]

Modern interpretations of Shaka's mentality have inevitably sought some indications in his childhood. A psychological approach toward understanding Shaka has turned the attention of scholars and other writers to the formative period of this great African ruler. What made him so cruel while at the same time so courageous and daring?

Zulu boys at that time went completely naked until they were initiated. Legend has it that one day, when Shaka was eleven years old, two older herd-boys flung the historic insult at him: *"Ake ni-bone umtondo wake; ufana nom sundu nje"* ("Look at his penis; it is just like a little earthworm"). Shaka was enraged. He was now becoming increasingly conscious of the stumpiness of his genital organ. He flung himself at the two boys that had insulted him, and his pure fury and the element of surprise enabled him to inflict savage bruises and injuries on his two tormentors. The inadequacy of his sexual equipment, at least at that stage of the boy's growth, became a major factor in the shaping of Shaka's personality.

He began to brood deeply about his deficiency which, as all herd-boys paraded in the nude up to the age of puberty, was so painfully apparent. Nothing could be more humiliating to a Zulu than this. It led to a feeling of hopeless inferiority, and deep, resentful brooding, from which may well have derived that need to dominate first his family, then his tribe, at last a vast empire.[11]

As to whether Shaka's sexual organ later changed enough physically to be regarded as "normal," one version has it that by the time he was initiated only a few years after the first taunts, his organ had become sufficiently normal for Shaka to refuse to cover it even after the ceremonial rites of puberty. "He wished it to be known that he was now physically adequate."[12]

But other versions maintain that the stumpiness of his organ continued and affected important aspects of his behavior. By the time he became an all-powerful emperor he still insisted on having his bath on an open ground with his entourage in attendance.

We discussed earlier the role of initiation rites as confirmation of adulthood, manhood, and eligibility for warriorhood. Shaka is credited with having made some important changes in the initiation customs of the Zulu. One version credits him with having abolished circumcision among the Zulu though the practice continues among other members of the Nguni family of tribes.

But another version says that changes in circumcision ceremonies had begun just before Shaka assumed authority and power among the Zulu. The changes were deemed necessary for military reasons. Circumcision among the Nguni, though important as preparation for warriorhood, was nevertheless temporarily followed by a period of seclusion of a new initiate. In the words of Omer-Cooper,

> The circumcision ceremonies with subsequent period of ritual seclusion which deprived the tribe of part of its fighting strength for a considerable period and left the initiates very vulnerable in case of war were abandoned in response to conditions of more frequent fighting. At the same time tribal armies were recognized on an age-grade basis.[13]

Some records ascribe the changes in circumcision ceremonies to an order by Dingiswayo that circumcision ceremonies be postponed until his conquests were complete. Dingiswayo was the chief who gave Shaka some of his earliest opportunities and who was later succeeded by Shaka as supreme ruler.[14]

On balance it seems almost certain that the actual abolition of circumcision ceremonies among the Zulu came under Shaka's leadership. Again issues of manhood interacted with issues of warriorhood; a ceremony concerning the male organ became linked to military strategy. Some have even attributed Shaka's adoption of the short stabbing spear (assegai) not only to military considerations but also to considerations of symbolic male sexuality.

Whatever the actual facts concerning Shaka's life and policies, there is little doubt that in him we have a supreme example of the interaction between issues of manhood and issues of warriorhood, a link between a sense of sexual inadequacy and a policy of brutal assertiveness. In Shaka the warrior tradition as a fusion of virility and valor lacked an adequate balance. Yet in that very distortion the message of such a fusion became dramatized.

THE CELIBATE AND THE SPEAR

A related factor among the policies of Shaka was the principle of celibacy which he introduced for adoption by his warriors for as long as they were serving. In this sense we might distinguish between two senses of manliness in relation to sex. One sense implies virile promiscuity and the other implies sexual discipline. In the one case a man is he who can cope with either a number of women or a highly charged single woman. Capacity to perform well in sex becomes part of the very definition of virility in this sense.

The other sense of manliness regards a lot of sexual activity as being itself a form of weakness. The promiscuous male becomes a "playboy," without the will to conquer his games with his women. In this second sense of manliness, the warrior proves his manhood by renouncing for a while his sexual desires and concentrating instead on issues of courage, endurance, and discipline.

Shaka adopted the second sense of masculinity as the basis of his code for his warriors. He not only forbade his men to marry, which was one sense of celibacy, but also to have sexual relations at all with women until he gave them permission to do so upon retirement from active military service. There are tribes which forbid warriors marriage while giving them considerable license in extramarital sexual relations. As we mentioned earlier, the Nandi sometimes adopted matrimonial celibacy for their warriors without sexual abstinence. But Shaka imposed on his warriors both forms of celibacy. As a Sotho writer has put it:

> The reader must remember that above all else on earth the Black Races love to marry. Often in speaking of the good things in life people do not mention marriage, because marriage is life. Therefore we can understand well how hard the warriors of Chaka worked to gain this reward. To set his regiments an example Chaka remained a bachelor until the end of his life. This is . . . the most important thing that Chaka did.[15]

Shaka's adoption of this sense of manliness had its military rewards. The promise of a sexual paradise later on encouraged discipline while maintaining hope for the future. Nor was celibacy even in the sense of total sexual abstinence unknown among African societies in times of combat. What Shaka did was to distort this general principle and carry it to bizarre excesses.

He sometimes deliberately tested his warriors, stripping them naked in drill formations and then exposing them to the sight of naked maidens dancing before them. Those who showed any signs of genital erection were ruthlessly punished. When his mother died he carried it even further, forbidding for a while all intercourse in the kingdom. It is because of this and other excesses that scholars like Max Gluckman arrive at the conclusion that Shaka was "at least a latent homosexual and possibly psychotic."[16]

We see then once again in Shaka a distortion of a discipline which in other African societies legitimately forms, or could form, part of the warrior tradition. The demand on the warrior to exercise sexual self-discipline becomes converted into a demand not to have sexual feelings at all. The value of the discipline would normally have arisen out of the very ability to conquer temptation. But Shaka would not even permit the right to be tempted, let alone the privilege of satisfying that temptation.

Yet sexual celibacy does provide an important link between Shaka and the Mau-Mau movement in Kenya in the 1950s. Our analysis in this regard makes the Mau-Mau movement an important link in the chain separating the symbolic meaning of Shaka from the symbolic meaning of Idi Amin. The Mau-Mau movement, in rebellion against British rule and white settler occupation of African land in Kenya, constituted the first major resurrection of the warrior tradition in recent East African history. The Kikuyu mobilized themselves into armed rebellion against European settlerdom. The Kikuyu fighters in the forests and the hills of the Aberdares became for a while true heirs of that heritage of primary resistance. The Kikuyu went back to reactivate primeval symbolism, and to resurrect important elements of tradition Kikuyu virtues as a basis for establishing a military solidarity against the colonial presence in Kenya.

The connection between martial symbolism and sexual symbolism remains a major aspect of the oath of allegiance demanded from the Mau-Mau warriors. We have details of the Batuni oath. The new warrior initiate was first stripped naked and seated facing the oath administrator. Then a long strip of goat's meat was placed around the neck of the new initiate. One end lay across the chest of the naked man and the other dropped down his back around his waist several times, and then between his legs. The new initiate was ordered to hold this end of the goat's meat up against his penis. On the floor were the two eyes of an uncastrated he-goat, called a "kihei." The word itself meant "uncircumcised youth," but paradoxically it was used during the Mau-Mau insurrection to refer to a man who had taken the Batuni oath.

The oath itself did not demand total sexual abstinence but forbade the use of prostitutes and the seduction of "other men's women." These particular prohibitions were to discourage the danger of betrayal by temporary sexual companions, such as prostitutes. They were also designed to discourage the warriors from fighting with each other over women. But once the Mau-Mau fighters were in the forests, total sexual abstinence was demanded among some groups. And in some of the detention camps, where having intercourse with woman detainees was possible, special codes against sexual relations were self-imposed by the detainees.[17]

The Mau-Mau movement did use aspects of that old discipline which Shaka had demanded of his own warriors, but the movement did not push the particular discipline to total extremes.

There were other instances in the Mau-Mau movement linking sexual with martial symbolism including the use of menstrual blood for certain oath-taking ceremonies in at least some sections of the movement. What was happening was an attempt to provide a sense of sacred awe to counter-balance belief in the invincibility of the white man which the colonial experience had so far consolidated. Let us remind ourselves that the warrior tradition earlier in the century had been badly damaged by two terrors which had come with the white man—the terror of gunfire and the terror of hellfire. The terror of gunfire was what the new military technology of the white man was all about. Those early primary resisters against the European intrusion discovered before long the overwhelming superiority of the cannon as against the spear, the gun as against the bow and arrow. In the words of the English writer, Hilaire Belloc:

> Whatever happens we have got
> The Maxim gun, and they have not.

European technology soon overrode and demoralized the resisters. The new terror of gunfire initiated the decline in the warrior tradition.

The decline was reinforced by the terror of hellfire which came with Christianity. Death for millions of Africans was now given a new meaning. African ancestors were cut down to size, denounced as insignificant by the missionaries of the new religious order. A new god was proclaimed, and a new fear of damnation was propounded. Some African Christians, like many other Christians before them, accepted the concept of hellfire at its face value; others equated it simply with the threat of damnation after death. Whatever interpretation, literal or symbolic, the new religion had come with a new system of punishment and rewards. The power of all indigenous beliefs began to decline; the authority of the village medicine man was struggling against the challenges of local missionary schools. The old order was partially disintegrating—and with it, the warrior tradition.

Movements like that of Mau-Mau had to invent new forms of ritualized damnation in order to outweigh the combined demasculating effect of the fear of the white man's gunfire and the Christian priest's hellfire.

Christianity had in addition damaged the warrior tradition in Africa by proclaiming the ethic of "turning the other cheek." Meekness was regarded as a virtue even for otherwise virile and valiant men. A version of Christianity which had hardly even been truly implemented in Europe, and which had in part become anachronistic on its home ground, was now bequeathed to African school-children and peasants. The god of love was mobilized behind the task of "imperial pacification." The message of Christianity discouraged Africans not only from fighting each other but also from resisting the colonial presence.

Again, a movement like Mau-Mau had to help Kikuyu Christians transcend the conditioning of "turning the other cheek," as well as overcome the terror of eternal Christian damnation. Those oaths of Mau-Mau combining sexual symbolism with militant commitment were part of the process of countering the demasculating consequences of the colonial experience.

The Mau-Mau movement was militarily defeated by the British, but it was clearly a victory of the vanquished. The political triumph went to the African people, even if the military successes were retained by the colonial people. The stranglehold of the white settlers on Kenya was at last broken and before long Kenya was preparing for independence.

Mau-Mau was also the first great African liberation movement of the modern period. All the efforts which are now being made in southern Africa to consolidate resistance, organize sabotage, and seek to dispel white power and privilege, have for their heroic ancestry that band of fighters in the Aberdare forests of Kenya. The warrior tradition was at least temporarily revived at a critical moment in Kenya's history.

AMIN: THE QUEST FOR ADULTHOOD

Among those who fought on the British side in the Mau-Mau war was a soldier from Uganda called Idi Amin. He had been recruited into the fourth battalion of the King's African Rifles in 1946. When recruited, Idi showed all the signs of colonial conditioning into dependency. With him it was the terror of gunfire rather than hellfire that promoted his sense of allegiance to the British. Amin learned about hellfire from Islam rather than Christianity, but since Uganda was ruled by an imperial power associated with Christianity, and since the whole political culture of the country had already given considerable prestige to Christian values, there was in Idi Amin no sign of a pent-up *Jihad* spirit wishing to break out. He was no different from the bulk of the subdued population of Uganda. In some ways he seemed even more subservient upon recruitment into his branch of the British Imperial Forces in Africa.

> Within seven years he was promoted to lance-corporal and was displaying the qualities that so endeared him to his British superiors—instant obedience, fierce regimental pride, reverence towards Britain and the British, a uniform which crackled with razor-sharp starched creases and boots with toe-caps like black mirrors.[18]

The colonial experience had indeed undermined the sense of adulthood in Amin and Africa. On the one hand, there was the deep paternalism among even the most liberal of white men in Africa, and the tendency to see Africans as not quite mature. On the other hand, Christian missionaries once again looked upon their responsibilities in Africa virtually in parental terms. Africans were not only among the most heathen of God's children—they were in fact only grown-up children. Even a great humanitarian figure like Albert Schweitzer, while conceding that the African and the white man were brothers, went on to insist that the white man was the elder brother.

The ritualistic language of Christianity in terms of "children of God," and the whole symbolism of fatherhood in the organizational structure of the Catholic Church all the way from the concept of "pope" to the rank of "Father" among some priests, took on additional significance in African conditions. The metaphor of fatherhood within the Catholic hierarchy reinforced filial tendencies among African converts. Again the repercussions went beyond the particular members of that denomination and reinforced the dependency complex in the society as a whole.

While African culture encouraged respect for elders, the colonial experience made Africans subservient even to European children. It was almost instinctive to be deferential toward the white skin, whatever the differences in ages between the deferential African and the acknowledging European. When Idi Amin in the old colonial days invited the three sons of his commanding officer to Sunday lunch, Amin apparently insisted on collecting the three boys by car despite the fact that he lived only twenty yards away. "After lunch he solemnly drove them back again."[19]

The tendency to accept indignities was also pronounced and was a clear indication of the deep sense of servitude. Amin was again a child of this servile era.

> Inevitably, new African officers modelled themselves on the British, but a commission didn't mean an end to the traditional indignities they had suffered for years. The only African member of the Nile Rugby Club, Idi often travelled with the team to play in Kenya; but during the parties after the game he would be obliged

to sit in a vehicle outside the Europeans' only clubhouse. Such blatant discrimination did not prevent him from aping what he believed to be the established social
behaviour of European officers.[20]

The man was clearly not a Shaka. That militant self-confidence of the Zulu
despot, though lying latent in Idi Amin, had as yet to be activated. The
decline of the warrior tradition had made sycophants even of African soldiers.
In some ways it had made sycophants especially of African soldiers for at
least as long as the colonial era persisted.

The country became independent in October 1962. Little more than eight
years later Idi Amin was President of Uganda.

At first the dependency complex which had characterized his behavior
during the colonial period remained a factor in his behavior after assuming
the supreme authority. The two most influential foreign embassies in
Kampala were the British High Commission and the Israeli Embassy. Amin
reaffirmed his love for the British and demonstrated considerable deference
to the Israelis as his benefactors. Britain was in fact the first country in the
world to recognize Idi Amin's new regime, and Amin was not in the least
embarrassed by this imperial gesture.

It was not until 1972 that Amin at last began to assert a sense of
adulthood. His first major targets were the Israelis in Uganda, who probably
helped him to come to power and who had served him fairly well until then.
But it was indeed a dependency relationship, while it lasted. Uganda was in
some sense a client state of the Israelis for at least one year. Then Amin
decided to assert his independence. By April 1972 he had expelled all the
Israelis. By August 1972 he engaged in a major confrontation with the British
over the future of British Asians in Uganda. He gave British Asians three
months to leave the country, to the consternation of Britain and much of the
rest of the world. In the face of considerable pressure to reverse his decision,
Amin emerged triumphant.

By December 1972 he was then confronting the British on matters
connected with British businesses within Uganda. He was also trying to assert
a new independence on the issue of British advisors and teaching personnel
within Uganda. As the country entered 1973 a new challenge of adulthood
faced Uganda as a whole. Could the society survive the departure of so many
foreign businessmen? Could the schools maintain themselves in the face of
the Asian and European exodus? Would the country discover new economic
and professional energies within itself capable of consolidating a new level of
national adulthood?

The future is still uncertain, and the questions have yet to be conclusively
answered. Has Amin recovered his adulthood, or only his manhood?

The theme of masculinity is certainly pertinent here. Whereas Shaka had
defined manliness in terms of sexual abstinence, Amin has seen it in terms of

virile promiscuity. We should remember the Sotho writer's assertion that "above all else on earth the Black Races love to marry." Shaka's example did not prove that point; Amin's style lends greater support to it. He himself assumed supreme authority, equipped with four wives. To some extent he was making up for the prohibitions of the old colonial days when the British authorities would permit only one wife with him in barrack quarters. According to Amin himself, a British officer once came to inspect the quarters and saw two women in Amin's house. Amin introduced one of the women as his wife. The British officer asked suspiciously: "And who is the other one?" Amin answered that the second one was his own elder sister, "my *dada*," a Swahili word for elder sister.

Since he assumed supreme authority in the country Amin is known officially as President Idi Amin Dada. One story concerning the origins of the title "Dada" is that it goes back specifically to that incident of virile promiscuity when Amin was caught out by a British officer. When his fellow African soldiers discovered his quickwittedness upon being seen with a second woman in his barrack quarters they began to call him Idi Amin Dada.[21]

On attainment of independence Uganda's criminal code still technically regarded polygamy as a legal offense. The British administrators and missionaries, though fully recognizing that polygamy was widely practiced, nevertheless maintained the myth on the statute books that bigamy was against the laws of Uganda.

This anomaly had survived nearly ten years of independence. Obote's government had done nothing to restore legitimacy to a widespread indigenous institution. But by July 1973 General Amin had caught up with the anomaly. Announcing the legalization of polygamy, Radio Uganda said it was intended to orient the attitude of Ugandans toward "our cultural heritage, and regain our self-respect and dignity."

The polygamous marriages were to be contracted under the usual customary law and be in conformity with tribal regulations, including the payment of bridewealth.

But there was protection for Christian and Muslim inhibitions. A man could not have more than one wife if he had willingly opted for a Christian or civil marriage and a Muslim, marrying under Islamic law willingly, had to limit himself to the four wives permitted by Islamic law.

Apart from these concessions to the imported religions of Uganda, the decree on polygamy restored an important element in the old warrior culture of the different societies of the country.[22]

Even Amin's hostility to the Asians started in part as a reaction against the sexual and social exclusivity of the Asian community in Uganda. Amin's denunciation of the Asians first emphasized this exclusivity before he went on later to attack the economic preeminence of the community in Uganda.

Only six Asians had ever married black people, Amin claimed. Although there were more Asians in Uganda than there were Europeans, mixed marriages between Asians and Africans were fewer than between Africans and Europeans. If Mofolo is correct in that old assertion that "above all else on earth the Black Races love to marry," the barrier which the Asians of Uganda had erected against any intermarriage with Africans was an important aspect of their tragic fate under General Idi Amin.

A new Shaka has indeed cast his shadow across the African continent. But it is a Shaka committed to virile masculinity rather than celibate manliness.

But the sexual factor is itself symptomatic of something wider than that. What Fernandez said of the Shaka complex is also true of the Amin phenomenon:

> I would suggest that we are much closer to important perceptions if we analyze the Shaka complex, not in the terms of the problems of sexuality, but in terms of the problems of power. For it is this problem, if we can talk of a problem, that I feel to be more fundamental to African culture than the problem of sexuality. The Shaka complex is the drama of the working out of the impulse to power in human affairs.[23]

CONCLUSION

In discussing the pressures on a growing black child in the United States, two black psychiatrists examined the struggle against the forces of symbolic castration.

> For a white man in this country, the rudiments are settled at birth by the possession of a penis and a white skin. . . . For the black man in this country, it is not so much a matter of acquiring manhood as it is a struggle to feel it his own. Whereas the white man regards his manhood as an ordained right, the black man is engaged in a never-ending battle for its possession. For the black man, attaining any portion of manhood is an active process. He must penetrate barriers and overcome opposition in order to assume a masculine posture. For the inner psychological obstacles to manhood are never so formidable as the impediments woven into American society.[24]

In the case of the black American the impediments range from the multiple consequences of matriarchy as imposed by the slave experience to the sheer problem of getting a job and supporting a family. But underlying it all is again the factor of the dependency complex, the political castration implicit in being dominated by another.

The black American, too, to the extent that he is now struggling to find a new basis for his manhood, might be experiencing the beginnings of a reawakened warrior heritage from his primeval past.

Many black Americans have enthused over the warrior assertiveness of General Amin since 1972. And behind Amin lies a tradition which goes back to Shaka the Zulu and beyond—a tradition which has at times collapsed in exhaustion under the terrors of white hegemony, but which has also had its moments of resurrection. The Mau-Mau uprising was an important moment of such revival in the modern phase of African history and provides a grand precedent for the liberation movements of Southern Africa.

A warrior tradition, however, has also its brutal side. Both Shaka and Amin are among the more brutal of rulers in Africa's difficult history. Violence under the warrior tradition sometimes assumes a disproportionate air of sacredness and mystique. Manhood becomes equated with capacity for ruthlessness, as well as with potential for virility.

The warrior tradition in Africa is far from being as yet dominant once again, but there are signs of an important resurrection. As a reaction and rebellion against dependency, the resurrection wears the face of proud promise. But as an initiation into the culture of violent valor, the resurrection of the warrior tradition in African political culture also carries its own special hazards. As Africa seeks to consolidate its manhood and recover its adult-hood, it must also remember to conserve its humanity.

NOTES

1. Consult T. O. Ranger, "African Reactions to the Imposition of Colonial Rule in East and Central Africa," in L. H. Gann and Peter Duignan, *The History and Politics of Colonialism, 1870-1914,* vol. 1 (Cambridge: 1969): 293-324; John Iliffe, *Tanganyika under German Rule, 1905-1912* (Nairobi and Cambridge: 1969); Terence Ranger, "Connexions between 'Primary Resistance' Movements and Modern Mass Nationalism in East and Central Africa," parts 1 and 2, *Journal of African History* 9, 3 and 4 (1968): 437-453 and 631-641. Consult also Michael Crowder, *West African Resistance* (Ibadan: 1970), Robert I. Rotberg and Ali A. Mazrui (eds.) *Protest and Power in Africa* (New York: 1970); Terence Ranger, "The 'New Historiography' in Dar-es-Salaam: An Answer," *African Affairs* 70, 278 (January 1971): 50-61.

2. Although this description refers specifically to the Konzo, it also applies to a large number of similar cultures in Africa. For this particular quotation consult Kirsten Alnaes, "Nyamayingi's Song: An Analysis of a Circumcision Song," *Africa* 37, 4 (October 1967): 460.

3. Ibid.: 458-459.

4. G. W. Huntingford, *The Nandi of Kenya* (London: 1953); A. C. Hollis, *The Nandi, Their Language and Folklore* (London: 1909) and E. E. Evans-Pritchard, "The Political Structure of the Nandi Speaking People of Kenya," *Africa* 13 (1940): 250-268.

5. S. N. Eisenstadt, *From Generation to Generation: Age Groups and Social Structure* (New York: Free Press, 1971): 31-32.

6. Ibid.: 60.

7. Literature on the Nuer includes the following works: E. E. Evans-Pritchard, *The Nuer* (Oxford: 1940); Evans-Pritchard, *Marriage and Kinship Among the Nuer* (Oxford: 1951); and Evans-Pritchard, "The Nuer Age Sets," *Sudan Notes and Records, 1933-35,* vol. 19, part 2; and T. O. Beidelman, "Some Nuer Notions of Nakedness, Nudity, and Sexuality," *Africa* 38, 2 (April 1958).

8. Chinua Achebe, *Things Fall Apart,* chapter 7. The ritual killing of Ikemefuna was also discussed by Molly Mazrui, "Aspects of the Relationship Between the Individual and Society in Some African Fiction, with Special Reference to the Works of Chinua Achebe and James Ngugi," a thesis submitted in part fulfillment of the requirements for the degree of Master of Arts at Makerere University, Kampala, 1972: 258-263.

9. Eugene Victor Walter, *Terror and Resistance: A Study of Political Violence With Case Studies of Some Primitive African Communities* (London and New York: Oxford University Press, 1959 and 1972): 109-110.

10. Donald R. Morris, *The Washing of the Spears* (New York: 1965): 67.

11. E. A. Ritter, *Shaka Zulu: The Rise of the Zulu Empire* (London and New York: Longmans Green, n.d.): 14.

12. Ibid.: 16.

13. J. D. Omer-Cooper, *The Zulu Aftermath: A Nineteenth Century Revolution in Bantu Africa* (Ibadan History Series) (Longmans Green, n.d.): 27. Consult also James W. Fernandez, "The Shaka Complex," *Transition* (Kampala) 6, 29 February-March 1957): 12.

14. H. F. Fynn tells about Dingiswayo's postponement of circumcision ceremonies for military reasons. See James Stuart and D. McK. Malcolm (ed.), *Fynn's Diary* Pietermaritzburg: 1950); and John Bird, *The Annals of Natal,* vol. 1 (Pietermaritzburg: 1888): 60-71.

15. Thomas Mofolo, *Chaka, An Historical Romance,* trans. by H. F. Dutton (London: 1931): 137.

16. Max Gluckman, "The Rise of a Zulu Empire," *Scientific American* 202 (April 1960): 168.

17. Consult Karigo Munchi, *The Hard Core* (Richmond, B. C.: LSM Information Center, 1973): 19-22-43; Don Barnett and Karari Njama, *Mau Mau From Within* (New York and London: Monthly Review Press, 1966); and J. M. Kariuki, *Mau Mau Detainee* (London: Oxford University Press, 1963).

18. Alexander Mitchell and Russell Miller, "Amin: The Untold Story," *The Sunday Times Magazine* (London), October 29, 1972: 53.

19. Ibid.: 56.

20. Ibid.

21. For this version of the origins of the title "Dada" consult Judith Listowel, *Amin* (Dublin and London: IUP, 1973): 18. An alternative theory as to the origins of "Dada" is that it is a Nilotic concept denoting "patriarch," adopted as name by Amin's grandfather.

22. *Voice of Uganda* (Kampala), July 4, 1973. See also *The Washington Post,* July 4, 1973.

23. Fernandez, "The Shaka Complex," *Transition,* op. cit.: 13.

24. William H. Grier and Price M. Cobbs, *Black Rage* (New York: Bantam Books, 1969): 49-50.

Section V:

Policy-Making and New National Images

Chapter 11

NATION-BUILDING AND THE KINSHIP POLITY

We have defined *ethnocracy* as a system of government based on either ethnic exclusivity, or ethnic division of labor, or quantified ethnic balance.

We must now look more closely at this concept in a comparative perspective. In this chapter we are placing Amin's Uganda alongside Israel. Uganda is a military ethnocracy. Israel—because it has been a garrison state—has been a militarized ethnocracy. A comparison of the two countries should provide useful insights into the dynamics of the kinship polity.

Israel was born out of defensive ethnic consciousness. It was conceived as a state with an ethno-cultural definition. It was to be a Jewish state. The idea of *returning* to Palestine implied an ethnic descent from those who left Palestine more than a millenium ago.

General Idi Amin's conception of a new and exclusive Uganda has had important points of contact with the whole ideology of the Jewish state. Both the Jews and General Amin invoked primordial concepts of kinship as a basis for political organization and nation-building. And while there is a substantial difference in sophistication and intellectual rationalization between General Amin and Zionist theoreticians, that intellectual imbalance should not divert our attention away from certain fundamental similarities between these two ethnocratic systems.

The quest for ethnic exclusiveness in both countries has been conditioned by cultural and economic factors. What emerges is a shared concept of *ethnic self-reliance as a basis of nation-building.* As we hope to indicate in this paper, such an approach tends to obliterate the distinction between *nation-building* and *ethnic-building,* with important moral consequences.

By a curious destiny, the two countries have had significant points of historical contact. It all began when the nascent Zionist movement was first offered Uganda as the soil for the new state of Israel. Seventy years later Uganda had its first circumcized head of state, General Idi Amin—and the Israelis were for a while politically active in Amin's Uganda. Little more than a year later the Israeli presence in Uganda was suddenly ended. It is to this brief

[215]

historical interaction between these two countries that we should first turn, and see how it relates to the whole question of statehood based on ethnic exclusiveness.[1]

ISRAEL ON THE SOURCE OF THE NILE?

At the beginning of this century Joseph Chamberlain, on behalf of the British Government, offered "Uganda" to the Zionist movement as a home for the Jews. Chamberlain's offer to the Zionists was probably not entirely of Uganda but also of the highlands of Kenya, parts of which were at that time sometimes included within the territory designated as "Uganda." But Uganda's name has remained more pertinent in the historical recollections of Zionism.

Theodor Herzl, the towering European founder of the Zionist movement, gave the idea of an Israel on the source of the Nile, in East Africa, some serious consideration. He later conceded that Uganda might be eminently suitable for an *extension* of Israel, but not suitable to be Israel itself. Herzl had said:

> Our starting point must be in or near Palestine. Later on we could also colonize Uganda; for we have vast number of human beings who are prepared to emigrate. We must, however, build upon a national foundation; that is why the political attraction of El Arish is indispensable to us.[2]

Joseph Chamberlain lamented this reluctance on the part of the Zionists to make Uganda the primary focus of their ambitions. On December 21, 1902, Joseph Chamberlain made the following entry into his diary: "If Dr. Herzl were at all inclined to transfer his efforts to East Africa, there would be no difficulty in finding suitable land for Jewish settlers.[3]

But the founding father of the Zionist movement continued to think of eastern Africa more as a possible extension of Israel than as the heart of the Jewish home. Given that there were large numbers of Jews who wanted to settle together in areas that they could themselves control and call a common home, it was conceivable that Palestine might not be adequate for all the Jews who wanted to settle together in this way. Herzl, therefore, like the India office in the 1920s and the 1930s in relation to Indian emigration, did conceive of East Africa as a potential area of the second wave of Jewish colonization, rather than the first.

Why did Herzl retreat from regarding settlement near the fountain of the

Nile as a meaningful alternative to Palestine? The debate flared up afresh in Uganda itself as recently as October and November 1971, after General Amin had come to power. The London staff reporter of the *Uganda Argus* transmitted a story from Jerusalem. That was before General Amin's break with the Israelis. As part of their contribution to nation-building in Uganda, Israel was reported at the time as planning to develop Karamoja district of Uganda. Karamoja covered an area larger than the size of Israel itself before the 1967 war. The scheme reported in the *Argus* involved the development of surface and underground water resources in that rather arid region of the country. The Israelis, because of their own experience in "making the desert bloom" in the Middle East, were supposed to be preeminently suited to undertake this greening of Karamoja. The London reporter of the *Argus* then referred to Britain's offer to the Zionist movement at the beginning of the century: "Ironically, the Jewish congress rejected the offer of Karamoja as an alternative to Palestine as a homeland some seventy years ago. Theodor Herzl's delegates surveyed the area and reported that it was totally unsuitable for settlement."[4]

A debate then started in 1971 as to whether the rejection of Uganda by the Zionist movement was because of the climatic and soil qualities of the country or whether it was concerned with the mere fact that Uganda was not Palestine. Margaret-Anne Mackay wrote a letter to the *Argus,* published on November 2, 1971, putting forward the simple proposition that Palestine was the ancestral home from which the Jews had dispersed to the rest of the world.

A. S. Schick wrote in return to the Ugandan newspaper, explaining that the original impulse behind the Zionist movement was to establish a Jewish home somewhere in the world, not necessarily Palestine. Schick also asserted that Herzl's own predisposition had not at first been oriented towards Palestine as such but had emphasized the right to independent autonomy rather than a right to ancestral return. But Herzl was overruled in this endeavor and later became converted to the thrust for a return to Palestine itself.

Schick's account, though basically correct, underestimated Herzl's own leaning towards Palestine. Nor is it really correct to suggest that Joseph Chamberlain was offering the Zionist movement the arid areas of Karamoja on their own. The offer, as we indicated, included parts of what later became the White Highlands of Kenya. Julian Amery has used this to make the point that the land which was being offered to the Jews in East Africa was, from the point of view of climate and richness of soil, richer than what they could conceivably find in Palestine. According to Amery, there was, in fact, "no better white man's country anywhere in the Tropics" than the East African land which was offered at the time to the Zionist movement.[5] What made the Zionist movement insist on Palestine was therefore not the lure of a more fertile soil than in Karamoja, not the attraction of a better climate than Uganda's, but ultimately a link with the past. Herzl, himself basically a liberal and humanitarian, moved gradually towards an ethnically defined nationalism. He regarded the Jews as a biological group and not merely a religious or cultural community. The whole idea of creating afresh a Jewish state carried implications of exclusiveness which Herzl himself did not fully comprehend.

Are the Jews a race or a religious group? The idea has been debated for centuries. But the biological definition of Jewishness has persisted as a force in international discourse to the present day. C. P. Snow, the distinguished British scientist and novelist, said in March 1969 that he was prepared to believe that the Jews were *genetically* superior to other people. He was addressing a primarily Jewish audience at the Hebrew Union College, Jewish Institute of Religion, in New York. Lord Snow posed himself the question as to why the Jews had been so successful in scholarship, the arts, and the sciences.

> Well, take any test of achievement you like—in any branch of science, mathematics, literature, music, public life. The Jewish performance has been not only disproportionate, but almost ridiculously disproportionate. To use a crude criterion, run your eye down the lists of Nobel Prize winners for the last twenty-five years. You will find something between a third and a quarter have Jewish names.

Lord Snow asserted that roughly the same astonishing performance turned up whatever kind of human excellence one was examining. But why had this happened? Was there something in the Jewish gene-pool which produced intellectual talent on quite a different scale from, say, the Anglo-Saxon gene-pool? Snow's answer was: "I am prepared to believe that may be so."[6]

It is clear that both Herzl and Snow fall within a tradition of regarding the Jews as a biological group. From this point of view the idea of establishing a Jewish home was therefore oriented toward creating a purposefully exclusive state as far as possible.

Herzl acquired his concepts of nationalism partly from German intellectual traditions. According to a prevailing German theory of nationhood at the time, people of common descent should form one common political community. Pan-Germanism was substantially based on the idea of making statehood coincide with a presumed consanguinity. The beginnings of Nazism lie deep in the history of German conceptions of nationality in relation to blood. Nazism was an equation of nation-building with race-building. And Zionism in its infancy borrowed substantially from precisely these Teutonic concepts of racially defined national entities. In the words of Morris R. Cohen:

This constant tendency to emphasize the consciousness of race, tragically intensi-
fied by the increased persecutions of recent years, has thus led newly emancipated
Jews to adopt the very popular racial philosophy of history, represented on the
Teutonic side by Chamberlain's *Foundations of the Nineteenth Century,* or, on
the Russian side, by Slavophiles like Katkoff. Zionists fundamentally accept the
racial ideology of these anti-Semites, but draw different conclusions. Instead of
the Teuton, it is the Jew that is the pure or superior race.[7]

The celebration of the twenty-fifth anniversary of the establishment of
this ethnically defined Jewish state coincided with the pursuit of an exclusive
ideology by a person drawn from an entirely different cultural tradition,
General Idi Amin of Uganda. It is to this latter phenomenon that we must
now turn in further comparative analysis.

THE ISRAELI EXPERIMENT IN UGANDA

When General Idi Amin overthrew the government of Milton Obote in
Uganda in January 1971, the Israelis seemed to be on Amin's side. When
Milton Obote gave his first press conference in Dar-es-Salaam after his
overthrow, he explicitly blamed the Israelis for the success of the military
coup which had overthrown him. Observers were understandably skeptical.
Why should the Israelis have any special interest in overthrowing Milton
Obote? Obote had, after all, been the man who had invited the Israelis in
Uganda as advisors and teachers for Uganda's air force and the military.
But then, as the situation unfolded, there was circumstantial evidence in
support of the proposition that the Israelis were more than casual friends of
General Amin's regime. In the early ceremonies celebrating the military coup,
the Israelis were the only foreign country prepared to be conspicuous as
participants in the celebrations. Before long it was quite clear that the two
most influential embassies in Kampala were the British High Commission and
the Israeli Embassy. In a former British colony it is not difficult to discover
reasons as to why a British ambassador or High Commissioner should be
influential. The British in their former colonies either continue to be extra-
influential or are deeply resented. Either attitude has substantial historical
reasons behind it. But why should an Israeli embassy be influential in
Uganda?
Then Amin left on his first trip abroad. Considering that he overthrew
Milton Obote while Obote was abroad, it could be deduced that Amin's own
first trip abroad was bound to be preceded by considerable contemplation.
The risks of being absent from Uganda could be significant. If it was

necessary to leave the country, the choice of destinations had also to be especially significant. When Amin left Uganda on his first trip abroad, he had appointments with two distinguished ladies. He was due to have discussions with Mrs. Golda Meir in Israel, and then proceed to London to have lunch with Queen Elizabeth II. The two most influential foreign countries in Uganda were also those of the two countries which Amin visited when he left Uganda for the first time as President. There were extensive discussions both in Tel Aviv and London about relations between these two foreign countries and their protégé, General Idi Amin Dada.

Israeli interest in Uganda was derivative rather than direct. The Israelis were interested more in supporting the separatist movements in southern Sudan than in Uganda for its own sake. And since Idi Amin came from a tribe which was partly Sudanese and partly Ugandan, his role in facilitating Israeli strategy along the Nile Valley from Uganda into southern Sudan was for a while significant.[8]

For a while there were no special indications of any strain between General Amin and the Israelis. On the contrary, there was considerable evidence of firm patronage from and possessive concern on the part of the Israelis for General Amin and his government.

Did Amin regard the Israelis as "white people?" A question like this could have important relevance in determining the roots of Amin's conversion to racial self-reliance in Uganda. The shift in 1972 first against the Israelis, later against the Asian communities, and later still against the British presence in Uganda, all amounted to a major reorientation in the direction of black self-reliance. Why had Amin turned against the Israelis?

The evidence is still inadequate, but there is already some evidence that the Israeli presence in Uganda had taken a turn toward being defined as a form of "white racist arrogance." Were the Israelis white men? If they were, their behavior in independent Uganda seemed to some observers to be as arrogant as anything experienced from the British in half a century of colonial rule. Again, the question now arises whether Amin's experience with the Israelis was an important factor behind his rapid conversion in the months which followed to a doctrine of black self-reliance, and as a second alternative, continental self-reliance between African states both north and south of the Sahara.

But the personality of General Amin includes an orientation toward religions and supernatural concerns. Amin is caught between Jehovah and the Ju-Ju. It is not clear precisely what sorts of dreams or supernatural warnings the General had about the Israelis once the cumulative evidence of domestic concern about their presence began to be brought to his notice. No doubt other factors helped to shape Amin's attitudes towards the Israelis in the remaining few months before his honeymoon with them was well and truly over. Amin's later hysteria about the Israelis ranged from his fear of conspiracy from Rwanda (because Rwanda had diplomatic relations with Israel) to his remarkable letter to the Secretary-General of the United Nations in support of Hitler's policies on the Jews. Later evidence certainly tended to confirm a deep-seated psychological worry in General Amin. The evidence would seem to suggest that as the domestic resentment of Israeli arrogance, especially in the President's own home district, increased, Amin began to reconsider the whole role of the Israelis in Uganda. His economic debates with his Israeli advisers played an important but by no means fundamental part. Amin's hysteria with regard to the Jews and the Israelis can only be explained by a simple proposition haunting his mind—"Those who helped to make me may help to break me!" Circumstantial evidence does support Obote's claim that Amin's success in the coup, in spite of having only a minority of Ugandan soldiers on his side, was partly attributable to advice from some of his Israeli friends. There was probably an important difference of opinion on the eve of the coup between the Israeli Embassy in Kampala and the Israeli military advisers close to Amin. The embassy was probably on the side of normal orthodox diplomatic inhibitions, opposed to intervention in changing the government of Uganda. But the Israeli military advisers, in the face of President Obote's increasing pro-Arab orientation in his last year in office, were inclined more toward *real politique.* If Amin was going to carry out a military coup anyhow, there was a case for helping him to succeed. The tactics which enabled him to control the mechanized battalion in Uganda, and tilted the balance of effectiveness between his minority of supporters and the majority of pro-Obote soldiers, probably owed a good deal to the advice of sophisticated Israeli tacticians.

And yet Amin could not expel the Israelis for as long as the Sudanese Civil War was still being fought. Amin had relatives and allies among the Anyanya who were fighting the government in Khartoum.

In February 1972 a peace settlement for the Sudan was at last reached between contending Sudanese parties at a meeting in Addis Ababa, Ethiopia. Reports from southern Sudanese sources at that time indicated that the Israelis were almost the only ones of their major advisers who were opposed to the peace settlement. Be that as it may, the very fact that a settlement had been reached provided a potential new basis for Amin's relations with the Israelis.

It has been suggested by Israeli officials in Tel Aviv and by observers elsewhere that Amin became anti-Israeli as a result of visiting Libya. The sequence and causation were probably in the reverse order. Amin visited Libya because he was already calculating to expel the Israelis. But if he was going to expel the Israelis, it made good economic and diplomatic sense to extract advantages from Israel's enemies. The causes of Amin's rejection of the Israelis did not lie in the Arab world. They lay in the history of southern Sudan, the personality of Idi Amin, and the fear he had that those who had helped to make him could so easily break him. Amin did owe the Israelis considerable amounts of money, but these were subsidiary factors which the Israelis later decided to exploit in their own face-saving operation after their expulsion from Uganda. By the end of April 1972 there was not a single Israeli left in Uganda. It was not merely military advisers or airport builders who were required to go. It included other personnel, some of them doing superb developmental work in rural areas and overcrowded schools.

Amin's expulsion of the Israelis turned out to be a dress rehearsal for the expulsion of Asians less than five months later. Amin's conception of continental self-reliance within Africa, involving the substitution of Libyans and Egyptians for the departing Israelis, was in turn a dress rehearsal for his sharper commitment to *black* self-reliance in the months ahead.

Underlying the latter attitude was the kind of defensive race consciousness which bore striking similarities to the Jewish concepts of ethnic self-reliance which led to the creation of Israel in the first place.

If, then, the expulsion of the Israelis was the first major assertion of defensive consciousness by General Amin, that very expulsion was ironically taking Amin on an ideological road similar to Zionism. To this extent, Amin's rejection of the Israelis in April 1972 was, paradoxically, a dress rehearsal for the "Israelization" of Uganda in the sense of embracing the principle of group exclusiveness.

Behind both Zionism and Amin's black nationalism is a special concept of citizenship. In the Middle East this concept of citizenship created the problem of Palestinian refugees; while Amin's version of the same concept more than two decades later created the problem of Asian refugees. It is to this *Zio-Aminist* idea of citizenship that we must now turn.

ZIONISM AND "IDI-OLOGY"

Herzl, in his original idea of a Jewish home, did indeed see a state populated almost wholly by Jews at first. But his original solution was in terms of finding vacant territory which the Jews could then populate—"to give to the people without land a land without people." These were the days when Herzl could allow for the possibility of an Israel in South America. But by the time Joseph Chamberlain offered him Uganda, the lure of Palestine as the proper home for the Jews was too strong. And yet to Herzl himself the vision was that of a state where non-Jews might still live in an open society, and where the Jews and their religion would not constitute a privileged group.

It would be immoral if we would exclude anyone, whatever his origin, his descent, or his religion, from participating in our achievements. For we stand on the shoulders of other civilized peoples. . . . What we own we owe to the preparatory work of other peoples. Therefore, we have to repay our debt. There is only one way to do it, the highest tolerance. Our motto must therefore be, now and ever: "Man, you are my brother."[9]

Herzl was more liberal but certainly less logical than the Zionists who later triumphed. The idea of having a Jewish home where everybody else was equal, and where others could be admitted even to the extent of tilting the balance of population, was to some extent a contradiction in terms. Morris R. Cohen captured this dilemma when he asked:

Indeed, how could a Jewish Palestine allow complete immigration, without soon losing its very reason for existence? A national Jewish Palestine must necessarily mean a state founded on a peculiar race, a tribal religion, and a mystic belief in a peculiar soil.[10]

As Zionism gathered strength a strong preference for an ethnically and religiously purist state for the Jews began to gain ascendency, though this concept was up against considerable diplomatic difficulties on the international arena.

The Jewish Agency of Palestine, the shadow Jewish government before the creation of Israel, played down the notion of an ethnically and religiously purist state. The Agency was even embarrassed during World War II when significant members of the Labour Party in Britain went to the extent of demanding that the Arabs should be forced to leave Palestine to make way for Jewish immigration.[11] Early discussions on the best solution for the Palestine problem sometimes envisaged a federation of Jewish and Arab states. This was deemed to be one realistic solution which would reconcile the interests of both groups and fulfill the British Balfour Declaration of 1917.

His Majesty's Government views with favour the establishment in Palestine of a national home for the Jewish people, and will use their best endeavours to facilitate the achievement of this object, it being clearly understood that nothing shall be done which may prejudice the civil rights of existing non-Jewish communities in Palestine, or the rights and political status enjoyed by Jews in any other country.

At the diplomatic and international level a compromise seemed to be emerging. In 1947 a United Nations' Special Committee on Palestine (UNSCOP) left to make a new study of the problems involved in Jewish-Arab relations and conflicting ambitions involved. But when UNSCOP completed its work, it was only the minority report which favored a federation of Jewish and Arab states. On September 3, 1947, the majority report of UNSCOP recommended that the League of Nations' mandate, initiated in 1919 after the Ottoman Empire lost control of its Arab territorial possessions, should now be terminated, and that Palestine should be partitioned into sovereign Arab and Jewish states. That school of Zionism which was militantly purist in its conception of a Jewish home had triumphed. On November 29, 1947, the General Assembly of the United Nations—by a vote of 33 to 13, with 10 abstentions—confirmed their vision. The state of Israel was given a global birth certificate in imminent anticipation. A new political community, explicitly defined in terms of descent from the ancient Hebrews, was about to enter world history.

What did this concept of an ethnically defined Jewish state have in common with General Amin's own redefinition of Uganda in 1972? Both conceptions of citizenship were in an important sense pre-modern. This is what the compound concept of Zio-Aminism is all about. C. G. Montefiore was surely right when he argued as long ago as 1899 in relation to at least Zionism:

> There is no *apriori* reason why in any one state men of different races and creeds should not be ardent citizens living in peace and harmony with each other. The trend of modern thought, in spite of backwaters and counter currents, is surely in that direction. A Russia which must be purely Slav and of the orthodox Greek church strikes us as an anachronistic effort which in the long run will inevitably break down.[12]

As we have indicated, Amin's conception of citizenship borrowed from pre-modern African indigenous ideas. Citizenship in such indigenous polities was inseparable from kinship. A person could not belong to a social or even ceremonial collectivity if he did not have kinship status. In many an indigenous society both in Africa and elsewhere "there are no non-relatives." All roles are allocated and activities organized in relation to kinship status broadly defined.

This pre-modern conception of citizenship is sometimes better illustrated in some South Pacific island societies and among aboriginal tribes in Australia than in African political communities, but the element of similarity is strongly there all the same. Certainly many societies in Amin's part of the African continent organized themselves traditionally by kinship, either real or conferred. A new citizen became one either through complete cultural assimilation or through mixing his blood with members of the community concerned. What Meyer Fortes said of Kariera society is true of many traditional political communities in Africa as well.

> Outsiders can be incorporated into a society or a community, or more generally, brought into the ambit of sanctioned social relations, by having kinship status

ascribed to them. Different communities, even those of different tribal or linguistic provenance, can exchange personnel by marriage, and can fuse for particular ceremonial occasions by, so to speak, intermeshing their kinship fields. . . . Herein lies the essence of the kinship polity.[13]

Idi Amin, being a rustic man drawn from the countryside, assumed supreme political power in Uganda with political ideas still deeply conditioned by his peasant and rural origins. The fate of the Asians in Uganda was partly an outcome of Amin's primordial idea of citizenship. Idi Amin could conceive of different black tribes "intermeshing their kinship fields." Amin was capable of seeing other *black* people as kinsmen in a single society, though even that black empathy was sometimes severely strained. But the demand to take a leap and recognize Gujeratis and Punjabis as kinsmen in a shared kinship polity called "Uganda" was in some ways too modern for this rural rustic and rugged President. When he moved to expel "aliens" from Uganda, he originally included among them citizen Asians of Uganda. The cultural and kinship distance between Indians on the one side and the President's own tribe, the Kakwa, on the other side, was too great for this warrior's imagination. The result was a speedy equation between nation-building and race-building.

But here an important difference does present itself between "Idi-ology" and Zionism, between Idi Amin's conception of citizenship and the Jewish approach. For Amin readiness to intermarry is an important precondition for jointly belonging to the same political community. The already mentioned refusal by Asians to intermarry made it difficult for this rustic President to see them as genuine fellow citizens.

The Zionist approach to citizenship is in some ways quite the reverse of Amin's. Their capacity to see themselves as a group descended from the ancient Hebrews, and therefore as a group entitled to return to Palestine, was facilitated by their traditional goal of endogamy. When religion and descent are so intertwined, both ethnic intermarriage and religious intermarriage become additionally constrained and inhibited. Again Montefiore saw this as a problem for the modern Jew already in the nineteenth century.

I admit that in the case of the Jews religion and race are practically co-extensive. A Roman Catholic Czech of Bohemia may perhaps be united, so far as the Czech part of him goes, with his fellow Bohemian Protestant, and *qua* Catholic he will marry a German of the same religious denomination. Among the Jews, religion and race play into each other's hands, and the common refusal of intermarriage, however justified as the only means of maintaining the life of a tiny minority, preserves and strengthens the alleged isolation and difference.[14]

Today in Israel problems of defining the rights of Jews as against the rights of others have been bedeviled both by militant nationalism and by Judaism's hostility to interreligious marriage. Cases have come before the courts in the last few years in Israel involving children of mixed descent. The political forces that are still capable of being mobilized against the liberalization of Israel's laws of descent are still significant. Both the government of Israel and the courts in Israel have felt the pressures of ethnic purity as a political force in the Jewish state. And the pressures are partly religious and partly emanating from the psychology of the garrison state.

Amin's concept of citizenship is less purist than the orthodox Jewish approach. Amin himself claimed to be acting out this doctrine of "mingling blood" by providing a personal example. As a Muslim, Amin was permitted to have up to four wives. He availed himself of this Quranic latitude and took four wives from four different ethnic groups in Uganda. When his own is added, five ethnic groups in the country were mingling blood and "inter-meshing their kinship fields" in the matrimonial experience of a single man. The Kakwa, the Baganda, the Lango, the Basoga and the Lugbara, all found a moment of kinship identification through the married life of the rustic President of Uganda. Amin's conception of a political community as involving readiness to mingle blood found a moment of illustration by personal demonstration.

To this extent Amin's approach to the creation of a purist state is broader than that of Zionism, both because Uganda is in any case a polyethnic state even if uni-pigmentational, and because Amin carries the African vision of kinship as something ultimately designed to extend the frontiers of empathy. For the Jews, on the other hand, kinship is ultimately designed to maintain internal cohesion and exclusiveness. After all, had not the K'ai-feng Jews of China disappeared from the map of world Jewry mainly because they had permitted themselves to intermarry freely with the Chinese? And had not the Jews of northern Ethiopia become so *black* that for centuries rabbis had found it difficult to accept them as Jews? It was not until 1972—the year of Amin's expulsion of the Asians—that the Sephardic Grand Rabbi Ovadia Yosseff decided to save the black Jews from the fate of the Chinese Jews— total disappearance. Recognition was at last reluctantly conceded to the 25,000 members of the Falashim tribe of northern Ethiopia as a group biologically descended from "genuine" Jews who went to Ethiopia centuries ago.[15]

THE REFUGEES: PALESTINIAN AND ASIAN

The ethnic "purification" of Israel after its creation in 1948 was helped considerably by the military ineptness of the Arab states. The original Israeli boundaries as defined by the United Nations gave Israel 5,400 square miles with a population of 963,000 of whom 500,000 were Jewish. The Arab state partitioned out of Palestine had 4,500 square miles with a population of 814,000 of whom 10,000 were Jewish. Jerusalem, with a population of 206,000 had 100,000 Jews—and was turned into a separate body.

On May 14, 1948, the day on which the state of Israel was formally proclaimed, the Arabs launched a military attack. They were defeated near the controversial borders of partitioned Palestine. The Israelis had their first moment of triumphant expansionism. They occupied more than half the territory allotted to the Arabs, and increased the size of their state from 5,400 to 7,722 square miles.

Technically their territorial expansion should have resulted in a further ethnic dilution of the population of the new Israel. After all, the original Israel had little more than half its population Jewish, while the new lands which were conquered had a preponderance of Arabs.

But the Arabs of both the newly conquered territories and the original Israel were encouraged to flee. Who encouraged them to become refugees? The Israelis claim that Arab broadcasting stations instigated the flight of the Arab inhabitants within areas controlled by Israel. But there are claims that the Arabs had begun to run before the fighting broke out, partly as a result of the conditions of terror deliberately created in some areas by Israeli militants. One of the most notorious of such operations of intimidation was the "Deir Yassin Massacre," committed on April 9, 1948, which cost 245 lives.

One investigation made into whether Arab broadcasting stations had instigated the Arabs of Palestine to flee was made by the Irish writer, Erskine Childers. From the records of the British Museum Childers examined and listened to the tapes of Arab radio stations monitored during the first Arab Israeli war in 1948. Childers claims to have found nothing to substantiate the Israeli claim that the Palestinian refugee problem was created by Arab radio stations.

The Israeli government had promised Childers concrete proof about these broadcasting instigations. Childers visited Israel again in 1958, but was shown no proof of the point in dispute. On the contrary, he claims he had found on listening to the tapes of Arab broadcasts evidence of appeals from Arab countries asking the Palestinians to stay put as a way of ensuring their claims.[16]

One set of sources claims that the refugees have swollen in numbers since 1948 to over a million. Technically some of these refugees should indeed be regarded as Israeli citizens, to the extent that they were part of the population of Israel on the day Israel was created and were deemed by the United Nations to be citizens of the country. The United Nations was the body which had brought the state of Israel into being. The Geneva Convention which Israel signed in 1949 recognized the right of refugees to return to their homeland, whatever the reasons for which they originally fled.

But the doctrine of an Israel consisting of Jews was not easily compatible with the readmission of thousands of non-Jewish citizens. The Israeli immigration laws—especially from 1950 with the Law of the Return—are prepared to admit large numbers of Jews from Russia, Eastern Europe, and elsewhere, and complain if the Russian government makes it difficult for those Jews to get to Israel. And yet the same government so keen on Jewish immigration is at the same time militantly opposed to the resettlement of some of its own Arab citizens who fled twenty-five years ago. The Jews of Russia have never known Israel and would technically be alien to this part of the world. But the Arabs in tents next door to Israel were part of Palestine until Zionism triumphed, and an ethnically exclusive state came into being. The Israeli government says it has no responsibility for the Arabs who fled from Palestine, since Israel has replaced them with Sephardic Jews from Arab countries. The doctrine of ethnic purification continues to color the ideological legitimation of the Jewish state.

Israel has continued to have its Enoch Powells, its defenders of an ethnically exclusive state, to the present. There are strong voices even today not only defending permanent exclusion of those non-Jews who were terrorized into leaving the country in previous years, but also urging the further de-Arabization of Israel as it now exists. Life as a garrison state has taken its toll of Jewish tolerance. More than two decades of continuous military preparedness have sharpened Israeli chauvinism and Jewish consciousness.

Of the present population of three million in Israel, 10 per cent is Arab. But an additional one million Arabs have fallen under Israeli control as a result of the 1967 June war and the new lands conquered by Israel at the time. The Jews still outnumber the Arabs almost two-to-one even including the conquered territories. But many Israelis are already worried about the survival of Israel's Jewishness. A survey commissioned by the Israeli government in 1972 pointed out that the Arab population was growing faster than the Jewish, and that by 1985, if present trends continued, the Arabs would constitute 40 per cent of the combined population of Israel and the occupied lands. This is what has come to be called "the demographic nightmare."

Finance Minister Pinhas Sapir represented an important school of thought among Israelis when he said that he would rather give up most of the territory now conquered since 1967 than see the Arab population of Israel come up to 40 per cent before the end of this century. In a television interview in 1972 he said: "If I have to choose between a binational state which will include the town of Hebron, in the West Bank, and a Jewish state without Hebron, I shall prefer the latter."[17]

Sapir has repeated that a binational state would be a "tragedy". Former Defense Minister Moshe Dayan is in some ways less purist in his conception of Israel than are some of his compatriots. He would rather keep the conquered lands even if he has to put up with non-Jews. Dayan has been known to express the view that after ten years of economic union with Israel, the occupied Arab lands might voluntarily want to remain part of the Israeli state. But even Dayan has to think in terms of a solution which would ensure a permanent majority in the Jewish state.

In reality Dayan's vision includes a preference for the availability of cheap labor within Israel or cheap labor for Israeli industry within the occupied territories. Arab workers pour into Israel from the occupied territories in a manner fundamentally similar to the migration of cheap labor from Turkey into the Federal Republic of Germany. Within Israel itself, it is quite clear that these workers would be the first to be laid aside should there be an economic recession. It is quite true that the Arab workers are better off with the wages that they earn than they would be in their original areas; just as the Turkish laborers in the factories of West Germany are better off than they would be at home. But profound moral problems are raised by a situation where cheap labor is imported on a temporary basis, and on the clear understanding that never would it be allowed to affect demographically the Jewish state. They want the availability of non-Jewish labor, on the one hand, and the guarantee of perpetual Jewishness of their state on the other. The dilemma has posed for many Israelis and humanitarians profound moral unease.[18]

The similarity with Amin here lies in Amin's ambition to import temporarily personnel from other parts of the world, including conceivably the Indian subcontinent itself, on a temporary basis, provided the long-term black nature of Uganda is not compromised. Of course Amin expelled relatively affluent Asians in 1972, whereas Israel facilitated the flight of thousands of Arab workers from their homes in 1948. The purification that Amin undertook hit a group which was relatively privileged economically within Uganda, whereas the purification undertaken by Israel at the beginning of its history in 1948 hit a relatively bewildered and primarily underprivileged Arab sector of the Palestinian population.

But both Amin and Dayan want to combine the economic blessing of alien personnel without compromising the ultimate exclusive principle of their own conceptions of statehood.

Amin has sent recruiting agents to a number of different countries, expressing a preference for black labor, but still unwilling to give up non-black personnel for as long as there is a need for their expertise in Uganda. Recruitment in the Indian subcontinent itself was briefly explored by Amin's agents, at least until the hideous anomaly of the enterprise was understood, and the hostility of many sectors of Indian opinion within the Indian subcontinent to the Amin regime was more clearly sensed.

Again Amin's need is for sophisticated expertise. The foreigners he requires to replace the Asians are those who would have to be paid very well to work in Uganda. The foreigners that Israel requires are those who are cheap labor as compared with local citizens.[19]

> They come in the early morning, before most Israelis are awake, from the West Bank of the Jordan River and the Gaza Strip. Wearing Arab headdresses and work boots, they commute each day in overcrowded buses and taxis to construction sites and factories all over Israel. They are Israel's migrant workers—about 50,000 to 60,000 Arab laborers from the occupied territories who have come in steadily increasing numbers since the 1967 war to find jobs in Israel's overheated economy. In the last few years they have become an indispensable ingredient in Israel's economic boom—the cheap labor on which the economy has volted forward since the six-day war.[20]

The principle of kinship polity is up against the dictates of economic convenience in both Israel and Amin's Uganda. Economy and culture exert a mixed influence on these approaches to nation-building.

CONCLUSION

The days of Afro-Israeli cordiality were the early 1960s. Israel made considerable progress then in establishing new friends in black Africa. When one East African visitor was a guest of the Israeli government, Prime Minister David Ben-Gurion had occasion to remind him of the old plan which would have settled the Jews in "Uganda" instead of Palestine. The East African visitor replied: "It is a good thing that the plan was never implemented; otherwise the Jews would have been kicked out by now."[21] The East African visitor underestimated the resilience and determination of his Jewish hosts. What saved Uganda from the fate of Palestine was the Jewish preference for the soil of their ancestors. But with that consciousness of ancestry went the notion of an ethnically defined state. And Zionism triumphed in that ambition.

But history came to play her games of irony in a different way. The Uganda which might have become the home of an exclusive Jewish community fell into the hands of a racially exclusive African soldier. It was a soldier who owed something to Israel in his rise to ultimate preeminence in his country. But it was also a soldier who expelled the Israelis and began the process of racially "purifying" his country.

General Amin developed into a black nationalist, finding greater bonds with black Americans than with Ugandan Asians. Israel, on the other hand, has refused to accept the claims of 300 black American Jews who wanted to emigrate to Israel. And behind both Amin's black nationalism and the nationalism of the Jews was a conception of citizenship still basically premodern, drawing heavily from notions of kinship and shared descent. There were differences between Amin and the Zionists even in this kinship approach to citizenship, preeminent among the differences being the contrast between Jewish endogamy, on the one hand, and Amin's belief in the functions of intermarriage as a basis of national integration, on the other. But the idea of a Jewish state nevertheless remains basically similar to Amin's idea of a militantly black Uganda even if the non-blacks have to be expelled.[22]

Amin has been able to carry out the expulsion of large numbers of non-black Uganda citizens by a number of devices ranging from terror to the threat of making Asian citizens live the life of rural peasants (like the majority of Africans), in spite of their having no tradition of such a life in the Ugandan context.

Again life as a garrison state carried Israel to some similar excesses. In Israel the range of devices used towards "purifying" the population has included terror, both following the 1948 war and more recently against the background of Palestinian terrorist resistance. At least until the October war, 1973, the Israelis had shown a cynicism toward using terror on an official basis at least as elaborate as that of General Amin's. Terror by private groups is always to be distinguished from terror by governments. If the British Army in Northern Ireland were to use the same tactics of brutalization as those used by their opponents, the Irish Republican Army, the world would rise up in justifiable indignation. If British commandos were to enter the Irish Republic to try and root out and kill terrorists of the Irish Republican Army before any more sons of England were shot in the back in the streets of Belfast, again both the Irish Republic and the world as a whole would be outraged. But in 1973 the Israeli prime minister was capable of congratulating Israeli commandos who had moved into Beirut, carrying forged British and other passports, in order to break into homes of Palestinians and kill them in their beds. The fact that the Palestinians carry out such terrorist activities is not an adequate reason for official brutality by a government. Terror tactics by Ugandan guerrilla refugees operating from Tanzania could never justify the brutalization that Amin himself has committed in alleged self-defense against Obote's supporters. But once again the logic of a militarized kinship polity has its excesses. Both Amin and his Israeli counterpart have, in their different ways, at times embraced moral codes of their own, willing to invoke security and self-defense as legitimation for acts of officially sanctioned terror.[23]

The big difference for the time being between Israel and Amin's Uganda is

that at least for the Jews themselves within Israel the country is still a
democracy and a basically open society, whereas Amin denies not only
non-Africans but also black Ugandans an adequate arena of political freedom.
Because Israel is a freer society, voices of rationality and dissent are heard.
The case for greater liberalization of the laws of citizenship and emigration
has its champions. There are even isolated Israelis who are prepared to spy for
Arab countries in order to break the ethnic exclusivity of their society and
propagate their views of greater social justice. The Jews as an international
community have been in the vanguard of liberal and humanitarian thought.
But the fulfillment of the Zionist ambition, and the creation of Israel, started
a new era of Jewish identification with the forces of power.

Perhaps one day the commitment to a Jewish state might wane, and Arab
refugees be readmitted, and conceivably a federation of Arab and Jewish states
at last be consummated. The haunting voice of Herzl might once again remind
the Jews of another vision.

> It would be immoral if we would exclude anyone, whatever his origin, his descent,
> or his religion, from participating in our achievements. For we stand on the
> shoulders of other civilized peoples. . . . There is only one way to do it, the
> highest tolerance.

Perhaps both General Amin and his former Jewish benefactors in Tel Aviv
might one day come to sense the power of such a vision and retreat from too
rigid a conception of the kinship polity. Sooner or later two critical and
strangely related distinctions have to be drawn by both Israel and Uganda:
one is indeed between nation-building and ethnic or race-building, the other is
between toughness and terror. When those distinctions are at last made and
operationalized in policy, national endeavor in those countries might at last
cease to wear the ominous face of militarized ethnic exclusivity.

NOTES

1. Under Prime Minister Whitlam, Australia has at last abandoned an immigration
policy based on a "White Australia" tradition. Israel's immigration policies are more
exclusive than Australia's were at their most "purist."

2. See Julian Amery, *The Life of Joseph Chamberlain,* vol. 4 (London: Macmillan,
1951): especially 262-265. Consult also John H. Davis, *The Evasive Peace: A Study of
the Zionist Arab Problem* (London: John Murray, 1968).

3. Ibid.

4. *Uganda Argus* (Kampala), October 28, 1971.

5. See Amery, op. cit.

6. *The New York Times,* April 1, 1969.

7. Morris R. Cohen, *The Faith of a Liberal* (New York: Holt, 1946).

8. Consult also Ali A. Mazrui, "Is the Nile Valley Emerging as a New Political

System?" Paper No. 21 presented at the 1971 Social Sciences Conference of Universities of Eastern Africa, held at Makerere University, Kampala, December 14-17, 1971.

9. Cited by Hans Kohn, "Zion and the Jewish National Idea," *Menorah Journal* 46, 1 and 2 (Autumn-Winter, 1958).

10. Cohen, *The Faith of a Liberal,* op cit.

11. Dan Kurzman, *Genesis 1948, the First Arab-Israeli War* (New York: New American Library, 1970): 23.

12. See C. G. Montefiore, "Nation or Religious Community?" reprinted in *Zionism Reconsidered,* ed. by Michael Selzer (London: Macmillan, 1970): 61. Montefiore's discussion of these issues originally appeared in *Transaction of the Jewish Historical Society of England,* vol. 4, 1899-1901 (London, 1903).

13. Meyer Fortes, *Kinship and the Social Order* (Chicago: Aldine, 1969): 104.

14. *Zionism Reconsidered,* op. cit.: 51.

15. See "Israel Acknowledges Jewishness of Tribe of Northern Ethiopia," *The Washington Post,* January 5, 1973. For an alternative interpretation of why the K'ai-feng Jews of China got assimilated in China, consult Song Nai Rhee, "Jewish Assimilation: The Case of Chinese Jews," *Comparative Studies in Society and History* 15, 1 (January 1973): 115-126. For further discussion concerning Amin's attitude to the Asians in relation to kinship factors see Mazrui, "The De-Indianization of Uganda: Does It Now Require an Educational Revolution?" paper presented at the Social Science Conference of Universities of Eastern Africa, held at the University of Nairobi, December 1972. The issues of racial exclusiveness in relation to Amin's attitudes to the Asians were also discussed in Mazrui, "Sex and Indophobia," lecture delivered at Makerere University, Main Hall, January 1972. When taken in a historical perspective, of course, neither the Indians nor the Jews have fully observed their taboos against intermarriage. A major reason why Jews look more like other people in the specific countries they have adopted than like each other lies precisely in the history of illicit race mixture. On the question of the limits of the cultural assimilation of the Jews in foreign lands consult also Maurice Samuel, *I, The Jew* (1927) (New York: Harcourt Brace, 1954).

16. For a recent discussion of Childers' findings and their relevance for the present militancy of the Palestinian refugees consult the illumination series of articles carried by *The Guardian* (London) in October 1972. See especially Paul Balta, "Palestinian Refugees: A Growing National Consciousness," *The Guardian,* October 21, 1972.

17. See article by Yuval Elizur (Washington Post special), *Chicago Sun Times,* August 16, 1972.

18. Consult Terrance Smith, "Israelis Debate Morality and Economics of Using Arab Laborers," *The New York Times,* April 12, 1973.

19. For a discussion of Amin's efforts as an attempt to transcend dependency consult the chapter on the soldier, the socialist, and the soul of development.

20. Terrance Smith, *The New York Times,* April 12, 1973, op. cit.

21. Cited by Mordechai E. Kreinin, *Israel and Africa: A Study in Technical Cooperation* (New York and London: Praeger, 1964): 4.

22. While Israel refused to accept black American Jews, Rabbi Ovadia Yossef conferred recognition after centuries of debate on the Falashim Jews of Ethiopia. These latter, though black, were regarded as having genuine Jewish blood from long ago. See *The Washington Post,* January 5, 1973.

23. For the case of an Israel rabbi trying to promote a system of giving economic incentives to Arabs to get them to immigrate consult *The Times* (London), January 12, 1972.

Chapter 12

ECONOMIC TRANSFORMATION UNDER

A MILITARY ETHNOCRACY

From Uganda's own point of view perhaps the most fundamental question that arose following President Idi Amin's decision to expel non-citizen Asians was, quite simply, what the economic life of Uganda would be like without the Asians. Would there be a smooth adjustment after initial dislocations? Were black Africans likely to be as effective in commerce and the professions as the Asians had been? Or were there fundamental cultural and sociological differences between the two races that would make it very difficult for the Asians to be effectively replaced?

THE ORIGINS OF INDOPHOBIA

This lecture does indeed start from the premise that the Asians attained their levels of economic and professional success partly because of historical factors which favored them in the colonial period, and also because of cultural factors relevant to business success in a situation of minority status. As so often happens in the case of immigrants in new societies, there is a preselection involved. Many of the Indians that came to Uganda were, almost by definition, drawn from the more ambitious and the more enterprising sectors of the population of the Indian subcontinent. Their very readiness to uproot themselves from their ancestral soil and try their fortunes in lands fundamentally different from their own implied that the Indians who came started off with a high degree of ambition and enterprise.

The Indians of East Africa might therefore be said for a while to have evolved a distinct sub-culture of their own, different both from the culture of their immediate neighbors in East Africa and from the dominant value

[234]

systems of the Indian subcontinent itself. Again, this is not unusual for a minority group which transplants itself to another part of the world. Differences begin to emerge between that minority group and the bigger entity from whose womb that group was initially born. The Indians of East Africa had therefore developed an economic sub-culture which was more enterprising than the dominant cultures of the Indian subcontinent, but which of course also drew a good deal from those parent cultures.[1]

The British colonial authorities sharpened the entrepreneurial factor in the local economic sub-culture of Asian immigrants. They did this by forcing the Asians away from certain areas of endeavor, especially farming and food production. In Kenya the white settlers monopolized the field of cash crops and kept the Asians at bay. In Uganda some Indian participation has been very important in selective cash crops, but the principle of maintaining black ownership of land drastically reduced Asian potential in agriculture and diverted their energies even more purposefully into commerce and the professions.

The Asians did become successful in the business world, the liberal occupations, and in the clerical, managerial and administrative areas of specialization. They became too successful for their own safety in the long run. Certainly not long after independence measures were being considered by the new African government of Uganda to reduce the Asian factor in the national economy. The policy of drastically reducing the Indian presence in East Africa was by no means invented by General Amin.

It became clear quite early after independence that three distinct elements were involved in this entire endeavor. First, there was the deep race consciousness which had been building up for half a century, and which emphasized people's awareness of each other's color of skin; secondly, there was the fragile but growing territorial nationalism attached to the new entity called Uganda; and thirdly, there was a genuine desire to create an effective African entrepreneurial culture and a successful African business class.[2]

The race consciousness made Asians vulnerable, whether or not they adopted local citizenship. The territorial nationalism exposed black Africans from neighboring countries working in Uganda, while at the same time protecting those Asians who had adopted citizenship. In other words, when Ugandans adopted policies based on territorial nationalism, Rwandese, Kenyans, and Tanzanians, however black they may have been, were more exposed than Asians who adopted local citizenship. This was certainly the case in the last eighteen months of Obote's rule, when his new labor policies resulted in a large exodus of black Kenyans, many of whom had lived and worked in Uganda for many years. President Obote seemed to be embarking on policies similar to those which had been adopted by Dr. Busia when he was Prime Minister of Ghana. Busia in 1969 and 1970 initiated a series of measures which resulted in the expulsion of thousands of Nigerians and other non-Ghanian West Africans who trekked forth, uprooted from their normal areas of residence, often impoverished in the very act of removing themselves from Ghana.

Similarly in Uganda under Obote, cooks, porters, houseboys, large numbers of whom were from Kisumu and surrounding areas in Kenya, were forced out of the country, while the future of Asians who were citizens remained secure for the time being.

The third factor in this entire Asian question was the ambition to create a local entrepreneurial private enterprise system. Independence had brought effective African participation in government, administration, university life, managerial work, the clerical professions, law and increasingly medicine and other professions. But African participation in the higher reaches of the commercial life of the country was still modest. Again Obote's government, partly following Kenya's lead, started a series of measures to promote the Africanization of commerce in Uganda. The measures ranged from special loans to enable Africans to enter the commercial world to a request by the Uganda government to Makerere University that a School of Business be established as quickly as possible. In 1969 the Trade Licensing Act was passed in Uganda and a new Immigration Act was also passed under Obote's government, both of which were designed to contain and circumscribe the Asian presence in business, and to promote more rigorously an effective African entry into this area of national endeavor.[3]

Then in January 1971 the army overthrew Obote in Uganda, and before long Indophobia entered a new phase. We define *Indophobia* as a tendency to react negatively towards people of Indian extraction. Cultural Indophobia is a reaction against aspects of Indian culture and normative habits; economic Indophobia in East Africa has been a resentment of Indians as a successful economic group.

By August 1972 General Idi Amin had decided to push the logic of Indophobia to its extremity and create a purer ethnocracy. Why not throw out the Asians altogether? The original estimates placed the total number of Asians at 80,000, of whom about 23,000 were thought to be Uganda citizens. The rest were mainly British Asians (once estimated at over 50,000), and a few thousand from India, Pakistan, and Bangla Desh. Actually, by 1972 far more Asians had already left the country than had been assumed. The non-citizens were now given ninety days beginning August 8, 1972, in which to wind up their businesses and depart. The Uganda citizens had their papers subjected to a new scrutiny—and many lost their Uganda citizenship.

In the wake of the expulsion of Asians, could black Ugandans now take over successfully? Much continues to depend upon whether black Ugandans are capable of evolving an economic culture as relevant to success in these spheres as the Indian sub-culture among the immigrants was. If there are unfavorable cultural factors in the systems of values of black Ugandans, adequate success in this economic sphere could presumably presuppose some basic cultural changes. Can those cultural changes be brought about without a major educational revolution?

We would argue that a major "educational revolution" is needed if the Asians are ultimately to be effectively replaced in their roles and functions, but by the term "educational revolution" we have to mean more than just changes in schools, colleges, and the University. Important changes in the formal educational institutions may indeed be needed for this purpose, but even more fundamental is the task of making structural changes in the wider society and promoting new forms of economic acculturation in the population as a whole. The changes in the wider society must include new attitudes to acquisition and consumption, new perspectives on economic risk-taking as against bureaucratic security, a more modernized form of citizenship, and a transvaluation of the values themselves.

But in the long run, will Uganda adequately recover from the departure of the Asians? It is too early to conduct an adequate cost-benefit analysis of the de-Indianization of Uganda. There have been societies in history that never fully recovered from the consequences of their intolerance toward minorities. Spain is one such society.[4]

But Ugandans have a duty to try and salvage what they can. Even natural disasters can sometimes be put to creative purposes where there is a will to do so.

What part can the educational system play in all this? What aspects of the changes which have already taken place in Uganda stand a chance of yielding long-term benefits? It is to these questions that we must now turn.

THE ROLE OF THE SCHOOL

Any changes in the educational institutions have to be thought out carefully and would of course include a re-examination of syllabuses in schools and colleges and at Makerere University. But a less obvious, and yet perhaps quite fundamental, educational change which might be needed is quite simply a greatly increased number of government scholarships in secondary schools as well as an expansion of those schools. The aim in this case should be to make secondary education free as quickly as possible. Many countries in Africa started by making university education free, then moved on to universal primary education and seemed to tackle the issue of secondary education last. In the Ugandan situation, particularly in the wake of the Asian exodus, enormous resources should be diverted toward building up the level of *secondary* education in the country. We could almost "let primary education fend for itself!" There is enough motivation in much of Uganda to make parents and young people work hard to get into primary schools. But once the parents have successfully got a child beyond the primary stage, every attempt should be made by the state to facilitate the secondary education of that child without undue financial strain on the family.

Two important considerations provide the case for widespread free secondary education. One concerns the comparative advantages between free primary education and free secondary education. There is growing evidence that in African conditions primary education on its own is only modestly relevant to the economy and sometimes leads on to a relapse into illiteracy among those whose newly acquired reading skills are not adequately utilized. Secondary education provides a firmer basis for the acquisition of modern practical skills and helps to avert the danger of relapse.

But an even more fundamental consideration concerns the psychological consequences on a child who has had to struggle too hard for his education. Every week schoolboys turn up at Makerere trying to get jobs as garden-boys or cleaners in exchange either for some modest accommodation at the back of a staff house or a contribution towards school fees. Large numbers of Ugandan schoolchildren have to walk for miles every day in pursuit of an education. Many of them have to do their homework in little hovels, badly lit, full of the noise of other children and wondering where the fees for the coming term will come from. The parents themselves calculate from term to term whether they can continue to pay the fees.

In short, African children—unlike Asian children in East Africa—have quite often to work very hard indeed for an education. The question that arises is whether the strains that have to be undergone to acquire an education create a state of mind which, upon the completion of the educational process, makes the black Ugandan a bad entrepreneur. Does an excessive struggle in youth in pursuit of a particular goal create an excessive attachment to economic security at the end of the enterprise? Are well-educated Africans inclined toward more leisurely jobs, partly because the acquisition of an education requires victory over so many handicaps?

There is certainly evidence that sophisticated Africans are disproportionately security-conscious in their adult economic life and unwilling to take risks which might lead to the loss of their jobs. By the same token, they are reluctant to engage in economic enterprises which combine potential high returns with actual high risk. The question which arises is whether this kind of psychological mentality has been consolidated by the peculiar difficulties of acquiring an education in Africa, and by the high premium given to education as a passport to the world of secure privileges.

If this kind of analysis is correct, a great expansion of free secondary education in Uganda could help reduce excessive security consciousness among future Ugandans as well as lay the foundation of certain functional skills. The ease with which many Indians in East Africa have had access to good primary and secondary education could have been a fundamental factor behind the kind of economic sub-culture which made them so successful in this domain.

As regards replacing the Asians in such professions as law, medicine, architecture and the like, what is needed primarily is a quantitative expansion of manpower, and only secondarily a qualitative transformation of the skills involved. Africans have already demonstrated that they are quite capable of becoming excellent lawyers and doctors. The educational institutions should gear themselves toward preparing more black Africans to enter these professions.

In short, the problem of replacing Indian professionals with African professionals is more straightforward than the problem of replacing Indian businessmen with African businessmen. It is the latter task which requires a closer examination of the entire economic picture of the country, and of the educational and cultural presuppositions behind that economic picture.

Related to this problem is the replacement of those intermediate categories of manpower, such as clerical, managerial, and administrative personnel. The skills which the Asians had went toward providing an infrastructure for certain services and general development in the country. Again, the question arises whether drawing out these clerical and managerial skills from the African population might not itself also require the kind of fundamental cultural change necessary for the related area of entrepreneurial endeavor. Certainly new vocational schools will be needed—and also new attitudes to occupations such as carpentry, shoemaking, and so on.

But apart from direct changes in the formal educational institutions themselves, what other factors in the society at large need to be subjected to cultural transformation?

Some of General Amin's policies outside the economic domain may themselves have great relevance for solving the problem of replacing the Indians. Sometimes consciously and sometimes unconsciously President Amin has dislocated certain patterns of behavior and expectations in Uganda in a manner which, in the long run, could help to fill with local Africans the void left by the Indians. A process of national change has been let loose in Uganda in the Second Republic whose long-term consequences are still incalculable, but which nevertheless provides possibilities of a creative national response in the years ahead.

What other areas of national life in Uganda have been disturbed in a manner which is potentially creative? What patterns of expectations which were stabilized until the Second Republic have been disrupted in a manner which could in time release the entrepreneurial energies of black Africans?

The expansion of free secondary education and the enlargement of opportunities for technical and vocational training are important preconditions for the task of *economic reculturation.* But even more fundamental is the tilting structure of the society as a whole.

It is now to these issues that we must turn, remembering once again that our concept of an "educational revolution" is a concept that addresses itself not just to classroom situations in formal schools but also to the wider experience beyond.

THE DESTABILIZATION OF THE CIVIL SERVICE

A foreign researcher working among Makerere students in 1967 and 1968 analyzed the career preferences among the students and drew the conclusion that Makerere students put a high premium on *security* in their choice of a career. The evidence seemed to suggest that there was a low readiness among Makerere's students to take risks with the future. The most popular jobs at that time were in the civil service, with all the security of tenure afforded by that service, and the assurance of promotion on minimum exertion.[5]

In the first decade of independence Uganda had for its most creative sector of the population a group of security-conscious graduates produced by Makerere University from year to year. The civil service was by far and away the largest employer of the graduates. There was an ease of entry into the civil service which was in many ways staggering, as each new B.A. or B.Sc. stepped out of the Makerere campus into a government office with relatively little competition. Within that government office there was a solidity of expectations, an assurance of prospects difficult to equal in any other profession.

The private sector of Uganda's economic life could not compete effectively for the best brains emerging from the universities. This was not simply because the government needed the graduates, but even more so because the graduates wanted to go into government.

That old problem of risk-taking as the precondition of a vigorous entrepreneurial culture asserted its own relevance in the Ugandan situation. On the one hand, the Uganda government under Milton Obote was trying to promote an indigenous entrepreneurial culture and private enterprise system while, on the other hand, the most promising products of the educational institutions of Uganda betrayed a marked preference for very limited risk-taking as an approach to life.

Economic writers have sometimes distinguished between the passive investor and the entrepreneur. Alongside this distinction has been the distinction between interest and profits. The passive investor as an ideal type therefore prefers the assurance of regular interest on capital, or regular rent on land or housing. But the entrepreneur is prepared to bear more systematically the burden of uncertainty. In the words of at least one school of economic analysis:

> In so far as uncertainty as to the future is an integral feature of economic change, the bearing of uncertainty must necessarily be identified with the making of the ruling decisions in the economic system. Hence the entrepreneur is in a very special sense the key factor in economic life.[6]

Both Kenya under President Kenyatta and Uganda under Milton Obote groped for a while to create from among indegenous populations effective risk-takers in the economic domain. There was encouragement to the extent of providing easy loans for investment. In Kenya the Ministry of Commerce even undertook elaborate ways of distributing shares in important industries and business as a way of inculcating the very impulse to invest, even passively. Kenya succeeded to some extent in releasing entrepreneurial energies among certain sectors of the population, especially among the Kikuyu. The commercial life of the country is beginning to sense a Kikuyu presence. The Kikuyu community has displayed not only a readiness to take risks but also a readiness to travel far and open up new areas of commercial endeavor.

But, although Kenya's performance was still considerably better than Uganda's under Milton Obote, both countries still displayed signs of an economic culture that was cautious and inclined towards low risk-taking. In the Ugandan situation the dominant attraction of the civil service as a solid bulwark of security was an additional factor militating against entrepreneurial experimentation.

Even taking a gamble on politics rather than economics was more clearly illustrated among Kenyan civil servants in the 1969 elections than among Ugandan civil servants in the months which were supposed to lead on to the elections under *Document No. 5* by A. Milton Obote. Both in Kenya in 1969 and in Uganda in 1970 and 1971 civil servants seeking to be chosen as candidates for elections had to relinquish their jobs with no guarantee of getting them back should they lose in the elections. On balance there were many more civil servants in Kenya who were prepared to risk the loss of their civil service jobs in pursuit of political rewards on the open electoral market than there were Ugandans prepared to take similar gambles. Again the solemn solidity of the Ugandan civil service was itself part of the stranglehold on the entrepreneurial energies of the local people.

It is true more and more Ugandans were prepared to be at least passive investors, or to build houses for the sake of rent. But judged by the standards emanating from Asian performance, black Ugandans fell far short of entrepreneurial rigor.

And then the Second Republic came into being with the army coup of January 1971. Some of Obote's socialistic measures of nationalization were modified without being renounced. The rhetoric of socialism disappeared in domestic arrangements, but part of the socialistic infrastructure which Milton Obote had begun to build was retained.

Obote himself had combined socialistic pursuits with that imperative to create an indigenous private-enterprise system. A basic contradiction had bedevilled Obote's economic policies for quite a while. The year of *The Common Man's Charter* as a socialistic blueprint was also the year of the Trade Licensing Act as a piece of legislation to help the emergence of an African business class. For quite a while Obote lay himself open to the charge that he loudly emulated Nyerere's socialism and silently imitated Kenyatta's capitalistic experimentation.

General Amin maintained the ambivalence for a while but renounced the socialistic speechmaking except in foreign affairs. Then gradually Amin seemed to be moving toward emphasizing afresh the aim of fostering an indigenous private-enterprise system, partly for its own sake as a potentially creative economic culture, and partly as a way of helping Uganda to rely less on alien business interests.

But what about the bureaucratic tendencies of the elite? What about the low capacity for risk-taking? What about the overwhelming temptation inherent in the security of a civil service career?

In fact, General Amin had begun to undermine that security. Milton Obote in his *Communication from the Chair* addressed to Parliament in 1969 had reduced the privileges of the civil service in terms of car loans and even automatic annual increments, but he had left untouched the security of the job itself.

Amin basically reversed this procedure, reinstating some of the privileges which had been lost as a result of Obote's *Communication from the Chair,* but at the same time asserting that security of tenure could now no longer be guaranteed if performance on the job was deemed to be inadequate.

The most dramatic implementation of this new policy came with the sacking early in the second year of the Second Republic of twenty-two senior civil servants. The technical language was that they were "pensioned off," which in the majority of cases did apparently mean genuine retirement benefits, but in the minority of cases just the end of a career with nothing further to be derived from it. The sacking of the twenty-two senior civil servants was the most dramatic shock on issues of tenure within the service, and an impressive assertion that the attractiveness of the service simply in terms of security was now under challenge.

The sacking and pensioning off of certain police officers in August 1972 reinforced the new era of vulnerability for public servants.

The question which arose was whether this vulnerability could in fact turn out to be the shot in the arm needed for the private sector. Is the decline of the security of the civil service the beginning of an entrepreneurial climate in Uganda? Will there be greater readiness now on the part of gifted Ugandans to try their luck outside the public service? Now that the risks within the civil service are beginning to be comparable to the risks of private investment, will the domain of private investment attract into its fold some of the creative skills which previously sought the lazy comfort of bureaucratic security? This might well be so—provided the new professional insecurity in the civil service is not aggravated by *physical* insecurity for those who show other forms of initiative.

Amin's ideas on the administrative provincialization of Uganda also raise further issues concerning tenure for civil servants. The new provinces which Amin is trying to create are the nearest equivalent so far by Amin to that aspect of Obote's *Document No. 5* which sought to detribalize the political system by making each member of Parliament stand for election in four constituencies. Amin's attempts to create provinces which are not defined in ethnic terms but which instead seemingly seek to create administrative units of ethnic mixture, could be deemed to be his own version of detribalizing the administrative system of the country.

But will the new provinces continue to be headed each by a Military Governor? And will this interplay between a Military Governor and civilian Commissioners create new questions about the attractiveness of the civil service in the days ahead? If the proposed provincialization of Uganda does help to further de-romanticize the civil service, once again the private sector might ultimately gain.

A researcher working among Makerere students in 1976 may discover less infatuation with the public service than his predecessor discovered eight years earlier. The gap might thus be narrowed between the high entrepreneurial tendencies of the Asians while they were in Uganda, and the more restricted performance of black Africans.

An entrepreneur has been described as "simply a gambler in the economic lottery". Most Asians in Uganda converted even citizenship itself into an economic lottery. On attainment of independence they seemed unique in being confronted with three choices, as indicated in Chapter 4. No other group in East Africa was fortunate enough to have such a tripartite choice of insurance policies.

The Asians who adopted British citizenship did so purely and simply as an exercise in the economic lottery. They had no special feelings for Britain, and the great majority of them had never been to Britain and did not even intend to go there. The calculation was in terms of acquiring the British economic umbrella to ensure them economic security within East Africa while they themselves continued to live there. The Asians had carried the entrepreneurial culture to its logical extreme—citizenship itself became an exercise in cost-benefit analysis, a theorem in profit and loss. The Asians had at times proved to be excessively entrepreneurial; black Africans had often turned out to be inadequately so.

THE COMMERCIALIZATION OF THE MILITARY

Connected with these problems of cultural difference and bureaucratic insecurity is the whole problem of the militarization of ethnicity. Because foreigners are traditionally regarded in some African societies as potential enemies, and because different ethnic groups within the same society continue to regard each other as foreigners even when they are all black, an acute danger does persist in the relations between these ethnic groups. And these relations in times of stress could degenerate into a militarized confrontation.

This has in turn to be linked to the simple fact that African soldiers tend to be recruited from those strata of society which are still bound by traditionalist values. The Africans that have undergone a process of de-traditionalization are those who have either moved physically for a long time to situations where they have no kinsmen nearby, or those who have undergone a system of secular education, usually of the Western style. The armed forces in Africa recruit from strata of societies different from the more highly educated. It could be argued that the real problem with soldiers in Africa is not that they are very politically conscious, but that they are under-politicized. The level of political consciousness among recruits is often frighteningly low, and there is a marked lack of sensitivity to the political implications of their actions. President Nyerere of Tanzania staggered on to this fact after the 1964 mutiny, and Tanzania took active steps to raise the level of political education among the rank and file of its reconstituted army.[7]

When President Milton Obote of Uganda was shot at and wounded on December 19, 1969, roadblocks were set up around Kampala to control the movements of some of those who might have been implicated in the attempted assassination, and to contain any civil strife which might follow the attack. The soldiers had a job to do, and many of them performed their task with competence and humaneness. But there were also reports of the sense-less brutalization of people stopped at roadblocks, and even of the pointless killings of innocent civilians.[8]

These incidents in some ways echoed the experience of the previous month. When the ex-Kabaka of Buganda died suddenly in exile in London, the government of Uganda was presented with a delicate problem. Since the Kabaka was the leading opponent of the regime there could be no question of officially recognizing his death as an event of any importance, and yet to prevent the Baganda from mourning their late leader would have been to run the risk of serious popular disturbances. The government adopted a con-ciliatory stance, and mourning was permitted. However, when large crowds assembled outside the Royal Tombs at Kasubi, they were dispersed by the army and for several days afterwards soldiers molested civilians going about their business in the area. The government may have been involved in the original decision to prevent the formation of large crowds of emotional mourners, but there can be little doubt that it was embarrassed by the way in which the decision was implemented. The actions of some elements in the armed forces were counter-productive in terms of the realization of govern-ment policy.

Uganda has not been unique in these problems concerning discipline in the armed forces. Several other African governments have encountered com-parable difficulties. Uganda experienced some of the stresses of having created rather rapidly a new army for independence which was then allowed to expand quite quickly. The rawness of some of the recruitment aggravated the difficulties of socializing the troops.

Throughout much of Africa there is the phenomenon of a rugged mili-tariat, relatively unsophisticated politically, and unaware quite often of the possible consequences of its acts. These are compatriots who are under-politicized in the sense of not having been subjected to a process of socializa-tion which would have made them conscious of the nature of citizenship and its rights, the meaning of individual protection, the boundaries of authority, and the concept of national interest.[9]

In a sense the most fundamental of the processes of political socialization are those which relate to national integration, on the one hand, and to the consolidation of political authority, on the other. Soldiers become nationally integrated when they become capable of recognizing bonds of shared na-tionality and respecting the rights of federal citizens. Soldiers become absorbed into the system of authority when they learn to measure physical force against legitimate need, when they recognize their place in the pattern of roles and functions within the social system, when they learn to respect socially sanctioned frontiers of authority, and when they are sensitized to the broader concept of national welfare.[10]

In addition, the training of the soldiers during the colonial period presupposed a pattern of military duties which would involve dealing with distant foreigners as enemies. The techniques transmitted were techniques of maiming and killing. While soldiers of the developed countries in the West may indeed have their primary military duties defined in terms of foreign wars, soldiers in much of Africa find themselves dealing most of the time with fellow citizens of the same country. Here are people drawn from traditionalist norms, tending often to regard total foreigners as potential enemies, inadequately sensitized as yet to regard people from other ethnic groups as compatriots. And yet these same people were trained by the colonial authorities not in the soft arts of dealing with troublesome fellow citizens within, but in the harsh skills of destruction. Again, a paramount educational revolution from the point of view of the soldiers is a revolution which would at last recognize that the previous philosophy of military training inherited from the imperial power is inappropriate in countries which have very few foreign wars to fight and few international alliances to maintain. The most immediate duties of soldiers in a country like Uganda involve relations with their own compatriots.

But the process of politicizing the soldiers in terms of moral sensibilities to their new political systems may not be separable from a process of economicizing those soldiers. The two processes are indeed substantially different. The consequences of soldiers becoming political animals are to be distinguished from the consequences of their becoming significant economic agents. Nevertheless, it may well be that the two processes, like politics and economics at large, need each other for mutual reinforcement, as we have indicated in a previous chapter.

In the Ugandan situation, the issue which arises is whether the entry of soldiers into the world of business and commerce will create among them new perspectives concerning the value of stability. Where soldiers regard themselves as a group apart, in a relationship of economic warfare against the bourgeoisie, the soldiers' interest in commercial stability would not be paramount. For them other issues would intrude and demand more immediate attention. But, to use fictitious names, when Lieutenant-Colonel Mutindo and Captain Hamisi become, in addition to their military roles, shareholders in this industry, or actual owners of that shop, these two military figures will evolve a productive interest in commercial stability in its own right. And commercial stability is often an aspect of general political stability.

Not all the businesses and shops previously owned by Asians have in fact been bought or acquired by the soldiers. The soldiers are likely to become only a fraction of the total size of the national bourgeoisie. There will be many civilian businessmen to every one military entrepreneur. But the economic interpenetration between the civilian and economic sectors of society should help to reinforce the bonds between them. That old sociological theory of cross-cutting loyalties, as Lugbara soldiers find a point of affinity with fellow shareholders among the Baganda, could help both to demilitarize ethnic confrontations and reinforce the trend toward the bonds of modern citizenship.

For the time being, General Amin himself has categorically asserted that he would not personally go into business. Some of his statements also seem to encourage civil servants and soldiers to enter business, but as an alternative career to their present one. But in the actual operation of the Africanization of commercial activity in Uganda, the possibility of civil servants and soldiers being at the same time investors can hardly be ruled out.

As soldiers enter the culture of calculating profit and loss, the whole system of analyzing in terms of cost and benefit, their attitudes to the virtues of procedure and predictability might indeed undergo a change. Through the commercialization of the soldiery, a process of re-stabilizing Uganda might be set in motion.[11]

CONCLUSION

We have attempted in this chapter to see beyond the heartaches of the present situation in Uganda. We have accepted the drastic de-Indianization of Uganda as a given, and then sought to discern both the signs of hope and the lines of future reforms demanded by the situation. Uganda must continue to live with herself, now that the bulk of the Indians have departed.

But although the de-Indianization of Uganda is now, on the whole, irreversible, reservations remain as regards the way it was done.

It is true that General Amin invented neither the psychology of Indophobia nor the policy of economic de-Indianization in East Africa. General Amin's measures to expel Asian non-citizens were an acceleration of the policies of his predecessor, Milton Obote. But in that very acceleration lay the special dangers of the policies. A phased-out de-Indianization program could have been conducted without an excessive dislocation of services and needs in Uganda, and without too much disruption of the lives of the Asians involved. Indeed, the de-Indianization program should have been accompanied with a manpower program for Uganda. Uganda should indeed have refused the unilateral British quota system, devised by London with an eye mainly on protecting the British domestic situation from political problems connected with the entry of citizens who belonged to a different race. Uganda should simply have introduced a quota system of its own based on some rough manpower projections, oriented toward helping Uganda to realize its policies without dislocating some of its own services. The Uganda government could have said that one particular category of British Asians (for example, bank managers) should leave, say, by June 1973; another category (for example, lawyers) should leave by December 1973; a third category (for example, shopkeepers in specified cities) should leave by August 1974; and the bulk of the rest of the population of Asians from Britain, Bangla Desh, and Pakistan should leave by, say, December 1975. But the government of Uganda should still have allowed for a system of exemptions, even after December 1975. These exemptions could have been either on the basis of Uganda's continuing need for some particular categories of manpower (for example, doctors and teachers), or for humanitarian considerations in special individual cases. These latter humanitarian exemptions would surely include Asians too old to be expelled to a new and strange environment.

If by 1975 the Asian population of Uganda had been reduced from the peak of 80,000 to a mere 10,000 and the latter figure consisted overwhelmingly of Uganda citizens themselves, the government could have proceeded to use creatively these very gifted people as citizens and at the same time promote a new indigenous business class. The Asians who have adopted citizenship in East Africa are basically greater East Africans, as we mentioned earlier. They have made the impressive move from kinship to citizenship.

In any case, it makes sense that the few that are left should be rewarded as simply one additional African tribe. Kinship culture should be used in a new way. If Indians are overrepresented in commerce and some of the professions, so are the Baganda in the civil service, and the northern tribes of Uganda in the security forces. There is a case for restoring the balance in commerce and the professions, just as there is a case for such a restoration of balance in the armed forces and the civil service. The methods used in that restoration should be as considerate as those that might be devised to deal with other problems of ethnic arithmetic in the nation.

But there is another balance that needs to be struck—a healthier balance between race consciousness and human toleration; between territorial nationalism and the larger African view; and between the promotion of an indigenous private enterprise system and the dictates of economic and social justice.[12]

But even this balance cannot be effectively struck without social reform and new modes of economic acculturation. The educational institutions have to respond with a new emphasis on *free* secondary education and *expanded* vocational training. Hopefully, the civil service may never again become a fortress of complacent security, devouring disproportionately the skilled manpower of the country. Above all, ethnicity in Uganda needs to be demilitarized, and the soldiers have to acquire a new awareness of the costs and benefits of what they do. The partial politicization of the soldiers may indeed need to be accompanied by a partial commercialization.

The owl of Minerva hovers over Uganda's dark hours—while the cockerel of Masaka is hopefully waiting to announce a new dawn.

NOTES

1. We use the adjective "Indian" in this chapter mainly to refer to the Indian subcontinent as a whole, including Pakistan and Bangla Desh, rather than just the Republic of India on its own. The more popular word in East Africa for this group of people is of course the word "Asian."

2. I have discussed this third ambition more fully in Mazrui, *Cultural Engineering and Nation-Building in East Africa* (Evanston: Northwestern University Press, 1972), especially chapters 12 and 13. See also Mazrui "Sex and Indophobia," lecture delivered at Makerere University in Main Hall, January 1972.

3. For the Kenya experience consult Donald Rothchild, *Racial Bargaining in Independent Kenya: A Study of Minorities and Decolonization* (London: Oxford University Press, 1973).

4. See Mazrui, "When Spain Expelled the Jews and the Moors," *Transition* 42 (1973): 21-22.

5. See *Transition* (Kampala) 37 (1968).

6. Maurice Dobb, "Entrepreneur," *Encyclopaedia of Social Sciences,* vols. 5 to 6 (New York: Macmillan, 1967): 558-560.

7. For details of some of the problems involved see Henry Bienen, *Tanzania: Party Transformation and Economic Development* (Princeton: Princeton University Press, 1967): 374-481.

8. These issues are discussed in a related context by John D. Chick and Ali A. Mazrui in "The Nigerian Army and African Images of the Military," paper presented at the Seventh World Congress of the International Sociological Association at Varna, Bulgaria, September 14-19, 1970.

9. Refer also to Mazrui, "Political Science and Social Commitment Across Two Republics of Uganda," Universities Social Science Conference of Eastern Africa, Makerere University, Kampala, December 1971.

10. For a neo-Marxian interpretation of the Uganda coup consult Michael F. Lofchie, "The Uganda Coup—Class Action by the Military," *Journal of Modern African Studies* 10, 1 (1972).

11. Consult also chapter 7 on "The Rise of the Lumpen Militariat," above.

12. This critique of Amin's style of de-Indianization was first published in Uganda in my feature article, "Exodus, 1972," *The People* (Kampala), September 9, 1972.

Chapter 13

RELIGIOUS REVIVAL UNDER

A MILITARY THEOCRACY

In 1969 Pope Paul visited Uganda. He was the first reigning Pope to visit black Africa. In 1971 General Idi Amin "returned" the visit. He was the first executive Ugandan President to visit the Vatican. Behind both visits was the religious factor in Uganda politics. Neither President Milton Obote—who played host to Pope Paul—nor President Idi Amin were Roman Catholics. Obote was a Protestant, Amin a Muslim. But their diplomatic courtesies with the Vatican were connected with deeper issues in the political history of their country.

What were these deeper issues, and in what way do they relate to Amin's role as a military ruler?

If Obote on independence was heir to the colonial administration, Amin has in part become heir to the Christian missionaries. Uganda under Idi Amin has re-entered the era of puritanism and fear of God as principles of state-craft. If Max Weber's state was one which could successfully claim a monopoly of the legitimate use of physical force, Amin's state goes on to claim a monopoly of the legitimate use of *spiritual* sanctions as well. The government under Amin has aspired to create a devout society and to participate in transmitting the gift of religious leadership. It is in this sense that Uganda soldiers might be deemed to be "apostolic successors." Under Amin's inspiration, they have at any rate become pretenders to that divine role.

Rudolf Bultmann has argued that the term "apostle" once referred to all missionaries and was later narrowed down to the twelve disciples of Jesus in order to help establish the formal theory of apostolic succession. It was not until the end of the second century A.D. that "apostolic succession" was given a sacramental interpretation in the sense of uninterrupted transmission of a special gift of consecration and sacred leadership, descended from one or more of the original Twelve Apostles.

[250]

Our sense of "apostle" is the older one which refers to missionaries and messengers of God. A. Richardson distinguished between apostles who had received their commission directly from the Lord, such as the Twelve, and those who were emissaries of local religious establishments. The distinction becomes difficult with General Idi Amin, since he claims to derive some of his policies from divinely-inspired dreams. But whatever sense of "apostle" might be appropriate for the General, his regime has included an important theocratic factor, partly derived from the impact of the Christian missionaries on Uganda society as a whole. Again, it is in this sense that Amin stands "in apostolic succession" to the European founders of the imperial religious culture of Uganda.[1]

Against a background of state sponsorship of religious ceremonies, the banning of mini-skirts, newly-imposed drinking hours, a ban on certain forms of "teenage dancing," and the enforcement of religious unity, several questions have arisen concerning the Second Republic of Uganda under Amin. Has Uganda under him been evolving into a military theocracy? Is the country experiencing an extension of the ethos of military discipline in the form of a puritanical mood? Has the Second Republic become the *Sacred* Republic? What does Uganda's experience tell us about the interplay and interrelationship between politics, religion, and the military?

There is little doubt that certain theocratic factors have indeed been at play in the political style of General Idi Amin since he assumed power. These theocratic elements are related to the triple capacity of the General in this regard—the General as a soldier, as a religious man, and as a political activist. But we propose further to argue in this chapter that the origins of theocracy or neo-theocracy in Uganda do not lie merely in the military coup of 1971 but are more deeply rooted in the history of the country as a whole. The politicization of religion in Uganda has been a feature of the country's politics from way back in the colonial era, but has entered a new phase under military rule.

That is why the soldiers of the Second Republic are in an important sense successors to the early missionaries of Uganda. The early missionaries of Uganda were also profoundly sensitive to issues of piety, decency, and propriety, and engaged in forms of moral censure which have had long-term consequences on the entire life-style of the people of that country. The origins of the elaborate Kiganda dress, the *busuti,* and the ban on mini-skirts form one continuous moral thread in the history of that country. The ultra-modest busuti dress came into being partly in response to the moral puritanism of the early missionaries; the mini-skirt has disappeared in Uganda partly in response to the moral puritanism of the military government.

What follows from this is that we may be witnessing a militarization of traditional missionary activity, as new standards of decency, morality, and propriety are set by the soldiers.

But does the impact of the Christian missionaries hold in spite of the fact that the General himself is a Muslim? The General's own religious style and convictions are indeed based on the Islamic religion, but the impact of the Christian missionaries was not only on those they converted but on the society as a whole. Euro-Christian standards were often the reference point for Christians and non-Christians alike. Those Ugandans who were converted to Christianity acquired educational advantages, prestige, and influence. The socially prominent Christians influenced other Ugandans in a variety of ways. And even when Uganda Muslims were being defensive in the face of Christian influence, the Muslim reaction was itself a manifestation of Christian influence.

Today, with a Muslim President in power, the country has witnessed a remarkable interplay between the heritage of politicized Christianity and the beginnings of military puritanism.

But there is an additional factor which this chapter would seek to bring out. And this lies in the degree to which a military theocracy can have points in common with a socialist state in matters connected with conceptions of decency and sexual discipline. Since 1971 Amin has been moving to the left. In this regard we shall compare briefly Uganda under General Amin with Tanzania under Mwalimu Nyerere.

WHAT IS A THEOCRACY?

First, what is a theocracy? For our purposes we define a theocracy as a political system which uses God as a point of reference for policy-making and makes God the focus of political morality. Political wisdom in a theocracy is ultimately divinely inspired. The world of politics and the world of religion in a theocracy are profoundly intertwined.

We shall be discussing later the concept of a secular theocracy. When a theocracy is secularized the center of the system becomes not a God in the literal sense but a sacred focus of another kind. Certain schools of socialism, as we hope to indicate, provide potential foundations for neo-theocratic arrangements. The sacred focus may be a special interpretation of the concept of man as an abstraction. It was after all Karl Marx himself who argued "The Supreme Being for man is man." There are schools of dedication to man as an idealized abstraction which come quite near to being religiously inspired movements. Socialism at times is a deification of the worker, a conversion of the concept of the proletariat into a divine principle of reference. A socialistic state could become a theocratic state if to all intents and purposes the concept of the worker becomes almost dehumanized as this assumes the status of mystical significance.[2]

For at least a year before the military coup General Idi Amin was already beginning to make an impact as a religious man. He was attending special *Mauledis* and had begun the sustained refrain that he feared no one but God. There were times when President Obote betrayed his anxiety about the style of the new Amin. Was the General beginning to build for himself a political base among the Muslims of Uganda? Did the General have political ambitions? Or was he simply building up a popular following as a way of discouraging President Obote from taking stern action against him? Amin already had a substantial following within the armed forces. Was his adventure in image-building among the populace as a whole an exercise designed to give him extra protection against Obote's arbitrariness?

A supreme game of political survival started between the General and his commander-in-chief, President Obote. In that supreme game Amin won. The Second Republic of Uganda came into being on January 25, 1971.

Soon the religious factor in Amin's personality as a political activist began to emerge. The General expressed an interest in establishing a Ministry of Religious Affairs. He was finally persuaded to establish a Department of Religious Affairs, but with a full permanent secretary at its head. Amin's language included a theme of religiosity. He organized a major religious conference at the International Conference Centre in Kampala, designed to bring the different and mutually suspicious denominations of Uganda into something approaching national harmony. Each major session of that conference, even when subdivided into committee groups, was chaired by no less a figure than a cabinet minister. The chairman of a session was seldom a member of the religious denomination over whose session he presided. That very trans-denominational technique of organizing a conference was itself an exercise in promoting a new attitude towards religion in Uganda as a nation.

What began to emerge was that General Amin wanted to go down in history as the man who tried hard to come to grips with the religious factor in Uganda and attempted to forge national unity out of warring factions.

It was out of those initial moods that Amin appeared as a man committed to creating an ecumenical state in Uganda. An ecumenical state is to be distinguished both from a secular state and from a state with an established church. A secular state is one which systematically asserts that the duty of the state is to keep out of religious affairs and insists that the churches should similarly keep out of affairs of state. A secular state tries to translate into reality the dictum that citizens should give unto Caesar that which is Caesar's and to God that which is God's. The United States is a secular state in this sense.

The United Kingdom, on the other hand, is not a secular state. The head of state, Her Majesty the Queen, is also the head or governor of the Church of England. The Archbishop of Canterbury is appointed by the Prime Minister. Major doctrinal changes in the Church of England cannot be made without the approval of the British Parliament, either directly given or derivatively granted. There is no pretense in the British formal system of government to separate church from state. On the contrary, the very concept of an established church is a repudiation of such a separation.

The third type of state is ecumenical. In this case the state neither favors one denomination against others, as the state does in England, nor does it keep out of religious affairs as a major constitutional imperative, as the federal government does in the United States. The ecumenical state by contrast maintains a role for government in religious affairs, but not in favor of any one particular denomination. In the ecumenical state the thrust is toward state participation in serving as a referee among denominations, and in the systematic promotion of greater harmony. In the Middle East, the Lebanon is an ecumenical state, elaborately institutionalized. Different denominations hold different ministries in government; different denominations hold different percentages in Parliament. The Lebanese have since the 1920s attempted to provide their Christian and Muslim groups with a system of government that has institutionalized political balance based on religious affiliation.

General Amin seemed to have embarked on a similar policy when he first organized the religious denominations into a historic conference at the International Conference Centre. Among the denominations that turned up at the Conference, the Catholics were the most united internally. Though Amin later came to fear Catholic unity, he was initially impressed by it. Among the most divided internally were the Protestants and Muslims, each group having deep cleavages which went back several decades.

General Amin committed himself to promoting Protestant unity, Muslim unity, as well as unity between Muslims, Protestants, and Catholics. When a certain section of the Anglican Church tried to make a bid to secede and form a diocese of its own, the government of General Amin intervened. Amin's government categorically asserted that the Anglican Church was to remain intact, and no subsection was going to be permitted to secede.

And when Muslims were in disagreement as to when to celebrate Idd el Fitr, the government of Idi Amin chose a common day for all Muslims to observe as Idd el Fitr.

With regard to both the imposed unity of Protestants and the imposed unity of Muslims, observers might have had reservations about the legitimacy of the government to interfere in this way in the turmoil of power relations within religious bodies and in disagreements about theological issues.

I for one was greatly concerned about the implications of an announcement which came on Radio Uganda on the eve of Idd el Fitr in 1971. The announcement not only said that a particular day had been chosen by the Uganda government as the day for the Idd el Fitr holiday, but went on to threaten anyone who observed Idd el Fitr on any other day with unspecified consequences. It was one thing for the government to say that it would grant only a particular day as a day of rejoicing, off work. It was quite another to threaten retribution to those who went to the Mosque for Idd prayers on another day.

Uganda had witnessed a variety of forms of interference with freedom. But there was a danger that freedom of conscience might itself be interfered with for the best ecumenical motives in the world. And in fact the most serious risk of invading religious conscience so far has not been with reference to Christians but to Muslims. The secessionist movement within the Anglican Church was an exercise in power politics within the Church rather than a doctrinal issue of theological interpretation. But the issue of Idd el Fitr in its very simplicity, perhaps in its very frivolity, was an issue which concerned how long the Muslims observed the fast of Ramadhan and on which particular day they were to break that fast. The issue was much more purely religious than the bid for secessionism within the Anglican Church. The fast of Ramadhan was a fast for simple people, based according to some on when the moon was sighted with the naked eye in the very country in which the fast was being observed; and according to other versions the month of Ramadhan was to be counted in precise astronomical calculations. Which side one belonged to was quite clearly a matter of deeply held conviction.

On the day I heard on the radio that any Muslim who attempted to pray on the day other than that prescribed by the government would face an unspecified retribution I was deeply disturbed. I attempted to contact members of the Uganda government. I also attempted for several hours to contact His Excellency the President himself. My purpose was not to challenge the desirability of promoting harmony and unity among religious factions in Uganda. My ambition was simply to try and persuade our policy-makers to be careful lest the pursuit of religious unity should result in a violation of the freedom of conscience.

General Amin did find out about my reservations on this issue. I later discussed it in a related context in my own fortnightly column in *The People*.[3]

Regardless of these reservations, however, we have in these instances part of the story of Amin's ecumenicalism, struggling against the sectarian history of the country and against Amin's own inadequacies and lack of sustained sense of direction.

But at what point does an ecumenical state become a theocracy? Both the state with the established church and the ecumenical state could become a theocracy when the center of the political system becomes markedly God-conscious in its policy formulation. Where the state merely tries to promote religious harmony, without directly engaging in defining the boundaries of spiritual purity and moral behavior, the state could be ecumenical without being theocratic. But where the state invokes God as the fountain of political morality and specifies directions of moral puritanism symptomatic of religious fervor, the state has become not only ecumenical but also theocratic in spirit.

The question which now arises is whether the nature of theocratic trends in Uganda is due to special innovations of the Second Republic or whether they are due to some deep-rooted traditions within the country as a whole.

My own argument in this chapter is to the effect that the roots of these theocratic trends lie in a fragile interaction between a nascent military puritanism, the personality of Amin, and the longstanding historic interaction between religion and politics in Uganda. In spite of Amin's upbringing as a Muslim, the theocratic trends and the moral puritanism in his Second Republic of Uganda have, in historical terms, a Christian genesis. But the puritanical element under army rule has been reinforced by certain aspects of the military ethos itself, with its theoretical emphasis on "barrack austerity" and discipline. In reality the Ugandan army is not among the most disciplined and self-denying in the world. Yet even that may help to explain Amin's search for a wider climate of discipline. Amin seems to feel that his army will sober up only when society as a whole becomes more sober.

Lastly, the personality of the General has itself played a part in defining the boundaries of these theocratic and puritanical elements. The General's style includes elements of religious leadership. He makes use of dreams and pre-vision as ingredients in political image-building. The utilization of dreams and inspired pre-visions is often more a characteristic of religious leaders than of political ones in the modern period. General Amin lies astride both traditions. Sometimes he defines a dream only partially, leaving the important factors undefined and adding to the mystery of what is forecast. Indeed the General cannot be excluded as a factor in his own right behind the theocratic trends in Uganda. He does claim a special divine gift—an apostle in uniform.

Some countries have Pilgrim Fathers among their founders. Uganda can now count on one Pilgrim Dada in a formative period of its history.[4] Will the General go down in history as a religious unifier or was this particular "dream" too much for this rough-and-ready Muslim soldier? We shall return to this later in the analysis.

THE CHRISTIAN ORIGINS OF UGANDA'S PURITANISM

But more important than Amin's religiosity is the deeper history of Uganda as a sacralized polity. Indeed, Amin's religiosity might itself have been profoundly influenced by that older interplay between religion and politics in the life of Uganda since the 1890s.

Professor B. A. Low once argued that Uganda's receptivity to Christianity was facilitated by the prior coming of Islam. Citing an argument of David Livingstone's brother-in-law, John Smith Moffat, Low shared the view that a new religion found it easiest to take root in a place where traditional values had already been disturbed. In the words of Moffat,

> It is where the political organization is most perfect, and the social system still in its aboriginal vigour, that the missionary has the least success in making an impression. Where things have undergone a change and the old feudal usages have lost their power, where there is a measure of disorganization, the new ideas which the Gospel brings with it do not come into collision with any powerful political prejudice. The habits and modes of thinking have been broken up, and so there is a preparation for the seed of the Word.[5]

Applying this reasoning especially to Buganda, Anthony Low suggested that the Christian missions would have encountered the prejudice of deep-seated Buganda traditional religions had the atmosphere for change not already been prepared for them by the Arabs. The first Arabs to enter Buganda were later expelled by Kabaka Suna. The Arabs were allowed to return by Suna's successor, Kabaka Mutesa I, at the beginning of the 1860s. The fortunes of Islam and the Arabs fluctuated. But the Arab intrusion was itself a preparation for what came later. As Low expressed it:

> Though Islam had been the first to make its way in, Christian missionaries arrived at a singularly opportune moment. For Islam was not firmly entrenched, so that Christianity did not have to compete with another world religion—always a difficult matter; but Islam had set many minds agog; it had brought an era of change, and this helped to give Christianity its entree more particularly because the first question was usually whether Christianity was a better version of religion than Islam—and here the Christian denunciation of Arab slave dealings was clearly important. Certainly the relatively exemplary character of the missionaries had its influence.

The merits of the Koran and the Bible were hotly debated, and the degree to which the Koran and the Bible sometimes agreed as against the local values of traditional Buganda also entered the arena of theological disputation. But the central point which Low was making was, quite simply, Islam disturbed the ethical world of the Baganda sufficiently to prepare the way for Christianity.

By the time that Uganda as a whole had its first Muslim President, Christianity in turn had mixed religion and politics in Uganda for long enough to prepare the way for General Amin's theocratic tendencies. Would the earlier Christian arrogance of Uganda in turn lead to a new Muslim intolerance?

And as a final touch of foreign policy ironies, the Israelis in the Second Republic of Uganda had, by default, prepared the way for the Arabs. The dialectic of history had indeed been at work, as one rival religion had cleared a path for another and one rival political entity made way for its own enemy.

But in what manner did Christianity lay the foundation for the theocratic styles of the Second Republic of Uganda under Amin? And in what manner did this in turn relate to the problem of moral puritanism and its demands on individual behavior?

From this point of view the Christian impact on Uganda has to be seen as a two-pronged impact. Uganda witnessed what might be called the *Christianization of sexual relations;* and Uganda also witnessed the *politicization of Christianity.* The Christianization of the world of sex prepared the ground for moral puritanism; the politicization of Christianity in Uganda initiated the theocratic process. Let us take each of these two trends in turn.

The Christianization of sexual relations arose out of the widespread belief among the early missionaries that the world of sex in African societies was a little too loose; that inadequate discipline was exercised over sexual appetites. The missionaries were bringing the Gospel to "heathen communities" steeped not only in superstition but also in sinful desires. The first behavioral imperative therefore was to control those areas of African life which helped to whet those appetites and desires. Discipline was of the first order, and a new regularity needed to be imposed. Even when the missionaries accomplished successfully the excellent mission of rescuing victims of slave-traders and establishing settlements for them pending their rehabilitation, the opportunity was taken by the missionaries to transform the moral ways of these liberated victims. The British historian, Roland Oliver, wrote this about such settlements for Africans in East Africa under missionary tutelage:

> Within the enclaves there was no social ostracism to be endured for Christ's sake.... There were no sexual initiation rites and no ceremonial debauches to enflame the passions beyond their normal vigour. Instead, there was a new social solidarity calculated to support the ethical doctrines of Christianity. Monogamy, the greatest stumbling block, was a condition of residence [in these enclaves], and polygamy in the new economic conditions lost much of its significance as the only means to wealth and power.[6]

The new schools which came into being proceeded to discourage important areas of African cultural life, on the assumption that these contributed to moral laxity and sinful appetites. Africa experienced its own interrupted symphony—the interruption of certain kinds of dance, music, and drama as these were banned by missionary intervention.

When in 1972 Amin banned what he called "teenage dancing," he was as firmly within a Christian tradition in Africa as he was within an Islamic one. Amin's regulation of drinking hours in the Second Republic was also as firmly Christian and missionary as it was Islamic. Missionary disapproval of alcohol for Africans went deeper than the American experience of prohibition.

Behind it all was the wider puritanism concerning "appetites," including disapproval of sexual longings.

A liberal and deeply Afrophile modern missionary who worked at Makerere was F. B. Welbourn. Welbourn cited the lament of a deeply Christian English woman who said, "We are told to make friends with Africans and to invite them to our houses. But I cannot bring myself to regard as social equals men who are polygamists. Perhaps I'm out of date and ought to go back to England for good."

Trying to understand both sides, Welbourn attempted to define the dilemma for the Church in Africa. The dilemma arose in the clash between Western Christianity and firmly-rooted African customs. Welbourn observed that

> The first missionaries . . . found a society that was polygamous by conviction. Bride wealth was an important aid to the stability of marriage. . . . They found a society where drunkenness was rife. Dances not only were an essential contribution to social wellbeing but often ended in unrestrained sexual promiscuity. . . . The first impact of Christianity on Buganda led to the banning of all traditional dances as potentially obscene. All African music was felt, in some way or other, to be connected with paganism and were therefore "of the devil."[7]

The banning of certain traditional forms of dancing and music has remained in many East African schools to the present day. Some changes have indeed taken place in some respects. Increasingly attention is given to the possibility of using some traditional music for church services. Welbourn referred to the adoption of the traditional Royal Dance of Acholi, with suitable modifications, for use at Christian festivals. Today it is possible to see on Uganda television Acholi dancing by Acholi girls from schools which bear names like "the Immaculate Virgin." Of course, the girls are covered from neck to toe quite often, and not just across their breasts. But the movements of the traditional dance are now actually being permitted, duly covered up, on television under the sponsorship of a religious school.

And yet it was an Acholi poet, Okot P'Bitek, who put into the words of Lawino the lament concerning Africa's interrupted dances. Okot captured the clash of interpretations concerning which kind of dancing was near to obscenity and which was not. Okol, a Westernized Acholi husband and apparently Christianized in his inhibitions, denounced to his wife, Lawino, traditional dances. Those dances were, in Okol's view, "mortal sins." Lawino's own description of these dances does reveal why missionaries had reservations about them. The dances according to Lawino are held in broad daylight so that things can be seen openly.

> All parts of the body
> Are clearly seen in the arena,
> Health and liveliness
> Are shown in the arena!
>
> When the daughter of the Bull
> Enters the arena
> She does not stand there
> Like stale beer that does not sell,
> She jumps here
> She jumps there.
> When you touch her
> She says "Don't touch me!"
>
> The tattoos on her chest
> Are like palm fronds
> The tattoos on her back
> Are like stars on a black night;
> Her eyes sparkle like the fireflies,
> Her breasts are ripe
> Like the full moon.
>
> When the age mate of her brother sees them,
> When, by accident,
> The eyes of her lover
> Fall on her breasts
> Do you think the young man sleeps?
> Do you know what fire eats his insides?[8]

But Lawino then moves on to indicate how the ballroom dancing which her Christian husband approves of is to her more shameful than anything performed in a traditional Acholi arena. In the words of Lawino:

> My husband laughs at me
> Because I cannot dance white men's dances;
> He despises Acholi dances
> He nurses stupid ideas
> That the dances of his People
> Are sinful,
> That they are mortal sins.
>
> I am completely ignorant

Of the dances of foreigners
And I do not like it.
Holding each other
Tightly, tightly
In public
I cannot.
I am ashamed.
. . .
Each man has a woman
Although she is not his wife,
They dance inside a house
And there is no light.[9]

What we have here are competing interpretations of obscenity, Acholi and Euro-missionary versions.

CHRISTIAN ORIGINS OF UGANDA'S THEOCRACY

But it is not merely the moral puritanism of the Second Republic that has its genesis in the missionary influence; it is also the sacralization of the state.

Religion became politicized in Uganda in the modern period quite early partly because competitive proselytism was also competitive imperialism. The British became identified with Protestantism; the French with Catholicism; the Arabs with Islam. Proselytism might have been a competition for the souls of men; but imperialism was a competition for the control of societies. The Catholics became *Bafranza;* the Protestants became *Baingleza*—each denoting the national origins of the missionary thrust.

At first the Catholics and the Protestants were united as Christians against the Muslim threat. The most important unifying factor for Christians was Islam. Arab and European immigrants struggled for supremacy in Uganda toward the end of the nineteenth century. In the words of an official of the British East Africa Company in 1888 when Arab influence was on the ascendancy in Buganda: "These events render the question now paramount: is Arab or European power henceforth to prevail in Central Africa?"[10]

This was in many ways the time of maximum amity between Protestants and Catholics in Uganda. When Lugard came he managed to rally the Christian armies of both denominations and put an end to the Muslim "threat" and the power of the Muslim party. But in so doing Lugard "thus dissolved the last link binding the Catholics and the Protestants."[11]

The stage was set for a continuing dialectic between church and state in the public life of Uganda. By the eve of independence religious affiliation was already an important factor conditioning people's political responses. Uganda had at times already been viewed as "the Ireland of Africa," more susceptible to religious animosities than almost any other black African state.

The last elections held in Uganda were in 1961 and 1962. In both elections sectarian differences were evident. The Democratic Party became identified with the Roman Catholic Church and, though to a lesser extent, the Uganda People's Congress under Milton Obote became identified with the Protestants.

And yet the ethnic factor in Uganda was always straining to reassert its primacy. With the emergence of Kabaka Yekka as the royalist party of the Baganda, ethnic loyalties momentarily superseded religious forms of solidarity. The 1962 elections showed a reduction in the influence of religion in the voting compared to the 1961 elections, but that might well have been mainly because Kabaka Yekka had come into being and competed in 1962, and ethnic loyalties within Buganda and against the Baganda affected the balance of support for the two other parties. The alliance between the so-called Protestant party, the Uganda People's Congress, and the party of the Baganda, the Kabaka Yekka, helped further to obfuscate the religious dimension. After all the majority of the Baganda were Catholics—though in the ultimate analysis they were probably Baganda first and Catholics second.

By 1970 Obote was designing a new method of election which would dilute the ethnicity which had characterized the 1962 elections, and perhaps start a process which would help to keep tribal considerations out of the political behavior of parliamentarians. Obote emerged with a scheme known as *Document No. 5,* whereby each Member of Parliament was to stand in four constituencies. One of these constituencies was to be in the north, one in the south, one in the east, and one in the west of the country. The Member of Parliament would thereby be compelled by the quadruple nature and multi-tribal composition of his electorate to look for areas of trans-ethnic interest and trans-regional popularity rather than for platforms of a more parochial appeal. But the question arose with *Document No. 5* whether if Obote succeeded in de-tribalizing Parliament, he would by that same result re-sacralize it. Elections would be spared ethnicity, but at the cost of lending new importance to religion. After all, the voters had to choose their candidates by some criterion or another. In a situation where none of the two or three candidates standing was of their ethnic group, the second point of solidarity might well be that of denominational affiliation. Members of Parliament might once again be chosen, perhaps more clearly than ever, on the basis of whether they were Catholic, Protestant, or Muslim. A resurgence of sectarianism was feared should Obote's ambition to de-tribalize politics succeed. The fear arose precisely because the Uganda polity had for so long retained this heavy religious intrusion.

But a curious factor began to be observable. On the one hand the

Democratic Party was indeed the party which had the closest correlation between political support and religious affiliation. It was a party which had indeed been helped to come into being by church organizations. It was a party which was nearly named the Christian Democratic Party, similar to Christian Democratic Parties in Europe. The identification of DP with Catholicism was certainly much clearer than the identification of the UPC with Protestantism.

And yet in some ways the Democratic Party had a vision of establishing a secular state years before the UPC was radicalized in the same direction. There was a populist theme in the policies of this Democratic Party, opposed quite often to monarchical privilege at Mengo in Buganda years before Obote had the political courage to engage in similar denunciations.

The Democratic Party was also quite early opposed to the idea of giving special posts and jobs and ministries on the basis of religious affiliation. After all, Buganda, like the Lebanon, had itself devised a semi-ecumenical state to the extent that an attempt was made to distribute political offices partly with religion in mind. On the one hand Buganda had a clear Protestant establishment at the top, headed by the Kabaka himself who by the time of independence could not conceivably have been anything else but Protestant. But on the other hand, ministries in the Kabaka's government were distributed partly on a religious basis.

It was not Obote's Uganda Peoples' Congress which denounced this system at the beginning; it was in fact the Democratic Party.

On the eve of independence Mr. W. Senteza-Kajubi, personal advisor to the president of the Democratic Party, released the manifesto of the DP for Buganda. On the question of religion the Democratic Party manifesto promised that the party would work for the abolition of the system by which religion was used as a criterion for the appointment of people to responsible posts. The system of appointing the Katikiro, the Omuwanika, and the Omulamuzi (different portfolios) in the Kabaka's government on the basis of religion would be subject to speedy abolition if the DP won.

The party was in favor of allowing church organizations, like any other organized group in the society, to have a say in politics. Just as trade unions and students felt free to put forward their own interests on matters affecting personal preferences, so should church organizations be granted the right of interest, articulation, and participation in the discussion of public issues. But that was different from appointing individuals to posts or ministries on the basis of which religion they belonged to. The Democratic Party committed itself to the abolition of the latter system.[12]

On balance the Catholics in any case stood to gain by a system of undiluted democracy. They outnumbered Protestants and Muslims put together in both Buganda on its own and Uganda as a whole. A system of government which did not award special privileges on the basis of religion but permitted numbers to determine democratically the distribution of posts and power was a system which would have served the Catholics well in any case. But whatever the reason for the commitment of the Democratic Party to a purer secular state than that championed by the UPC at the time, we should not forget that this was indeed the public preference of DP at that time.

The Democratic Party was also concerned about the relatively underprivileged status of Muslims in Uganda. After an initial period of bungling by Mr. Benedicto Kiwanuka in his relations with the Muslims, DP was getting wiser to the implications of an unequal distribution of social advantages and social opportunities as between the different religious denominations.

There was no doubt that Muslims were the least privileged of the three denominations. Muslims were less educated, less prosperous, and had less than a proportionate share of the influential liberal professions. Their conviction that Christian missionary schools were designed to convert young Africans to Christianity had resulted in their distrust of secular schools generally for quite a while. Muslims were relegated to the ranks of the politically marginal on many issues.

Muslims clung to the small privileges they had. Among these was special access to jobs as butchers.

When Benedicto Kiwanuka was in power under self-government, his desire to establish a secular state went to the extent of wanting to abolish a system whereby those who slaughtered animals for food were Muslims. After all, only Muslims among Ugandans have a prescribed ritualistic way of killing animals for food. It had therefore made sense to let the butchers be almost exclusively Muslims, especially if they were involved in the actual slaughter of the animals.

And yet to reserve a special area of occupation even as modest as that of a butcher to followers of a particular religion detracted from the principle of secularism. And so the Democratic Party's government in the year prior to independence fell foul of the Muslims partly because of this policy on the distribution of jobs in butchering. Muslims began to be afraid that a government under Benedicto Kiwanuka might not only force them to eat beef which was not *halal* but might in time force Muslims to eat pork.

When he was the President of an Opposition party, Benedicto Kiwanuka began to sense the limitations of being too doctrinaire even in the commitment to secularism. His change of position was coming rather late, perhaps too late, but by 1964 greater efforts were being made by the DP to make inroads into the Muslim sections of the electorate. The President-General of the party, Mr. Benedicto Kiwanuka, began to concede to Muslims that they too had been underprivileged in Uganda, holding the more menial positions on the social ladder, enjoying more modest economic and educational advantages.

Addressing Muslims in Busoga in the January of that momentous year of 1966, Kiwanuka lamented the handicaps suffered by Muslims in education, health, and other social services. He promised to rectify the situation if he were returned to power and help the Muslims recover equality of opportunity with other citizens. He denied that he had ever intended to force Muslims to eat pork. He also promised the Muslims their rightful share in political power.[13]

But while the evidence does indeed demonstrate that the Democratic Party had a vision of a secular state before the Uganda People's Congress embraced such an aim, it should also be remembered that the Democratic Party was in favor of a society where religion was taken seriously, without necessarily favoring any particular denomination. On the one hand, the party was against the distribution of offices and advantages on the basis of religion; on the other, the party was mortally afraid of irreligiosity. On the one hand, no religion was to be favored, but on the other, religion itself was not to be destroyed.

We might say that the Democratic Party stood for a combination of a *secular state* and a *religious or devout society*. Religion was to be kept out of certain areas of state activities and political affairs; but religion was to be kept alive in the life of the ordinary man and in the texture of morality.

Analytically there was no contradiction between the principle of a secular state and the principle of a religious society, but human behavior is not easily subject to analytical compartmentalization. When religion is held very seriously by society, it affects the state and the polity. It is because of this that the DP often appeared to be the party of religious fervor, in spite of its commitment to political secularism.

THEOCRACY AND NEO-McCARTHYISM

It is because of this dual commitment of the DP to a devout society and a secular state that the supporters of the party very often drifted towards tactics of neo-McCarthyism. Neo-McCarthyism is a style of political innuendo which seeks to discredit political opponents by associating them with communism. The song of neo-McCarthyism has been an important feature of the Ugandan scene, at least since the 1950s, and certainly featured prominently in the early years of the 1960s.

Milton Obote was often up against two accusations which normally should have been mutually incompatible. One accusation was that his political party, the UPC, was a Protestant party; the other accusation was that the UPC was leaning towards ungodliness and an atheistic ideology. Both accusations tended to come from supporters of the Democratic Party, and sometimes from people associated with the Roman Catholic Church itself. The fear that the UPC was moving Uganda toward a life of ungodliness offended that side of the Democratic Party which stood for the consolidation of a devout society. But the tactics of discrediting political opponents by such innuendoes were themselves in conflict with the Democratic Party's desire to remove sectarianism from the center of political activity in Uganda.

In March 1962 the organizing secretary of the UPC issued a statement concerning a two-hour interview which two leaders of the UPC had had with an official of the Catholic Secretariat. The UPC press release reported that Mr. Grace Ibingira, the party's legal adviser, had been invited to meet Father Augustino of the Catholic Secretariat at Nsambya. Mr. Ibingira took with him Mr. Felix Onama, a prominent Catholic member of the UPC from West Nile and later Minister of Defence in the First Republic of Uganda.

It was reported that in the course of the conversation Father Augustino admitted that the Catholic Secretariat feared the UPC because of the party's apparent "Communist tendencies." Father Augustino was even reported to have said that the Democratic Party would be prepared to disband and join the UPC if the UPC got rid of Milton Obote as president and John Kakonge as secretary-general. With those in control, Father Augustino was reported to have said, there was a genuine fear that the UPC would "nationalize mission schools and property."

Mr. Grace Ibingira assured the Father that the UPC did not intend to nationalize anything and was fully appreciative of the work of the missionaries in education and health. Moreover, there was nothing communistic in the manifesto of the UPC.

Felix Onama, carried away in enthusiasm, commented that judging from the friendly atmosphere during the talks, there was a possibility that the Catholic Secretariat would withdraw its support for the Democratic Party and the Democratic Party would subsequently disband.[14]

The Catholic Secretariat later issued a statement accusing the UPC of having distorted the conversations which Father Augustino had had with Mr. Ibingira and Mr. Onama. Father Augustino in a personal statement said his views had been misrepresented. He had simply expressed an opinion to Ibingira and Onama that the UPC and the DP might be able to meet and discuss matters calmly after the elections, and that if there were some changes in the party leadership within the UPC this might make it easier for more Catholics to join the UPC. Perhaps certain changes were needed in the

Democratic Party, too, to facilitate their endeavor to attract Protestants, the Catholics suggested.[15]

Even in his denial, the Father conceded the identification of the Democratic Party with the Catholic community. Reading between the lines in the denial, it did appear clear that the Catholic Secretariat had indeed expressed worries about the leftist orientation of some of the leaders of the Uganda People's Congress.

Meanwhile the Democratic Party itself continued periodically to invoke neo-McCarthyist tactics. The publicity secretary of the party once claimed to have "concrete proof" that Milton Obote went behind the Iron Curtain soon after the London Constitutional Conference of 1961. Obote had denied repeatedly having gone to any Communist country, but the Democratic Party then claimed to have evidence that Obote "disappeared" from Vienna where he was attending an international conference in October 1961. It was alleged that Obote had been to East Germany.

The publicity secretary of the Democratic Party produced an East German monthly pictorial magazine published in October 1961 which carried a picture of Milton Obote with Hassan Wani, president of the Kenya Students' Union in East Germany, and Gerald Goetting, member of the East German People's Chamber and vice-president of the Germany-African Society in East Germany.

Milton Obote again issued a statement denying categorically that he had visited East Germany in October 1961. In a statement from the UPC headquarters Obote said that he stayed in London and in Scotland until October 28 when he went to Sweden. He returned to London on November 1, and stayed there until he left for Uganda on November 5. Obote said: "I have not seen the photograph produced by Mr. Paulo Semogerere [of the DP] but a lot of pictures were taken of me in London during the conference by all sorts of journalists from all over the world."[16] A few days later the UPC at last identified the place where the photograph had been taken. The UPC having examined the photograph and the people in it, issued a statement saying that the picture was in fact taken in London during the conference outside the Cumberland Hotel in the course of a meeting between Mr. Goetting and Mr. Obote about a textile order and the possibility of twenty-five scholarships.[17]

Obote went through much of the first five years of Uganda's independence with a deep cautiousness concerning the danger of neo-McCarthyism. The last thing Obote wanted was to be portrayed as a man who wanted to take God out of the value systems of the people of Uganda. And even when Obote moved in a leftward direction in 1968, he repeatedly betrayed a great concern for religious approval. He was keen to ensure that socialism should not be equated with sin, and that it should in fact be deemed to be consistent with a commitment to the service of God as well as of the nation. His Holiness the

Pope visited Uganda against a background of the declared aim of a move to the left under Obote's leadership. Symbolic gifts were given to religious leaders. The face of Obote and the face of the Pope competed for attention on hundreds of shirts worn around the country and stacked in warehouses.

The furthest to the left Obote moved was on May 1, 1970, with the Nakivubo pronouncements. In those pronouncements he nationalized or partially nationalized a number of industries and declared plans to give workers control in some sectors of the economic life of the country, and peasants control in other sectors. The song of socialism was then being sung at its most ambitious by the man who had once been all too anxious to deny that he had ever gone behind the Iron Curtain.

As Obote stood there in Nakivubo Stadium announcing a series of social-istic measures, the question was still with him whether this move to the left might be misunderstood as ungodliness. Was there a risk that neo-McCarthyism might once again sow the seeds of discontent and religious suspicion in the population? Obote rose to the occasion in that very speech of Labor Day, 1970. The national motto of Uganda provided him with a suitable line of reassurance. He concluded that historic speech with the simple sentence: "Fellow citizens, I have decided upon the matters I have told you, 'For God and my Country.' "[18]

With his "move to the left" Obote was in fact trying to move Uganda from a country with politicized religion to a country with a political creed. In this sense a political creed like socialism can be a secular religion. Was Obote taking Uganda towards a system of secular theocracy?

If Alexander Dubcek in 1968 was trying to give Czechoslovakia "socialism with a human face," Obote in 1969 and 1970 was trying to give Uganda "socialism with a divine face."

Behind the Obote experiment was Julius Nyerere's example in Tanzania. And when Obote was overthrown, ideological tensions developed between Nyerere and Amin. What must not be overlooked was the shared link of puritanism and missionary styles between the soldiers in Uganda and the socialists in Tanzania. It is to these links that we must now turn.

SOCIALISM AS A SECULAR THEOCRACY

Of the three countries of East Africa the first to have had something approaching a state religion was Tanzania—but Nyerere called it not a state religion but a "national ethic." Of course, Tanzania's socialism has not carried the same passionate attachment to theological issues that one sometimes finds among Marxist socialists. It is far easier to portray communism as such as a kind of secular religion than it is to portray *ujamaa*. Communism has, after all, definitely carried in its history strong theological disputations on doctrinal matters. Communism has also accumulated a collection of ideological ancestors who command from followers a deep ancestor worship. Marx and Lenin are not mere figures in the history of communism—in their very death they continue to exert the kind of influence which wins deep religious reverence.

Nyerere on the other hand has been all too conscious of the theological excesses of some schools of socialism. Nyerere has indeed asserted that socialism is not a theology and has described any attempt to create a new religion out of socialism as "absurd." Marx was a great thinker but not an infallible man. In the words of Nyerere:

> We are groping our way forward towards socialism, and we are in danger of being bemused by this new theology, and therefore of trying to solve our problems according to what the priests of Marxism say is what Marx said or meant. If we do this we shall fail. Africa's conditions are very different from those of the Europe in which Marx and Lenin wrote and worked. To talk as if these thinkers provided all the answers to our problems, or as if Marx invented socialism, is to reject both the humanity of Africa and the universality of socialism. Marx did contribute a great deal to socialist thought. But socialism did not begin with him, nor can it end in constant re-interpretations of his writings.[19]

Nyerere was prepared to be an admirer of Karl Marx, but not one of his worshippers. But was Nyerere himself becoming the center of a personality cult? Nyerere has not sought to become himself a prophet for popular reverence or a founder of a new religion. On the contrary, there is a good deal of evidence to show the extent to which he has discouraged this trend towards a personality cult.

The atmosphere in Tanzania has increasingly discouraged even alternative schools of socialism and to that extent the ideological monopoly bears comparison with theocratic righteousness. The one-party state itself was basically an attempt to institutionalize ideological monopoly. It certainly amounts to an assertion of ideological righteousness.

We might therefore say that until the advent of the Second Republic of Uganda, Tanzania was in an important sense moving in the direction of a secular theocracy, forging link with the African ancestors of socialism as practiced in kinship systems, and seeking to bring to fruition a collection of gospels at the center of which was the Arusha Declaration. Kenyatta once described Document No. 10 of African Socialism in Kenya as the new Bible of the country. But if it was a Bible, it was more often honored in the breach than in the observance.

The same is not true of the gospel of Tanzania's socialism, with the central text of the Arusha Declaration itself. Ujamaa as a nostalgic link with African communalism seeks to introduce a little of the reverence of ancestors into Tanzania's socialism. Ujamaa as a broad national ethic seeks to create a parallel code of behavior to that afforded by the traditional religions. Ujamaa as an exercise in documentary radicalism seeks to give this secular theocracy something approaching a holy scripture. There are Tanzanians who have walked more than a hundred miles as a form of prayer to the Arusha Declaration. Nyerere himself has walked such long miles on a pilgrimage to affirm the national ethic and its scriptural foundation, the Arusha Declaration.

Colin Leys, a former Professor of Political Science at Makerere University, was right to see in Nyerere a style very reminiscent of Gladstone in England. Gladstone was the grand moralistic statesman, tending in his style to see great spiritual issues involved in the banality of day-to-day politics. In the view of Colin Leys:

We have to understand Nyerere's style—the relentless magnification of the moral aspects of each and every policy decision—in terms of his need to sustain the moral basis of his own leadership, vis-à-vis both the party cadres and the public at large; it is his *stock-in-trade,* as it was also Gladstone's.[20]

But the analogy should go beyond Gladstone and include some of the founders of British socialism. The genesis of the Labour Party lies as much in Methodism as in Marxism. The genesis of Nyerere's puritanism may, in turn, lie as much in his socialism as in his "missionary" upbringing in colonial Tanganyika.

The national ethic of Tanzania before long was tackling not just the issue of who owned what but also the issue of who *wore* what. Even before the advent of the Second Republic of Uganda, Nyerere's Tanzania had already experienced debates on mini-skirts. Indeed, it might even be argued that the most important shared characteristics between the Second Republic of Uganda and the socialist Republic of Tanzania lie in the realm of moral puritanism.

It was in October 1968 that some girls wearing mini-skirts were manhandled by members of the TANU Youth League in Dar-es-Salaam. Riot police had to be called in to handle the youths. A resolution (entitled "Operation Vijana") was proposed to ban mini-skirts, wigs, and tight trousers from Tanzania with effect from January 1969, but younger members of the ruling party thought January was too far away and embarked on measures to speed up the change.

The Afro-Shirazi Youth League in Zanzibar soon endorsed the move by their sister organization on the mainland. In a resolution marking the close of a three-day seminar the Afro-Shirazi Youth League pledged they would work resolutely to eliminate such remnants of foreign culture in the country. In the background of these resolutions was the memory of Kariokoo market place, Dar-es-Salaam, a few days earlier when these youthful gangs stopped girls wearing mini-skirts and tight dresses and insulted them, and riot police carrying guns and tear gas helped disperse huge crowds at the market place.

In a way, the excessive enthusiasm of the young militants helped later to promote greater toleration in Tanzania towards those who fell short of these rigorous standards. But what had happened was precisely the rapid extension of the fires of political puritanism from the socialist cabinet to the private wardrobe, from issues of state to matters of taste.

A related instance of Tanzania's puritanism in this regard was the country's decision to abolish in 1968 the beauty contest for Miss Tanzania. The display of female bodies in competition for the title of beauty queen belonged basically to the same area of moral sensibilities as the display of thighs below the mini-skirt.

THE MASAI AND THE KARAMOJONG

Would all this puritanism have also manifested itself in Uganda had Obote continued on his own path towards socialism? After all, other aspects of Tanzania's National Ethic had found an echo in Obote's Uganda. Some of these questions can never be fully answered since Obote was overthrown. What we do know is that Obote's successors—the soldiers—have shared certain forms of puritanism with Obote's friend, Julius Nyerere.

The disapproval of the mini-skirt is not the only area of moral sensitivity shared between the military government of Uganda and the socialist government of Tanzania. It is not even the only issue connected with nakedness, real or asserted. Both the socialist government of Tanzania and the military government of Uganda have shown a certain embarrassment over those traditions among their people which accepted customary forms of nakedness and nudity. President Nyerere's government was concerned about the ancestral naked ways of the Masai; and President Amin later was concerned about the naked ways of the Karamojong. How much of the leaders' embarrassment was Euro-Christian in origin?

It was in 1968 that the authorities in Tanzania decided that the Masai had been permitted naked indulgence for far too long: that their withdrawal from normal attire constituted a withdrawal from the mainstream of progress in their country. It was therefore decreed that no Masai men or women were to be allowed into the Arusha metropolis wearing limited skin clothing or a loose blanket. The Masailand Area Commissioner, Mr. Iddi Sungura, kept on issuing a number of warnings to the Masai threatening retribution if they clung to awkward clothing and soiled pigtailed hair.[21]

From a prominent Masai across the border in Kenya came protest. A Kenya Masai Member of Parliament holding a ministerial position, Mr. Stanley Oloitiptip, asserted that Tanzania was denying the Masai the right to be themselves. Another Kenyan, Mr. John Keen, threatened to turn up at Arusha, the capital of the East African Community, dressed in his Masai attire and see what the authorities there would do to him.

Tanzanian authorities in turn replied in this debate across the border that such interference in the policies of Tanzania toward modernization and national integration was totally unacceptable. The Masai of Kenya could remain in their pristine traditionality, but the Masai of Tanzania were to be converted to the trappings of modernity.[22]

Not long after the military coup in Uganda a similar policy was pursued by the new government with respect to the Karamojong. Again a shared puritan-ism with regard to bodily exposure seemed to be influencing both the soldiers and the socialists. The question which arises is what sort of factors were at play behind this area of shared sensibility.

Of course, objections to the kind of nakedness implied by the mini-skirts were fundamentally different from attitudes to the nakedness of the Masai and the Karamojong. The denunciation of the mini-skirt was in part because it was alien to African culture, an ominous and unwelcome intrusion from a foreign universe of fashion.

On the other hand, to force the Karamojong and the Masai to wear trousers and shirts was to force them away from their own traditions and customs into styles of imported attire.

It is also worth distinguishing nakedness as an attempt to contrive a sexual impact, as the mini-skirt often sought to do, from nakedness as a natural state without any contrivance at sexual impact. When the Karamojong go about their daily business completely unclothed, they are not engaging in obscene exhibitionism. They are just being themselves.

While it is therefore arguable that the discouragement of the mini-skirt in Tanzania and its ban in Uganda are motivated by a pursuit of moral propriety and discipline, it is less persuasive to portray the policies towards the Masai and the Karamojong in similar moralistic terms outside the Euro-Christian missionary framework.

Where the mini-skirt and Nilotic nakedness might conceptually touch is within the conceptual relationship between *cultural decadence* and *cultural retardation*. Cultural decadence is a stage of decay, a situation which comes after the full flowering of a civilization. Cultural retardation, on the other hand, implies being socially arrested in one's development, stopping short of the full flowering of civilization. Ancient Rome first rose to grandeur and then declined and fell. The period of decline was a period of descent into decadence, as values became diluted, as principles became abused, as moral restraints became looser.

Social critics of capitalism see also a period of decadence setting in in the entire capitalist civilization. Although many of those who wear mini-skirts, or who profess to be hippies, are ideologically leftists situated in Western countries, Communist observers have been known to see in this very trend the beginning of the end of capitalist civilization, the rot setting in.

The mini-skirts become by this interpretation a manifestation of Western decadence, while the Masai blanket and Karamojong nudity are a manifestation of cultural retardation, defined in Euro-Christian terms.

We could therefore argue that for TANU Youth Wingers the attack on the mini-skirt was in part an attack on the cultural guise of capitalism. As for the motives behind the same policy in the Second Republic of Uganda, this came in a period of a general radicalization of foreign policy, with an expanding rhetoric of anti-imperialism. Opposition to the mini-skirt was in part an aspect of foreign policy, constituting a posture of resistance to cultural imperialism. Both the TANU Youth Wingers and the policy-makers in Amin's Uganda were extending their radicalism to encompass a particular form of attire.[23]

The policies concerning the Masai and the Karamojong, on the other hand, could be seen in terms of the pursuit of equal opportunity. Within the ideology of Tanzania this is even clearer. Nyerere's concern for the Masai included the worry that they would continue to be relatively underprivileged in Tanzania unless certain important aspects of their life style were transformed. To get the Masai into the future stream of economic prosperity in Tanzania required at least a partial cultural transformation. Dress is one symbolic aspect which could be tackled first, in the hope that it would result in other changes of attitudes. Ataturk, the architect of modern Turkey, saw very clearly that the Westernization of the dress culture of Turkey could itself help to start a process of Westernizing other attitudes in the life style of the Turks. In some ways Ataturk oversimplified the connection between dress and other aspects of culture—but that there is a connection was itself a revolutionary premise from which Ataturk started.

Likewise, Julius Nyerere has concluded that dress for the Masai could not be separated from the issue of equal opportunity in Tanzania. The ability of the Masai to compete effectively in the job market was certainly connected with whether or not they wore anything. And in any case economic justice must not only be done, it must be seen to be done. And the visual aspects of economic justice range from whether people own cars, and if so which kinds, on one side, to the issue of whether they wear clothes and if so what kind, on the other.

If every Tanzanian were naked, this would itself be an assertion of equality. But since the great majority are already dressed, should the Masai be encouraged to enter that mainstream of economic culture?

The policies on the Karamojong in Uganda were less ideologically coherent, but an egalitarian factor was certainly present. General Amin certainly seemed to feel that the north as a whole in Uganda needed to establish parity of esteem with other parts of the country. And each section within the country needed to assert credentials of respectability and equal status. Amin's concept of egalitarianism was interregional and inter-ethnic. It might even be described as a nationally oriented form of egalitarianism. Nyerere's egalitarianism, on the other hand, was clearly socialistically derived. But both showed a Euro-Christian influence in their origins.

CONCLUSION

President Amin and I were sitting together on a couch late in 1971 when I quietly raised the issue of religion. "Is it true, General, that you intend to bring up two of your children as Roman Catholics and prepare them for the priesthood?" I asked. The news had been announced publicly by Amin's Chief Justice at the time, Mr. Benedicto Kiwanuka. Justice Kiwanuka was himself a Roman Catholic.

When I raised the issue with the General a few days after Kiwanuka's announcement, my voice must have betrayed some surprise. It was as difficult to imagine a relatively devout Muslim committing himself to bring up a child of his as a Roman Catholic as it would have been to hear a Roman Catholic planning to have his eldest son converted to Islam and trained as a mullah.

General Amin turned to look at me and began saying rather defensively "It was the Chief Justice . . . !" He never finished the sentence. He suddenly remembered that we were not alone. There were some Roman Catholic citizens within hearing distance in the same room. The General lowered his voice further and said: "We shall talk about this some other time."

Whether or not Idi Amin wanted to bring up any child of his as a Roman Catholic, it was clear that he did not want to deny it publicly in spite of the surprise the announcement had caused in Muslim circles in Uganda. What was at stake was Amin's ambition to forge Uganda into an ecumenical and yet devout society. Religious leaders of all denominations would have to share with him the burden of such a task. Was he also prepared to offer his children in the same apostolic cause? He left this latter question open.

Behind Amin's ambition was the momentum of Uganda's history since the 1890s when rival missionary groups started competing for the soul of the nation. We have sought to demonstrate in this paper that the origins of both the moral puritanism of the Second Republic and the evolving theocratic pattern are part of a tradition which has its genesis—in spite of the Muslim religion of General Amin—in the longer term impact of Christianity on Uganda. Sexual relations in African societies in Uganda, as elsewhere in the continent, became to some extent Christianized. They became subject to the puritanical restraints and inhibitions of missionaries, self-consciously committed to a cause to save Africa from some of its own presumed moral laxity.

The ban on mini-skirts is in part a child of cultural nationalism and has been shared by radical countries like Tanzania. But it is also possible to see the disapproval of mini-skirts as part of the same tradition which had banned certain kinds of African dances and led to the invention of the *basuti* as a style of modest attire.[24]

What should be noted is the additional puritanizing effect of army rule. In reality Ugandan soldiers are normally over-indulgent rather than austere. General Amin himself used to be a heavy drinker at one time. He is now much more temperate, though not a total abstainer. But how is he to deal with the rest of his army? He has harangued them often on the virtues of moderation and discipline. He seems also to grope for societal sobriety as an answer to military inebriation.[25]

The other theme of this chapter has been the tradition of politicized religion in Uganda, and the strange dialectic it played when political parties came into being and the politics of electoral disputes entered the scene. We have argued that just as Islam once prepared the way for the reception of Christianity in Uganda in the nineteenth century, so Christianity in the twentieth century prepared the way for the religious style of the first Muslim President of Uganda. Uganda as a neo-theocracy did not emerge quite simply from the upheavals of January 25, 1971, but formed part of the flow of history which went back to Lugard, Mutesa I, and beyond.

Amin was a self-conscious Muslim partly because the Uganda in which he grew up was so self-consciously sectarian. Historically, the Christians least patient with Muslims in Uganda were the Catholics. When in 1972 Amin found himself drifting towards religious intolerance, he became in turn more patient with the Protestants and Muslims than he later became with Roman Catholics. He came to regard the Roman Catholic Church as the least African of the churches, partly because it was a centralized church answerable to a European religious pivot, the Pope. When Amin moved toward expelling mainly Catholic missionaries and Catholic Archbishop Nsubuga, denouncing his ecumenicalism was struggling for breath under the heavy weight of the sectarian history of Uganda.[26]

There are times when military heirs to church missionaries are at the same time rivals to the missionaries. The competition is for the soul of the nation. Religious leaders in Uganda—as in Zaire—are up against a state which seeks to assert a monopoly of the legitimate use of spiritual force. Yet to the extent that Amin stands for some of the values of the old missionaries, history has indulged its own ancient sense of humor once again. A rustic warrior from the womb of the African countryside has symbolically presented his ecumenical credentials to share in the gift of the apostolic succession.

NOTES

1. R. Bultmann, *Theology of the New Testament* (1952) and A. Ehrhardt, *The Apostolic Ministry* (1958).

2. For a discussion of Marxism as a religion consult John Plamenatz, *German Marxism and Russian Communism* (London: Longmans, 1954). Consult also Robert C. Tucker, *The Marxian Revolutionary Idea* (New York: Norton, 1969).

3. For a report at the time about my protest concerning Idd el Fitr see *The Daily Nation* (Nairobi). For my discussion of these issues in my fortnightly column see my essay "General Amin and Archbishop Makarios," *The People* (Kampala), March 3, 1972.

4. President Idi Amin's decision to adopt the title of *Dada* (Patriarch or Father) was inspired by a familial interpretation of a political system—that a polity is a family writ large.

5. Moffat to Unwin, September 4, 1869, in Wallis (ed.) *The Matabeli Mission*, Oppenheimer Series No. 2 (London, 1945): 70-71. Cited by Low, *Religion and Society in Buganda, 1875 to 1900* (Kampala: East African Studies, No. 8, East African Institute of Social Research).

6. Roland Oliver, *The Missionary Factor in East Africa* (London: Longmans, 1952 2nd Ed. 1965): 64.

7. F. B. Welbourn, *East African Christian* (London: Oxford University Press, 1965): 104-105, 114-115.

8. Okot P'Bitek, *Song of Lawino* (Nairobi: East African Publishing House, 1966): 34-35.

9. Ibid.: 41, 35.

10. Cited by Roland Oliver, *The Missionary Factor in East Africa,* op. cit.: 133-134.

11. Ibid.: 142.

12. "Religious Ministries Must Go; D.P. Outlines Aims for Lukiiko Role," *Uganda Argus* (Kampala), February 13, 1962: 3.

13. See *Munno,* January 25, 1966. It was Kiwanuka who became Chief Justice under the Second Republic, but in September 1972 he was picked up by soldiers, "disappeared," and is now believed dead.

14. *Uganda Argus,* March 19, 1962.

15. *Uganda Argus,* March 21, 1962.

16. See *Uganda Argus,* January 13 and 15, 1962.

17. *Uganda Argus,* January 18, 1962.

18. For the full text of the Labour Day speech of May 1, 1970, see either the *Uganda Argus* or *The People* (Kampala) of May 2, 1970. The speech later came to be known as Document No. 4 of the Move to the Left.

19. Julius K. Nyerere, *Freedom and Socialism: A Selection from Writings and Speeches, 1965-67* (Dar-es-Salaam: Oxford University Press, 1968): p. 15.

20. Colin Leys, "Interalia—or Tanzaphilia and All That," *Transition* (Kampala) 7, 34: 53.

21. See for example the *Daily Nation* (Nairobi), February 6, 1968.

22. See *Daily Nation*, February 8 and 16, 1968. This issue is placed in a wider context in my essay "On Revolution and Nakedness," chapter 14, in Mazrui, *Violence and Thought: Essays on Social Tensions in Africa* (London: Longmans, 1969): 281-305.

23. Nor should it be taken for granted that banning mini-skirts is peculiarly radical or socialistic. Even before Operation Vijana got under way in Tanzania, President Banda of Malawi had already expressed his distaste of the mini-skirt. The disapproval of the mini-skirt has been championed by regimes as diverse as Dr. Banda's on one side and President Nyerere's on the other, and by soldiers as diverse as the Greek colonels and the Ugandan warriors.

24. Amin also banned long hair. For an earlier discussion see Mazrui, "Political Man and the Heritage of Hair," *British Journal of Political Science* 2 (1971).

25. For a discussion of indulgence versus puritanism in another African army consult Robert M. Price, "A Theoretical Approach to Military Rule in New States: Reference-Group Theory and the Ghanian Case," *World Politics* 23, 3, (1971): especially 416-419.

26. The Pope had finally to make a cautious appeal to President Amin for greater toleration towards servants of the Church. See *The Times* (London), December 2, 4 and 5, 1972.

Chapter 14

THE SOLDIER, THE SOCIALIST, AND THE

SPIRIT OF DEVELOPMENT: AMIN AND

NYERERE IN COMPARATIVE PERSPECTIVE

In the first half of the 1960s every African state seemed to be a potential socialist society. By the second half of the 1960s every African state seemed to be on the verge of having a military regime. The first decade of African independence was a dialectical experience involving ambitious soldiers and aspiring socialists. In Arab Africa the soldiers and the socialists were often in alliance; in Black Africa they tended to be torn apart.

It is not clear yet whether the second decade of African independence is to be the decade of radicalized black soldiers. What we propose to examine in this paper are two particular leaders, one a soldier and the other a socialist, and their efforts to transcend dependency.

We start from the normative concept of *the spirit of development.* We mean by this the ultimate values which define both the ends of development and the means by which they are sought. In African conditions the spirit of development concerns issues of autonomy and dignity.

In their drastically different ways, General Idi Amin of Uganda and Mwalimu Julius K. Nyerere of Tanzania signify the beginnings of Africa's rebellion against her heritage of dependency. Their experiments still betray remnants of this heritage. We propose to examine these remnants in a wider perspective not only of comparative politics but also of comparative psychology.

DEPENDENCY AND CULTURAL SCHIZOPHRENIA

The most serious problems of dependency in Africa lie in the minds of individual men and women. And these problems arise partly out of the West's

[278]

cultural impact on Africa. After all, colonialism was an experience more fundamental in its cultural repercussions than in its political. African systems of thought, of values, and of beliefs have been irreparably disrupted. As a style of direct political domination, colonialism has been retreating. But as a process of cultural conquest, colonialism is for the time being triumphant. And this cultural triumph may interfere with Africa's psychological readiness to assume control of its own destiny. In the economic sphere Africa is still a continental dependency. Africa's capacity to change soon may be modest. But Africa's political *will* to pursue such a change could be greater than it is were it not encumbered by problems of *cultural schizophrenia.* [1]

We define cultural schizophrenia as the tense ambivalence which arises out of the interplay between dependency and aggression in the process of acculturation. Attitudes to the conquering culture produce a confusion between fascination and repulsion, emulation and defiance, among the recipients. A dependency complex struggles with a longing for distinctiveness at a certain stage of acculturation.

We accept for our purposes in this paper the definition of acculturation which views it as the process by which an individual or a group acquires cultural characteristics of another through direct contact and interaction.

> From an individual point of view this is a process of social learning similar to that of adult socialization in which linguistic communication plays an essential role. From a social point of view acculturation implies the diffusion of particular values, techniques and institutions and their modification under different conditions. [2]

The process of acculturation in Africa has resulted in the crisis of psychological inadequacy, sometimes manifesting itself in indiscriminate imitation of Western culture, sometimes emerging in the form of aggressive hostility towards that dominant culture. Both cultural aggression and cultural imitation in contemporary African conditions could be symptoms of an inner dependency complex, still struggling with itself.

The experience of Black America may be a prophecy for Africa in this regard. There is indeed the persistent problem of white arrogance as an aspect of the North American racial scene. But in relation to the dependency complex, it is black behavior which concerns us here. We see in Black America a residual dependency problem and an intermediate problem of anomie. The residual dependency problem may be manifested in "Uncle Toms," a breed of human beings who are taken to be or mistaken for blind imitators of Western, usually Anglo-Saxon, norms, and who usually feel uneasy about being abandoned by their Western reference group. But the dependency phenomenon in North America could take more subtle forms than that of blatant imitation. It sometimes takes the form of aggressive reaction against what is taken to be white indifference to the black man.

But aggression among blacks in North America may also be due to the subsequent stage of anomie. This is a stage which could be post-dependency but pre-adjustment. It comes in the agony of rejecting the cultural and protective embrace of Anglo-Saxon liberality, the agony of groping for an inner autonomy and a more self-confident relationship with one's former superiors.

This latter kind of problem is, in a way, the most acute manifestation of the crisis of identity. It is not really the Uncle Toms and securely integrated black men in North America that are devoid of identity. Such Uncle Toms do have an identity—that of imported black people, assimilated culturally in certain directions, and accepting certain expectations in the new society in which they themselves were born. The Uncle Toms are often secure in the identities they have acquired. The militants might not like their identities, but it is not the Uncle Toms who are suffering from a crisis. Very often it is the militants. And their crisis arises because they are in an intermediate position between shedding off an old intermediate personality and acquiring a new autonomous self-conception. In between this leap from the role of an Uncle Tom to a new, autonomously satisfying alternative self-image lies that painful period of anomic bewilderment.[3]

Africa has not yet reached the stage of identity crisis that Black America is currently experiencing—at least, not the same kind of crisis. On the other hand, cultural schizophrenia in Africa is more clearly defined. There are still active indigenous cultures struggling for survival against the challenge of the Western heritage. There are still indigenous languages co-existing with metropolitan English and French. Yet the prestige and influence of the metropolitan languages creates schizophrenic problems for those who have acquired competence in them, as well as creating problems of relative deprivation for those who have not had a chance to do so.[4]

The dependency complex can be either submissive or aggressive. Submissive dependency is deferential towards the metropole and imitative in its inclinations. Aggressive dependency is excessively abusive about the metropole and incapable of permitting Africa the capacity to be evil on its own initiative. Aggressive dependency is particularly marked among radical African intellectuals when they display total unwillingness to accept responsibility for almost *any* of the things which go wrong in Africa.

On one side, it is indeed true that Africa is a prey to historical and economic forces over which she has no control and which are sometimes consciously manipulated by powerful nations in the international system in cynical disregard of the interests of anyone but themselves. But aggressive dependency among Africans can only be transcended when Africans recognize that the most pressing problems in their societies are capable of at least preliminary amelioration by determined domestic resolve.

The black movement in the United States seems to have moved from a stage of submissive dependency to a stage of aggressive dependency. Some parts of English-speaking Africa are also entering the initial phases of aggressive dependency; but much of French-speaking Africa is probably still in a mood of submissive dependency.

Having placed Amin and Julius Nyerere within this broad context, let us now turn to these individuals themselves and their struggles to transcend dependency.

GENERAL AMIN: FROM SUBMISSION TO AGGRESSION

On January 25, 1971, the Uganda army overthrew President A. Milton Obote, and General Idi Amin assumed the supreme authority of the state. The date of the coup was uncanny. It celebrated precisely the seventh anniversary of that impressive illustration of submissive dependency at the Jinja barracks on January 25, 1964. In January 1964 British troops, without firing a shot, disarmed mutinous Uganda soldiers and recovered the armory at Jinja. The local mutineers capitulated like lambs to a few hundred Scots guards.

Would Amin as President maintain this tradition of deferential orientation towards the metropole? The initial evidence amounted to an affirmative answer. It was soon clear that the two most influential embassies in Kampala were the British High Commission and the Israeli Embassy. Britain had indeed been the first country to extend formal diplomatic recognition to General Amin's government. Amin's repeated expressions of deference to the British in the early days of his regime seemed to mark a direct continuation of a dependency phenomenon which went back to the Jinja affair in 1964 and beyond.[5]

In its own specialized way, a military career in the Ugandan army was a semi-Westernizing process for Amin. The rituals of the military in Uganda, from the drill to the ceremonial music, were overwhelmingly British derived. Amin himself became a typical product of British military training. As a British newspaper recorded after Amin fell out with the British in 1972:

> British officers in the 4th Battalion, King's African Rifles, thought the world of chaps like Sergeant-Major Idi Amin. He was keen, loyal, respectful, immaculately turned out and stamped his feet as if determined to shake the continent. A first class type altogether: fanatically pro-British *and* a useful forward on the rugger field.[6]

Amin carried this deferential anglophilia not only into independence but also into the Second Republic of Uganda under military rule, a decade after independence. He became one more illustration of what Robert M. Price has called the "emulation paradox" among African soldiers—something intimately related to cultural schizophrenia. The military in long-established states of the West tend to be among the ultra-patriotic sections of the population. In the words of S. E. Finer, a "strong sense of nationalism and national identity, with pervasive tones of xenophobia . . . adheres to the military as a profession."[7]

But among soldiers in newly independent countries, attachment to the former metropole could be more compelling than sympathy with civilian nationalists in their own midst. Basically this is the "emulation paradox" referred to by Price.

Robert Price also invokes psychological categories to explain the phenomenon. He uses reference group theory to explain the emulation paradox.

> An individual's reference groups are those social groups to which he psychologically relates himself, with which he identifies. To become a member of a group in the psychological sense implies the internalization of its central norms and values—for to be a member implies certain modes of thought and behavior.[8]

Applying the theory to the Ghanaian military especially, Price argued that the training process undergone by the officer corps was "such as to produce reference-group identifications with the officer corps of the ex-colonial power and concomitant commitments to its set of traditions, symbols, and values."[9]

Although Price was providing an important new perspective on the behavior of African soldiers, he overlooked three important factors. He assumed that Ghanaian soldiers had internalized the *"central* norms and values" of their British model. Price was begging the question. The soldiers had internalized *some* norms and values from the British military tradition, but these might have been peripheral within the British model. In other words, the most important of the values which were effectively transferred need not have been the most important to the British themselves.

The second factor to bear in mind is that an African's *perception* of the British tradition need not, in any case, be the British tradition itself. The values undergo a change in the cross-cultural transference. The result is that even those originally peripheral "British" values which were indeed internalized by Africans might have become something quite different in that very process.

A third factor which Robert Price seemed to have overlooked was that values are not only capable of being internalized; they are also capable of being neutralized by newly internalized competing values. Structural changes in the polity or the economy of a country could generate new values and dispositions competing for acceptance. And the internalization of these latter could neutralize a previous normative orientation.

All these three factors may have to be borne in mind in assessing General Amin's transition from submissive anglophilia to the new paradox of *aggressive anglophilia*. Aggressive anglophilia is to be differentiated from real anglophobia. General Amin has maintained a love-hate attitude towards his former reference-group, the British. He mercilessly and at short notice expelled thousands of Asians carrying British passports; he nationalized dozens of British economic enterprises with next-to-no guarantee of compensation. He harrassed some British technical assistance personnel into leaving Uganda before the end of their tour. And yet almost simultaneously he sent a high-powered delegation to Britain to assure British investors and exporters that Uganda was still worthy of their trust, and to assure the British people of his own continuing affection and friendship. After all, how could he ever forget that the Queen's own father, King George VI, had been Amin's own commander-in-chief not so long ago? The phenomenon of aggressive anglophilia continued to be a feature of Amin's cultural schizophrenia.

And yet Amin may recover sooner from some of these complexes than some of his more Westernized African critics. In the words of Martin Walker: "Amin . . . is perhaps the first widely known black leader who is totally African. No European education, no credibility for white intellectuals, Amin is a man of the people, speaking their language in a way that Nkrumah, Kenyatta, Kaunda, Senghor, and Nyerere could never do."[10]

Amin is not even semi-Westernized; he is at the most *sub-Westernized* simply because he experienced British colonial authority and entered a profession with a self-conscious British tradition. Amin's rudimentary Westernism is therefore the more fragile. He may recover sooner from cultural schizophrenia as a result.

But in the course of 1972 Amin evolved his own concept of economic self-reliance, different from but at least as fundamental as Nyerere's socialistic experiment across the border in Tanzania. In his own way, Amin gradually arrived at the conclusion that the essence of exploitation for Africa was not capitalism but racial stratification. The uniqueness of Africa's experience dictated first and foremost an uncompromising strategy against racial stratification within Africa itself.

Part of Amin's tribe, the Kakwa, was in the Sudan. The Sudanese civil war broke out partly because of a de facto heritage of racial stratification in the Sudan. Amin's first rebellion against racial stratification took the form of his sympathy with the southern Sudanese movement. His friendship with the Israelis was also connected with shared connections with southern Sudanese fighters. His friendship with the Israelis later stood him in good stead in his coup against Obote, but the initial bond of sympathy between Amin and the Israelis did not arise purely from the Uganda situation.

Some of Amin's earliest statements after he assumed power as President of Uganda included a denunciation of the stratification system in the Sudan. Amin even compared the Sudanese problem with apartheid in South Africa.

Yet for a while there was a basic inconsistency in Amin's ideological universe. He disliked the Sudanese heritage of racial stratification and resented the economic dominance of the Asians in Uganda. Yet Amin remained fond of the British and conciliatory towards South Africa. He even allowed for a possible dialogue with South Africa under certain conditions. He was going to nominate me as one of a group of ten people from Uganda to go to South Africa and assess the sincerity of the South African government on this question of dialogue. But the South African government rejected the idea of such a delegation on the grounds that it smacked too much of a commission of investigation.

After a while the radicalization of General Amin got under way, especially following the end of the Sudanese civil war in February 1972. The Sudan had at last confronted the problem of racial stratification in its midst and given the southern provinces a chance to assert racial parity. With the end of the Sudanese civil war, Amin's relations with the Israelis entered a new phase. By April 1972 he had expelled all Israelis from Uganda.

His attitude to southern Africa as a bastion of racial stratification was also getting radicalized. He then moved from a strategy of conditional dialogue to a strategy of offering to train liberation fighters in Uganda, and raising a special national appeal within Uganda for funds as a contribution to the guerrilla effort in southern Africa.

But could he oppose racial stratification in the Sudan and southern Africa without confronting it in his own country? It was not long before the fate of the Uganda Asians was sealed.[11]

But what about the British presence itself in Uganda? It was one thing to expel British Asians; but what about white Britons? Amin nationalized a number of British industries and firms and encouraged a number of British professionals to leave, but Amin's basic anglophilia has prevented the anti-British strategy from going much further for the time being. Yet he may already have done enough to start a process of voluntary British withdrawal from several sectors of Uganda's national life.

But what about racial stratification within religious organizations? Amin turned next to them, expelling 58 foreign missionaries and warning the rest of the expatriate religious leaders that their days in Uganda were numbered. After the expulsion of the 58, there were still 1,238 expatriate Roman Catholic mission personnel, 93 Protestant, and 67 expatriate missionaries from other denominations. Addressing a conference of women's organizations in November 1972 in Kampala, Amin again emphasized "the need to Africanize the churches" and promised to convene a conference of religious leaders to discuss with them the best approach.[12]

The Africanization of the churches was beginning to assume as much importance as the Africanization of the economy. The spiritual as well as the temporal domains of Uganda's national life were to be stripped of non-indigenous leadership. Racial stratification in Uganda had not only to come to an end; it had to be seen to have ended. The actual expulsion of non-indigenous leadership in economic and church affairs was one way of making racial de-stratification in Uganda clear and unmistakeable.

Certain aspects of Amin's strategy are not only simplistic but unjust. Especially unfair was his treatment of those Asians who had become Uganda citizens and attempted to identify with the aspirations of independent Uganda. Racial stratification is wrong because racism as a whole is wrong. Some of Amin's anti-Asian policies could not but contradict his moral opposition to racial stratification. But Amin is not the first black man to have felt it necessary to resort to what Léopold Senghor has called "anti-racist racism." This rationalizes the resort to black racialistic militancy as a response to the racism of others. In some cases *anti-racist racism* is a form of aggressive dependency complex, but even then it could be a stage towards a subsequent modus vivendi among the races.[13]

By December 1972 there were signs that even Tanzania, a longstanding critic of Amin as President, was beginning to take the General seriously as a genuine economic nationalist. In a widely studied editorial in the Tanzanian Government newspaper, the *Daily News,* the point was conceded that from whatever angle the economic actions of General Amin were looked at, "they contain some elements of economic nationalism in them."[14]

Yet even in that single editorial there were features which indicated the differences between the two concepts of self-reliance, Nyerere's and Amin's. It is to these comparative factors that we must now turn.

FROM ECONOMIC NATIONALISM TO SOCIALISM

Nyerere was a nationalist before he became a credible socialist. One of the most important questions confronting the Second Republic of Uganda by the end of 1972 was whether Amin, too, would undergo a transition from economic nationalism to socialism. Let us look at these two propositions more closely.

But an even prior point to note is that both Nyerere and Amin started their political careers as "moderates." It is not often remembered that Nyerere was the political darling of relatively conservative Western opinion for more than a decade of his political career. To some extent, Nyerere showed clear signs of cultural schizophrenia. His calm and gradualist approach as a fighter for Tanganyika's independence won him wide acclaim in the West. He was definitely put in a different category from "militants" like Kwame Nkrumah and later Sékou Touré. When independent African states were for a while divided between radical Casablanca states and moderate Monrovia states, Tanganyika was drawn towards the Monrovia group.

Curiously enough, even as compared with Tom Mboya and the image of Jomo Kenyatta still in detention, Nyerere was regarded as a much more moderate African leader than his Kenyan neighbors.

And then Nyerere's economic nationalism began to be aroused, at first somewhat slowly. A major disappointment came early in independence when his hopes for substantial economic aid from the West were not fulfilled. He even complained at that time that his own political moderation had made the West take him too much for granted. The carrot in the diplomacy of those days was dangled before naughty boys to tempt them towards moderation. But those who were moderate from the start got more applause than aid. The origins of Nyerere's economic radicalization may well be connected with that initial disappointment over aid from the West. But the very issue on which he started getting radicalized betrayed a form of dependency orientation. The question was whether this orientation would change from a semi-submissive state to a new aggressive militancy.

The pace of Nyerere's radicalization was much slower than Amin's even in the domain of economic nationalism. Nyerere's first major area of diplomatic emphasis was not the quest for economic self-reliance but the quest for regional integration. In June 1961 he even offered to delay Tanganyika's independence if this would facilitate the formation of an East African Federation, but he underestimated the mood of his colleagues in Dar-es-Salaam on this issue. The offer to delay independence was never put to a real test, but it did signify Nyerere's earliest scale of priorities. His leadership in the Pan-African Freedom Movement for East, Central and Southern Africa, was another illustration of his emphasis on political regionalism at this stage of his ideological evolution.

However, unlike Amin, Nyerere paid at least lip service to socialism from the start. His essay, *Ujamaa: The Basis of African Socialism,* has become a classic in East African political thought. The essay goes back to the very beginnings of Tanganyika's independence.

Yet even in his resort to kinship ties (*ujamaa*) as a basis for the ideology of a modern state, Nyerere's original political thought has points of contact with the later reasoning of General Amin. Nyerere used kinship solidarity as the foundation of socialism; Amin came to use kinship solidarity as the foundation of citizenship. The idea of non-indigenous Ugandans was to Amin a contradiction in terms partly because his conception of citizenship was primordial. With a slight imaginative leap Amin could see all black Ugandans as being in some sense kinsmen. Their Adam and their Eve were both black. But Amin could not take the kind of imaginative leap which would make Asians also into fellow *jamaa*.

The problem of cultural schizophrenia had come to touch the issue of citizenship. Traditional conceptions of citizenship among African societies implied either biological intermingling among members of each society or cultural assimilation into the society. Asians in Uganda had neither intermarried with black Ugandans nor identified culturally with them. To Amin the question arose: How could Asians be "real" Uganda citizens in such circumstances?

Did Nyerere once share this kind of reasoning? There was a time when only black Africans could become members of the Tanganyika African National Union. Both the colonial heritage and primordial concepts of *ujamaa* had conspired to make the nationalist movement in Tanganyika explicitly racialistic in its original membership rules. The word "African" in TANU's name was, at the beginning, conceived in terms of color and race.

But Nyerere's commitment to a modern, rather than primordial, concept of citizenship emerged before long. His early assurances to Asians and Europeans might have promised them too much (including security for their property), but even those promises seemed inspired by a modern sense of citizenship—a sense which more readily accommodates racial and cultural pluralism within the same society. "Socialism is not racialism," Nyerere came to assert.

He internationalized this attitude when, on the eve of independence, he threatened not to take Tanganyika into the [British] Commonwealth if South Africa was still a member of it. Joint pressures by Nyerere and Nkrumah contributed toward forcing South Africa out of the Commonwealth.

Four years later Nyerere rediscovered how "very, very British" the Commonwealth was. He was reminded of this upon returning from a Commonwealth meeting of heads of government. Yet the cultural ambivalence remained—for Nyerere obstinately refused to leave the Commonwealth even after severing relations with Britain over Rhodesia. He correctly asserted that the Commonwealth did not "belong" to Great Britain.

It was precisely this period of strain with Britain which gave Nyerere's growing radicalism the extra push it needed toward the climax of the Arusha Declaration. British aid was frozen as a result of the break-off of relations over Rhodesia. Nyerere became more convinced than ever that a moralistic style of politics such as his could only be sustained in conditions of national self-reliance. He got an intimation of this lesson in 1961 when his efforts for aid from the West yielded so little, but at that time it was his moderation rather than his militancy which seemed to explain this. Then there was the wrangle over the Hallstein Doctrine, as West Germany insisted on the expulsion of East Germany's embassy from Tanzania. When Nyerere promised only the compromise of limiting East Germany's representation to a consulate-general, Bonn decided to terminate certain kinds of aid to Tanzania. Nyerere responded by terminating all other aid-relations with West Germany. Once again a lesson had been brought home to Nyerere concerning the indignities of dependency.

The suspension of British aid to Tanzania following Tanzania's break with Britain over the Rhodesian issue was the proverbial last straw. It probably affected profoundly the whole doctrine of self-reliance as a principle to accompany Tanzania's socialism. The Arusha Declaration sought to awaken Tanzanians to a realization that their own most important resource was human labor, and their strategy for development should therefore be based on the efficient utilization of that labor instead of on the persistent supplication for capital from others.

In reality the doctrine did not mean economic autarky, but it did mean a combination of genuine economic nonalignment (balancing the West with China) and greater domestic efforts, with communal exertion through ujamaa villages.

Nyerere, then, is indeed a case of wounded economic nationalism leading on to greater radicalization. Once again an African socialist was born out of the womb of African nationalism.

But is not socialism itself a form of ideological dependency? It is to this puzzle that we must now address ourselves.

SOCIALISM AND CULTURAL SCHIZOPHRENIA

The most disguised form of Europe's cultural dominance is the Marxist heritage. Because the governments of the Western world have on the whole been anti-Marxist, cultural nationalists in the Third World have often forgotten that Marx himself was a European. It is not unusual to find African intellectuals who, on the one hand, are militantly hostile to Europe's cultural infiltration into Africa and, on the other, are tending toward expressing that hostility in Marxist vocabulary. To be an African cultural nationalist and a Marxist at the same time is a contradiction not only from the point of view of Marxism but also from the point of view of African cultural nationalism. Embracing Marxism is a process of de-Africanization in this sense.

This question has haunted the ideological life of Julius Nyerere from quite early. In his more moderate days, Nyerere's cultural nationalism still had the upper hand. He was already fascinated by the concept of socialism, but was keen to link it to indigenous African traditions: "We in Africa, have no more need for being 'converted' to socialism than we have of being 'taught' democracy. Both are rooted in our own past—in the traditional society which produced us."[15]

This is the language of a cultural nationalist even more than that of a socialist. It was therefore not surprising that this was a period when Nyerere was criticized in Soviet literature for putting his main ideological stress on the "African originality of views and outlook."

Nyerere had explicitly rejected the Marxist concept of "class struggle" as being inapplicable in Africa. In 1965 he was criticized by Soviet writers for what in the Soviet Union is sometimes referred to as "distributive socialism"— the idea that exploiting relationships can be eliminated by perfecting the system of distribution of the goods produced. Even as late as 1966 Nyerere—as a partisan of "African socialism"—was unfavorably contrasted with "revolutionary democrats . . . carrying out radical social and economic reforms."[16]

In this refusal to be drawn into Marxist preconceptions, Nyerere had domestic as well as distant critics. There were Tanzanians who preferred the language of historical and dialectical materialism and insisted on discerning a continuing "class struggle" in Tanzania whatever policies Nyerere pursued. These were usually more severe cases of cultural schizophrenia than Nyerere himself had even been.[17]

As Nyerere became more radicalized he did in fact begin to narrow the gap between himself and the Marxists. Even his Soviet critics began to make concessions. Soviet readers were informed that Nyerere had borrowed many of his views from "utopian socialism, Gandhism and also various modern sociologists, laborites and social democrats." During the first few years of independence he had sought "an intermediate position, a middle way between capitalism and socialism," as his memorandum of June 1966 on principles of development had shown. But there were now indications that the views of Tanzanian leaders were "coming nearer to scientific socialism."[18]

Nyerere's discovery of China, following the aid treaties between Tanzania and China, also increased his interest in aspects of Maoism. Both the new strategy of self-reliance and the concept of ujamaa villages might have received additional inspiration from the Chinese experience.

But for Nyerere there was such a thing as *ideological* self-reliance, as well as general economic self-reliance. Though still vulnerable to cultural ambivalence, Nyerere was at least aware of the hazards of ideological dependency.

THE SOLDIER AND THE SOCIALIST: A CONCLUSION

What about Idi Amin in Uganda? Was he also a case of wounded economic nationalism leading on to greater radicalization? The question entered a new phase in December 1972. It had become pertinent to ask whether Amin's economic nationalism would in time mature into some kind of socialism. That editorial of the Tanzanian official newspaper, the *Daily News,* raised the issue in those terms following Amin's nationalization of a number of British firms: "Tanzania can only wish that he takes over the remaining foreign capitalists properties, such as the banks and insurance companies."

Of course Amin's motives for the takeovers were very different from what Tanzania would have preferred. For the time being Amin hated even the word "nationalization" in its socialistic sense. He kept on affirming that government was a temporary trustee, pending the emergence of indigenous private buyers and investors. But the Tanzanian government nevertheless saw Amin's action as "a significant shift":

> Tanzania can only wish that these properties are truly run in the interest of the people of Uganda as a whole and not a few Black exploiters. Tanzania can only wish that General Amin, with the help of the workers and peasants of Uganda, will convert these properties into socialist property. Tanzania can only wish that in case of difficulties, Uganda will ask for help and seek Tanzania's experience in running such people's enterprises.[19]

As the Asians departed and the British cut their losses, Uganda did need a new spirit of self-reliance. The question which remained was whether, in the absence of adequate private capital and entrepreneurial personnel among indigenous Ugandans, the government would be forced to assume and *consolidate* state ownership. To the extent that such state ownership would be a reduction of private property in a potentially powerful area of the economy, Amin would indeed be moving in a leftward direction. Socialism by default may be Uganda's destiny if Amin's initial efforts toward indigenous capitalism do not find an adequate infrastructural support.

But socialism by default would at least be dictated by the situation rather than by a borrowed bag of ideological tricks. For the time being Amin has been responding to a concrete African situation, and his strategy has had a rustic independence all its own. Both liberals and radicals have been aghast. Amin has made more enemies in the Western world than in the Communist world, and yet his quest has been for an indigenous private enterprise system. Because he is not an intellectual, Amin's schizophrenia has in any case not been as pronounced as that of his more Westernized critics. And by being spontaneous and brazen, Amin has been striking out for ideological autonomy.

It is not as yet clear whether the Uganda experiment launched by this rustic soldier will succeed. It is not even clear whether it will have as long a period of trial-and-error as the Tanzanian experiment has had. Nyerere has played around with a decade of experimentation; Amin's entry is still fresh.

And yet, in a curious way, Amin's impact on the future of Uganda may already be deeper than Nyerere's impact on Tanzania. There is a quality of *irreversibility* about some of the actions which Amin has taken which is greater than that inherent in most of Nyerere's projects in Tanzania. The ujamaa villages may collapse when Nyerere goes, if not before. Or Nyerere and his colleagues may change their minds and dismantle the present socialistic superstructure in Tanzania. But not even Amin himself could ever bring the Asians back to their previous position in the country even if he wanted to. There is a *finality* about some of Amin's actions, including aspects of civil-military relations, which seems to be more convincing than almost any socialistic experiment on mainland Tanzania. In this respect the changes in Uganda are nearer to the changes in Zanzibar in their irreversibility than they are to those of Nyerere's mainland.

But both Amin and Nyerere must be seen as Africans who decided that development itself had to have a spirit. The spirit was to relate to issues of dignity and autonomy. Starting with a rough distrust of racial stratification from the Sudan to southern Africa, Amin gradually emerged from his sub-missive dependency complex and entered a process of radicalization. The manifestations of this ranged from the break with the Israelis to a new toughness on southern Africa, from the expulsion of the Asians to the Africanization of church leadership. An aggressive anglophilia persisted in this former sergeant of the King's African Rifles, but he had at last emerged from easy submission, deference, and imitation.

Julius Nyerere, a staunch critic of Amin for so long, had an ideological history which could bear comparison with Amin's experience. Starting from moderation and trust in Western intentions, Nyerere's economic nationalism was gradually aroused. It was through his economic nationalism that he found his way to socialism—but without stumbling into the ideological encumbrance of a Marxist straightjacket.

In absolute terms, the struggle against dependency, the quest for cultural and economic autonomy, has only just started. Amin and Nyerere are part of a larger picture. A restless continent is trying to rediscover its soul, reassert its sanity, and recreate itself.

NOTES

1. Our use of these terms is not, of course, clinical. It is an attempt at psychological approximation.

2. See G. Duncan Mitchell, *A Dictionary of Sociology* (London: Routledge and Kegan Paul, 1968). Consult also Dent Ocaya-Lakidi and Ali A. Mazrui, "Secular Skills and Sacred Values in Uganda Schools: Problems of Technical and Moral Acculturation," paper presented at conference on "Conflict and Harmony between Traditional and Western Education in Africa," School of Oriental and African Studies, University of London, March 1973.

3. Consult also Mazrui, "Educational Techniques in Plural Societies," *International Social Science Journal* 24, 3 (1972): 149-165.

4. Some of these ideas concerning a cultural dualism anticipate my book *A World Federation of Cultures: An African Perspective,* sponsored by the World Order Models Project, the World Law Fund and Carnegie Endowment for International Peace. (forthcoming)

5. The initial influence of the Israelis in Amin's Uganda had more complex political reasons. Consult Mazrui, "Is the Nile Valley Emerging as a New Political System?" paper presented at the Annual Universities Social Science Conference of Eastern Africa, Makerere University, Kampala, December 1971. Consult also Selwyn Ryan's paper about external intervention in Eastern Africa, paper presented at the conference of the International Institute of Strategic Studies, Italy, September 1971.

6. Alexander Mitchell and Russell Miller, "Amin: The Untold Story," *The Sunday Times Magazine* (London), October 29, 1972: 53.

7. S. E. Finer, *The Man on Horseback* (New York, 1962): 63-64.

8. Robert M. Price, "A Theoretical Approach to Military Rule in New States: Reference-Group Theory and the Ghanaian Case," *World Politics* 23, 3 (1971): 403-404.

9. Ibid.: 407.

10. Martin Walker, "Political Super-Star in the Making," *The Guardian Weekly* (London), January 13, 1973. I made a similar point not long after the coup in 1971. Consult chapter 16 in Mazrui, *Cultural Engineering and Nation-Building in East Africa* (Evanston: Northwestern University Press, 1972): 263-76. For a further elaboration refer also to Mazrui, "The Lumpen Proletariat and the Lumpen Militariat: African Soldiers as a New Political Class," *Political Studies* 21, 1 (March 1973).

11. For some reservations concerning Amin's style of expulsion consult Mazrui, "The De-Indianization of Uganda: Does It Now Require an Educational Revolution?" paper presented at Social Science Conference of Eastern Africa (USSC), University of Nairobi, December 1972.

12. The conference of women's organizations was chaired by Elizabeth Bagaya, former Princess of the Kingdom of Toro who was later briefly appointed Foreign Minister by General Amin after the coup. At the conference Chairman Elizabeth recalled the General's efforts the previous year to foster religious amity in Uganda, and appealed to him "not to allow the achievements he has so far made by bringing the religious groups together to be destroyed overnight." See *The Times* (London), December 1, 1972.

13. For my defense of those Asians who had taken Uganda citizenship consult my newspaper feature article "Exodus, 1972," *The People* (Kampala), September 9, 1972. An earlier defense was made in "Sex and Indophobia," public lecture delivered at Makerere University, Main Hall, January 1972 (mimeo).

14. See *Daily News,* December 21, 1972; *Daily Nation* (Nairobi), December 22, 1972; and *Sunday Nation* (Uganda edition), December 24, 1972. The Uganda government issued a statement welcoming the change of tone in Tanzania as signified by the editorial.

15. Nyerere, "Ujamaa: The Basis of African Socialism," *Présence Africaine* (Paris) 18, 47, third quarter, 1963.

16. "Tanzania: Soviet Views on the Arusha Programme," *Mizan: Journal of Sino-Soviet Policies* (London) 9, 5 (September-October 1967): 197. See also William Tordoff and Ali A. Mazrui, "The Left and the Super-Left in Tanzania," *The Journal of Modern African Studies* 10, 3 (October 1972): 442-445.

17. Julius K. Nyerere, *Freedom and Socialism: A selection from Writings and Speeches 1965-1967* (Dar-es-Salaam: Oxford University Press, 1968): 17 and 22-3. See chapter 13 for full discussion.

18. *Mizan,* op. cit.: 201

19. *Daily News* (Dar-es-Salaam), December 21, 1972.

Appendix

The Human Cost of Amin's Rule

Appendix

THE HUMAN COST OF AMIN'S RULE   *May, 1973*

Letter from A. Milton Obote to
The Assembly of Heads of State and Government,
The Organisation of African Unity,
ADDIS ABABA.

1. As a signatory of the Charter of the Organisation of African Unity, I salute the advent of the Tenth Anniversary of the Organisation. I also write to report on the grave situation which has persistently existed in Uganda for the last twenty eight months.

2. Ten years ago, thirty one African Leaders launched a new epoch of African history and image when they signed the Charter of the OAU. The Leaders proclaimed on that occasion, a total struggle to liberate the whole of Africa. They bonded Governments and Regimes in the liberated areas of Africa to harness the resources of Africa for a better life for the peoples of Africa. Eight of the original signatories to the Charter are no longer on this earth to share in this year's celebrations and the review of the past ten years, or the consideration of future. I join the Assembly of Heads of State and Government in recording my deepest respect to the memories of Abdul Nasser, Kwame Nkrumah, William Tubman, Abubakar Balewa, Leon Mba, Milton Margai, Cyrill Adoula and Fulbert Youlou. What these eight helped to create, namely, a platform and instrument of African oneness, dignity and freedom will grow in strength and will triumph.

3. Already on the board of history, and since the founding of the OAU, Africa has won and then recorded great victories particularly in the fields of Liberation and good neighbourliness. Every square kilometer of Africa recovered from the imperialists and colonialists, and the fact that the white-racialists are spending more and more Rand in their desperate and futile endeavour to delay the day of reckoning, are all items for celebrations on this auspicious occasion.

4. Africa's victories are, however, also Africa's greatest challenges. To recover a square kilometer from the imperialists is a victory. To develop that land for the good of the people is a challenge. To free a village or a country from the yoke of foreign serfdom, vassalage and oppression is a great victory. It is also a great challenge to create conditions in which the people of such a village or country can live and work with dignity and in peace. Africa has accepted to meet that challenge in Article II of the OAU Charter.

5. As millions of the peoples of Africa in the Liberated Countries now represented in the Assembly of Heads of State and Government celebrate with hope the inauguration of the second decade of the OAU, ten million people in Uganda are wailing. I report and bring to the CONSCIENCE of the Leaders of Africa and to humanity at large the fact of MASS MURDER and HUMAN DEGRADATION of the most heinous type which obtain in Uganda. I do also predicate that the said bestialities are being perpetrated by a murderous clique in the Uganda Armed Forces under the direction of Idi Amin.

6. Some of the methods of mass murder, torture and other forms of atrocities perfected by Idi Amin or his agents are too horrible to describe. These methods include the sticking of bayonets into unmentionable parts of the human body and the placing of embers in the reproductive organs of women victims. The most widely used method is to torture and then shoot the victim. Another method is to line up the victims in single file and then the victim at the head of the line is ordered to lie down. The next victim to the one on the ground is then given an axe to crush the head of the person on the ground; knowing full well that it is his turn next. The last victim on the line is then either bayoneted or shot. There are cases where victims had their eyes plucked out before being killed. In numerous cases, bodies of victims were dismembered and the parts thrown about in different places. Some victims have been disembowelled in public often in market places. Some have been decapitated and their heads were then put on public display. There are cases where the victims are first tortured, tied and then herded onto and driven into the bush to die there. It is horrible, but it is a fact that some victims were forced to be cannibals in orgies where Amin's soldiers cut parts of the bodies of the victims, roasted the human flesh and fed the starving victims on their own flesh until they died. Africa and, indeed, the world at large must have been shocked by the public executions carried out in February this year. The families of the victims were forced to witness the executions and the victims were stripped of their clothes before they were murdered in public. Other methods, although known, are too macabre and bizarre to describe.

7. The nature of the outrage on humanity in Uganda being practised by Idi Amin and his agents is in fact genocide. This genocide and other atrocities against humanity are being perpertrated in violation of the Universal Declara-

tion of Human Rights and the provisions of the Uganda Constitution on the fundamental human rights. The extent of this outrage is such that there are in every part of Uganda widows and orphans in their thousands.

8. This genocide began in January 1971 and has persisted to the present day. It began with the systematic killings in the barracks and with Lake Victoria and the Nile being the graveyards. The Army Chief of Staff, Brigadier Suleiman Hussein and ten Army and Air Force Officers of the rank of Lt. Col. and above as well as over two hundred officers from Major down to Lieutenant and NCOS were among the very early victims. There were also civilians amongst the very early victims such as Prefessor V. P. Emiru of Makerere Medical School and Dr. George Ebine of Mulago Hospital, the State House Chief Driver Albert Masurubu and hundreds of others some of whom can be named. These men did not die during the heat of a coup d'etat. They were all killed in cold blood.

9. In early March 1971 over 30 Officers were herded in a small hut and the hut was blown up by dynamite. The explosion was heard all over Kampala, and Radio Uganda broadcast a statement from "The President's Office" which said that the general public should have no fear, and that the explosion they had heard was caused by the detonation of old bombs. A member of the OAU Council of Ministers was present in Kampala when this massacre was perpetrated.

10. At the end of March 1971 Amin ordered the recruitment of sixty men into the army on the pretext that they would be given special duties at the burial of Sir Edward Mutesa. The men were to come from Buganda Region and had to be true supporters of Edward Mutesa. All the sixty men were executed by a firing squad in early April at an army training ground called Kabamba in Western Uganda. The men were not guilty of any crime except that they were too eager to show their support for traditionalism.

11. During the same month—April—when the number of civilian as well as military victims became very large, hundreds of people decided to seek refuge in the Sudan. Over 600 of these were apprehended when they tried to cross the border and were massacred in the presence of Idi Amin. Photographs of this mass murder were taken and Amin went throughout Uganda showing these photographs in public rallies.

12. At the beginning of May, 1971 Amin came out openly in his true brutal and rapacious colours. He licensed mass murder and empowered his henchmen to shoot any person on sight if any henchman suspects such person "to have committed or is about to commit a crime," no matter how small, or whatever the henchman may imagine to be a crime. Amin himself is on record as having said repeatedly in public and in various parts of Uganda beginning in May, 1971 that politicians and civil servants, in particular, found holding meetings or suspected of being anti-Amin, should be treated as "kondos"

(armed robbers) and should therefore be shot on sight. Many citizens of Uganda have been murdered as a result.

13. On May 11th, 1971. Amin issued a decree providing for detention without trial. The decree was meant to achieve two objects. First, it was to "legalise" the status of over 800 men whom Amin had thrown into jail soon after the coup. The second objective was even more sinister as it turned out to be in reality. It was to enable soldiers to openly arrest any person, detain the person and then murder him in prison. A glimpse of Amin's over developed sense of dissimulation and lies may be gauged from the fact that his very first of the so-called eighteen reasons for his coup was about detention without trial. I quote the first reason Amin gave as ground for his coup. It was as follows:

"1. The unwarranted detention without trial and for long periods of a large number of people, many of whom are totally innocent of any charges."

In terms of principle any detention law or decree in any country is detested irrespective of the number of people detained under that law, or decree. In principle therefore there is no difference in the fact that at the time of the coup there were 25 detainees who were all released by Amin after the coup and detention on Amin's orders of 817 persons immediately after the coup. The real and clear difference is that my ministers and I never tortured nor ordered torture nor killing of any detainee whereas the majority of Amin's detainees have been murdered in jail. The fate of the 817 detainees mentioned here will be told in another paragraph of this letter.

14. June 1971 was characterised by extensive purges in the Army and diabolical killings in the country side. In Mbarara Barracks alone some 500 soldiers were tortured, tied up, herded onto lorries and driven and deposited at a ranch to die. Two survived the ordeal and foolishly and to the surprise of all, returned to the Barracks. The two were well received by their tormentors. The latter quoted texts in the Koran and Bible on how God loved the two. The unfortunate two were showered with an abundance of concern and good-will by the murderers. The two were immediately taken to the battalion's Dispensary. At night, they were dragged out and murdered. During the first half of July, two Americans—one a journalist and the other a lecturer at Makerere University heard and went to investigate the Mbarara massacre of June 1971. The two Americans on reaching Mbarara, were murdered to silence them for good for their "impudence" to ask questions. For months, even to the wife of one of the murdered Americans, Amin pretended not to have known nor heard anything. A subsequent inquiry by Mr. Justice Jeffrey-Jones, though ordered by Amin himself, was so much frustrated by Amin that had it not been for the tenacity of the Judge, no one would today know

of the attempts to cover up the murder of the two Americans who were killed in their attempt to record the massacre of some 500 Ugandans.

15. On July 3rd. 1971, Amin announced and it was widely published that he had cancelled a visit to Malawi on account of alleged uneasy situation on the Uganda border with Tanzania. He alleged that from January to June 1971, some 70 officers and 600 soldiers of his army had lost their lives fighting on the Uganda/Tanzania border. He did not name the enemy they were fighting. However, that was the first time Ugandans first heard of the imaginary battles and which have since been fought almost monthly. Amin's statement was an attempt to explain the massacre of officers and men but the figures he gave were for those he had decided to liquidate not the thousands who were already dead. He was also about to go to Israel and Britain. The invention of the imaginary battles at which many were killed gave him a convenient explanation for the massacres. Thus, on 8th. July, 1971, he threatened that he would not hesitate to strike deep into Tanzania by land, air and water. He left for Tel Aviv en route to London on 11th. July.

16. Within 24 hours of Amin's departure for Israel, reports were received of killings in Jinja, Soroti, and Moroto. These reports were first denied by "a spokesman from the President's Office." However, on 14th. July, Amin then in London, confirmed the story of the massacres. He added that the killings were occasioned by guerrilla attacks in which the Chinese were physically involved. Like many of his utterances, that was a blatant lie. The victims were officers and soldiers and members of the Police Para-Military Unit who belonged to certain tribes particularly but not excusively Acholi and Lango. Over 1,000 people were killed.

17. The whole of Africa was startled by the news that fighting had broken out in August 1971 along the Uganda/Tanzanian border. What Africa did not know was the fact that the people of Uganda were at that time very perturbed about the massacres. Amin had to find some way of detracting attention from his terror in which many people were being massacred. The way he found was to attack Tanzania. It was during the same August that Martin Okello, a Member of Parliament, together with several other persons, were massacred and buried in shallow graves. No investigation has ever taken place as to the circumstances of their deaths; a fact which points to the complicity of the Army under Idi Amin in these killings.

18. During the month of September, 1971, Amin became very bold and arrogant. He established a network of terror and murder squads in what he calls Military Intelligence, Public Safety Unit, State Research Centre and Military Police. At the beginning of this new wave of massacres and terror under the four organisations, Ugandans living and working in Buganda (Southern Region) bore the brunt of the atrocities. This was because the four squads had their headquarters in Buganda Region where also the highest

numbers of Uganda's Civil Servants, politicians, intellectuals and successful businessmen are to be found. The first victim of the newly established murder squads was Michael Kagwa, the President of the Industrial Court. He was found burnt in his car. The atrocities committed in Buganda Region involving massacres and plunder during the last quarter of 1971 (September to December) by the four specialised murder squads, have since spread throughout Uganda.

19. The four squads mentioned above are all directly responsible to Amin. The Head of each of the squads gets from Amin a list of persons to be liquidated. This is called the "official" list to differentiate it from lists compiled by each of the Heads or general purges in the army and the slaughter of the masses. Amin's "official" list is normally drawn to a thousand at a time. There are people everywhere, particularly in towns, whose job is to find victims whose names are to go onto the "official" list. The job of the squads is to ensure that those on the "official" list "disappear" or "swim." Thus in Uganda the words "disappearance" and "swimming" have acquired ominous meanings. "Disappearance" means that the victim has been kidnapped by members of one of the four murder squads, very often in the presence of other people, and the victim is subsequently killed; but the murder is then completely denied, always by "a spokesman from the Office of the President." "Swimming" on the other hand, means that the victim is lured to some place by members of the murder squads and is immediately killed but the body is found in some place, be it a house, a street or some public place. The aim in both cases is to terrorise the masses into submission.

20. During the month of December 1971, Amin had over 600 political detainees in the maximum security prison known as Luzira, near Kampala. An order was given by Amin for the transfer of these detainees, who included military personnel—officers and men—Police Officers, and civilians to a Prison Farm at Mutukula near the Tanzania border. The detainees were handcuffed as they left the Prison and boarded buses. Amin's statement at the time regarding this odd transfer was that the men were to be court-martialled and that the court-martial was to be held at Mutukula. Why a Police Officer or a civilian should be court-martialled in a State which is not under martial law was not explained.

21. In January 1972, my Minister of Commerce and Industry, William Kalema was kidnapped by members of Amin's murder squads. He has since not been seen. During the same month, there began a systematic pogrom at Mutukula Prison. By the beginning of February, 1972 less than 200 of the 600 odd detainees were still alive. The rest had all been axed to death. On the 5th. February, 1972, the remainder knowing that in any case all were going to die, resolved to break out from Prison. Only 23 managed to get to Tanzania to tell the story of this diabolical atrocity against Africa. The

Mutukula victims included almost the entire leadership of the C.I.D. Mohammed Hassan who was Head of the C.I.D. and his deputy Festus Wauyo were both like the other victims, tortured and then killed.

22. In February, 1972, District Commissioner Mulekezi and Hotel Manager Shekanabo were both dragged out of a hotel at Tororo in the presence of several guests. They were immediately killed. During the month three employees of the Coffee Marketing Board—Esaku, Oyamu and Omana—were kidnapped and have not since been seen. Amin then launched one of his periodic massacres in the town of Soroti. The town was sealed off by soldiers who then went from house to house beating up the residents. Many died that night and others died later in hospital. Amin threw the blame on Lt. Col. William Ndahendikire as the officer who had arranged to harrass the residents of Soroti. Ndahendikire was in Nairobi at the time and knew nothing about the planning and the execution of the Soroti massacre.

23. On 21st March, 1972, Amin disbanded the Police Special Branch and C.I.D. He ordered officers and men of the two departments to wear uniform when on duty and empowered men of his murder squads to "detect crimes," wear plain clothes and combat armed robbery. The disbandment of the Special Branch and the C.I.D. followed staggering reports received by the Police about missing persons and the attempts by the Police to investgate the reported cases. Seven days later, on 28th March, a large number of people were rounded off from Bugisu and Bukedi Districts in the Eastern Region and taken to Tororo Barracks. Amin went there and addressed the "prisoners." None left the Barracks alive.

24. On May 1st 1972, Idi Amin boasted at a public rally that he was such a good man that his Army did not have any Ugandan in detention. Yes, the General indeed boasts and it is true that at that time and ever since there have been no detainees in Uganda. He has no need to detain anybody. He simply orders the murder of the victim within a few hours of the arrest, and then the famous word "disappearance" follows the demise of the victim. The brutal and barbaric atrocities have compelled thousands of Ugandan peasants, students, civil servants, lawyers, businessmen and politicians to flee from their homes—homes which have become infernos. Thus, Ugandans who had to flee for their lives are to be found not only in the neighbouring sister States, but also far beyond. Some Ugandans have sought refuge as far as Europe and the Americas.

25. When Amin says as he emphasised on May 1st 1972, that his army is disciplined, it is true in so far as his terror squads are concerned. Members of the terror squads act precisely according to Amin's directives. Thus during 1972 a barbaric and tragic plot was launched against the well known Leaders. It began with a decree issued on 3rd. May, 1972, absolving Amin and all his henchmen from any massacre or murder committed by them in the past or to

be committed in the future. Anil Clerk a Member of Parliament was the first victim under the new decree of genocide. Capt. Avudiria who had begun to oppose the decree was murdered in June. Ambassador George Kamba was dragged from the Nile Hotel in Kampala in the presence of many guests and subsequently murdered.

26. The murder of Benedicto Kiwanuka, Amin's Chief Justice in September, 1972, has received world wide publicity. Amin began to plot the murder of Kiwanuka in March 1972, possibly earlier. On March 3rd. Amin accused Kiwanuka in public of having attempted to influence the appointment of certain persons as Judges of the High Court. Kiwanuka as Chief Justice, was also the Chairman of the Judicial Service Commission, a body which recommends, inter alia, the appointment of Judges. Thereafter, Amin went about accusing "a high ranking official from Masaka District" who, Amin alleged was not pro-Amin. Kiwanuka was born in Masaka District. When he was openly "arrested" in his Chambers in the High Court building, Radio Uganda did not report the "arrest" for almost 36 hours! Kiwanuka was forcibly taken from the High Court by a group of armed men at about 8:30 a.m. on 21st September. It is surprising that the entire press in Uganda never got the "Story" in time for their editions of September 22nd. Amin has accused "guerillas" of having kidnapped and killed Kiwanuka. Those "guerillas," if they exist, must be controlling Radio Uganda and the entire Press in Uganda to have succeeded not only in kidnapping a Chief Justice in broad day light but also to have gagged the Radio and the Press for more than 24 hours.

27. During the same September, Amin ordered the murder of Nekemia Bananuka who at time of the coup in January, 1971 was the elected (not appointed) Leader of the Local Administration in Ankole District. Bananuka was murdered after a torture in which his legs were first cut off.

28. Francis Walugembe who was the Mayor of Masaka (the fourth largest town in Uganda) had perhaps the most foul torture followed by his murder. He was arrested at a village outside the town where he had gone to visit a friend. His tormentors carried him in the boot of a car to the Masaka market. Residents of Masaka were ordered at gun point by "Major" Maliyamungu— Amin's cousin—to gather at the market. What was done to Walugembe at the market is odious to describe. Having been tortured for hours, his male part was cut off by Maliyamungu who asked the victim to state whether he (the victim) was a man! The piece was then put into the mouth of the victim. Hours later, after more tortures, he died.

29. The murder of Basil Bataringaya my Minister of Internal Affairs, will always, for years to come, ashame army uniform in Uganda. Bataringaya was decapitated. The rest of his body without the head was dismembered, cut into pieces and scattered in and around the town of Mbarara. His head was

carried throughout the town by soldiers who stopped at different places to ask groups and individuals whether anyone could recognise whose head the soldiers were holding. This orgy went on for hours and hundreds of the residents of Mbarara were gravely nauseated by the orgy.

30. Ben Otim, like Bananuka, was the elected Leader of the Local Administration in Lango District. In September, 1972, Amin sent a message requesting Otim to go to Kampala to see Amin. Otim complied but as he was boarding a vehicle going to Kampala, he was shot and killed by Amin's men. Otim's body was dismembered and he has no grave.

31. Simayo Oryem was at the time of Amin's coup and in September 1972, the Administrative Secretary (Head of the Local Civil Service) of Acholi District Council. Oryem was axed to death on the orders of Amin and was dismembered. He has no grave.

32. James Buwembo was a pharmacist. While driving with a friend along Kampala's main street, he was stopped, "arrested" and has never been seen. He was the brother of my wife. Amin has since callously stated that he believes that Buwembo "went to join his brother-in-law in Tanzania." That means a certificate that James Buwembo is dead.

33. Some of Uganda's and I believe Africa's finest and most capable Prison Officers were murdered by Amin in September and October 1972. They include Peter Oketta and Adam Ochitti. None has a grave.

34. Frank Kalimuzo was the Vice-Chancellor of the University of Makerere, Kampala. He was arrested by the Military Police in September 1972 and then released. There are eye witnesses of his second arrest in early October 1972 by members of Amin's so-called "Public Safety Unity." Kalimuzo has since not been seen or heard of.

35. Joseph Mubiru was the Governor of the Bank of Uganda at the time of the coup. Amin threatened to imprison Mubiru but later ordered his murder.

36. Local Administrations in the Districts of Acholi, Ankole, Lango and Bugisu have collapsed due to the massacres of Senior Officials including Chiefs. Local Administrations in other Districts are also about to collapse due to the same reason. The extent of the massacres of the Chiefs alone may be gauged from Amin's decision to appoint 128 "soldiers" to replace the murdered chiefs.

37. The situation has developed to such an extent that in 1973 even persons who were very close to Amin, including some of those he designated as Ministers, have had to run for their lives. The Minister of Education has resigned and is now a refugee. The Minister of Foreign Affairs has also resigned. Fearing that the rest of his "Ministers" would follow the examples of Rugumayo and Kibedi, Amin ordered them to go on two month com-

pulsory leave and then called them back when he insulted and humiliated them and ordered them to work as clerks. Not many are likely to live for long.

38. Before the barbaric executions of February 1973, Idi Amin unleashed a reign of terror in and around the town of Mbale in the Eastern Region. The town and its suburbs were sealed off by troops for three weeks and some 300 people—men, women and children were massacred.

39. In Kigezi District in the Western Region nine men were buried alive by men of the Public Safety Unit during the month of February 1973.

40. In March Idi Amin turned his attention to Busoga District in the Eastern Region. Amin hates to have an intended victim slip through his hands. When my wife and children did so he ordered the murder of my brother-in-law and my cousins. The murder of the innocent people in Busoga, which began in March and continued into April, was on account of the fact that Wanume Kibedi, who comes from Busoga, cannot be reached by Amin.

41. The instances of massacres, the figures and names, I have given in this account are far from being exhaustive. Amin is the greatest brute an African mother has ever brought to life. His terror and callous disregard for human life have made some of Uganda's most capable and highly trained men to flee to other countries. They are all witnesses to the greatest outrage, disregard and contempt for human life perpetrated in Uganda.

42. The people of Uganda are most appreciative and very thankful to all African States and all countries across the world who have been kind and generous enough to host the Ugandan refugees. It is an earnest request in this letter that I now address to all Leaders of Africa, to be as kind and generous as their brothers in Zaire, Rwanda, Sudan, Kenya, Tanzania and Zambia, who have already received Ugandan refugees. This is a matter of life and death. To remain in Uganda is to be a potential victim of a murderous clique that cares nothing about human life. Amin is determined to unleash unceasing terror over Uganda and to bleed Uganda dry of its life. It is my submission to the Leaders of Africa that a continuation of this kind of terror and crime against humanity needs to be checked and censured by the Assembly of Heads of State and Government of Member States of the OAU.

43. Genocide has been a fact in the very heart and belly of Africa for the past 28 months. The people of Uganda have had their lips sealed by the gun. African Leaders, however, are not threatened by that gun. They can at least speak for Africa if not for humanity. To condone Amin's atrocities against the people of Uganda is to condemn Uganda to a slow death.

44. Africa today is on a precipice and Africa now stands to be judged and condemned forever on conspiracy of silence over the trampling of human rights or the active assistance if given by any African State to a murderous

clique in Uganda which is engaged in committing genocide. There is a distinct danger of Africa being charged with employing double standards in considering and pronouncing upon the oppressive measures of the racialist regimes in Southern Africa, while keeping silent whilst the same type of oppression goes on at least in Uganda.

45. During 1972 Amin announced and carried out a racialist exercise in which he expelled from Uganda, within 90 days, nearly 50,000 persons of Asian origin. Many of those expelled are Uganda citizens. However, solely because of the colour of the skin of these victims of tyranny, statements have been made in some parts of Africa welcoming the expulsions. To uproot so many thousands of people within such a short time, and to do so because of the colour of the skin of the victim, is an exercise in racialism and is definitely contrary to the provisions of the Universal Declaration of Human Rights.

46. It is true that there are still to be found in Uganda some persons of Asian origin. Amin's racialism, however, comes out clearly in the fact that he has ordered those remaining not to settle in any part of Uganda as they please, but to be settled by the military in remote parts of the country. It follows clearly, therefore, that to Amin, Uganda citizens are of various classes. The honoured class has the gun and uses it to oppress the rest. The second class consists of victims of his continuous reign of murder and pillage, whose families, on Amin's orders are not allowed to even report the fact of such murders to the Police. The third class is that of Uganda citizens of Asian origin who have to leave their residences, business or places of work and are either expelled or rusticated into remote parts of the country. Some States have been reported to have promised to give assistance to Idi Amin in the implemention of this policy.

47. Racialism apart, Amin's so-called economic war is a facade for fascism and an exercise in the enrichment for a lustful clique. Even before the seizure of the "Asian" properties, the same clique had looted and plundered extensively through Uganda, killing and maiming the victims. The seizure of the "Asian" properties was followed by a dramatized charade which was called allocation of business. The businesses were allocated to and not bought by the new "owners" who are in the main, Amin's friends, favourites and relations.

48. Amin is an avowed anti-Socialist and a fervent fascist. Amin is on record as having praised and endorsed the policies of another fascist—Adolf Hitler. Thus the "Asian" properties seized by the gun have been "allocated" to a few hundreds but the compensation monies are to be the burden of the common man. Amin hopes to get assistance from other countries so as to build in Uganda an aggressive fascist elite whose bond is murder and looting

and whose survival depends upon a continued reign of terror and massacre of the masses—the same masses who are to pay for the new riches of their gun-bearing tormentors.

49. Assistance to Amin has also been given in a form which is directly contrary to the OAU principle of non-interference in the internal affairs of another State. In September 1972, during a conflict involving purely Ugandans, including some Ugandan exiles who were exercising their rights to self-determination, the Libyan Arab Republic rushed troops into Uganda to prop up a murderous clique. To the people of Uganda this was a clear case of interference by Libya in the internal affairs of Uganda.

50. Assistance to Amin in his mission to liquidate thousands in Uganda has also come from Palestinian Organisation. Cases are known in Uganda in which Palestinians, together with Amin's murder squads, kidnapped and subsequently murdered their victims—all of whom were Uganda citizens of African stock.

51. It is contrary to the principles embodied in the OAU Charter that assistance be given by one State to another in order to perpetrate crimes against the peoples of Africa.

52. African unity cannot exist in a vacuum, and indeed African States as such are not just territories, waters and mountains, animals and birds. The substance of African unity and the bedrock of the OAU are the African peoples—their freedom and their welfare. That being so, it would follow that a large-scale slaughter of Africans in any part of Africa must concern every African and every Member State of the OAU. Paragraph 1(b) and 1(e) of Article 2 of the OAU Charter is specific on the important question of "a better life for the peoples of Africa." Quite clearly the provision envisages the honouring of the inviolability of the right to life. It is on the promise that every Member State subscribing to the OAU Charter shall value human life that the Charter makes provision for co-operation among African States. The substance is not co-operation regardless of the violations of the provisions of the OAU Charter, the Charter of the United Nations, the Universal Declaration of Human Rights or the fundamental rights in the municipal laws of each Member State. The OAU Charter calls for co-operation to enable the peoples of Africa to live and to enjoy a better life, not co-operation in the destruction of African lives. Furthermore, The Charter, because of its insistence on the acceptance of the Charter of the U.N. and the Universal Declaration of Human Rights, demands co-operation on the basis of the "recognition of human dignity and of the equal and unalienable rights of all members of the human family." Co-operation in this sense is therefore conditional on the observance of the principles and the goals set out in the Charter of the OAU. . . .

53. It is necessary for the purpose of enabling Africa to understand the

tragedy which now envelopes Uganda, to dwell briefly on the history of Amin's coup. The Amin coup of 1971 was a crime against Uganda and against Africa as a whole. Amin resorted to a coup in order to frustrate enquiries then being conducted on specific crimes about which evidence of his complicity in those crimes was coming to light.

54. There was the crime of murder. A senior Army Officer and his wife were murdered on 25th January 1970—exactly one year before Amin's coup in 1971. The suspects were arrested by the Police. The suspects claimed that it was Amin who hired them to commit the double murder. While this was being investigated by the Police, Amin staged a coup and released the suspects, including one amongst them who had been convicted and sentenced to death in another case.

55. In collusion with a notorious mercenary who had committed crimes against Africa in Algeria, Zaire and Nigeria, Amin was engaged during 1970 in waging war against the Republic of Sudan. The mercenary, Colonel Rolf Steiner, was arrested during that year, and in early 1971 was deported for trial in Khartoum. Amin saw that trial as his own and therefore hurriedly staged a coup so as to destroy evidence which Uganda Police had compiled against Steiner.

56. It is pertinent to recall that the issue of mercenaries has been of grave concern to the OAU from the very inception of the organisation. There are strong resolutions on the matter, the latest of which was passed in Lagos in 1970, requiring every African State to arrest any mercenary and to deport such mercenary to any other African State in which the mercenary is known to have operated. The Government of Uganda, in pursuance of these resolutions and the principles of the OAU Charter, arrested Steiner and deported him to the Sudan. However, the man who was in collusion with Steiner, Idi Amin—and who by that very fact was subverting the Charter of the OAU—is now the murderer of the people of Uganda and is the same man who is welcomed and embraced by some of the world Leaders.

57. In the afternoon of 25th January, 1971, someone who identified himself as a Sergeant in the Uganda Armed Forces, uttered on Radio Uganda the following words:—"The Uganda Army has taken over the Government of Uganda and Dr. Obote's Government has been overthrown. The Parliament is banned." Soon after, the Nation was addressed by Major General Idi Amin, who said, "I have been on a hunting trip 300 miles away from Kampala. There was mutiny in the Army and the Army took over the Government and have given it over to me to run the new military Government." In addition to these statements a very long list of alleged reasons for the coup was read over the radio.

58. On the next day, 26th January, 1971, Amin gave a totally different reason for the coup. He said there had been no mutiny and that the coup had

not been planned in advance. The new reason given by Amin was that "the soldiers of the Acholi and Lango tribes wanted to kill me and also to kill all the soldiers of other tribes. I therefore commanded loyal troops from the Command Post to defeat the ENEMY completely." Such was the beginning of the Uganda tragedy involving unceasing lies, intrigues and killings.

59. On January 25th 1971, the day of the coup d'état there were 19 Ministers in the Uganda Government. Today seven are dead.

(i)   WILLIAM KALEMA–Kidnapped and murdered by men of the Military Police in January, 1972.

(ii) JOSHUA WAKHOLI–Arrested by the army in Masaka District in September, 1972 and murdered by "Major" Mali Ya Mungu.

(iii) ALEX OJERA–Arrested by the Army in Masaka District in September, 1972. He was marched almost naked to a diplomatic Reception at State House where Amin proceeded to question Ojera and put up a show of cruelty for the diplomats and the OAU Secretary-General. On October 13th. Amin himself shot Ojera, Picho Ali, Capt. Oyile and six others at Malire Barracks, Kampala. Next morning Radio Uganda announced that the "War captives" and other detainees broke out of jail in Bondo, West Nile; and that thirty-five were killed but seven including Ojera, Picho Ali and Oyile managed to escape. Three days later, Radio Uganda reported that the jail in question was sited between Masaka and Mbarara nearly 200 kilometers West of Kampala and not at Bondo some 500 kilometers North of Kampala.

(iv) BASIL BATARINGAYA–Brutally tortured and murdered by the army in Mbarara in September, 1972. Bataringaya knew too much about Amin's crimes which led to the coup and which are described in this letter.

(v)   JOHN KAKONGE–Arrested in Kampala in November, 1972 in broad daylight by men of the "State Research Centre." He was murdered in Malire Barracks.

(vi) JAMES OCHOLA–Arrested in Tororo by men of the "Public Safety Unit" in November, 1972. He was murdered in Tororo Barracks.

(vii) HAJI SHABAN NKUTU–Arrested in the presence of hundreds of people at Jinja by men of the "Public Safety Unit" on 12th. January, 1973. The same day, Radio Uganda reported that Nkutu had fled the Country. A few days later his body was found on the banks of the Nile. At his burial the army stormed the the mourners and killed nearly 200 people for their "audacity" to bury a "guerrilla."

60. In January, 1973, Amin issued a statement in which he gave some names of some of his victims. His account is most revealing in the repeated assertion that **"nobody knows where he went"** which is to be found against the names of the victims. His statement was meant to show Ugandans how others will also "disappear." Seven young men from Tanzania who went for job interviews at the Headquarters of the East African Posts and Telecommunications Corporation in Kampala were quickly made to "disappear." Father Clement Kiggundu, editor of a local newspaper, was burnt in his car. Dr. F. G. Sembeguya a member of Parliament and a Medical Practitioner was kidnapped from his Nursing Home during day time and later murdered. Dr. Edward Kizito, Acting Head of the Dental School was kidnapped and

murdered. Kenyans working in Uganda, particularly those working for the East African Railways Corporation, were harassed and some murdered. Terror and lies continue in Uganda.

61. The Uganda situation is a grave challenge to the OAU Member States. That challenge revolves around the morality of conducting "normal" relations with Uganda when there is abundant evidence that a clique in the Armed Forces of that Country is based on mass murder. A section in the preamble of the OAU Charter enjoins the OAU Member States to uphold the principles contained in the Charter of the United Nations and those in the Universal Declaration of Human Rights which "provide a solid foundation for peaceful and positive co-operation among States." Co-operation with Uganda when the provisions of the said Universal Declaration of Human Rights are being flouted daily and the populace subjected to a brutal reign of terror would appear to be co-operation with the gun-man and not with the people of Uganda. The moral issue is on the desirability to co-operate with a band of murderers and to thereby strengthen them in their diabolical scheme to depopulate a part of Africa through mass slaughter.

62. It has not been during the past 28 months part of my method to express to the world the grave situation existing in my country through public statements nor do I intend to do so in future. In this letter, I have tried to place before you a genuine and a serious matter of concern and not propaganda since I know that each of you can find out the truth independently. It is with that in mind that I now make reference, for record, to the Mogadishu Agreement signed in October last year between Tanzania and Uganda. Article 2 of this Agreement provides that the two States agree "to effect an immediate cessation of hostile propaganda directed against each other through the radio, television and press."

That is the published document but I would like to draw your attention to the agreed minute. This reads:—

"After prolonged discussions, Article 2 was accepted as initially proposed. Tanzania made it clear it was accepting the Article on the understanding that genuine comments on Government policies shall not be construed as hostile propaganda. Uganda expressed reservations on the proviso by Tanzania regarding 'genuine comments' and stressed that everything should be done."

Thus there is proviso to Article 2. It is within the terms of this proviso that I have addressed you in this letter on the grave matters of murder, massacre and degradation of Ugandans by Idi Amin.

63. One of the men who served under Amin as a Minister has written a memorandum on the Uganda situation copies of which I believe a number of you received from him directly. Amin's Ex-Minister raised in that memorandum an important question of principle when he wrote:—

"Too many nations regard what is happening in Uganda as an internal matter. Is systematic genocide an internal matter or matter for all mankind? The Sharpeville massacre was condemned by the entire civilised world, but nobody has yet condemned the wholesale killings and disappearances of innocent people in Uganda."

64. In the same memorandum, the Ex-Minister stated that at a conservative estimate—and stresses conservative—the death toll in Uganda in Amin's first two years of terror was 80,000 to 90,000 people! It is an incredible statistic and I must point out that it comes from one who was in Uganda and a minister in the "government" during those years. It is difficult not to take seriously his conservative statistics. I do not ask Africa or humanity to believe me but how can Africa or anybody else also disbelieve scores of Ugandans who are fleeing every week because they believe their lives are in danger. They include ministers and civil servants who have been serving under Amin. There are also scores of Kenyan employees of the East African Community who have fled this year and have refused to return to Uganda. They cannot all be imagining a non-existent danger of exaggerating isolated cases of murder. The danger is real and present.

65. In April, 1973, Amin was reported to have said that Ugandans who have fled the country including myself are free to return to Uganda and that none would be molested or harmed. It was reported that Amin had given that assurance in a document, addressed to me and which was to be delivered to me through the good office of a Member State of the OAU. I can say truthfully and categorically that at the time of writing this letter—May 1973—I have not received the said document and that he who believes what Amin utters, is a dreamer.

66. In conclusion, I affirm that I have brought the grave matter of genocide in Uganda for the sake of Africa. I have no doubt whatsoever that the Assembly would not want Africa to stand condemned by its enemies of double standards and hypocrisy. I therefore plead that even if as Africans you feel you cannot materially and morally support Ugandans in their determination to overthrow Amin, do not materially or morally support him and do not arm him; for to support him and to arm him is to give him the international certificate to massacre the people of Uganda at will and on his whims. Finally, I and thousands of Ugandans who are now refugees, are at your disposal to verify what has been happening in Uganda.

A. MILTON OBOTE.

SELECT BIBLIOGRAPHY

I. RELATED WORKS BY ALI A. MAZRUI

This book has benefitted from earlier essays by the author about Uganda and has borrowed from some of these essays. Of particular relevance are the following:

1. "Leadership in Africa: Obote of Uganda," *International Journal*, Vol. 25, No. 3, June 1970.
2. *Cultural Engineering and Nation-Building in East Africa*, (Evanston, Illinois: Northwestern University Press, 1972).
3. "The Lumpen Proletariat and the Lumpen Militariat: African Soldiers as a New Political Class," *Political Studies*, Vol. 21, No. 1, March 1973.
4. "The Militarization of Charisma: An African Perspective," SSIP (*Sozialwissenschaftlicher Studienkreis fur Internationale Probleme*), Mitteilungen Bulletin, No. 38/39, January/June, 1974.
5. "The Social Origins of Ugandan Presidents: From King to Peasant Warrior," *Canadian Journal of African Studies*, Vol. 8, No. 1, 1974.
6. "Piety and Puritanism under a Military Theocracy: Uganda Soldiers as Apostolic Successors," chapter in Catherine M. Kelleher (editor), *Political-Military Systems: Comparative Perspectives*, (Beverly Hills and London: Sage Publications, 1974).
7. "The Resurrection of the Warrior Tradition in African Political Culture," *The Journal of Modern African Studies*, Vol. XIII, No. 1, scheduled for publication in March 1975.
8. "Ethnic Stratification and the Military-Agrarian Complex: The Uganda Case," chapter in Nathan Glazer and Daniel P. Moynihan (editors), *Ethnicity in the Modern World*, (Cambridge, Mass.: Harvard University Press, 1975).
3a. "Racial Self-Reliance and Cultural Dependency: Nyerere and Amin in Comparative Perspective," *Journal of International Affairs*, Vol. 27, No. 1, 1973.

II. BOOKS AND MONOGRAPHS BY OTHERS

1. Apter, David E. *The Political Kingdom in Uganda*, (Princeton, N.J.: Princeton Univ. Pr., 1961).
2. Beattie, John *The Nyoro State*, (London: O.U.P., 1971).
3. Brett, E. A. *Colonialism and Underdevelopment in East Africa*, (Nairobi: H.E.B., 1973).
4. Fallers, Lloyd A. (ed.) *The King's Men: Leadership and Status in Buganda on the Eve of Independence*, (London: O.U.P., 1964).
5. Gukiina, Peter M. *Uganda: A Case Study in African Political Development*, (Notre Dame and London: Univ. of Notre Dame Pr., 1972).

6. Ibingira, G. S. K. *The Forging of an African Nation: The Political and Constitutional Evolution of Uganda from Colonial Rule to Independence, 1894-1962,* (New York: The Viking Pr. and Kampala: Uganda Publishing House, 1973).

7. The Kabaka of Buganda [Edward Mutesa] *Desecration of My Kingdom,* (London: Constable, 1967).

8. Kabwegyere, Tarsis B. *The Politics of State Formation: The Nature and Effects of Colonialism in Uganda,* (Nairobi: East African Literature Bureau, 1974).

9. Kasfir, Nelson M. *Controlling Ethnicity in Ugandan Politics: Departicipation as a Strategy for Political Development in Africa,* a thesis presented to the Dept. of Government, Harvard Univ., in partial fulfillment of the requirements for Doctor of Philosophy, Sept. 1972.

10. Kiwanuka, M. S. M. *From Colonialism to Independence,* (Nairobi: East African Literature Bureau, 1973).

11. Leys, Colin *Politicians and Policies: An Essay on Politics in Acholi, Uganda, 1962-1965,* (Nairobi: East African Publishing House, 1967).

12. Listowell, Judith, *Amin,* (London and Dublin: IUP, 1973).

13. Mamdani, Mahmood *From Citizen to Refugee,* (London: Pinter, 1972).

14. Martin, David *General Amin,* (London: Faber and Faber, 1974).

15. Ministry of Internal Affairs, Uganda Government *Evidence and Findings of the Commission of Enquiry into Allegations made by the Late Daudi Ocheng on 4th February, 1966,* (Kampala: Uganda Publishing House, 1971).

16. Obote, A. Milton *The Common Man's Charter and Appendices,* (Entebbe: Government Printers, 1970).

17. O'Brien, Justin (pen-name for Yashpal Tandon), *Brown Britons: The Crisis of the Ugandan Asians,* (London: Runnymede Trust Publication, 1972).

18. Patel, Hasu H. *Indians in Uganda and Rhodesia—Some Comparative Perspectives on a Minority in Africa,* (Denver: Center on International Race Relations, University of Denver, 1973-1974).

III. ARTICLES AND PAPERS

1. Brownlee, Robert J. "Uganda: Employment Consequences of the Economic War," paper presented at the annual convention of the African Studies Association of the U.S.A., Syracuse, N.Y., November 3, 1973.

2. Campbell, Horace "The Rise of the Lumpen Militariat in Uganda," paper presented at the annual convention of the African Studies Association of the U.S.A., Chicago, November 1, 1974.

3. Cohen, Dennis L. "Ryan on Obote," *Mawazo,* (Kampala), Vol. 3, No. 2, December, 1971.

4. Cohen, Dennis L. and Parson, J. "The Uganda People's Congress Branch and Constituency Elections of 1970," *Journal of Commonwealth Political Studies,* Vol. XI, No. 1, 1973.

5. Doornbos, Martin "Kumanyana and Rwenzururu: Two Responses Ethnic Inequality," chapter in *Protest and Power in Black Africa,* edited by Robert I. Rotberg and Ali A. Mazrui, (New York: Oxford University Press, 1970).

6. Gershenberg, Irvine "Slouching Towards Socialism: Obote's Uganda," *African Studies Review,* Vol. XV, No. 3, 1972.

7. Gertzel, Cherry "The Uganda Coup of 1971," unpublished paper, School of Humanities and Social Sciences, Univ. of Zambia, 1972.
8. Gingyera-Pinycwa, A. G. G. "A. M. Obote, the Baganda and the Uganda Army," *Mawazo,* Vol. 3, No. 2, December, 1971.
9. Jacobs, B. L. "The Second Republic of Uganda," *Africa Today,* Vol. 20, No. 3, 1973.
10. Kasfir, Nelson "Cultural Sub-Nationalism in Uganda," chapter in *The Politics of Cultural Sub-Nationalism in Africa,* edited by Victor A. Olorunsola (Garden City: Doubleday, 1972).
11. Kironde, Erisa "Aminism" unpublished seminar paper at the Center for International Affairs, Harvard Univ., 1973.
12. Kiwanuka, M. S. M. "Nationality and Nationalism in Africa: The Uganda Case," *Canadian Journal of African Studies,* Vol. 4, No. 2, 1970.
13. Lofchie, Michael "The Uganda Coup—Class Action by the Military," *Journal of Modern African Studies,* Vol. 10, No. 1, 1972.
14. Martin, Michael "The Uganda Military Coup of 1971—A Study of Protest," *Ufahamu,* Vol. 3, No. 3, Winter 1972.
15. Michel, Alexander and Russell Miller "Amin: The Untold Story," *The Sunday Times Magazine,* (London), October 29, 1972.
16. Mittelman, James H. *The Uganda Coup and the Internationalization of Political Violence,* (Pasadena, Calif.: Munger Africana Library, 1972).
17a. Obote, A. Milton "Language and National Identification," *East Africa Journal,* Vol. 4, No. 1, April 1967.
17b. Obote, A. Milton "The Footsteps of Uganda's Revolution," *East Africa Journal,* Vol. 5, No. 10, October 1968.
18. Ravenhill, F. J. "Military Rule in Uganda: The Politics of Survival," *African Studies Review,* Vol. XVII, No. 1, April 1974.
19a. Ryan, Selwyn "Economic Nationalism and Socialism in Uganda," *Journal of Commonwealth Political Studies,* Vol. XI, No. 2, July 1973.
19b. Ryan, Selwyn "Uganda: Balance Sheet of the Revolution," *Mawazo,* Vol. 3, No. 1, June 1971.
20. Southall, Aidan "Amin's Coup in Uganda: Great Man or Historical Inevitability?" *The Journal of Modern African Studies,* Vol. XIII, No. 1, March 1975.
21. Tandon, Yash "The Expulsions from Uganda: Asians' Role in East Africa," *Patterns of Prejudice,* Vol. 6, No. 6, 1972.
22. Twaddle, Michael "The Amin Coup," *Journal of Commonwealth Political Studies,* Vol. X, No. 2, July 1972.

INDEX

A

Abboud, Ibrahim, 108-09
Acculturation, 279
Achebe, Chinua, 200
Acholi, Kigezi (Acholi), 33, 117; under
Amin, 48; and coup of 1971, 112,
113-14, 116; and imperialism, 195; and
Lango Master Development Plan,
113-14; and Pan-Nilotism, 103-04; in
Ugandan army, 40, 49, 113, 116, 131
Adoko, Akena: and coup of 1971, 112-13,
116, 117-18, 152-53; and Pan-
Nilotism, 104
Africa: acculturation of, 279, 282-83; age,
reverence for, 7, 207; armies of, the
emerging modern, 127, 244-46, 278;
and black majority rule, 68, 278; and
chiefdoms, 72-73; Christian impact on,
196, 205-07; civilian supremacy in, 55;
and colonialism, resistance to, 195,
205-06; demilitarization of, 165, 196,
207-08, reasons for, 55-57, 149-165;
dependency of, see Cultural schizophrenia; independence of, and education, 55, 238, 244; leadership styles in,
7, 155-59, 278, and political regimes,
139, 278; nationalism in, 25, 56, 68,
224, 226, 231; partitioning of, 102-03;
sexual attitudes in, 150, 203, 258, 259,
272; violence in, political, 23-24, and
radicalism, 278; warrior societies of,
196-99, 207; warrior tradition of, 149,
166, 187-88, 195 et seq., 203, 205,
207-08, resurgence of, 211
Afro-Shirazi Youth League, 270-71
Agreement: Uganda, of 1900, 34-35,
57-59, 60-61, 63, 68; Uganda, of 1955,
63; of Extraterritoriality (Japan), 59
Ali, Mahomet, 188

Alliance: extraterritorial, 192; Four
Power, 110; of intelligentsia and military, 30-31; 42-43, 50; intelligentsia
and peasantry, 43, 50; intelligentsia
and traditionalists, 42; and military-
agrarian complex, 31, 41, 50; political,
57; and political survival, 16; of UPC
and KY Parties, 10-11, 12, 16, 17, 18,
42, 182
America. See United States. See also
Blacks, American.
Amery, Julian, 217-18
Amin, Idi: accused of complicity, 13, 174;
and Asians in Uganda, 45-48, 66, 71,
78-79, 141, 158-61, 208-10, 222, 235,
287, 291; and Battle of the Palace,
175; and the British, 283-84; as bureaucratic leader, 45; as charismatic
leader, 148-49, 151; and coup of 1971,
43-45, 98, 111, 127, 135, 155, 170,
174, 219, causes of, 44, 112, 114; and
deposed Obote regime, 112-13,
115-18, 183, 185; and deruralization,
33; diplomatic relations of, 46-47, 123,
166-67, 220-21; education of, 183-84;
ethnic origin of, 33, 49, 170, 172, 185,
188-89; ethnicity under, 48, 49, 71,
215, 231, 284; freedom under, 232,
255; first cabinet of, 45; as intimidatory leader, 48, 161-63, 164-66,
211; and Islam, 206, 209; and the
Israelis, 123, 208, 215, 217-22,
283-84, 291; military background of,
42, 173-75, 207-08, 281; and military
recruitment, 30, 49, 50; as mobilization leader, 46, 48; and Mutesa,
176-77, 190-91; under Obote, 42, 50,
151-53, 154; as patriarchal leader,

77-78; personal characteristics of, 42, 47, 133, 135, 154-55, 158-59, 164, 167, 172, 175, 188, 207-08, 251, 256, 275; and polygamy of, 77, 150-51, 209, 226; political attitudes and tactics of, 46, 76-79, 160-62, 164, 176, 184, 193, 208, 221, 229-30, 253, 273, 284, 286; and racism, 76-77, 79, 230-31, 232, 235, 284-85; and religion, 158, 160, 162-63, 220, 240-51, 253-256, 259-276, 277n, 284-85, 291, 292n; as reconciliation leader, 163-64; and socialism, 284-286, 290-91; as symbol, 166, 196, 204; and warrior tradition, 148, 195, 198, 206-210, 211; Westernization of, 283

Ankole, 39

Apartheid, basis of, 71

Apter, David E., 148-49, 159

Arabs: in Africa, 104, 105-06, 121, 124, 160, 187, 257-58, 278, 261; Amin policy towards, 221, 222, 232; and Israel, 71-72, 104-05, 222-24, 227-29, 232

Armed Forces Decree (Power of Arrest), 129

Army. See Military, the.

Arusha Declaration, 8, 269-70, 287-88

Arua. See West Nile.

Ashanti, 73-74. See also Ghana.

Asians in Uganda: and citizenship, 78-79, 225, 235-36, 243-44, 248; economic success of, and Indophobia, 236; economic success of, reasons for, 234-35, 239, 242; expulsion of, by Amin, 79, 158-61, 208, 222, 231, 236-37, 247-48, 283-84, 285; population of, 248; sexual exclusiveness of, 66, 71, 76, 78-79, 158, 209-10, 225, 233n, 287; as urbanizing influence, 47-48

B

Bataringaya, Basil, 11, 118

Battle of the Palace, 15, 64, 175

Beattie, John, 74

Bennett, George, 9

Blacks, American, 210-11, 231, 279-81

Britain, See Great Britain.

British Balfour Declaration, 223

Buganda (Baganda): and coup of 1971, 11, 163-64, 262-63; demilitarization of, by British, 34-35, 57-61, 64, 68, 180, by Obote, 139; and ethnicity, postcolonial, 12, 262; and ethnicity, precolonial, 66; as heartland tribe, 9-10, 34, 49, 68, 189; Japan compared with, 57-61, 64; kabakaship, abolition of, 19, 176, 193; law enforcement in, 91-92, 117, 180; and "lost" counties, 12-13; militarism in, 37-39, 48, 174; military vs., 17-18; and murder of Okoya, 152-53; pre-eminence in national affairs, 10-12, 34, 50, 68, 103-04, 170, 176, 180, 182, 192, end of, 15, 28, opposition to, 20, 104; and religion, 257-58; repoliticization of, under Obote, 17-18, 28, 41-43, 117, 139-40, 170, under Amin, 151, 176; and Westernization, 180-81, 190. See also Mutesa, Edward II.

Bugangazi. See Bunyoro.

Bultmann, Rudolf, 250

Bunyoro, 35, 37-38, 66, 195; "lost" counties of, 12, 13, 63

Burma, 31

Busoga, 77, 226

Buyaga. See Bunyoro.

C

Capitalism, and imperialism, 56, 143

Cantril, Hadley, 156

Chamberlin, Joseph, 124, 216, 217, 219, 222. See Also Zionist movement.

Charismatic leadership, 8, 35, 57, 165-66, 168n; military vs. civilian, 147-48; as political masculinity, 150. See also Weber, Max.

Childers, Erskine, 227

Christianity: in Africa, 57, 90, 106, 206-07, 258; in Uganda, 64, 206, 251-52, 257-59. See also Religion; Missionary influence in Africa.

Chwa, Baudi II, 172, 174, 177

Circumcision ceremonies, 55, 150, 167n; and age-grade systems, 197-98, 202; Shaka and, 202; significance of, 196-98, 202; and warrior tradition, 197-99

el-Azahry, Sayed Ismail, 108, 109
Embourgeoisment, 128, 140-42, 144, 246-47
Engels, Friedrich, 136
England. See Great Britain.
English. See Languages.
Ethnicity: and discrimination, 117, 244; and the intelligentsia, 43-44; Jewish, 218-19, 222-226; in the military, 30, 38-41; and military-agrarian complex, 40-41; and Pan-Nilotism, 104; as political influence, 12, 22, 31-32, 41, 48, 69-70; and political stratification, 39; in post-coup (1971) ambience, 114-118, see also Military, the; as tribalism, 23, 36, 48, 50, 51, 73, 186; and warrior tradition, 66
Ethnocracy: balanced, 28; and Document No. 5, 43; forms of, 66, 215; and heartland tribes, 10, 34; Israeli, compared with Uganda, 215-19; precolonial, 66
European Common Market, 70
Evans-Pritchard, E. E., 67, 74

F

Fallers, Lloyd, 38, 59, 60, 181, 190
Family, extended. See Kinship; Nationhood.
Farouk I, 100, 101, 102, 107-08, 184
Finer, F. E., 282
Fortes, Myer, 74, 224-25
Four Power Alliance, 110
France, 33, 46, 105
France, 33, 46, 105
Friedrich, Karl J., 88

G

Gallagher, J., See Robinson and Gallagher
Galtung, Johan, 34
Ganda. See Buganda.
George IV of England, 173
Ghana, 73-74, 112, 163, 235-36, 282
Gluckerman, Max, 204
Goli, 25-26, 28
Goody, Jack, 130
Great Britain: and Asians in Uganda, 208; and Buganda, 57-61, 180, see also

Agreement, 1900 of Uganda; colonial army recruitment of, 37-38; demilitarization of Africa by, 34-35, 55-56, 65, 84, 174, 196; impact of, on Amin, 281-83, 284, on Uganda, 189-90; and Israel vote, 120; kinship in, 70; and "lost" counties, 12; monarchy of, compared to Uganda kingdoms, 73; and Mutesa, see Mutesa, Edward II, Westernization of; and regional integration effect of, 124; and Suez Canal, nationalization of, 105, 108; and Unity of the Nile, 102-03
Grunitzky, Nicolas, 184-85
Gulu, 174
Gun tax, 61-62

H

Heartland tribes. See Buganda; Kikuyu.
Herzl, Theodor, 216-17, 218, 222-23, 232
Hitler, Adolf, 156, 221
Hobbes, Thomas, 90
Huntington, Samuel P., 30-31, 43

I

"Idi-ology." See Zio-Aminism.
Immigration. See Asians in Uganda; Israel.
Imperialism. See Great Britain.
Independence: African, 27, 55; Kenyan, 26; Sudanese, 108; Ugandan, 26, 42, 49, 50, 243. See also Constitution of 1962.
Indophobia, defined, 236. See also Asians in Uganda.
Initiation rites. See Circumcision ceremonies.
International Conference Centre, 253, 254
Interpenetration, 121-122; economic, 99, 124; in Nile Valley, 118, 122; in Sudan, 100, 101; by violence, 99-100, 118, 121, 123-24, 125; in Zanzibar, 187
Iraq, 31
Islam. See Muslims.
Israel (Israelis): and Arab war, 101, 104-05, 120-21, 227, 231; citizenship and kinship in, 71-72, 225-26, 228-29,

P'Bitek, Okol, 259-61
People, The, 18, 20, 255
Perham, Margery, 56
Polity, the: under Amin, 45; and civilian supremacy, 55; militarization of, 18, 29, 38
Polygamy. See Amin, Idi, polygamy.
Population: of Asians in Uganda, 236, 248; dispersal of in Tanganyika, 9; of Israel, 227-28; of Palestine, 227; of Falashim tribe, Ethiopia, 226
Power rivalry, 22, 23-24, 107-08. See also Coups d'etat.
Price, Robert M., 282
Puritanism. See Religion. See also Amin, Idi.

R

Racial stratification, 283-85. See also Class structures.
Racism, 47, 222, 285. See also Asians in Uganda.
Radcliffe-Brown, A. R., 74
Radicalism: in Egypt, 105; in Kenya, 8; in Sudan, 109-110; in Uganda, see Obote, Apolo Milton, and Amin, Idi; in UPC, 10-11
Ranger, Terence, 195
Religion, impact of, in Uganda, 189-90, 275; of the "living dead," 90; and socialism, 22, 270-71; and puritanism, 250, 251, 258-59, 270-71, 275; and the state, 253-54; 256, 261-68
Renan, Ernest, 176
Republic of Uganda: First, see Obote, Apolo Milton; Second, see Amin, Idi.
Responsibility, collective, 117
Richardson, A., 251
Robinson and Gallagher, John, 102, 103
Royal Guard Corps, 60
Rural areas: definition of, 32; and development, 33; and economics, 36-37; 49; and military recruitment, 36, 37-41, 49; and urban tensions, 48; and vigilantism, 184-85

S

Sadat, , 118
Saidi, Augustine, 14
Salisbury, Lord, 102
Sapir, Pinhas, 225-29
Sartori, Giovanni, 148, 149
Scalapino, Robert, 40
Schapera, I., 73

Schick, A. S., 217
Sexuality. See Warrior tradition, sexual symbolism in. See also Shaka of Zulu; Amin, Idi, and celibacy.
Sexuality and Christianity. See Religion, and puritanism.
Shaka of the Zulu, 196, 200-04, 205, 208, 210-11
Shils, E. A., 148
Singapore. See Obote, Apolo Milton.
Socialism, African, 77, 104-06, 144, 289; ideology of, 22, 252-53. See also Radicalism.
Soldiers as businessmen. See Embourgeoisement.
Somalia, 116
Sorel, George, 136-37, 142
Statehood: effect of military on, 127; purposes of, 85; and use of force, 86, 91
Succession: apostolic, 250-51; by coups d'etat, 170, 186-88, 276; by election, 170-71; in kingdoms, 73, 170-71, 177
Sudan, 49, 99-101, 103, 104, 105-07, 108-110, 118-19, 120-122, 123, 160, 185, 188, 220-21, 283-84
Swahili. See Languages.
Syria, 110, 118

T

Tanganyika, 44, 67, 138, 187-88. See also Tanzania.
Tank Hill Party, 26, 27, 28
TANU (Tanganyika African National Union) Youth League, 270, 273, 287
Tanzania, 8, 9, 14, 17, 20, 27, 67, 69, 113, 115-16, 122, 125, 137-38, 195, 252, 268, 276, 277n, 290; effect on, of Uganda violence, 98; as uniting of Tanganyika and Zanzibar, 187
Technology, 129-30; and capitalism, 135-36; and coups d'etat, 131. See also Weaponry.
Territoriality, 74-75. See also Kinship; Nationhood.
Things Fall Apart, 200
Third World. See Africa.
Third World, Maoist, 33, 34
Togo, 184-86
Toure, Sekou, 56, 286
Tradition. See Warrior tradition.
Transition, 19, 20
Treaty. See Agreement.
Treaty complex, 62, 63-64. See also Demilitarization.
Tribal politics. See Ethnicity.

NOTES

NOTES

NOTES